ROYAL MARRIAGES

Diana, Camilla, Kate, Meghan

and princesses who did not live happily ever after

SUSANNA DE VRIES

AUTHOR OF

ROYAL MISTRESSES OF THE HOUSE OF HANOVER-WINDSOR

Digital distribution by Ebook Alchemy

ISBN: 9781925283624 - paperback
ISBN: 9781925283648 - ebook

DEDICATION

To those who provided information for this book, Sylvia Alison and her husband, the Rt Hon Michael Alison, a member of the Queen's Privy Council, Philippa Lester-Wilson, friend of Earl and Countess Spencer. Lady Elsa Bowker, confidante of Princess Diana, Professor Sir Martin Roth, President of the British Royal College of Psychiatrists, former psychiatrist to the royal family, and mentor of my late husband, Dr Larry Evans, Professor of Psychiatry at the University of Queensland.

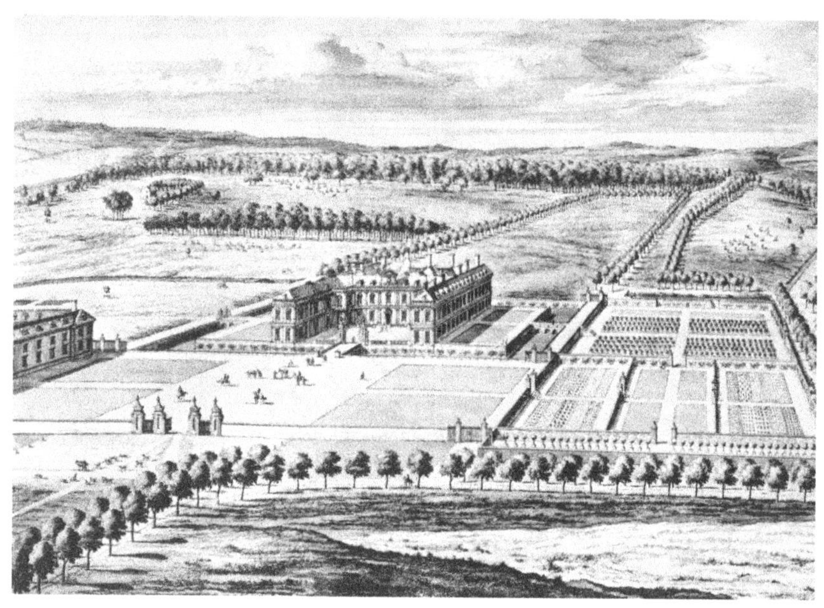

Althorp in a seventeenth century copper engraving showing the old formal garden (private collection) contrasted with Althorp in the late 20th century when Diana lived there.

CONTENTS

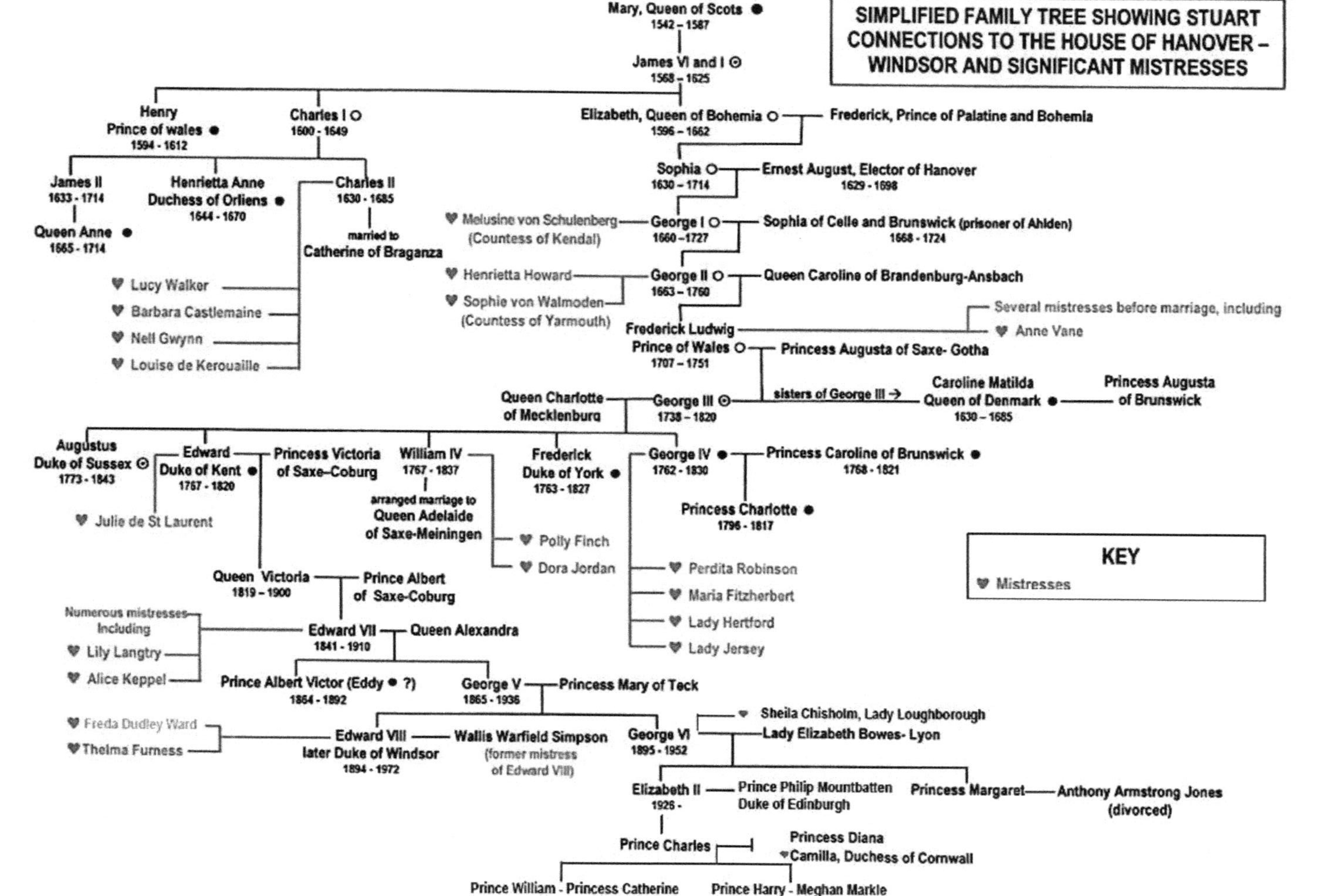

SIMPLIFIED FAMILY TREE SHOWING STUART CONNECTIONS TO THE HOUSE OF HANOVER – WINDSOR AND SIGNIFICANT MISTRESSES
Mary, Queen of Scots ● 1542 – 1587
James VI and I ⊙ 1568 – 1625
Henry Prince of wales ● 1594 - 1612
Charles I ○ 1600 - 1649
Elizabeth, Queen of Bohemia ○ 1596 – 1662
Frederick, Prince of Palatine and Bohemia
James II 1633 - 1714
Queen Anne ● 1665 - 1714
Henrietta Anne Duchess of Orliens ● 1644 - 1670
Charles II 1630 - 1685
married to Catherine of Braganza
♥ Lucy Walker
♥ Barbara Castlemaine
♥ Nell Gwynn
♥ Louise de Kerouaille
Sophia ○ 1630 – 1714
Ernest August, Elector of Hanover 1629 - 1698
♥ Melusine von Schulenberg (Countess of Kendal)
George I ○ 1660 – 1727
Sophia of Celle and Brunswick (prisoner of Ahlden) 1668 - 1724
♥ Henrietta Howard
♥ Sophie von Walmoden (Countess of Yarmouth)
George II ○ 1663 – 1760
Queen Caroline of Brandenburg-Ansbach
Several mistresses before marriage, including
♥ Anne Vane
Frederick Ludwig Prince of Wales ○ 1707 – 1751
Princess Augusta of Saxe- Gotha
sisters of George III →
Caroline Matilda Queen of Denmark ● 1630 – 1685
Princess Augusta of Brunswick
Queen Charlotte of Mecklenburg
George III ⊙ 1738 – 1820
Augustus Duke of Sussex ⊙ 1773 - 1843
♥ Julie de St Laurent
Edward Duke of Kent ● 1767 - 1820
Princess Victoria of Saxe–Coburg
William IV 1767 - 1837
arranged marriage to Queen Adelaide of Saxe-Meiningen
♥ Polly Finch
♥ Dora Jordan
Frederick Duke of York ● 1763 - 1827
George IV ● 1762 - 1830
Princess Caroline of Brunswick ● 1768 - 1821
Princess Charlotte ● 1796 - 1817
♥ Perdita Robinson
♥ Maria Fitzherbert
♥ Lady Hertford
♥ Lady Jersey
KEY
♥ Mistresses
Queen Victoria 1819 – 1900
Prince Albert of Saxe-Coburg
Numerous mistresses Including
♥ Lily Langtry
♥ Alice Keppel
Edward VII 1841 - 1910
Queen Alexandra
Prince Albert Victor (Eddy ● ?) 1864 - 1892
George V 1865 - 1936
Princess Mary of Teck
♥ Freda Dudley Ward
♥ Thelma Furness
Edward VIII later Duke of Windsor 1894 - 1972
Wallis Warfield Simpson (former mistress of Edward VIII)
George VI 1895 - 1952
♥ Sheila Chisholm, Lady Loughborough
Lady Elizabeth Bowes- Lyon
Elizabeth II 1926 -
Prince Philip Mountbatten Duke of Edinburgh
Princess Margaret
Anthony Armstrong Jones (divorced)
Prince Charles
Princess Diana
♥ Camilla, Duchess of Cornwall
Prince William - Princess Catherine
Prince Harry - Meghan Markle

CHAPTER ONE

Princesses in arranged marriages who did *not* live happily ever after

'The only books Diana ever read were mine, she confused them with reality and they weren't good for her.' – Barbara Cartland, popular writer of romantic novels and Princess Diana's favourite author.

French lawyer-turned-author Charles Perrault published a collection of mediaeval fairy stories to amuse his children. Their favourite story was that of Cinderella, about a sweet-natured girl used as a housemaid by her ugly half-sisters who manages to attend a ball where a handsome prince falls in love with her. The complex plot involving a fairy godmother, a pumpkin coach and a glass slipper is a story of how true love prevails. The prince marries Cinderella, the girl he loves, and they live happily ever after. However, in real life this was impossible.

Charles Perrault's rags-to-riches story enchanted romantic young girls unaware that princes obeyed their fathers and married princesses or wealthy aristocrats with large dowries.

Three centuries after Perrault wrote the fairy story Cinderella, former journalist Barbara Cartland added a modern twist to the tale with novels about virginal girls in humble jobs like governesses or nannies. These virginal heroines defeat their sexually-experienced rivals, win the love of a prince, marry him and live happily ever after.

Although Princess Diana was not aware of this, in the past many princesses had led unhappy lives, victims of arranged marriages who were used as baby factories, something Diana would claim on her 'Secrets Tapes' had happened to her.

In the twelfth and thirteenth centuries, English princes married French princesses to strengthen peace treaties and prevent frontier conflicts, as England owned Brittany, Normandy, Anjou, Poitou and Gascony and that gave them a large part of France from the North Sea to the Pyrenees. Disputes over borders were often settled by treaties in which marriage of a virginal French princess to a prince from the ruling Plantagenet dynasty sealed the deal.

Child brides, betrothed as toddlers and married at thirteen or fourteen were pawns in these treaties, and no one cared about their homesickness or their happiness. Brides had to be virginal, and it was standard practice in royal families during the Middle Ages that the bed sheets of the bridal bed were examined the morning after the wedding for bloodspots from the bride's hymen. This was proof the bride had been a virgin. These teenage princesses were seen as 'baby factories' to produce heirs who, once they were old enough, would lead armies into battle.

Many brides only met their bridegrooms for the first time a few days before their weddings.

England's worst monarch, King John (infamous for signing the Magna Carta and then refusing to comply with it) made both his young wives unhappy. His first wife, Isabella of Gloucester, daughter of an English earl, was even younger than Lady Diana (daughter of Earl Spencer) when she married Prince Charles.

Lady Isabella's avaricious husband took possession of her dowry in land and gold and held on to it, keeping Isabella of Gloucester short of money to buy clothes and food and pay her ladies-in-waiting. This was the reason her father had given her a dowry.

In spite of her husband's efforts to impregnate her, Isabella did not produce an heir, and John continued to be a philanderer who was able to attract women through the power of royalty. Isabella kept no diary, so it remains unknown what she felt about her husband as he prowled around his court seducing the wives of his courtiers.

After ten years without an heir, King John wanted to exchange his wife for a much younger French princess with a large dowry. There were as yet no divorce courts, so King John consulted three French bishops who favoured his French marriage. They advised that his marriage to Isabella of Gloucester could be annulled on the grounds of *consanguinity* (a legal term for the closeness of blood line) even though King John had been aware that Isabella was his first cousin when he married her.

In the year 1201, King John managed to have his marriage to Isabella of Gloucester annulled, falsely claiming he had received the Pope's permission so was free to court Princess Isabella of Angoulème who was thirteen or fourteen – the births of mere girls were rarely recorded in this sexist era.

On a hunting trip in France, John convinced the innocent young princess that Count Hugh de Lusignan (the widowed friend of her father to whom she had been betrothed) was too old for her. He told her that she would have a wonderful life as Queen of England and she should marry him.

The naïve Princess Isabella believed him, and they married in France. She was unaware that King John was after her large dowry and was a clever liar. John had already betrayed his brother King Richard the Lion Heart and ordered the murder of his nephew, young Prince Arthur to attain the Crown.

John now showed his real character. The marked differences in their ages and John's relentless womanising made Isabella very unhappy. She wrote to her father complaining her husband had taken her dowry and kept her short of money. However, they did have a sexual relationship and the beautiful Isabella eventually bore her husband five children.

Meanwhile, Count Hugh de Lusignan complained about King John's conduct to the King of France. He raised an army and repossessed some of John's English territories in France, and King John unfairly blamed his French wife for their loss. Matters went from bad to worse, and as John was an adulterous king, Isabella took a lover to console her.

Husbands could take mistresses but for a wife to take a lover was considered treason and punishable by death. John ordered his bodyguards to murder the lover and drape his corpse across his wife's bed as a warning to her. Fortunately for Isabella King, John died in 1216 having lost most of his empire in France.

After her husband's funeral, Queen Isabella returned to her native France with her daughter Joan who was intended to marry Hugh de Lusignan's son. To the surprise of everyone, the young Count de Lusignan married the still beautiful Queen Isabella, and she managed to marry off her daughter to the widowed King of Scotland.

⁂

Tall, golden-haired 23-year old Prince Edward, a member of the Plantagenet dynasty since his boyhood, was in love with an employee of his father named Piers Gaveston. The prince knew that he had to marry young Princess Isabella of France to whom he had been betrothed since she was in the cradle.

It is highly unlikely when the teenage princess arrived in England by sea that she was aware of her husband's passionate sexual relationship with Piers Gaveston, the handsome Gascon horseman with little money and boundless ambition who was a year older than Prince Edward. (Homosexuality [or sodomy as it was known in Biblical terms] at that time was regarded as a heinous crime punishable by death.)

Years earlier, when Prince Edward told his father he wanted to donate an entire French province to his close friend Piers Gaveston, King Edward I was furious believing his son to be homosexual and banished Gaveston to his birthplace of Gascony, determined that Prince Edward would honour the marriage contract struck with King Philip IV of France. No one cared about Prince Edward's feelings, and he and Princess Isabella were pawns in a treaty that the old king hoped would bring peace to both countries involved in a dispute over England's possession of Gascony and unresolved claims over the French duchies of Anjou, Aquitaine and Normandy.

There is no large-scale portrait of Queen Isabella, as women rarely rated this honour.
The closest rendering of the beauty of her embroidered wedding gown, jewels and silken coif comes from one of the few great mediaeval artworks depicting a French aristocrat.
This is one of the tapestries from the Lady and the Unicorn series in the Cluny Museum in Montparnasse.
Photographed on loan to the Art Gallery of New South Wales in 2018 by the author.

King Edward I, the old warrior king, died in July 1307.

After being crowned as Edward II, his son promptly recalled his boyhood lover to court and honoured him with the title of Lord Gaveston, Earl Duke of Cornwall, a title previously reserved for members of the royal family.

Princess Isabelle was only twelve when she was sent by sea to meet her husband. The naïve young princess must have been puzzled that her tall, fair-haired husband took so little interest in her and spent his time with his boyhood friend, Piers Gaveston who had already been banished once by Edward's father who believes he was corrupting his son.

But after the old king died and his son was crowned as King Edward II, Gaveston returned to court and was made Earl of Cornwall by Edward II who gave him the right to collect annual rents from Cornish farmers. The money went to Gaveston's head making him very arrogant, and this increased after the king insisted he make an arranged marriage' to Edward's niece, Margaret de Claire, in 1307 and the couple had a child five years later.

Gaveston was hated by a group of noblemen who he taunted by giving them nicknames based on their physical appearance. He mocked them in front of the king and humiliated them by playing practical jokes on them for the king's amusement.

But like every king and Prince of Wales, Edward II knew it was his duty to sire an heir for the nation. In fact, Isabella had four children, two boys and two girls, in this very complex relationship. By 1312, Piers Gaveston's arrogance and his conduct towards the barons was deemed insufferable. In secret conclaves, the barons plotted how to get rid of Gaveston, inviting him to take part in a tournament in which they planned he would be killed. But Gaveston surprised them by revealing he was an expert swordsman and won every sword fight in which he had participated. Eventually, he was kidnapped and murdered by a group of barons in a plot masterminded by the Earl of Warwick.

For a time, it seemed that Lord Gaveston's death meant Edward would draw closer to his beautiful wife and mother of his four children. However, Edward II soon found a new 'favourite' in handsome young Hugh Despenser, who he lavished with money and gifts. Despenser hated Isabella and made her life difficult, and also he hated Margaret, the widow of Piers Gaveston, and vandalised her properties by having men set fire to them.

There was trouble in Edward's French territory of Gascony, and Isabella, hating the Despensers, father and son, convinced her husband to let her travel to Gascony as she was the ideal person to negotiate on his behalf.

The Queen and her son, young Prince Edward, were allowed to travel to France. Here she fell in love with a handsome but very angry nobleman called Roger Mortimer. He had been imprisoned by Edward II in the Tower of London where Edward had him committed for treason and had his lands confiscated. Roger Mortimer vowed vengeance on King Edward II.

Isabella and Mortimer became lovers, and she turned against her husband. They raised an army in the province of Hainault, and in 1326 they invaded England and defeated the king's forces. Mortimer and Isabella governed England as co-regents in the name of Isabella's son Edward III until he came of age four years later, but they were accused of taking money from the Treasury to support an extravagant life-style. Isabella purchased many properties including the exquisite Castle Rising near Sandringham in Norfolk.

The former King Edward II was imprisoned in remote Berkeley Castle and murdered in the dungeons on the orders of Roger Mortimer. It was later alleged he planned dreadful revenge for his imprisonment in the Tower and the loss of his estates in a way that would leave no marks on the king's body so that Queen Isabella would think her husband had died a natural death. Mortimer ordered the deposed king to be skewered through his anal passage with a red-hot roasting spit which burned out his intestines. It has never been established how much Isabella knew about Mortimer's gruesome method of killing her husband or if this is only a legend.

Castle Rising. In a strange twist of history, the mother of Princess Diana hired this ruined but picturesque castle for the coming-out dance of Diana's elder sister, Lady Sarah Spencer. Today this beautifully situated castle is open to the public at times shown on its website.

The young King Edward III was outraged at the death of his father and had Mortimer beheaded. He imprisoned his mother in the remote but beautiful Castle Rising but allowed her children and grandchildren to visit her. She requested that she be buried in her exquisite wedding dress with her husband's heart contained in a silver casket beside her.

⁂

Another very unhappy princess was red-headed seventeen-year-old Princess Katherine of Aragon. Betrothed to Henry VIII's sickly older brother, Prince Arthur, their marriage was intended to establish an alliance between England and Spain at a time when England was a Catholic country.

A great deal of money was spent by King Henry VIII on the spectacular wedding of the young couple. England had just emerged from the misery of the Wars of the Roses and, having deposed a previous king, Henry VIII wanted to establish the legitimacy of his Tudor line and gain popularity.

As Arthur's title was Prince of Wales, the young couple were sent to live in a remote castle on the Welsh borders to placate the king's Welsh subjects where, without proper medical care, Arthur wasted away and died of what was known as 'the sweating sickness'.

Princess Katherine claimed later that her husband had been far too ill to consummate their marriage.

Prince Arthur's avaricious father, Henry VII, did not want to return Katherine's large dowry to her parents. He selfishly kept the homesick unhappy Spanish princess at court when she wanted to return to Spain.

After seven years living in poverty while the Tudors enjoyed spending her dowry, Katherine was married off to her deceased husband's brother who was five years younger than she was.

Her bridegroom, Prince Henry, was not the gross figure who appears in portraits by Holbein many years later. When he married, Prince Henry was tall, handsome and muscular. Katherine fell deeply in love with him, was a devoted wife and this was the only really happy period in her life.

While Henry was occupied fighting in France, Katherine, daughter of a warrior queen, defeated a planned Scottish invasion at the battle of Flodden Field in 1913.

But Henry VIII still felt threatened by the way his father had won the Crown and was increasingly desperate for a male heir. Katherine longed to give her husband a son. She had aged, and five years older than her husband, now looked lined and drawn after so many miscarriages and stillbirths, but she manages to produce a daughter named Mary.

The idea of a woman ruling England was intolerable to Henry VIII who persuaded himself that God had turned against him for breaking the ecclesiastical law and marrying his late brother's wife. But Katherine continued to swear her marriage to Arthur had never been consummated. By now, her life was turning into a nightmare as the king she loved set about divorcing her, creating the Anglican Church to achieve this.

Now very unhappy, Katherine was banished to remote Kimbolton Castle with her ladies-in-waiting and became increasingly religious.

Dark-haired sophisticated Anne Boleyn, whose father owned Hever Castle and had been one of Katherine's former ladies-in-waiting on her return from the French court, was now enchanting the king. Anne was very clever and refused to have sex with the king unless he promised marriage. This left Henry mad with lust.

Anne Boleyn's elegance, quick wit and French sophistication soon bewitched Henry, and learning from her sister's mistake of giving herself too easily, Anne Boleyn cleverly refused the king's gifts of jewels and money by insisting she was virtuous. She said demurely she greatly respected the king but could only accept gifts from a future husband. This made him keener to win her. While Mary Boleyn had sought love, Anne Boleyn sought power and had no intention of becoming one of Henry' s discarded mistresses like her sister.

During a long courtship which left Henry mad with lust, Anne only allowed him to fondle her breasts and was determined to retain her virginity. Henry did everything he could to please the capricious, hot-tempered Anne. He made her father Earl of Wiltshire and gave her magnificent jewels.

In 1526, after courting Anne in vain for a year and a half, Henry wrote to her promising that if she gave herself to him, she would be his only mistress and he would never take another. Anne was playing for higher stakes and refused.

Only when Henry promised to have his marriage annulled to the unhappy Queen Katherine the following year did Anne agree to accompany him to a meeting with the French king. To do this, she needed a title, and Henry gave Anne Boleyn the extinct title of Lady Pembroke. Anne now had the use of the Privy Purse to buy whatever clothes, jewels and furs she wanted.

Looking elegant, Anne Boleyn was welcomed back at the summit meeting held at French court as though she was royal. She wore magnificent jewels that had once belonged to Queen Katherine of Aragon, and the French king, seeing which way the wind was blowing, gave her a diamond as an official gift.

Two imagined likenesses of Anne Boleyn by artists who never met her, painted some 50 years after her execution, as Henry VIII had ordered every portrait of Anne to be burned. An impression of how she might have looked in the National Portrait Gallery shows her with red hair like her daughter. Contemporaries claim Anne Boleyn had black hair and large luminous eyes like those in an unnamed portrait by Frans Pourbos the younger.

Anne Boleyn and Henry VIII spent a week alone together on the French coast in a short holiday. And finally, after seven years of teasing, Anne surrendered her virtue after a firm promise in writing from Henry VIII he would marry her.

Anne, now 32, soon informed Henry she was pregnant. Henry lied to the distinguished churchman who conducted the ceremony claiming he had a document from the Pope Clement VII permitting him to marry. His marriage to his brother's wife had never been legal in the eyes of God, so it should be annulled. Henry cited a passage in the Old Testament Book of Leviticus which claimed that a brother who married his dead brother's wife was sinning.

Initially, Henry had sought an annulment as divorce was unheard of for a king. Pope Clement refused. Hot-tempered Henry VIII ignored the papal verdict, and at the risk of being excommunicated, decided to divorce Queen Katherine who protested that she loved him as his queen and as a woman and had done no wrong. But women had no power, and Katherine's marriage was declared null and void to her great distress.

Aided by the wily Thomas Cromwell, Henry proclaimed himself Head and Defender of the Church of England, and granted *his own* divorce. In January 1533 he then married Anne Boleyn in a secret ceremony in the

Tower of London. He was aware the populace loved Katherine and hated Anne, who they called a whore and a witch. Anne did not care. She was convinced the child in her womb would be a boy and her hold over Henry would be total. Instead, Princess Mary was born and was declared a bastard and could not use the title of Princess. The shock that her father did not love her affected Mary deeply and would have severe long-term effects.

Anne was crowned Queen in Westminster Abbey, the folds of her luxurious fur-trimmed robe covering the signs of her pregnancy. The pious Katherine was heartbroken by the divorce. She retreated into seclusion at Kimbolton Castle with her Spanish ladies-in-waiting until she died of cancer.

On the day of Katherine's funeral which Henry refused to attend, Queen Anne had a miscarriage. Anne realised that giving Henry a son was vital. She fell pregnant again and miscarried and became more difficult and demanding as her marriage soured.

Anne's third attempt also failed, and she gave birth to a healthy red-headed daughter they named Elizabeth. Anne's hot temper grew worse, and her enemies called her 'a demanding shrew'. Henry was tired of Anne's tantrums and attracted by the placidity of Jane Seymour and paid court to her. But Jane feared the consequences and retired to the home of her parents to escape him. Henry visited Wulfhall, Jane's home, where he received a warm welcome from the ambitious Seymours, eager to enrich themselves and unite Jane and the king.

The obliging Thomas Cromwell, who had helped Henry obtain a divorce from Katherine, realised that Henry must have a son or Mary, a Catholic like her mother, would inherit the throne and the country might be plunged into war.

Cromwell realised Anne Boleyn must be replaced by Jane Seymour. As Chief Minister to the king, he had Anne accused of adultery, incest with her brother and of being involved in a conspiracy to kill the king, which was clearly ridiculous.

Henry chose to believe Anne had cuckolded him, and her trial went ahead. Opinions are divided on whether these were trumped up charges with adultery admitted under torture by those men accused of being her lovers. Anne Boleyn was found guilty and in May 1536 was executed on Tower Green and buried in the Chapel of St Peter and Vincula inside the Tower of London. She had been queen for only a thousand days.

⁂

Three weeks after divorcing Anne of Cleves because he was unable to have an erection when he went to her bedchamber, Henry married the teenage Catherine Howard. Catherine was poorly educated with a childlike naivety. She was happy to have dressmakers make her sumptuous gowns with detachable sleeves and the jewelled hoods that were fashionable in the Tudor era. She saw all the gifts as compensation for having to make love to a corpulent elderly husband with an ulcerated leg which reeked of putrefaction.

The teenage queen enjoyed dining with the king and dancing with her husband's courtiers and flirting with a young aristocrat called Thomas Culpepper, a distant relative of her mother. Ironically, Frances Dereham, her lover before she married Henry VIII, had independently secured a minor post at court.

Henry VIII was now so vast and unsteady on his feet that dancing with his young wife was impossible, so he looked on while his young wife danced with Thomas Culpepper and Frances Dereham. Foolishly in his cups, Dereham boasted about their previous relationship.

Archbishop Cranmer heard rumours about Queen Catherine's past, indicating she was not a virgin before she married – a necessary adjunct for royal wives with the fear they might be pregnant by another man when they went to the altar. He started making investigations. He learned about Catherine's past with Frances Dereham from Mary Lascelles, the maid at her grandmother's house. A suggestive letter dictated by the illiterate Catherine was found in the room of handsome young courtier Thomas Culpepper. In the letter Catherine confided her growing passion for the handsome young man and how she feared what her husband would do should he learn about it.

After the letter was discovered, Catherine Howard was accused of leading a 'base carnal and voluptuous life before her royal marriage' and behaving like a common harlot while at Hampton Court.

She was sent to the tower, tried, and protested her innocence but was found guilty of treason and adultery and beheaded. Thomas Culpepper being noble met the same fate. Dereham, as a mere commoner, was hung, drawn and quartered. The severed heads of both young men were placed on pikes on London Bridge for all to see as proof of the king's power.

⁂

In the seventeenth century, English kings looked further afield, and their sons married Spanish and Portuguese princes. These virginal young princesses arrived in England with marriage contracts arranged by ambassadors and notaries. Their dowries were sacks of gold coins or entire ports like Tangier and Bombay, gifted to the rakish Charles II by his virginal teenage bride Catherine of Braganza, daughter of King of Portugal.

The teenage Princess Catherine of Braganza, daughter of the King of Portugal who wanted military aid from England, was given a large dowry and married the cash-strapped but handsome Charles II. However, she made the fatal mistake of not understanding this was purely an arranged marriage even though her husband met her when she arrived in England accompanied by Barbara Palmer, his tall, beautiful and pregnant mistress. The petite, swarthy Portuguese princess was unfortunate to fall in love with a husband who did not find his wife physically attractive. He spent his time with the voluptuous Nell Gwynn, the arrogant and unfaithful Barbara Villiers and blonde Louise de Kérouaille.

⁂

The unhappy Princess Anne of Denmark found herself trapped in an arranged marriage to the bisexual James VI of Scotland (later James I of England). He preferred men and was in love with charismatic, handsome George Villiers, Duke of Buckingham. Divorce was out of the question. Crowned as Queen Anne, she consoled herself by acquiring expensive hand-embroidered dresses and jewels and having her portrait painted. Like Princess Diana, the young Danish princess consoled herself by changing her hairstyle frequently and dressing elegantly.

A miniature portrait by Paul van Somer shows the Danish queen with her hair in a towering creation held in place on a wire frame. Her hair and court dresses were copied from those in fashion at the French court.

When not busy hunting stags and fondling handsome young male courtiers, tall, spindly-legged King James I visited his wife's bedchamber where he did his duty by siring three children in what has been referred to as a 'lavender' or inter-gendered marriage.

Anne of Denmark seems to have dealt with a difficult situation with no divorce possible in an adult way and made the best of it. She remained on good terms with her husband and when they moved to London after James became King of England, they set up a joint arts programme including funding performances by the company to which Shakespeare belonged and watching performances of new works like *Macbeth* and *King Lear*.

There was great sadness for Queen Anne when her eldest son Henry, Prince of Wales, died aged 18 leaving his younger brother Charles to inherit the throne.

Anne of Denmark, painted by Paul van Somer

Royal lover, handsome George Villiers, Duke of Buckingham, created a Knight of the Garter. Attributed to William Larkin (National Portrait Gallery, London)

The new King Charles I married the elegant French Catholic Princess Henrietta Maria, and initially, she was upset when he showed little interest in her. As his reign became more difficult, he came to depend on his wife, and they grew very fond of each other. Queen Henrietta Maria sold her jewels to raise money for her husband's royalist army and was devastated when Charles I was captured by Cromwell's forces and executed on a scaffold at the Palace of Whitehall. She spent the rest of her life relatively poor and unhappy.

Elizabeth, daughter of Charles I and Queen Henrietta Maria, married Frederick, Prince of the Palatinate, and their arranged marriage produced a daughter named Sophie who married the ruler of Hanover.

Elizabeth, Princess of the Palatinate, had a grandson named Prince George of Hanover who had a small amount of Stuart blood in his veins, and since he was Protestant rather than Catholic, he was invited by Parliament to rule England, Scotland and Ireland after Queen Anne died childless.

He had treated Princess Sophia Dorothea brutally, had spent her dowry and humiliated her by living with his mistress and two illegitimate children in Hanover's royal palace.

Thoroughly miserable, young Princess Sophia Dorothea retaliated by taking a lover after which the adulterous Prince George of Hanover had her arrested for treason. Sophia Dorothea was regarded as a chattel or property of her husband.

Princess Sophia Dorothea's lover, handsome Count Philip Königsmarck, disappeared without a trace. Many years later, one of George I's bodyguards made a deathbed confession that he had helped his fellow bodyguards murder Count Königsmarck on the instructions of Prince George, the future George I, who became the founding father of the Hanover-Windsor dynasty.

Prince George of Hanover, an adulterous husband, imprisoned young Princess Sophie for the rest of her life in remote Ahlden Castle. He was crowned in Westminster Abbey by the Archbishop of Canterbury on 20 October 1714 and took up residence in Kensington Palace with his German-speaking mistress and their only unmarried daughter.

To reward his mistress and make Melusine more acceptable to the English, he gave her the English title of Duchess of Kendal and founded the Hanover-Windsor dynasty.

George I's son hated his father for the brutal treatment of his mother and founded a dynasty whose heirs hated their fathers.

Kensington Palace in the Victorian era (engraving from a private collection)

⁂

Another very unhappy princess was Princess Caroline of Brunswick-Wolfenbütel. Prince George Augustus, the spendthrift heir of the pious George III, was deep in debt when he agreed to marry her, aware she would be provided with a large dowry and Parliament would pay his debts if he agreed.

Princess Caroline arrived by sea at the port of Dover three days before her wedding, scheduled for 8 April 1795 in the Chapel Royal of St James's Palace.

Although warned by an equerry that the Prince of Wales was fastidious, Princess Caroline for reasons unknown did not bother to bathe before her first meeting with the portly George, Prince of Wales. Princess Caroline made her future husband a deep curtsey as she had been instructed to do. He lifted her to her feet, found her body odour repellent, turned to his equerry, Lord Malmesbury, and told him he was unwell and asked for a glass of brandy.

The Prince of Wales drank the brandy and without any explanation left the room.

The next ordeal was their wedding which was unhappy for both of them as it was clear they were not going to live happily ever after.

On 7 January 1706, weeping into a large red handkerchief and with a severe hangover from his stag party, the Prince of Wales managed to survive the ceremony propped up by his ushers. But he was still so drunk he needed help to propel him into the bridal chamber. Once inside the room Prinny slumped semi-comatose on the floor.

However at some stage during the night the Prince of Wales managed to stagger to the marital bed and consummate his marriage in order to do his duty as Prince of Wales and provide the royal House of Hanover with a legal heir. Nine months later, Princess Caroline gave birth to Princess Charlotte, but the marriage was now seen to be a disaster. This mismatched couple were unable to divorce in what became known as the first War of Wales which was humiliating to both the prince and princess.

Nearly three centuries later, there would be a second War of Wales ending with a divorce. This would change the old rules for royal marriages, and the sons of Prince Charles and Princess Diana would be able to marry for love alone.

Queen Victoria had been assiduous in arranging the marriages of her numerous children into Europe's ruling royal families, without any thought about compatibility although she had insisted on making a love-match and been very happy with Prince Albert until his premature death.

In the context of the recently changed approach to royal marriages involving 'commoners' rather than aristocrats, Diana, Princess of Wales is important. Her story is the main one in *Royal Marriages* because Diana broke the mould of royal wives who suffered their husband's infidelities in silence. She alone dared to reveal in public the unhappiness and emptiness at the core of a marriage which she admitted involved three people. The very public failure of Diana's marriage caused immense sympathy for her and a huge outpouring of grief over her death. These factors led the Queen quietly to relax the centuries old requirements of blue blood and virginity for the wives of those in the direct line of succession.

In telling Diana's story I have emphasised how her unhappy childhood deprived of a mother led to her overly-idealistic expectations of a blissfully happy marriage. Diana's revelations about the real state of her 'fairy-tale' marriage would lift the curtain on the ancient practice of arranged royal marriages.

Continuing grief over Diana's death and the much stronger role for women in western society led to the Queen relaxing the rules governing the marriages of princes in the direct line of succession. In a totally new departure for royalty, Prince Charles was allowed to wed his first love, the divorced Mrs Parker Bowles. A few years later his sons, Princes William and Harry were allowed to marry 'commoners' in popular marriages which have made the monarchy seem far more relevant to the public.

CHAPTER TWO

Lady Diana – ancestry & a troubled childhood

I disappointed my parents by being a girl and disappointed my husband who was in love with someone else… I felt a failure, and no one loved me. It was a very unhappy childhood. – Princess Diana on tapes made for her voice coach Peter Settelen.

'Diana has been accused of making too much of losing her mother through divorce, but her loss ran deep within her.' – The late Lord William Deedes who accompanied Princess Diana on anti-landmine missions to Angola and Bosnia.

Born at Park House on the royal Sandringham estate on 1 July 1961, the Hon Diana Spencer was a very pretty baby. But her parents and her grandfather, the seventh Earl Spencer, were bitterly disappointed she was a girl as this meant she was unable to inherit the vast Althorp estate.

When he was telephoned at Althorp House with the news he had a *third* granddaughter, the seventh Earl yelled, 'Wrong sex,' slammed down the phone and cancelled the planned celebrations. When she was old enough to hear this family story it upset young Diana who felt unwanted and unloved.

Her christening in the small church at Sandringham was relatively modest compared to christenings of her elder sisters, the Hon Sarah and the Hon Jane Spencer. Earl Spencer feared that should Johnnie Althorp, her father, die without a male heir, Althorp House and its magnificent art treasures would pass to a distant male cousin and all the work he had done to preserve the treasures of Althorp for his heirs would have been in vain.

The years following Diana's birth were stressful for her mother, the former Frances Roche. Diana's mother was constantly reminded by her stern father-in-law it was her wifely duty to bear her husband a healthy son to inherit the Althorp estate.

The desperate efforts of Viscount and Viscountess Frances Althorp to produce a boy continued for years and marital relations became a wifely duty. Frances, Viscountess Althorp, whose money was supporting her husband until he inherited Althorp and the estate felt humiliated and angry by her father-in-law constantly blaming her for failing to produce a male heir.

Earl Spencer, her father-in-law and her husband insisted Frances take invasive tests conducted by a Harley Street gynaecologist which she found humiliating.

After three more years spent trying to conceive, Frances fell pregnant again. Meeting my school friend Philippa Lester, now Mrs Vere Davidge, owner of a smaller stately home near Althorp, at a maternity clinic as Philippa was pregnant with her son Peter, Frances, Viscount Althorp admitted 'I hope and pray it's a boy, I'm tired of being pregnant.

But finally, the wealthy former Frances Roche did produce the desired male heir. The baby boy with russet-coloured hair was much admired. He was baptised the Hon Charles Edward Maurice Spencer at a magnificent christening in Westminster Abbey with Queen Elizabeth II as his godmother. His expensive christening presents were on display at the christening party, and everyone was thrilled by his birth while little Diana was ignored.

The continuing appeal of the little boy who would become the ninth Earl had the effect of making the shy Diana feel unloved and that her parents had little time for her and she would later repeat the refrain, 'No one ever loved me.'

Diana grew up in an era when boys were valued more than girls. The two young Spencer children were looked after by a nanny but, unlike many aristocratic mothers, Frances spent a great deal of time in the nursery with little Charles and Diana. They adored her and looked forward to her bedtime stories and goodnight kisses.

Diana loved her paternal grandmother, Countess Spencer, who as a debutante had been considered a great beauty. Countess Cynthia was sweet-natured lady but treated badly by her husband, the hot tempered autocratic seventh Earl Spencer, Diana's grandfather.

As the daughter of the third Duke of Abercorn (an Anglo-Irish title), Diana's grandmother had made an arranged marriage to the seventh Earl, owner of one of England's largest estates. Countess Cynthia had royal Stuart blood. Her father, the Duke of Abercorn claimed descent from Sir Charles Lennox, the first Duke of Richmond, an illegitimate son of Charles II by his French mistress, Louise de Keraille (a Breton name).

When Diana was older, her grandmother told her stories about her Spencer ancestors, sheep farmers who under the Tudors started their rise to wealth due to their intelligence and capacity for hard work. After being ennobled, the Spencers became important figures at court of several Hanoverian monarchs, and kings and queens had been guests at Althorp House and palatial Spencer House in the centre of London.

The Spencers were closely related by marriage to the Spencer-Churchills who lived in splendour at Blenheim Palace. Diana's grandmother told her how a Spencer ancestor married the second daughter of the first Duke and Duchess of Marlborough. Because the Marlboroughs lacked a son, the daughter of the first Duke received a magnificent bequest of silver and gold tableware and great art when she married a Spencer ancestor.

Diana's maternal grandmother, Lady Fermoy, had the same mesmerising deep blue eyes as Diana. When wealthy Lord Maurice Fermoy first met Diana's grandmother, she was Miss Ruth Gill, an impecunious but talented music student with auburn hair, studying piano with the famous pianist Alfred Cortot. Ruth's father was a no-nonsense Scot who had set up a small paint factory before fighting in the Great War as an officer and eventually owned a rural property at Bielside near Aberdeen.

Diana's Irish, American & Scottish Ancestors

Lord Maurice Fermoy, whose full Irish title was Baron Fermoy of Trabolgan, was one of Britain's wealthiest aristocrats. He had inherited the vast fortune of his American stockbroker grandfather, Franklin Work who was the stockbroker to the Rockefeller and Astor families during the great American railroad boom.

Franklin Work educated his clever grandson and his twin brother at Harvard. Francis and Maurice in 1920 jointly inherited their grandfather's fortune. Maurice, the elder twin, inherited the Irish title of Lord Fermoy due to unexpected deaths in his family.

Having the title of Baron Fermoy of Trabolgan sounded impressive, but all that Maurice inherited were two crumbling Georgian mansions near Cork with Irish tenants too poor to pay their rents. In the same year, Maurice, now Lord Fermoy, and his twin jointly inherited the enormous fortune of Franklin Work, their deceased grandfather. The younger twin remained in America and the newly created Lord Fermoy moved to London with his American mistress where he was elected Member of Parliament for King's Lynn, paid for his mistress to return to America where he bought her a house and married young Ruth Fermoy.

Moving among aristocrats, the new Lady Fermoy carefully hid the fact her roots were middle class. As MP for Sandringham and Kings Lynn, and a good friend of the royal family, Lord Maurice was allowed an inexpensive Crown lease on the nine-bedroom Park House in the grounds of the royal Sandringham estate in the county of Norfolk.

So, Diana and her baby brother, Charles, grew up at Park House on the royal Sandringham estate. The attractive house with a swimming pool had once housed the overflow of guests from Sandringham House before the royal family enlarged it. As a toddler, Diana and her baby brother were invited to watch films with little Prince Andrew when the royal family were in residence at Sandringham House during the Christmas holidays. Lady Fermoy hoped pretty little Diana might eventually marry Prince Andrew as they played together happily.

Diana and her little brother, Charles Spencer, were guests at one of Prince Andrew's birthday parties and the teenage Prince Charles, home from boarding school for the holidays, made a brief appearance at the party. But like most teenage boys, Prince Charles did not fancy playing games with toddlers and soon departed.

Diana was too young to realise that her mother had become increasingly resentful of her husband for not defending her after her father-in-law, the seventh Earl insisted Frances visit a Harley Street gynaecologist for invasive tests, blaming her for producing three girls but no male heir. (Today doctors know that the male X chromosomes are responsible for the sex of the child, but this was not known in the 1960s).

Frances was paying to support her husband with her inherited fortune and resented that she was being blamed for producing girls. Frances, still a very beautiful young woman, was tired of a husband who spent his leisure hours shooting game birds with former Army cronies or with King George VI at Sandringham.

Diana's heiress mother Frances had been encouraged by her snobbish mother to marry Viscount Johnnie Spencer when she was a seventeen-year-old debutante straight out of boarding school. Johnnie was thirty-two, almost double her age and heir to thousands of acres the magnificent Althorp House in Northamptonshire.

The new Lady Fermoy had given her husband two daughters and a son, but aware he had a mistress in America, she had withdrawn from sex after she had fulfilled her side of the bargain and given him a male heir. Aware the aristocracy and major landowners of Norfolk looked down on her for being middle class, the new Lady Ruth Fermoy was rescued from social oblivion when the music-loving Queen asked her to give a recital after one of her Sandringham dinner parties and became a close friend of the new Lady Fermoy.

Now that her daughters were approaching marriageable age she was determined they would make brilliant marriages, her revenge on aristocrats who snubbed and ostracised her when she married Lord Fermoy.

Her second daughter Frances, (Diana's mother), was the family beauty and voted Debutante of the Year and Lady Fermoy hoped she would marry Johnnie, Viscount Althorp, heir to Earl Spencer, one of Britain's wealthiest landowners.

Lady Ruth Fermoy rented Londonderry House in Park Lane to give seventeen-year-old Frances a very romantic coming-out ball hoping that Viscount Johnnie Althorp (many years older than the Frances) would propose to her at the ball.

On the stroke of midnight on the instructions of Lady Fermoy, all the lights were turned out in the ballroom. In the romantic glow of hundreds of candles, Johnnie and Frances waltzed together, and at the end of the dance, he kissed her on the lips, said he loved her and asked her to marry him.

Frances carried away by romance was delighted by his proposal, although she was far too young to know what kind of man would make her happy. She already loved ballet and theatre and hated blood sports which aristocrats traditionally enjoyed.

Lady Fermoy was thrilled that her daughter was marrying the heir to a vast stately home. She persuaded Lord Maurice Fermoy to give their second daughter an enormous wedding in Westminster Abbey with royalty as guests of honour.

In June 1954, over 1,000 guests including the Queen and the Queen Mother watched eighteen-year-old Frances marry thirty-one-year-old Viscount Johnnie Althorp in the wedding of the year. Frances was the youngest bride to marry in Westminster Abbey for over a century.

⁂

Frances, Viscountess Althorp, 'The Bolter'

Now almost two decades later, vivacious, witty and highly intelligent Viscountess Frances Althorp was bored by her overweight husband and by acting as hostess at shooting weekends for him and his Army friends. She longed for a different type of life and a husband she could talk with about things that interested her.

Since the death of her father who had followed the American pattern and shared his fortune equally among his widow and his three children, Frances was now considerably wealthier than before and a major heiress.

Lady Fermoy now a very wealthy widow had become a close companion and confidante of the widowed Queen Mother (her official title for this honorary post was Woman of the Bedchamber). Lady Fermoy spent part of her time at Clarence House and the rest of her time in her luxurious apartment in Eaton Square.

Frances often left her younger children in the care of a nanny while she went to London to visit her mother or attend the theatre. Frances had been given the lease of Park House by her widowed mother, and it was her fortune that paid the staff, the heating bills, the children's clothes and other expenses of the marriage, which bored her.

Her husband Viscount Johnnie Althorp, educated at Eton and Sandhurst Military College, was a former Guards officer and attaché to George VI and the present Queen. He had many good qualities but was not an imaginative man with no interest in theatre, ballet or art – the things which fascinated Frances. Johnnie refused to accompany his wife to London to visit the theatre, the ballet or art exhibitions, telling her brusquely 'those arty farty things' which she enjoyed bored him stiff.

Her husband was waiting for his elderly autocratic father, for whom he had little love, to die. As the heir to the seventh Earl Spencer, Johnnie, would inherit the vast Althorp estate, one of the wealthiest in England but would have to pay the British Government several million pounds in death duties.

In the interim, his miserly father refused to sell off any of the valuable art or antiques in which Spencer wealth was tied up. When Johnnie left the army and had worked for his father learning how to run the estate, his stingy father kept him short of money.

Johnnie resented the fact that Frances, with her large private income, paid for the two older girls, Sarah and Jane, to go to West Heath, her former boarding school and was able to leave the two younger children in charge of their nanny and attend first nights and dinner parties in London.

At a dinner party given by friends, Frances was seated next to tall, handsome Peter Shand Kydd. He explained that Janet, his artist wife, had been unable to attend as she had to varnish her paintings for a forthcoming exhibition. Frances and Peter Shand Kydd spent the evening talking and laughing. He told her funny stories from his time as a naval officer, and she told him about Park House, their home on the royal estate of Sandringham and about the royal family.

Peter Shand Kydd was interested to learn that centuries earlier the Spencers had been England's most successful sheep farmers and bought the Althorp estate. After being ennobled by Tudors and Stuart, they became Lords of the Admiralty, Privy Councillors and Cabinet Ministers to Hanoverian kings who they served faithfully.

In my twenties as a keen skier and water-skier, I met Peter Shand Kydd's younger brother Bill in Switzerland where he was a member of the Olympic bobsleigh team. We met again at a country house party in England where Bill was riding in a point-to-point and he said he would like to learn to water ski so I invited him to come to Princes Water Ski Club where I taught him to water ski as was the current British water ski jumping champion and Bill became fascinated by the sport and I think he may have bought his own boat. I never saw him again, but I learned that the Shand Kydd brothers had inherited a successful business but sold it when their father died. Part of Norman Shand Kydd's fortune came from inventing and marketed a do-it-yourself product called Polyfilla which became a household name in the 1950s and 60s.

With his share of the money from the sale of the wallpaper and Polyfilla business, Diana's future step-father, Peter Shand Kydd bought a sheep property near Yass in New South Wales (now owned by Rupert Murdoch) and a 1,000-acre property on an island off the north of Scotland. While Bill remained in England with long holidays in Switzerland, Peter became a sheep farmer or grazier in Australia as well as in the remote north of Scotland.[1] He and Janet would escape from the northern winter to Australia and spend their summers in Scotland as she was Scottish.

To Frances, this handsome man discussing his new ventures on a remote Scottish island and in the Australian outback seemed more exciting than the overweight husband she had been encouraged to marry thirteen years earlier. Frances invited the Shand Kydds to visit them at Park House and dined with them at their home near London, and became a good friend of Peter's wife, the former Janet Munro Kerr, a Scottish heiress and a talented artist.

In the winter of 1967, as Peter Shand Kydd was an excellent skier, a sport she enjoyed, Frances persuaded her husband to rent a Swiss chalet and invite several married couples including Janet and Peter Shand Kydd as their guests.

The snow-covered Alpine village where cars were forbidden had winter sun, attractive restaurants and après ski evenings with mulled wine and dancing which made for a very enjoyable holiday. Frances and Peter were the best skiers in the Spencers' house party. They departed after breakfast with their skis over their shoulders, heading for the ski lift and the high slopes rather than accompanying Johnnie and the other married couples to ski classes with the local ski school on the nursery slopes, where Johnnie was not a star like Peter Shand Kydd.

Frances, with her slim figure and long legs, knew she looked good in ski clothes and flirted with Peter Shand Kydd. After a day's skiing, the group ate in picturesque chalet-restaurants where they dipped long forks into cheese *fondue,* drank spicy mulled wine and then went dancing. In the exciting atmosphere of the ski resort, Frances fell in love and believed Peter Shand Kydd was in love with her and Fate had thrown them together.

---

1 Bill Shand Kydd's wife was the sister of the wife of 'Lucky' Lucan, the English lord accused of murdering his nanny instead of the wife who refused to let him having custody of their children. After the murder as Lord Lucan's wife did have severe psychological problems the Lucan children came to live with Bill and his wife who adopted them.

Frances realised that when she married she had been too young and immature to know what kind of husband she wanted. She saw her husband as dull and regretted she had married so young. Frances was convinced Peter Shand Kydd was the kind of man she should have married: daring, dashing, amusing and keen for new challenges. Frances, head over heels in love, threw caution to the winds, believing in the power of love, just as reckless in its pursuit as Diana would be several decades later.

Arriving back at the rented chalet before the rest of the group returned from skiing, Frances and Peter became lovers. On their return to London, they continued their adulterous liaison in the small apartment in Cadogan Place, Chelsea that the besotted Frances purchased as a love nest for them.

Diana's mother, convinced she had found the love of her life, believed she and Peter would spend their lives together. Her two youngest children would live with them, and Sarah and Jane would join them for part of the school holidays, and she would use her inherited fortune to buy them a house by the sea where they could spend their holidays and be happy.

Frances, lost in a dream of future happiness, failed to realise that her virile lover was merely extending what had considered a holiday 'fling' with her and had no intention of leaving his wife and the three children he adored.

Janet Shand Kydd became suspicious of her husband's frequent absences and hired a detective to follow him. Janet loved her handsome husband and was furious when the detective produced a written report with photos of Viscountess Althorp's Chelsea apartment where the lovers met for afternoons of pleasure. Even worse was the fact her husband had deceived her with Frances Althorp who she had trusted, shared feminine confidences and regarded as a friend.[2]

Diana's mother was cited as the 'other woman' in a society divorce which received wide publicity. Janet Shand Kydd as the innocent party was granted a divorce on the grounds of her husband's adultery and, as was customary, awarded custody of their children.

Viscount Johnnie Althorp was humiliated and enraged by the sordid details of his wife's infidelity which appeared in the tabloids. One of their fiercest rows was witnessed by six-year-old Diana. Hearing her parents arguing, peering through the keyhole of their bedroom door she saw her father slap her mother hard across the face calling her a bitch. The little girl heard her mother cry out in pain while her father continued to yell crude names at her.

---

2 Information from Bill Shand Kydd.

Viscountess Althorp, later Mrs Shand Kydd, Diana's mother was tall, blonde and attractive, with the understated aristocratic elegance which Diana would inherit.

It was too much for little Diana: she became hysterical and had to be carried back to her bedroom. Her elder sister Sarah, seeing how much fights between their parents distressed Diana, tried to prevent her little sister overhearing their quarrels by turning up the volume on the radio as loud as possible.

The marital rows of Viscount and Viscountess Althorp continued after her elder sisters, Sarah and Jane, returned to their boarding school in Kent. Johnnie's rages and his bitterness over his wife's infidelity made life unbearable for Frances and upset little Diana.[3]

After another boiling row, Frances contacted her lawyer and moved with her children to her London apartment for a few months and sent them to a local nursery school.

Diana who had just turned six was confused by the situation which was never properly explained to her. They spent Christmas 1967 at Park House as a family with Johnnie and Frances pretending everything was normal for the sake of their children and this charade of a happy family was maintained until Johnnie once again insulted his wife over her infidelity.

---

3 Cited in Princess Diana's 'Secrets Tapes' recorded with the help of her voice coach Peter Settelen in 1992-3, selections from which were televised in England and Australia in August 2017.

Diana's birthplace Park House on the royal Sandringham estate (Private collection)

Without consulting a lawyer to learn her legal position if she left the marital home, Frances rashly told her husband she was in love with Peter Shand Kydd, feeling she had enough of paying most of the expenses of this marriage while waiting for her husband to come into his inheritance of the Althorp estate from his elderly father. She would sue her husband, obtain a divorce and marry Peter, live in her London apartment. Once the divorce was through she would send for her two younger children as the older girls were in boarding school.

Without realising the legal consequences of her actions, Frances instructed her maid to pack her clothes and jewels as she was leaving Park House for good, assuming she would be given custody of her two youngest children as had happened to Janet Shand Kydd.

Six-year-old Diana watched her mother's maid and her grim-faced father load her mother's leather suitcases into the boot of the car. Frances, her mother, near tears climbed into her car and without a word to her bewildered little daughter drove away, too emotional to face explaining to Diana why she was leaving or when she would return.

Diana heard the tyres crunch over the gravel, watched the car retreating down the drive and remained sitting on the stone steps of Park House, hoping her mother would return. Her hopes were raised whenever she heard a car in the distance and dashed when she realised it was not her beloved mother returning home.

For the next three days Diana sat on the steps waiting for her mother. At night she could not sleep and refused to eat. Her father refused to discuss the matter with her – a classic case of how not to treat a child during separation and divorce. At that time divorce was rare, and there were no books advising parents how to broach the topic with children so no one thought about the psychological damage of separation from her mother on Diana, a very sensitive child.

Diana's nanny and the rest of the staff obeyed her father's orders and refused to discuss the matter even if Diana howled, 'I want Mummy' and threw tantrums.

Diana's father showed little understanding of psychology in believing his little daughter could forget her mother. As a former army officer, he issued orders to his staff that all letters, birthday and Christmas letters and presents from Viscountess Althorp were to be burned. They must never mention this to little Diana, or they would lose their jobs.

Diana was convinced that the separation was all her fault as she had disappointed her parents by not being the boy that they all wanted. She concluded she was unloved by her mother, which was why she had left her. And as Diana claimed later, it was a very unhappy time as she was convinced that no one loved her.

Diana had recurring nightmares about her mother's departure, and memories of her mother's goodnight kisses and the smell of her perfume would haunt Diana for years. She was an imaginative child, always prone to over-dramatising events, blending truth with fantasy when recounting them and this would continue all her life, when recounting her marriage her descriptions of events although vivid colourful were not always correct.

Enforced separation from her mother for three years had a deep and shattering psychological effect on little Diana. At birthdays and Christmas, the motherless little girl would hope against hope for a card or a present from her mother to show she remembered her, but nothing ever arrived which made her suffer deeply. Her father sought to compensate his younger children by wonderful birthday parties with clowns, donkey rides and conjurers with their magic tricks, but for Diana, nothing could compensate her for the loss of her mother and even worse was the fact the staff were forbidden to speak about her as through her mother was dead.

Like many children of divorced parents, Diana became manipulative in order to get what she wanted from the staff, marooned from the outside world in the gated royal Sandringham estate.

Missing her mother, life at Park House with both sisters away at boarding school left Diana with no one in whom to confide her hopes that her mother would return, and her father refused to discuss the matter. So

Diana developed what is known as childhood separation anxiety, a psychological syndrome which continued into her adult life and left her fearing that she was unlovable and that *anyone* she loved would eventually abandon her.

The dark effects of divorce on Diana

Living in London, Frances was busy consulting divorce lawyers and making statements to be read to the divorce judge. It was unfortunate that her divorce lawyers incorrectly advised her she was certain to obtain custody of Diana and Charles because she was legally the guilty party having abandoned the marital home and her young children. Her husband was a respected member of the peerage who had served the Queen. He had not been unfaithful, was not mentally ill, and she had no photos which would prove she had received bodily injuries.

Viscountess Althorp was advised to take the third option and to sue for divorce on grounds of her husband's mental cruelty.

Frances had been raised to think of love and marriage as synonymous assumed that once she was divorced Peter Shand Kydd would marry her. They would set up home together, have Diana and Charles living with them and the older girls could spend part of the holidays with them. But events turned out very differently due to the meddling of Lady Fermoy. She loved titles and stately homes and wanted her grandchildren to enjoy these once the seventh Earl died, and had a soft spot for Johnnie, the future Earl Spencer.[4]

Lady Fermoy played a darker role in Diana's life than has often been acknowledged. Asked by her now cash-poor son-in-law to find nannies for the younger children, the wealthy Lady Fermoy found young untrained girls to look after them rather than mature well-trained nannies from the Norland College or the Princess Christian College who had learned how to cope with young children of divorcing parents, who at a stressful time needed special care and warmth from their nanny.

The young untrained nannies did not know how to deal with a distressed, anxious little girl like Diana, reacting to the loss of her mother by throwing angry tantrums, having panic attacks and sobbing fits. The motherless Diana burst into sobs whenever she thought about her mother

---

[4] Diana's adult relationship with her mother was often troubled. In the last four months of her life, Diana (with no idea she was to die in an accident) returned unopened her mother's letters, unopened due to a quarrel over an interview about her that her mother had given to a magazine donating the fees to charity.

or threw a tantrum when the staff acting under orders refused to discuss the topic with her. The nannies could not cope with Diana's hysterical tantrums which included kicking and screaming and beating the walls with her fists. After a few months of this they gave notice and departed.

An experienced fully trained nanny with some understanding of child psychology could have prevented Diana fearing she would lose the love of her father – now her sole parent – and developing the separation anxiety which would haunt her in later life when she married and hated her husband leaving and threw the same tantrums in private.

From London Viscountess Althorp started divorce proceedings against her husband citing mental cruelty, convinced she was bound to gain custody of her youngest children. Diana's older sisters Jane and Sarah away at boarding school for much of the year were not nearly as badly affected as Diana.

Frances Althorp, certain she would gain custody, planned to buy a large country house by the sea where her children could live with her and Peter Shand Kydd, although she still had no firm commitment that he would marry her. Frances was in a difficult position not yet divorced, with Shand Kydd now regretting he had left his loving wife and their three children and blaming Frances for initiating the holiday affair that had ended his marriage.[5]

Viscount Althorp was determined to punish Frances for humiliating him by leaving him for a very handsome, wealthy, younger man. He counter-sued for divorce on the grounds of his wife's adultery with Peter Shand Kydd.

Lady Fermoy had disowned Frances after the scandal of the Shand Kydd divorce but had a soft spot for Johnnie Althorp, her son-in-law in the marriage which she had encouraged when Frances was a schoolgirl, determined she would marry Johnnie and become the *chatelaine* of Althorp, one of England's grandest stately homes.

Lady Fermoy as a close friend of the Queen Mother, had buried her middle-class origins and become very snobbish; and now despised Peter Shand Kydd as *nouveau riche* and vulgar. She was mortified her daughter had renounced inheriting Althorp to live with a man who lacked a title and had made his money doing something as vulgar as selling wallpaper. (This was ironic in view of the fact that Lady Fermoy's father had made his money manufacturing tins of paint).

---

5 In *Charles versus Diana, Royal Blood Feud* (1993) journalist James Whitaker referred to Diana's father as a 'wife beater', claiming this featured in the divorce petition of Lady Frances Spencer but Diana's brother disagreed and claimed that his parents' divorce was granted on the grounds of mental rather than physical cruelty.

As a result, Lady Fermoy perjured herself in the divorce case brought by her daughter against her husband. She lied when she swore on the bible that her daughter was an 'unfit mother' so should not be given custody of the youngest children.

Frances saw this barefaced lie as a devastating act of treachery on behalf of her mother who should have been supporting her and it cost her the right to have custody of her children. Lady Fermoy committed perjury in order to help her son-in-law gain custody of his children. Lady Fermoy justified doing this by claiming she was doing her best for her grandchildren by keeping them in England.

It was tragic for Diana that Lady Fermoy failed to understand the situation. On the evidence given by Lady Fermoy, the family court judge granted custody of the four Spencer children to Diana's father while Frances, seen as the guilty party, had to pay the full costs of the divorce.

Frances was distraught by the verdict and used her inherited money to engage lawyers and a barrister and bring a custody case against her husband which went against her. She waited a few months and then instituted another lawsuit using a different law firm, hoping to gain custody of her younger children.

Lady Fermoy testified against her daughter claiming she was a 'party girl' unfit to care for her children and. Frances hated her mother even more for denying her access to her beloved children. Diana's mother was in fact desperate to see her two youngest children who she knew would be missing her badly. She defied the court order and risking a prison sentence drove to Park House. found the locks had been changed but knocked on the door and demanded to see Diana and Charles.

On the orders of her ex-husband, the butler denied her admission. It was traumatic for Diana and Charles to hear their mother sobbing outside the front door and know at last that she was alive but the fact they could not see her would torture Diana for a long time. At bedtime, they both missed their mother's hugs and goodnight kisses, and still received no letters or phone calls from her.

Their father was depressed that his wife had left him for a younger, much wealthier and more handsome man. He knew Frances and Peter Shand Kydd were living together and reacted by withdrawing into his shell and remaining in his study and ate alone in the dining room. Diana and her brother spent their days in the nursery with their nanny but loved the occasions when he came to the nursery to have high tea with them.

Frances pressed for another petition to gain custody, but by now the judge had lost patience with her and refused to hear a third petition for shared custody from Viscountess Althorp. As a result, Diana would not see her mother for the next three years or receive news of her whereabouts. Under the court order, all communication continued to be banned between Viscount Althorp and her children. At Park House, Viscount Althorp forbade his staff to mention his ex-wife's name in front of Diana and Charles.

Viscount Althorp knew that taking the children away from his ex-wife was cruel and regarded this as his revenge on her for humiliating him. He failed to realise that separating his youngest daughter from her mother for three years would cause her immense psychological damage.

In contrast, Diana's elder sisters were away at boarding school and had friends to lessen the bitter pain of maternal separation. Diana was the child most damaged by her parents' divorce and lack of maternal love as she and little Charles rarely saw their father. The nannies never stayed long, blaming Diana's ungovernable behaviour as they handed in their resignations.

Viscount Althorp ate alone in the dining room. Charles and Diana ate with their nanny in the nursery. Diana's elder sisters, being more mature and away at boarding school for most of the year, were not nearly as badly affected as Diana by the loss of their mother.

Frances, still uncertain whether Peter Shand Kydd would marry her, was upset to hear on the society grapevine that her mother told family friends and the Queen Mother that she was 'a bolter.' This was the term used in Nancy Mitford's novel *The Pursuit of Love* told from the viewpoint of a daughter whose mother had run away from the husband and became an uncaring mother.

His staff unquestioningly obeyed Viscount Althorp. All the letters, birthday and Christmas cards from his ex-wife continued to be burned as he hoped Diana would forget her mother. Each Christmas and birthday Diana hoped for a present or a card from her mother and burst into tears when she received nothing, convinced her mother no longer loved her.

Diana's father, a man of few words, still refused to explain their mother's disappearance and continued the ban on his wife's name, convinced he was doing the right thing to ensure Diana and Charles forgot their mother. As a result, Diana's feelings of loss and insecurity turned into full-blown separation anxiety causing her to throw violent tantrums, beat on the walls with her fists, break valuable ornaments and destroy things she thought her nannies valued. She feared her father might fall for one of the young nannies and marry her and this would ensure her mother would never return. Diana even flushed one nanny's engagement ring down the plughole of the nursery washbasin in revenge.

Things got worse when Diana, who had learned to ride when she was four, suffered a bad fall from her Shetland pony. She broke her arm which was slow to heal, and this developed a pathological fear of horses in Diana who now disliked all sports involving them. It would also cause problems when she made an unwise marriage to a prince who loved horses, fox-hunting and polo.

Diana's father, trained as a soldier, was not a demonstrative man. As the French have observed, the English upper classes often demonstrate more affection for their dogs than their children. Viscount Althorp never hugged or kissed his children but showed his love for them by giving them wonderful birthday parties.

Diana's paternal grandmother, Countess Cynthia Spencer, was the only person to give Diana the hugs and cuddles she craved when her grandmother visited Diana and Charles at Park House and read them fairytales.

Sometimes Countess Cynthia brought her friend Lady Elsa Bowker, the cosmopolitan Egyptian-born wife of a British ambassador, when she visited as a house guest at Althorp to see her grandchildren. The childless Lady Bowker grew fond of the pretty little blonde Spencer girl and realised she had been profoundly damaged by the loss of her mother and that Diana, always carried within her, the metaphorical 'hole in the heart' that never disappears.

Diana became attached to young Nanny Clarke, the only nanny who hugged her and kissed her goodnight and became a mother figure. But Mary Clarke left Althorp to get married and once again Diana suffered from childhood separation anxiety and for the rest of her life dreaded those around her leaving her. Years later Mary Clarke described Diana as a nervy, anxious child badly damaged by the loss of her mother.

If her father went up to London or took a holiday, she would cling to him *begging* him not to leave. In later life, she would re-enact the situation begging her husband not to go shooting or play polo. If he did not accede to her demands, she threw temper tantrums, lying on the floor and screaming and drumming her heels or beating her fists against the wall.

Much later, Diana's former nanny paid a surprise visit to Park House to see the little girl of whom she had been fond. In a memoir called *Little Girl Lost, The Troubled Childhood of Princess Diana by the Woman who raised her,* Mary Clarke revealed how Diana, who before her mother's departure had been a sunny-natured happy child had become obstinate, unhappy and temperamental. Diana confided to her former nanny that when she married it would be to a man who would adore her, and she would never divorce as the effects of divorce on children were so cruel.

Diana standing in doorway posing (Photo courtesy of the late Earl Spencer)

The wife of the local vicar gave Diana a lift in her car to the local kindergarten. She heard little Diana telling tall tales to make herself sound like a victim, (as many motherless children do). The vicar's wife called little Diana Spencer a liar and said that if she continued doing this, she would not give her a lift to the kindergarten.[6]

Intent on capturing her father's undivided attention, Diana loved posing for him as he was a keen amateur photographer. By doing this, she knew she was the undivided focus of his attention. Diana studied her sister's women's magazines and learned to pose like a model, a skill that she would use in adult life.

Reunion between Diana and her mother

Eventually, the court order against Frances expired, and Diana and her brother were allowed to stay with their mother. Viscount and Lady Althorp's divorce was not made absolute until 1969, and when Frances married Peter Shand Kydd, their wedding shattered Diana's hopes that her parents might get back together again.

---

6 The vicar's wife talked to Sally Bedell Smith author of *Diana, the Life of a Troubled Princess* and *Diana – in Search of Herself,* the first books to expose the darker side of Diana's character as a result of maternal deprivation. although the biographer was often vilified for revealing the truth behind the fairy tale.

When Diana and Charles stayed with their mother, Peter Shand Kydd as their new step-father was kind to them and bought them toys chosen out of the Hamley's catalogue. But Diana considered this as scant consolation for the hurt that lay deep inside. What Diana wanted was hugs and kisses every night from her mother and to have both her parents living together again.

On a visit to Althorp a decade later to see some of the paintings, I was shown photos in which Diana appears as a sweet little girl with the rosebud mouth who resembled the little girl in the poem by Henry Wadsworth Longfellow recited by my nanny when I was Diana's age:

There was a little girl, and she had a little curl,
Right in the middle of her forehead.
And when she was good, she was very good,
And when she was bad, she was horrid.

According to one nanny who only stayed at the Spencer household for a few months, there were two Dianas – the sweet-natured 'good' little girl who was kind and loving and the angry 'horrid' little girl, who threw temper tantrums, told lies and this dichotomy would continue into Diana's adult life.

When Diana was old enough, her grandmother visited Park House and played simple card games with her. Countess Cynthia was known for her kindness and empathy to patients at the local hospitals, and on several occasions, took Diana hospital visiting with her. Diana observed how good her grandmother was with these patients and wanted to be like her when she grew up.

Lady Cynthia Spencer, Diana's paternal grandmother, spent several days each month at Clarence House where, like her maternal grandmother, Lady Fermoy, they were both Ladies of the Bedchamber, (a higher-ranking post than a Lady-in-Waiting), acting as companions and confidantes of the widowed Queen Mother.

Aged nine, Diana was very upset when she learned her grandmother was ill with cancer and she would not be visiting her anymore.

Two years later, in 1972, Countess Spencer died from a brain tumour. Diana attended her funeral in Northampton and sobbed her heart out and from then on was convinced her grandmother was watching over her.

A Cynthia Spencer Hospice for cancer patients was funded and opened by the Queen Mother. Diana listened to the oration at her grandmother's funeral, praising her dedication to the welfare of others and wanted to follow in her footsteps.

After her grandmother died, Diana lost contact with Lady Bowker who spent some years in Ankara where her husband was appointed British Ambassador to Turkey.[7] Lady Bowker would not see Diana again for many years until as a widow she returned to live in Belgravia.

Having attended a local school in the town of King's Lynn until she turned nine, Diana was sent as a weekly boarder to Riddlesworth Hall, near Diss in Norfolk until she was considered old enough to board full-time at West Heath School in Kent, several hours drive from her Norfolk home.

On that first car journey to her new boarding school at the village of Diss, Diana burst into floods of tears, imploring her father not to leave her. He reassured his anxious young daughter she would come home at weekends, but Diana refused to listen, her sobs increased as she could not bear the thought of her father abandoning her in an attack of the separation anxiety caused by losing her mother and which would never leave her.

⁂

Diana and her young brother regarded their widowed grandfather, Earl 'Jack' Spencer, as an intimidating figure when taken to visit him at Althorp, their ancestral home. They ate in a large dining room situated so far away from the kitchen that the food was lukewarm when it arrived on a trolley. She and Charles were forbidden to touch anything as their grandfather, believed children should be seen and not heard. These visits were dreaded by Diana and her brother.

⁂

When staying with her mother and new stepfather in Scotland, Diana once again looked through keyholes and listened at doors and heard her mother and step-father arguing. Diana's relationship with her mother was never as close as it had been before she left. They were alike in many ways, and this made them argue. Diana felt resentful that her mother had been

---

7 A school friend of the author at St George's Ascot was Sylvia Haigh, eldest daughter of diplomat Anthony Haigh who was First Secretary under Lady Bowker's husband at the British Embassy in Ankara. Lady Bowker when widowed lived close to the Haighs who were now living in Eaton Terrace Belgravia while Lady Bowker lived in Eaton Square and we used to visit there here when I stayed with the Haigh family. Lady B as we called her liked the company of people younger than herself who she said kept her young and as she was bilingual and Sylvia and I had been at the Sorbonne she used to accompany us to French films at the Curzon Cinema in Mayfair and she would invite us to join her for a meal and talk frankly to us as Sylvia's father, Anthony Haigh was a trusted friend from her days at the British Embassy in Turkey, happy days about which she enjoyed reminiscing.

able to abandon her for three years not understanding the situation and still feeling her mother had not loved her enough, and a longing for love would continue all her life.

Diana regarded the domestic staff at Park House as family and enjoyed eating with them. The housemaids taught her how to iron clothes really well and she enjoyed doing housework.

Early in June 1975, after a period of illness, Diana's grandfather died. Her father became the eighth Earl, and she became Lady Diana rather than the Hon Diana which was confusing. Much worse was the fact that the motherless family were to leave Park House, the only home Diana had ever known which she loved.

She dreaded moving to Althorp House, the vast mansion lived in by fifteen generations of Spencers with its ninety rooms, some of which had not been entered for years with the doors locked and blinds drawn down over the windows. The whole idea of moving made her feel insecure.

CHAPTER THREE

Lady Diana at Althorp & at boarding school

I hate you so much. You've ruined our house, you spend Daddy's money and what for? Lady Diana Spencer to her hated stepmother.

'Lady Diana, a pupil with a defeatist attitude to schoolwork and very poor concentration'. School report from West Heath School.

About to turn fourteen and immature for her age, Diana hated leaving her birth place to live in her ancestral home of Althorp. The estate was made up of thousands of acres of rich farmland with dozens of farm cottages, many rented to estate workers whose families had worked for the Spencers for centuries.[8]

Althorp House had ninety rooms, many of which had not been lived in for some considerable time.[9] The Tudor manor house had been extended in the Georgian era with two side wings and a columned portico. The original brick façade had been refaced with pale tiles. Set in a walled park of 550 acres, the house was beside a formal *parterre* garden with ornamental statues which Diana loved and where she did her ballet practice in summer.

Diana was awed by the magnificence of her ancestral home, with its grand entrance hall and magnificent staircase — although at times she complained it felt like living in a museum as paintings, valuable antiques and *objets d'art* acquired by generations of Spencers were everywhere. Althorp had what was reckoned to be the finest private collections of paintings in England started by the second Earl Spencer, who as a young man made the Grand Tour and purchased art in Italy. Family portraits decorated the gallery that ran the entire length of the front hall, the magnificent staircase and the long passageways, and the highlights are two valuable paintings of the Stuart kings, James I and Charles I.

---

8 For a detailed history of Althorp, see Charles Spencer *Althorp, The Story of an English House*, St Martin's Press, London, 1999. The rooms are filled with the finest private art collection in England. For opening times see http://www.althorp.com

9 In the 2014 television documentary *Althorp, Secrets of the Manor*, Diana's brother, Charles, the current Earl Spencer, stated that Althorp had 90 rooms, but some books cite as many as 100 rooms.

Althorp Entrance Hall (courtesy the late Earl Spencer)

The Great Room had been used by the second Earl Spencer as a reception suite in the years when he was First Lord of the Admiralty and Home Secretary. It contained magnificent antiques and a rare portrait of Lady Jane Grey, the unfortunate young queen whose ambitious family had placed her in the position of ruling for a hundred days before she was executed.

Althorp's magnificent library, filled with rare first editions, held little interest for Diana who read nothing but romance novels by Barbara Cartland, Mills and Boon paperbacks and fashion magazines. With its large rooms and echoing passages, Althorp was cold in winter as efficient central heating had not been installed in most stately homes in the 1970s. Coal fires warmed the bedrooms, and there were no fitted carpets on the polished floors, only rugs. But times were changing. Diana arrived at Althorp in 1975 when domestic staff, chauffeurs and gardeners were demanding higher wages, so some staff had to be let go. Nevertheless, Diana's ancestral home still had a butler, a cook, a footman and seven indoor servants.

As her grandfather had warned Diana's father years earlier he had to pay enormous death duties on the estate. These were assessed at the staggering sum of two-and-a-half *million* pounds sterling, but the problem for the new Earl was that because of the divorce he lost his wife's money to help him pay the enormous death duties and this caused him a great deal of anxiety to find the money to do necessary restoration work to maintain his estate.

Diana was also awed by Althorp's grand bedrooms where several kings and queens had slept. The gallery that ran the full length of the house contained family portraits and some of Sir Peter Lely's famous portraits of ladies at the court of Charles II as there were family connections with several of the royal dukes who were ennobled as hey were the offspring of the king by various mistresses. A portrait of the 'Red' Earl Spencer showed him with a red beard and hair the same copper colour as hair of Diana's elder sister, Lady Sarah and her brother Charles as red hair ran in the family.

Diana was now able to spend time with her mother and stepfather in Scotland, although by now, her second marriage was having problems. Peter Shand Kydd's resentment over the loss of his children caused arguments between them, making Frances tense and unhappy. Diana watched them arguing and secretly hoped that her mother's second marriage would fail so her mother would return to live with them at Althorp, a forlorn hope as it turned out but which haunted Diana for years to make up for the misery she had endured when her mother left and she feared she might be dead.

⁂

The ambitious Lady Fermoy hoped that Diana, who was the prettiest of her three granddaughters, might eventually marry Prince Andrew but at this time did not see Prince Charles as a possible husband for her as he was thirteen years older than Diana and totally different in character.

Peter Shand Kydd found the idea of Diana marrying Prince Andrew was possible and, as a joke, nicknamed her 'Duch' short for duchess, as eventually Andrew would become the Duke of York, the name always given to the second son of the reigning king.

On one occasion Diana told her sisters she hoped to marry royalty or someone really famous or with a title, as she was surrounded by portraits of female ancestors who had married dukes and earls and her namesake had been briefly engaged to Frederick, Prince of Wales, a brief engagement facilitated by the large dowry offered by her grandmother, Sarah, Duchess of Marlborough.

In character, Diana resembled her mother being very emotional and romantic with a hot temper. Like Frances she hated blood sports believing they were cruel. So whenever her father held shooting parties at Althorp, Diana took refuge in the servants' hall, eating with the staff and reading their tabloid newspapers and exchanging local gossip with them, and soon enjoyed the same kind of warm relationship with them as she had done with the staff at Park House.

She continued to iron her own clothes, aware that with their numbers reduced, the servants had to work hard to keep Althorp House in order. She was disturbed by the gossip in the servants' hall emanating from Sandringham saying Prince Andrew was a couch potato who lay on the sofa watching sexually explicit videos. This made Diana remove the photos of Prince Andrew from her bedroom wall and concentrate her romantic dreams on Prince Charles. She continued to cut out photos of the young Prince of Wales from newspapers and magazines.

Due to her extreme shyness, Diana hated making polite conversation with guests and, rather than join them in the dining room, preferred to take a tray to her room and eat there alone watching *Coronation Street* or other television soaps.

As she grew up, Diana began to resemble her mother, with the same deep blue eyes under long lashes and long slender legs. She loved sweet things, so Mrs Smith the cook let Diana raid the fridge whenever she liked.

Bored and lonely when her sisters were away at boarding school, Diana would gorge on ice-cream, flavoured custards and cream cakes. Had Frances been there, her mother might have prevented Diana from binge eating, but no one checked what she was eating. Diana took food from the fridge on a tray up to her bedroom rather than eating in the dining room and this caused the shy sensitive little girl to have a brief episode of the eating disorder known as bulimia *nervosa.* By gorging on sweet 'comfort foods' but afraid she would put on weight and no one would love her, she would make herself vomit.

Bulimia nervosa had only recently been classified as a psychiatric disorder by the American Psychiatric Association, and few people in Britain were aware of the danger it posed as constant vomiting of food deprives the brain of essential vitamins and minerals and can cause severe mood swings. Diana's brief attack of this nervous eating disorder ceased once she became more accustomed to her new home.

Ashamed of what she later called a 'secret disease', she rarely talked about this brief episode of bulimia and in later life preferred to blame her long struggle with bulimia on the fear that her husband did not love her.

Once she had recovered from her bulimia Diana started to enjoy the advantages of Althorp when the weather turned warmer in summer. At Park House she had always enjoyed going to the beach or swimming in the pool and she was thrilled when her father arranged for a pool to be built at Althorp and spent a great deal of time swimming and practicing her diving skills.

She also enjoyed doing her ballet routines and posing for her father's camera which she knew secured his undivided attention and enjoyed posing beside one of the statues in the formal garden or being photographed diving into the pool, calling out excitedly, 'Look at me! Look at me!' as she longed for her father's attention.

At Althorp, Diana dressed very casually in jeans and baggy woollen pullovers or wore a favourite pair of green dungarees that matched her green Wellington boots or the flower-patterned 'milkmaid' clothes designed by Laura Ashley, so popular with teenagers in the 1970s.

She and Charles had their bedrooms in the former nursery suite, remote from the rest of the house that was so vast that for days on end both children saw little of their father. Earl Spencer ate in the main dining room, served by the household staff. Sometimes when he was alone, Diana and her brother were invited to join him there, but Diana was still very shy, and if her father had guests, she preferred not to eat in the dining room.

Her father had old fashioned values and was a firm believer in courtesy and good manners. Earl Spencer insisted his children write thank-you letters immediately they received a gift, no matter how small, and this was a habit that remained with Diana all her life. Apart from writing thank-you letters, there were few rules in this motherless household to discipline a teenager, and Diana lacked supervision in the school holidays.

With her father busy managing his estate and often away in London and her elder sisters at boarding school, she did virtually as she liked. Mrs Smith, the cook, did not see it as part of her job to discipline the often-headstrong young girl.

⁂

For years after his divorce, Diana's father had been lonely and depressed. Now as one of England's premier aristocrats with a stately home filled with art and antiques, he was seen as a 'good catch' by divorcées and widows who fancied themselves as the next Countess Spencer.

Diana's father, while serving on the heritage committee of the Westminster City Council, met Raine Dartmouth, wife of Bill Legge, the tenth Earl of Dartmouth who had been at Eton with him. As he and Raine shared an interest in old houses, he started taking photos for Countess Dartmouth's book on how best to preserve historic houses.

Diana's insecurity made her very manipulative, and she tried to stop her father leaving home as she had done during her childhood by throwing tantrums. However, this no longer worked as her father, having discovered this new interest, spent more and more time away.

Raine, sensing Earl Spencer's interest in historic houses, suggested Johnnie help her by taking photos for the booklet she was compiling. So they toured England taking photographs for the project, and this time away together staying in good hotels (as Raine enjoyed luxury) led to their clandestine love affair.

Diana pleaded with her father to stay home, trying the emotional blackmail tactics she had used years ago, telling him, 'If you *really* loved me you wouldn't leave me.'

On one family outing, Countess Dartmouth appeared as if by accident and was introduced to all four children. They greeted her politely but suspected that she had designs on their father and took an immediate dislike to her.

On several occasions, Raine came to stay at Althorp and was put in one of the best rooms in the house, known as the India Silk bedroom. She brought presents for all the children, but they were not grateful regarding these as bribes. Much later, Diana told her biographer, Andrew Morton, they knew even then that Raine wanted to marry their father and were determined to try to avert this.

The Countess of Dartmouth was a well-preserved woman in her mid-forties with four adult children. Her mother was the famous novelist, Barbara Cartland, whose romantic novels were often laughed at for their virginal heroines that Diana selected to be her role models in life.

Barbara Cartland had cleverly discovered a very popular formula for writing popular romance in which a pretty young heroine meets a handsome, powerful man who initially ignores her and pursues an older sexually experienced woman before he discovers that he really loves the innocence of the virginal heroine and proposes, and they marry and live happily ever after.

This winning formula for a romance novel had not been the case in Barbara Cartland's life. She had been a very good looking young woman with good social skills and was good at manipulating men. Her first marriage had ended in a bitter divorce with adultery on both sides, and she had often hinted to Raine that her birth father was the Duke of Sutherland, one of several high-profile lovers Cartland had had affairs with during her first marriage. Her second marriage was more successful, but as this husband was far from wealthy, Barbara Cartland began what became a brilliantly successful career writing sugary romantic novels which avoided the topic of sex by making the heroine determined to preserve her virginity at all costs. Cartland perfected a method whereby she could lie on a sofa and dictate these romances to a secretary. She wrote the staggering total of six hundred and fifty-five popular romances before the sexual revolution and the contraceptive pill made critics and readers fall about laughing as her novels were totally unrealistic.

Barbara Cartland did not care as she banked the money and spent much of it on expensive designer outfits, jewellery and beauty treatments. Always dressed in brilliant pink and loaded down with diamonds and pearls which she wore from breakfast until bedtime, in old age she was beloved of gossip columnists, as her appearance was so outlandish with long false eyelashes loaded with mascara resembling the legs of gigantic beetles, highlighted by brilliant green eye-shadow and fuchsia pink lipstick.

But these slushy romances that Diana adored had paid for Raine to have a London Season, as Barbara Cartland wanted her daughter to follow the path of her heroines and concentrate on making 'a good marriage.' Raine was smart so hid the fact she was very bright. She played the sweet ingénue, and landed what she thought was the big fish in the marriage stakes by marrying the Hon William Legge who was heir to the earldom of Dartmouth. But to her chagrin, by the time it took the old Earl of Dartmouth to die, the family fortune and estate had been dissipated and the stately home was sold. This was a bitter disappointment to Raine who, after twenty-eight years of marriage and raising four children, was bored by a husband who was not nearly as clever as she was and had carved out a successful career in local politics at a time when most men did not approve of women involving themselves in public affairs. She was clever at manipulating people, worked hard and became known as 'the woman who got things done' on the town planning and heritage committees of the Westminster City Council – and through working on this committee met and fell in love with Earl Spencer.

It is possible that, having been told by her mother she had been fathered by a duke, Raine felt she deserved a stately home like Althorp. Like most visitors to the Spencer's ancestral home with its art treasures, she must have believed the estate was worth many millions – as, indeed, it is today. But what Raine did not know was that death duties were still being paid on the estate, as Diana's father was cash poor but asset rich.

Raine was still very attractive in a very different way to Diana's mother and nothing like Frances with her bizarre outfits, large hats and garish make up. Raine became known for her elegant designer outfits, each one with a matching hat, and for wearing very high heels that showed off to good advantage her long shapely legs and trim ankles.

One of the main reception rooms at Althorp, hung with valuable pictures and antique mirrors. (courtesy the late Earl Spencer)

It took some time for the Earl of Dartmouth to suspect his former school chum was having an affair with his wife. But eventually the penny dropped, so the Earl engaged detectives to follow his wife and his former school friend from Eton. Raine's overnight visits to Althorp continued to the annoyance of the Spencer children and eventually a private detective obtained the necessary evidence for her husband's divorce action against Earl Spencer.

The fact the Countess of Dartmouth was often a guest at Althorp made Diana glad to get away by going to boarding school in Kent.

West Heath was an exclusive private school attended by Diana's mother and her daughters. The school had thirty-two acres of landscaped grounds near the market town of Sevenoaks and educated its fee-paying pupils to become good wives and mothers. They were not encouraged to study for university entrance in the 1960s when Diana attended the school and may have been the reason the school closed in the 1980s when debutante seasons were considered passé and many girls began thinking about tertiary education and well-paid careers.

As a new girl at West Heath, Diana was still very timid. She blushed and stammered if asked a question in class. Even if she knew the answer crippling shyness made answering it a problem.

Most girls aimed to do Cordon Bleu cookery or flower-arranging courses or attend private secretarial courses and do non-demanding jobs that gave them plenty of time for a good social life hoping to meet the man of their dreams.

Lady Jane Spencer had been a school prefect and achieved good exam results. Lady Sarah was just as intelligent, but her parents' divorce had affected her, and she was rebellious. Sarah smuggled vodka into her dormitory at West Heath and was found drunk by a senior member of staff, and as a result, Sarah was expelled and had to be sent to Switzerland to finish her education.

Had she been at school today, Diana would have been sent to an educational psychologist to treat her panic attacks in exams and her crippling shyness. Exams for Lady Diana were a nightmare. She was conscientious and took notes and revised them before the exam, but the panic attacks caused Diana's mind to go blank during the exams. Today she would be advised to relax with jogging or power walking on the morning of the exam and taught deep breathing and other relaxation techniques but these were not available to Diana.

Repeated exam failures eroded Diana's self-confidence and made her even more nervous. In her diary, Diana described herself as 'thick as two short planks' which was not true. She was intelligent but needed special tuition and counselling which she never received. Her subsequent career as a humanitarian revealed she had a good brain and was able to use it.

Even though her exam results were woeful, Diana enjoyed her time at West Heath and made many friends and was closest of all to warm-hearted, sensible Carolyn Pride and their friendship continued for years.

Frances Shand Kydd agreed to pay Diana's school fees as well as extra classes for ballet, tap and ballroom dancing. Dancing, considered one of the social graces, was taught at West Heath by Madame Vacani who had been teaching girls how to waltz, foxtrot and rumba.

Diana's ambitions were to join a ballet company followed by marriage and she pinned her hopes of happiness on marrying 'Prince Charming' determined to remain a virgin until she met him, believing from her reading of Barbara Cartland's books that men found virginity alluring as well as challenging.

Diana had inherited the talent of her maternal grandmother, Lady Ruth Fermoy, for the piano but was aware that although she played well her playing would never reach concert standard like her grandmother.

At West Heath, Diana practised the piano and developed a repertoire of classical works which she was able to play without the aid of sheet music.

But ballet was her chief passion. In spite of her shyness, she longed to perform on stage and receive applause, and as her later career shows, she did have many of the gifts for public performance which once she had conquered her nerves made her perform so brilliantly in public and in front of the camera.

This photo of Diana with some of her Barbara Cartland romances was used by Cartland's publicist (Private collection)

Each year before the school concert, Diana practised her ballet steps in front of the long mirrors in the school hall. She would sneak down to the hall in the middle of the night, turn on the lights and go through her routines. The fact that Diana was selected to perform each year in the school concert bolstered her dreams of joining a professional ballet company, despite the fact she was tall for her age and still growing. Lady Diana's ravenous appetite was a joke among her friends. She ate three kippers at breakfast and at dinner always had second helpings of dessert and between meals devoured boxes of chocolates.

Photos taken in her final year at West Heath show Lady Diana with plump rosy cheeks rather than the chiselled beauty of her mid-twenties. She knew that her best feature was her deep blue eyes under their long dark lashes. In the mirror she practised fluttering her lashes, looking upwards from under her fringe and giving her shy but brilliant smile, which she employed for the photos which would make her famous. But all that lay ahead.

⁂

'Touch them and let them see you feel their pain'

Important aspects of Diana's education at West Heath School were visits made by her class to the local hospital and the way she was taught to deal with patients by Miss Stevens, which would make this shy girl a success when she became Princess of Wales and behaved like no royal family member had ever behaved before.

A live-wire young teacher named Muriel Stevens took Diana's class to visit elderly patients at the Sevenoaks District Hospital and the grim Derwent Valley District Mental Hospital.

Even then Diana displayed remarkable empathy with the sick, the bereaved and those who were mentally ill. The influence of Miss Stevens on Diana was very important, and she praised Diana for the empathy she showed, which was genuine and came from her heart.

Miss Stevens' advice on how to deal with patients helped Diana later in life when hospital visiting became important to her and she discovered she had a gift for empathising with the sick and the elderly.

Miss Stevens explained to the class the importance of making eye contact with patients by crouching down at their eye-level. She explained how, whenever possible, the girls should sit on the bed or a chair beside the patient, hold their hands and touch them gently on the shoulders. They could stroke patients on the face if they seemed receptive as this provided comfort for the elderly and those who were bedridden. Many of the mental patients were widowed and rarely visited by family members. In some cases, no one had touched them affectionately for years, and being touched by someone young and pretty made them happy.

Diana never forgot Miss Stevens' words: 'Let the patients see you feel their pain. Touch is important and a comfort for those who are suffering.'

For a young girl from a privileged background, Lady Diana's empathy with the aged, the infirm and the mentally ill was astonishing. Many West Heath girls shrank from contact with patients who had cancerous tumours or signs of mental illness.

Diana exhibited no revulsion at seeing tumours or ulcerated sores and had no problems talking to mentally ill patients, even those who behaved in bizarre ways. She would chat happily to elderly people whose hands were shaking with Parkinsonian tremors or who had disfiguring facial cancers. Her empathy with the patients was remarkable, as was her gentleness towards the elderly. She loved children and was able to caress and comfort sick children and talk to them in ways they understood.

Miss Stevens gave Diana renewed confidence by telling her she had a very special gift for helping those in need and to talk to patients finding the right thing to say to put each patient at ease.

⁂

Diana and her siblings met Raine, Countess of Dartmouth, at Lady Sarah's coming-out ball. Frances surpassed herself by hiring the picturesque but ruined Castle Rising, filling it with flowers and hiring professional caterers and a disco for the night. Diana had hoped that the romantic setting might lead to a reunion between her parents. But her hopes were dashed when her father arrived at the ball with Raine and spent the entire evening dancing and talking to her ignoring Frances who was paying for the party and was the official hostess.

Diana and her sisters saw their mother was upset by their father's rudeness. Resenting the Countess of Dartmouth's presence, they made no effort to be polite to her.

Lady Sarah's romantic coming-out ball had cost Frances a great deal of money. Her partner for this important evening was handsome young Gerald Grosvenor, Duke of Westminster, Britain's wealthiest aristocrat, reckoned in debutante circles to be *the* 'catch of the season'.

Lady Fermoy was delighted at the prospect of such a brilliant match for her eldest granddaughter. At the end of the debutante season of lunches, balls, cocktail parties and country house weekends, Sarah was to fly to Australia to join her mother and stepfather for a three-month holiday on the Shand Kydd sheep property at Yass in New South Wales.

With her ticket paid for by her mother, Sarah felt she could not cancel the planned holiday. With mixed feelings, she left the handsome young aristocrat with whom she was in love hoping he would not forget her and flew to Sydney where her mother and Peter Shand Kydd met her at the airport and drove her to their country property.

However, absence did not make the duke's heart grow fonder. The young Duke of Westminster became involved with another girl who had no intention of giving him up.

After three months in Australia Lady Sarah flew back to London and was shattered to find she had lost her boyfriend. She refused to eat, developed *anorexia nervosa* and became skeletally thin.

Frances was sympathetic. Suspecting her second husband was unfaithful, she too had developed an eating disorder and lost a great deal of weight. Frances had Sarah admitted as an in-patient to a private psychiatric clinic under the brilliant young Dr Maurice Liversedge. Using behavioural techniques and a revised eating plan, Dr Liversedge helped Sarah overcome her eating disorder and regain some weight.

Sarah's friendship with Prince Charles began later at a house party at Windsor Castle during Royal Ascot week. She was still thin but no longer anorexic. The Prince of Wales found auburn-haired Lady Sarah witty and amusing and invited her to join a ski party he was organising in a Swiss chalet he rented along with a group of friends.

Young Diana, with her schoolgirl crush, longed to meet the Prince of Wales and was envious of her sister.

Unknown to Diana, the Countess of Dartmouth's divorce was finalised, and she was free to marry again. At Althorp the staff were under instructions from Diana's father to hide the newspapers that had covered the scandalous divorce case, so Diana was unaware of the extent of her father's involvement with a woman she disliked intensely.

On 13 July 1976, Raine, Countess of Dartmouth, and Earl Spencer married at Caxton Hall Registry Office in central London. Aware his children disliked Raine, Earl Spencer did not invite them to the wedding or to the reception that followed. Diana's brother was the first of his children to learn of his father's remarriage when he was informed by the head of his prep school.

Diana was distressed and jealous when she learned the news the following day from one of the staff at Althorp. Nothing had prepared her for the shock of discovering her beloved father had not only married the bossy woman she loathed but had not bothered to tell her about the wedding before setting out on his honeymoon.

Diana was furious at what she saw as her father's 'betrayal' of his children by marrying a woman they disliked. When her father arrived home with his new wife, as the chatelaine of Althorp, Diana refused to greet her stepmother. Diana seethed with suppressed rage, so dinner was fraught with ill feeling and veiled insults. Later when she was finally alone with her father, Diana slapped him hard across the face, yelling, 'That's from *all* of us, Daddy, for treating us so badly!'

Diana's stepmother was totally unlike her gentle arts-loving mother. Raine was a successful career woman with a commanding presence, her bouffant hairstyle held in place by a thick coating of lacquer. Johnnie admired Raine for her looks, her brains and her strength of purpose, but the more his children saw of her, the more they loathed her.

Confronted by four hostile stepchildren, Raine's lack of tact and the fact she was accustomed to being obeyed at work and secure in her position as the new Countess Spencer, she made little effort to win her stepchildren over.

Raine was an excellent hostess. When Lady Sarah told her she had invited Prince Charles to her father's next shooting party, Raine arranged for a ball to be held in honour of the Prince of Wales in the ballroom at Althorp.

Sarah had hopes that this friendship might turn into something more. Now aged sixteen, Diana was allowed to return home for the ball weekend – the first she had ever attended. She was photographed wearing a long blue and white strapless ball gown that showed off her bust to good advantage.

Diana's father and her stepmother, Raine, the new Countess Spencer, outside Althorp. (courtesy of the Late Earl Spencer)

At the ball, Diana described her elder sister as being 'all over Prince Charles like a rash' and dancing with her heartthrob. Although Diana hated shooting parties, she went out with the guns and laughed and joked with Prince Charles. He knew nothing about her childhood trauma over the departure of her mother and described her as 'jolly and bouncy', the impression Diana wanted to give.

At the ball on the Saturday night, Prince Charles asked Lady Diana for a dance as she was the daughter of his host. Diana was thrilled, dancing being her forte, and enjoyed dancing with the object of her schoolgirl crush. Later the prince asked Diana to show him around the Spencer's private art gallery. Diana blushed and said she would be delighted.

This raised the hackles of Lady Sarah, who intervened and told her younger sister to 'push off', as she was the one to show Prince Charles the family's magnificent art collection.

As Charles was saying his goodbyes, he mentioned another ball that would be held to celebrate his thirtieth birthday at Buckingham Palace and told Lady Sarah and Lady Diana they would be on the guest list. Diana was ecstatic at the idea of attending a 'grown-up' ball at Buckingham Palace and another chance to dance with the Prince of Wales. For months, she boasted about this meeting with her schoolgirl crush to school friends and pinned more photos of Prince Charles to the walls of her bedroom.

Prince Charles on horseback was one of the images Diana cut out and placed on her bedroom wall. (Private collection)

Sarah continued to see Prince Charles along with other friends and hoped the relationship might develop into a more romantic one. After watching the Prince of Wales play polo Lady Sarah expected he would invite her out to dinner, and they would drive back to London in his sports car. Instead, after the match, he flirted with an exotic South American and placed her in the front seat of his Aston Martin coupé for the drive back to London. Sarah spent the journey crammed into the back seat, fuming with rage.

The Prince of Wales then dropped an angry Lady Sarah at her London mews house and drove away with the beauty from the de Borsaga family, presumably to his suite at Buckingham Palace. Sarah realised that Prince Charles could not be serious if he was behaving like this and was mortified.

Unwisely, Sarah agreed to lunch with journalist James Whitaker, whom she had met on the ski slopes at Klosters when he had written an article about the prince's ski party suggesting Lady Sarah Spencer was in the running to become Princess of Wales.

Sarah should have been wary of Whitaker, but naively believed remarks made 'off the record' would not be published. Encouraged by the wily royal correspondent, Sarah became expansive, revealing she had been expelled from West Heath School for being drunk on vodka. When the journalist and gossip writer asked her about Prince Charles, annoyed by what had occurred with the South American girl, Sarah told Whitaker she would not marry Prince Charles even if he asked her, forgetting that divulging *anything* to the press about the royals was a cardinal sin.

Sarah's revelations appeared in the *Woman's Own* on 8 April 1978 under the by-line of 'Jeremy Slazenger', one of Whitaker's pen names and he quoted Lady Sarah as saying:

'There is no chance of my marrying Prince Charles ... I am not in love with him. If he asked me to marry him I would turn him down. Prince Charles is a romantic who falls in love easily.'

Prince Charles was having affairs with a large number of young women overcoming his disappointment that Camilla Shand, the girl he loved and had wanted to marry, had married his friend, Andrew Parker Bowles. But Sarah was ignorant of this and seeing her indiscreet remarks in print made her panic. She telephoned Prince Charles to make things better by explaining. But the prince had already been shown the article by a member of his staff, and his response was icy.

'Sarah, you've just done something *extremely* stupid,' he said before putting down the phone on her.

Diana learned a sharp lesson from her sister's experience. Never under any circumstances disclose anything about royalty to the press.

Meanwhile, at Althorp, Diana's stepmother had been funding repairs to their stately home out of her own funds and tried to improve the dire financial position of the estate by selling off valuable art treasures.

Diana and her siblings bitterly resented their stepmother selling valuable porcelain, silver and paintings at bargain prices in private sales rather than using one of the big international auction houses like Sotheby's or Christie's. Raine claimed she had made these private sales to avoid giving the impression the Spencers were strapped for cash. However, the art world is a gossipy place. Rumours spread rapidly that valuable items from Althorp were being sold way below market value. Diana and her siblings felt their heritage was vanishing under their noses and hated their stepmother even more.[10]

To pay for more renovations to Althorp, which secretly to her closest friends she called 'Gloomsville', Raine asked both major auction houses to value items she hoped to sell for big money.

---

10 At this period Sotheby's Art Courses were run by Derek Shrubb, and the author lectured there on Australian nineteenth-century art and was shown photos of paintings and antiques from Althorp, which were either sold or used as teaching aides for students in Sotheby's art history courses.

The fact that their stepmother was spending a great deal of Spencer money to redecorate Althorp in the way that pleased her angered her stepchildren. They hated what they regarded as Raine's vulgar alterations to their family home. New and very bright gilding took years to tone in with the mellowed splendour of Althorp. Years later, Diana's younger brother Charles described the gilding as 'better suited to the wedding cake vulgarity of a five-star hotel in Monaco than to Althorp'.

To add insult to injury, the woman the children now called 'Acid Raine' replaced the portrait of the first Earl Spencer at the head of the main staircase with a portrait of herself. Their stepmother also had the polished oak floor in the Picture Gallery covered with patterned wall-to-wall carpeting, which her stepchildren considered very vulgar. When her stepchildren told Raine they thought she had ruined the Picture Gallery, considered one of the splendours of Althorp, family relations deteriorated still further.

Raine aimed to make the debt-ridden estate pay for itself. She established a gift shop and a produce store that sold fruit and vegetables grown on the estate to visitors and also instituted guided tours of the house led by family friends and wives of local landowners like my school friend Philppa Davidge whose husband owned Little Houghton House, a Georgian residence with a lake in the grounds near Althorp. Philippa remembers Diana as always being polite to the volunteer guides, most of whom were family friends keen to help out and aware the estate was in debt.

Raine, aware of Diana's love of her mother's romance novels, let Diana accompany her on a visit to Barbara Cartland at Camfield Place which was the house where Beatrix Potter had written 'Peter Rabbit'. The famous romance writer described Diana as very pretty but very uneducated and with poor general knowledge. She commented sadly, 'The only books Diana ever read were mine, and they weren't awfully good for her.'

At Althorp Countess Spencer enjoyed playing the society hostess. She had the famous Marlborough table silver polished and filled the dining room with celebrity guests who were served delicious food. Seething with rage at Raine's extravagance and disliking having to make polite conversation at formal meals in the dining room, Diana retreated to her bedroom with her dinner on a tray.

When Raine demanded her stepdaughter attend another dinner party with celebrity guests, Diana arrived in the dining room wearing Sony Walkman headphones. She sat at the dining table with the sound turned up as loud as it would go refusing to talk to Raines' guests even when they tried to talk to her.

When Raine ordered Diana to leave the table, her stepdaughter gave her a murderous look and left, slamming the door behind her. To Diana, returning to boarding school was a relief from living with a strict stepmother.

Learning problems, panic attacks & exam failures

Miss Rudge, the headmistress at West Heath, observed that, in spite of her shyness, Diana could be very determined when she *really* wanted something. She was neat, well-organised, always on time and polite to the staff, and for these reasons, although her examination results were woeful, Diana was made a prefect.

In the summer term, Diana sat for six subjects in the Junior Leaving Certificate known as 'O' Levels. She failed every single paper but was allowed to do a re-sit of all the papers the following term. Her subjects included English literature, British history, geography and maths. Lacking any special tuition and fearing she would fail again, Diana's anxieties and nervous nail-biting grew worse, but she studied hard and felt that this time she must pass a few papers.

But once again in the examination room, Diana was subject to panic attacks and unable to concentrate. She had butterflies in her stomach felt queasy, and everything she had revised seemed to vanish from her head. Panicking, she read the question wrong and provided information the examiner did not want.

Later she burst into tears when Miss Rudge, the headmistress, called her into her office and told her that for the second time she had failed every single paper, aware her siblings would laugh at her and call her a dimwit and her stepmother would despise her. Miss Rudge did not realise Diana had suffered panic attacks. Diana's parents, still at loggerheads, agreed that having failed every single subject not once but twice in her 'O' Levels, there was no point in her staying on at West Heath. Diana would never pass exams, no matter how long she stayed at school.

So, at sixteen, Diana became a school drop-out without qualifications and little knowledge of the world around her.

At Althorp, as she had feared, Diana was teased by her siblings, who called her an airhead. Defiantly she declared that she didn't care about exam results and would join a ballet company, dance her way to fame and marry a man who was rich and famous.

A letter from Frances telling her that supermarkets demanded the girls on their checkout counters had the Junior Leaving Certificate was depressing. Diana, unhappy at home and constantly fighting with her stepmother, felt a total failure.

Diana's parents hoped that with her looks she would soon find an eligible husband. But where would she find 'Mr Right' – or even 'Lord Right'? The world had changed since Lady Sarah and Lady Jane had had their coming-out balls in what was then an exclusive upper-crust marriage market. Doing the London Season was now not very important as upper-class girls started to become more career-minded.

Both her parents were worried by Diana's lack of qualifications for anything other than child minding or housework. Her elder sisters had interesting jobs in London. Jane was planning to marry Robert Fellowes, a boyfriend she had known since her Norfolk childhood. Young Charles was doing well at Eton and planning to attend university.

Clearly, Diana could not remain at Althorp in constant conflict with her stepmother. Frances and Johnnie agreed to meet and discuss solutions to 'the Diana problem'. While her father had shouldered the huge financial burden of maintaining Althorp, Frances was still very wealthy, having invested her share of her father's fortune wisely.

Feeling guilty that Diana's problems could be her fault for abandoning her daughter at a young age, Frances agreed to pay for Diana to attend a Swiss finishing school that claimed it taught pupils to speak fluent French by what they called 'the total immersion method'. Frances hoped that after a year in French-speaking Switzerland, Diana would be speaking French fluently, and could then do a Cordon Bleu cookery course and support herself by cooking dinner parties for married friends until she got married.

Frances promised to buy Diana an apartment in London as soon as she was old enough to share it responsibly with friends. Until then she could live in her mother's small but luxurious Chelsea apartment, as Frances now spent most of her time in Scotland due to her matrimonial problems.

In 1978, Diana became a new girl at the Institut Alpin Videmanette near Gstadt. What her parents did not realise was that the 'total immersion method' meant students were forbidden to speak in their mother tongue and had to speak in French or remain silent. Most of the pupils were from Italy, Spain and South America and had a working knowledge of French so had no difficulty with this form of language teaching. Diana, with her learning problems and only a smattering of schoolgirl French, remained silent, isolated and homesick.

Dreading the prospect of another failure, Diana wrote to both her parents, pleading to be allowed to return to England. She was upset when both Johnnie and Frances replied urging her to stay in Switzerland until the end of the term as Frances had paid her fees in advance.

Once again, Diana felt unwanted by both parents and decided to abandon trying to learn French and concentrate on learning to ski which she enjoyed.

In spring, she was allowed to return to Althorp for a week for her sister's wedding to Robert Fellowes. Lady Jane was marrying the son of Sir William Fellowes, the Queen's land agent. Bob Fellowes was sixteen years older than his bride, hard-working and responsible who held the important position of Under-Secretary to the Queen.

The couple had known each other for years and had many friends, so the wedding was a very happy event. As chief bridesmaid, Diana looked pretty in a long pale pink dress with a circlet of rosebuds on her head.

The reception was held at St James's Palace. Lady Fermoy was in her element with the Queen Mother, Queen Elizabeth, the Duchess of Kent and the Duke and Duchess of Gloucester as guests of honour.

Frances paid for the wedding, the flowers and the reception but once again Earl Spencer and Raine ignored her. Their rudeness to her mother upset Diana but the fact that Frances and her former husband were not on speaking terms was obvious to most of the guests.

Journalist James Whitaker, now working for the *Daily Mirror*, was there to cover the wedding. Diana knew that Whitaker had damaged Sarah's friendship with Prince Charles by writing an article for *Woman's Own*, but instead of ignoring him, Diana, fascinated by the tabloid newspapers chatted to the young journalist, but it was clear he was not interested in her.

Years later when Diana was a celebrity princess, James Whitaker could have kicked himself for not foreseeing the tall slightly gawky bridesmaid would have such a brilliant future. But he found talking to Lady Diana boring and moved away to talk to more interesting wedding guests in search of a story.

Shy Lady Diana giggled nervously when talking to anyone she did not know but smiled happily when photographed beside the bride. When saying her goodbyes to Earl Spencer, the Queen Mother mentioned that perhaps it was time to think about his youngest daughter's future. Privately she and Lady Fermoy had reached the conclusion that the shy but very photogenic young Lady Diana would make a most suitable bride for Prince Charles, as she was fond of children and was certainly no rival to him.

Diana's advantages in the eyes of the Windsor's were her distinguished pedigree with two royal dukes in her family tree, her love of children and the fact it was known that, unlike most girls of her age, she had never had a proper boyfriend. The Queen Mother felt Diana was the 'right type of girl' to give the House of Windsor the heir they all wanted.

Aristocratic virginal brides of her age were hard to find now the contraceptive pill was available to unmarried girls.

Lady Fermoy was careful not to mention Diana's emotional problems or her disastrous exam record to the Queen Mother. No one took into account the enormous difference in age and education between the university-educated Prince Charles with his philosophical and environmental interests and shy, nervous Lady Diana, with no qualifications or intellectual interests, terrified of horses and hating 'horsey' events, her favourite pastime was watching television soaps. Any psychologist asked for advice would have said they were a mismatch.

Living in luxury at Clarence House with the Queen Mother as her Woman of the Bedchamber and confidante, the two Scottish widows were the best of friends, and wealthy Lady Ruth Fermoy encouraged the Queen Mother to borrow large sums from Coutts Bank to spend on luxuries.

Queen Elizabeth, more frugal than her mother, was worried as the Queen Mother's bank overdraft soared to more than seven million pounds. Sir Ralph Anstruther, Treasurer to the Queen Mother, nearly had a nervous breakdown, unable to stop his employer spending a small fortune on *haute couture*, jewels, racehorses and lavish entertaining.[11]

At Clarence House, the Queen Mother and Lady Fermoy enjoyed organising luncheon and dinner parties with a liveried flunkey behind every chair. A Cordon Bleu chef served guests with delicacies like soufflés, truffles flown in from Perigord the day before and lobster croquettes, accompanied by Veuve Cliquot or vintage Krug at three hundred pounds a bottle.

Lady Fermoy was in charge of arranging musical evenings for guests and occasionally gave a piano recital herself, or organised a group to visit a new play on in the West End. On quiet evenings at Clarence House over gin and tonics they discussed how to get Charles interested in Diana once she returned from Switzerland.

Lady Fermoy continued to emphasise to the Queen Mother that her youngest granddaughter was devoted to children and longed to have a family. This was very cynical because when Diana was being promoted to the Queen Mother as the ideal royal, Lady Fermoy must have known what everyone else at court knew, which was that Camilla Parker Bowles was Prince Charles' long-term mistress.

---

11 Compiling a book on art collectors, the author was shown the Queen Mother's collection, including a Monet of the Creuse River, illustrated in *Impressionists Revealed Masterpieces and Collectors*, Random House, USA, 1982 and Little Brown, London.

Clarence House, London (Photo Jake de Vries)

Just like Prince Charles, Lady Diana was also needy and longed for someone to love her. She disliked the cold and dreamed of holidays on warm beaches in the Carribean or the Mediterranean while Charles favoured chilly Balmoral or the Kalahari Desert. He enjoyed polo and shooting; she liked shopping at Harrods.

Leaving home for London & independence

Diana returned home, upset to learn her father had suffered a cerebral hemorrhage and was in the local hospital. But when complications set in, he was taken to a London teaching hospital.

Raine proved invaluable and somehow managed to obtain a new medical drug from Bayer in Germany that helped her husband make a partial recovery. The Spencer children were upset when Raine insisted that the children were tiring her husband and blocked them from visiting their father in hospital. Even when he returned to Althorp to convalesce under her care, she still limited the time they could spend with him.

Aware of Diana's unhappiness at Althorp and her quarrels with her stepmother, Frances allowed her youngest daughter to live in her Chelsea apartment entirely free as she was earning a pittance as a house cleaner.

Her eldest sister Lady Jane was expecting her first child while Lady Sarah was about to announce her engagement to Neil McCorquodale, a wealthy landowner who farmed in the north of England.

Diana still felt a failure due to her lack of exam qualifications and was self-conscious about her height. Aware she was taller than many men (including Prince Charles), she wore ballet slippers or low-heeled shoes, slouched and hung her head and experimented, not always successfully with clothes bought in second-hand shops. Her mouse-brown hair was soft and floppy, and not until Diana started having blonde highlights put in by a hairdresser did her hair began to have more body. The other advantage of going blonder was that it drew attention to Diana's mesmerising deep blue eyes under their long dark lashes.

Helped financially by her mother, Diana enrolled at Madame Vacani's Dance Academy in the Old Brompton Road in a course for dance teachers of young children. Diana hoped that by enrolling at the famous dance school, she might be invited to audition for the corps de ballet of a major company although she had already been told at school she was too tall to dance professionally.

Before the course started, needing pocket money, Diana spent a few weeks working as a cleaner for her sister Sarah and a girlfriend with whom Lady Sarah shared the mews house Frances had bought for her. In addition to mopping, dusting and using the vacuum cleaner, Diana did the ironing for both young women in return for the meagre sum of one pound a week. She also did some cleaning for a Knightsbridge domestic agency under the name 'Miss Diana Spencer', so her employers were not aware she had a title.

After completing two terms of the teachers' course, Diana plucked up courage to ask Madame Vacani if she could audition for a ballet company. Her hopes were dashed when Madame told her that although she had great talent, she was far too tall to be considered for any *corps de ballet*.

Bitterly disappointed, Diana wept in private but saw no point in continuing with the teacher's course. She did not want to teach but to *dance*. As a consolation, Frances paid for her to have a skiing holiday in Switzerland with a group of young Etonians and their Sloane Ranger girlfriends.

Using the excuse she had injured her foot in a skiing accident, Diana dropped out of the dance course. Many years later, when Diana had become famous, a journalist questioned Madame Vacani as to why the Princess of Wales had abandoned her teaching course abruptly. Madame Vacani replied diplomatically that Lady Diana had such a crowded social life it did not allow time for her to teach children to dance. This was a very tactful cover-up. At seventeen, Diana's social life was limited to window-shopping or lunching with school friends; scared of men, she still had no regular boyfriend.

Meanwhile, Frances Shand Kydd was having problems with her second husband due to his infatuation with a younger woman. She converted to Roman Catholicism and became involved with fundraising to help fishermen and their families on the Isle of Seil who were very poor and also took pilgrims to Lourdes on Catholic pilgrimages. Frances rarely came south to see her daughter, although they spoke on the phone.

Lady Fermoy, Diana's snobbish grandmother, decided to use her close friendship with the Queen Mother and her time at Clarence House in her honorary post as Woman of the Bedchamber to put the case for Lady Diana Spencer, her 'problem' but very pretty granddaughter to be regarded as a suitable bride for Prince Charles.

Lady Ruth Fermoy was an expert at arranging marriages; she had married Lord Fermoy nearly twice her age attracted by his money and his title when she was a penniless but talented music student. She had married off her beautiful daughter to a man with whom she had little in common.

Now she would spend almost a year beavering to secure the marriage of her shy, nervous granddaughter to the heir to the throne aware he loved a married woman he was unable to marry.

Lady Fermoy knew that the Queen Mother and Prince Philip were worried by Prince Charles' love for Mrs Parker Bowles and wanted to break up the relationship.

After several meetings at musical evenings at Clarence House arranged by Lady Fermoy, Charles pointed out that young Lady Diana was a sweet girl but far too immature for him to marry. The ambitious Lady Fermoy did everything she could to promote the marriage of her granddaughter to the Prince of Wales, but Charles did not seem interested.

Prince Philip with a tough childhood ruined by his father's dismissal as head of the Greek Army in the Greek Turkish war of 1920–1922 that ended in exile for over a million Greeks and the jailing of thousands more had fled with his mother to Paris where his father had abandoned his wife and children and left them virtually penniless. Then funded by wealthy mistresses, he pursued the life of a playboy in Monte Carlo.

Prince Philip's mother, a princess of the House of Battenberg, (now Mountbatten) suffered a nervous breakdown and was placed in a psychiatric clinic by her German relatives.

Mountbatten relatives in Britain took care of the almost destitute young Prince Philip and paid his fees to attend Gordonstoun, where he worked hard and became a great success and entered the navy, which he loved. In a meeting engineered by Lord Louis Mountbatten, young Princess Elizabeth fell in love with her handsome but penniless cousin and wanted to marry him, but to do this, he had to leave the life of a naval commander which he enjoyed and walk two steps behind his wife which made him unhappy. Philip felt his son was a wimp and told him so on many occasions with the result that Charles spent his time at dangerous sports to win the approval of his father but never gaining it.

In the early days of her marriage as the wife of a naval commander, the Queen adored Charles, her first baby and was able to spend time caring for him. But with the premature death of her father George VI, her life was changed. As Queen Elizabeth II, she promised to serve her people all her life at her coronation and became a very dedicated ruler with many responsibilities. The Queen relied on her mother and her husband to deal with problems among her four children and arrange their education.

After surviving a very tough childhood by sheer determination and hard work, Prince Philip of Greece demanded a great deal of his eldest son who did everything he could to please his father. Charles jumped out of planes, risked his neck on the hunting field, and even when he gained his pilot's licence, his father did not attend his passing out celebration. Prince Philip constantly criticised Charles for his lack of 'backbone' and his wilful refusal to do his duty and marry and produce an heir for the House of Windsor.

Charles had inherited the hot temper of his Hanoverian ancestors and his grandfather George VI. Prince Philip also had an alarming temper, which Charles feared when it was directed at him.

Charles was basically a kind and generous young prince who wanted to use the royalties from his Duchy of Cornwall estate to help those less fortunate than himself. Unable to marry Camilla for reasons of royal protocol and finding a ready supply of girls who were sexually available, he played the field. Eventually, Camilla, tired of her husband's many infidelities, re-ignited their former passionate affair although he realised that one day he would have to find a wife and sire an heir.

Charles considered Camilla his soul mate and best friend as well as his mistress – they enjoyed fast cars, fox-hunting, polo, yachting, flying and fishing. But Charles was also a workaholic, with a deep-seated need to justify his existence. He was prepared to work hard for the causes he believed in, such as saving Britain's architectural heritage, endangered wildlife and the environment, and helping disadvantaged young people.

The mystical and philosophical side of Prince Charles' complex nature was encouraged by his spiritual guru and mentor Laurens van der Post. The prince was on a lifelong spiritual quest to seek the truth in various religions including Greek Orthodoxy as well as in the doctrines of Islam. At Cambridge, Prince Charles had received a much broader education than his forebears and was the first member of his family to earn a university degree and develop intellectual and philosophical interests.

'My nephew Charles was *born* old and very *needy*,' Princess Margaret observed to close friends.

The fact that Charles and Diana were needy was not mentioned by Lady Ruth Fermoy when she enthused about Lady Diana to the Queen Mother, presenting her as an ideal bride: meek, pliable and smitten by Prince Charles since her school days.

Prince Philip backed the plan to marry Charles to Lady Diana as did the Queen who, due to enthusiastic reports from her mother, supported the idea.

The Queen liked Diana's father, was godmother to her young brother and was aware that generations of Spencers had been loyal servants of the Crown. The Queen's only reservation about young Lady Diana was what she called that 'bad Fermoy blood.' The Queen feared Diana's mother was unstable, as she had left her children to run off with her lover, unaware Frances had been told by her lawyers she would gain custody so was not planning to leave them.

Prince Philip reminded his son he was now thirty-two so must marry soon and produce an heir, the duty of every Prince of Wales.

Lady Ruth Fermoy spearheaded the campaign to make Prince Charles marry her granddaughter. She organised musical evenings at Clarence House, to which she invited Diana and Charles, but he still took no notice of the shy teenager.

Lady Fermoy did not give up easily. She organised a party to attend a play she thought Charles would like, with a post-theatre supper. Diana wore her prettiest dress, but Charles, who enjoyed the company of clever, witty women, had only a few words with Lady Diana who giggled nervously, tongue-tied with shyness. Charles assured Lady Fermoy he found Diana 'a poppet', but he was not interested in *marrying* poppets; he wanted a mature, intelligent wife with a knowledge of world politics when he met world leaders, but this was totally beyond Diana.

As head of the family, Prince Philip decided his son had been a bachelor for long enough and Lady Diana was the answer. He obeyed centuries of tradition and invited Diana's uncle to visit him at Buckingham Palace and asked Lord Edmond Fermoy to vouch for Lady Diana's virginity as though the royal family were living in the eighteenth or nineteenth centuries – which, when it came to the matter of the marriage of princes, they were.

Young Lord Edmond Fermoy, primed by his mother, assured Prince Philip his niece was a virgin.

No one in the royal family mentioned that very important word 'compatibility'.

CHAPTER FOUR

Camilla – ancestry & a happy childhood

The role of a royal mistress is to curtsey and jump into bed. Alice Keppel.

It would have been difficult to find another lady who would have filled the part of an intimate friend to King Edward VII with the same loyalty and discretion. Lord Hardinge of Penshurst.

Alice Keppel

One factor against Camilla was the fact that her great-grandmother, Mrs Alice Keppel, was the mistress of Prince Charles' great-great-grandfather, King Edward VII, formerly Bertie, Prince of Wales. Although Bertie was fond of his wife Princess Alexandra of Denmark, mother of his children, she became deaf and had gynaecological problems that affected their sex life. Bertie, who had a strong libido had not shared his wife's bed for years and was one of Britain's most adulterous kings.

The middle-aged Prince of Wales kept his beautiful young mistress, Mrs Alice Keppel, in the shadows while his mother Queen Victoria was alive. But after he became king, she was La Favorita, the woman he invited to court functions. She was widely respected for her calming influence on a monarch who when displeased would bellow with rage. Bertie and his wife knew royal marriages were for life and so the Queen had over the years turned a blind eye to all her husband's mistresses.

Mrs Keppel would never in her wildest dreams have imagined the Prince of Wales would give up his throne to marry her. She was almost as young as Edward VIII's third daughter. Alice was the seventh daughter of Admiral and Lady Edmonstone, and her childhood and adolescence were spent at Duntreath Castle near Strathblane, a Scottish baronial mansion, and she was educated by governesses.

Guests at the June 1891 wedding of Alice Edmonstone and the Hon George Keppel commented what a handsome couple they made. George's father had served as Household Treasurer to Queen Victoria, while his uncle was part of Queen Victoria's household. The uncle held out hopes of a post being created for George at Buckingham Palace. Alice persuaded her new husband to leave the army and move to London where they rented a small terrace house in Wilton Crescent, Belgravia. Unfortunately, the proposed post in the royal household never materialized and George had no private income.

Servants were vital as few private homes were connected to electricity. The Hon George felt that as an officer and a gentleman he should not work at anything as vulgar as trade or commerce. All they had to live off was Alice's small dowry and an even smaller income from George's father, as their debts mounted.

Alice soon realised that some aristocratic, but cash-strapped, wives of her acquaintance paid their enormous dress bills by taking wealthy men as their lovers. She was living in London in an era celebrated in the plays of Oscar Wilde where, as long as adultery was discrete and scandal was avoided, no one seemed to care.

Alice soon found herself a good looking and generous lover. William Beckett (soon to inherit the title of Lord Grimthorpe) was a widowed merchant banker, and a director of Beckett's Bank, which gave him access to unlimited funds. Besotted by Alice William Beckett, he gave the young Keppels generous bank loans with elastic dates for repayment.

He became a family friend, knew the rules of what was known as 'the game of love' and never threatened the Keppels' marriage. He was satisfied as long as he could spend a couple of afternoons each week in Alice's boudoir. So, in return for 'turning a blind eye' to his wife's leisure activities, the Hon George Keppel was able to lead the life of a gentleman of leisure which solved the money problems of the Keppels without Alice's husband having to soil his hands with work. Alice could afford to employ a butler, several maids, a boot boy and a nanny for young Violet, who was born a year after the couple arrived in London.

Enjoying life with an obliging and complacent husband, Alice became an accomplished hostess, widely regarded as one of the most beautiful and fascinating young women in London.

Introduced to Mrs Keppel at the races, Bertie, Prince of Wales, admired her long chestnut-brown hair, sparkling blue eyes and curvaceous figure, accentuated by the wasp-waisted gowns that were in fashion. He already knew that Mrs Keppel had had a wealthy lover and it was clear the

Hon George would make no trouble if the heir to the throne enjoyed an intimate relationship with his wife, as long as she was well provided for financially and discretion was observed.

When Alice became Bertie's mistress, he was almost sixty and weighed one hundred and ten kilograms (sixteen stone). Each afternoon the Prince of Wales sat in his horse-drawn brougham as they clip-clopped along the street from Marlborough House to Wilton Crescent and dropped the enamoured Prince of Wales at Mrs Keppel's front door. The coachman waited patiently in the street outside until the heir to the throne reappeared.

Needing money to support her household and maintain her position in society, Mrs Keppel, the family breadwinner, regarded the generous Prince of Wales as a sugar daddy sent from heaven. His devotion gave her prestige in the upper-crust circles among which the Keppels moved, so Alice was happy to 'curtsey and jump into bed' as she put it, with her generous lover and became fond of him. She would grace her husband's bed on occasions – but on her terms.

The besotted Prince of Wales, thrilled by the conquest of a beautiful woman young enough to be his daughter, showered Alice with jewels.[12] Bertie consulted his financial advisor Sir Ernest Cassel as to how he could support the cash-strapped Keppel household without anyone knowing.

Sir Ernest arranged a loan at a very low rate of interest so the Keppels could move from their small terrace in Wilton Crescent to a more imposing, six-storey house in Portman Square. Thanks to the generosity of the Prince of Wales and the intervention of Sir Ernest Cassel in obtaining the loan (much of which was never repaid), Mrs Keppel was able to employ several housemaids and a nanny for her children. She also employed a lady's maid to lace and unlace her corsets, so she could spend languorous afternoons in her boudoir with her lover.[13]

Aided by sound financial advice from Sir Ernest Cassel, Alice proved to be a shrewd investor and played the London Stock Exchange successfully during the stock market boom in the long period of peace and prosperity before the start of World War One.

Edward VII's gift to his married mistress of a parcel of shares in a rubber company caused much mirth among his ribald male cronies. Condoms made from vulcanised rubber were starting to be used by married couples but had previously been the preserve of prostitutes and courtesans. French courtesans had introduced Bertie to the practice, as they

---

12 The pearl choker that Bertie, Prince of Wales, gave Alice Keppel was later purchased at auction by Prince Charles for Camilla.

13 Diane Souhami, *Mrs Keppel and her Daughters*, HarperCollins, London, 1992, p21.

used condoms to avoid catching venereal disease.

Over the years, Mrs Keppel's shares in that particular rubber company soared in value and are alleged to have earned her fifty thousand pounds, equivalent to several million pounds today.

Famous for her tact and discretion, it was claimed that Alice never said an unpleasant word about anyone in court circles. One of her virtues was the fact that Alice managed to remain calm and unruffled even during a crisis, a skill her great-granddaughter, Camilla, Duchess of Cornwall, has inherited as well as the ability to soothe a moody or petulant Prince of Wales.

In May 1899, Alice Keppel gave birth to her second daughter named Sonia Keppel. The Prince of Wales added weight to the rumours that he was the father by lavishing Alice with flowers after the birth. Clever Alice allowed both Bertie *and* George Keppel to believe that they were the father.

In January 1901, on the death of Queen Victoria, the pleasure-loving Prince of Wales, after many years as monarch-in-waiting, succeeded to the throne as King Edward VII. For his coronation, Bertie made sure invitations were issued to favourite mistresses, past and present, so they could watch him being crowned. An area of Westminster Abbey near the altar was roped off for them. Lord Esher, a senior member of the Royal Household, dubbed this 'The King's Loosebox' (a stall for horses or, in the case of Edward VII, for mares).

Mrs Keppel, Lady Randolph Churchill, actress Sarah Bernhardt, courtesan Catherine Walters and the Duchesse de Cariocollo (allegedly the mother of one of Bertie's many ex-nuptial children) were seated in this special section of Westminster Abbey. It was ironic that royal mistresses, past and present, were assembled in a place of worship to see the adulterous Prince of Wales anointed as King and Defender of the Anglican Church. Edward VII, who had been breaking the Biblical commandment forbidding adultery for years, was now being awarded a key role in the Anglican Church, a body which regarded adultery as a sin.

In a front pew of the Abbey sat the Earl of Warwick and beside him, wearing scarlet coronation robes trimmed with ermine and the Warwick tiara glittering with diamonds on her head, sat Daisy, Countess of Warwick, the new king's ex-mistress.

Alice watched her lover being crowned by the Archbishop of Canterbury. Queen Alexandra, dazzling in diamonds and her scarlet coronation robes, was seated on a throne facing 'The Loosebox' beside her portly husband.

With Queen Victoria dead and the crown safely on his head, Bertie was able to acknowledge Alice's role in his life more openly. Journalists started discreetly referring to Mrs Keppel as the king's 'constant companion' or his 'favourite bridge partner'.

The grandeur of being a royal mistress went to Alice's head. From now on she wore nothing but expensive *haute couture* outfits from the House of Worth in Paris.

Mrs Keppel and Edward VII spent weekends together in grand houses like Chatsworth, Goodwood and Polesden Lacey where they were allocated adjoining bedrooms. George Keppel was allocated a bedroom in a separate wing to his wife and her royal lover.

The life of a royal mistress was not all roses and expensive jewels as royal gifts. Alice had to suffer the Prince of Wales' attacks of rage so extreme he ground his teeth, a propensity inherited by several of his male descendants. His courtiers were grateful to Mrs Keppel for soothing the monarch and charming him out of petulant moods, a skill Camilla has inherited from her great-grandmother.

However, Queen Alexandra disliked being upstaged by Mrs Keppel when they attended the same functions wearing the latest Paris fashions, aware that her husband was paying for both sets of designer clothes.

Prone to bronchitis in the cold, damp British winters, the ageing Edward VII was advised by Sir Francis Laking, his personal physician, to go south in search of a milder climate. So, the king took an annual three-week holiday in Biarritz from late March to mid-April. For many years, Alice joined him at this elegant French holiday resort. After visiting her favourite Paris couturiers and buying outfits for the coming season, Alice would travel south by train to Biarritz where she was treated like royalty by the French and officials used to royal mistresses of French kings and Premiers.

To preserve appearances, Alice never stayed at the same hotel as the king but was given an entire floor to herself in the holiday home of the king's friend and financial advisor Sir Ernest Cassel whose Villa Eugenie, overlooking the Atlantic, was fitted with every conceivable luxury.

In the spring of 1910, Edward VII set off for Biarritz, travelling separately from his mistress. That winter the king's bronchitis had been so severe that Queen Alexandra had tried without success to persuade her husband to enjoy a Mediterranean cruise with her on the royal yacht.

At Biarritz, Alice became alarmed when the king developed a chest infection, but he dismissed it as only a head cold and a cough. Instead of following their usual custom and attending the races, they went by car to Lourdes, so Edward VII could take the 'waters', which were alleged to have healing properties.

Alice was reassured by an apparent improvement in the King's condition. After seven happy weeks together, Edward VII returned to

Buckingham Palace on 27 April 1910. Queen Alexandra had remained in Corfu as a guest of her brother, the King of Greece, so Bertie travelled alone to Sandringham, expecting his wife to join him there.

Returning to her London home, Mrs Keppel stopped off in Paris to visit the House of Worth to commission the exquisitely embroidered ball gowns for which the celebrated designer was famous (and for which her royal lover paid the bills) and then returned to London by train.

On the evening of 2 May 1910, Edward VII dined and played bridge with Alice Keppel, Agnes Keyser and her sister.[14] The elderly monarch, still pale and racked by bouts of coughing, stopped playing bridge relatively early and returned alone to Buckingham Palace. As the monarch's condition continued to deteriorate, Sir Francis Laking telegraphed the news to Queen Alexandra.

The Queen hurriedly returned to London, and her husband rallied sufficiently to accompany her to a command performance of Rigoletto at Covent Garden – the last public engagement Edward VII would undertake.

The death of an adulterous monarch

By Friday, 6 May 1910, the king had suffered a series of heart attacks. Newspapers admitted the king was ill but did not provide details.

From Portman Square, Alice spread a story that Queen Alexandria had sent for her, implying that the Queen acknowledged her 'special relationship' with her husband. According to Lord Esher and the royal physician, Sir Francis Laking, this was a lie. Mrs Keppel had attempted to gain entry to Buckingham Palace, but the Queen had given orders she was *not* to see her husband and Mrs Keppel returned to Portman Square in floods of tears.

Alice was desperate to see her lover, having been advised by Sir Ernest Cassel that the previous day he had taken a large sum of money to the King's bedroom suite. It was believed to have been £10,000 in banknotes, the profit from a share trading deal Ernest Cassel, as the King's financial advisor, had carried out for the monarch. Sir Ernest told Alice that the king wanted her to receive this money from his own hands as a final gift.[15]

Lord Esher related how Mrs Keppel finally 'wheedled' her way into Buckingham Palace by a clever stratagem and sent a special messenger to

---

14 P. Lamont Brown, *Alice Keppel and Agnes Keyser, Edward VII's Last Loves,* The History Press, UK, 2005.

15 Theo Aronson, *The King in Love,* John Murray, London, 1988, p251.

the Queen enclosing a signed letter from Bertie, written years previously, just before Alice's lover had his appendix removed. The letter stated that Mrs Keppel was to be admitted to the royal suite as the king wished to say farewell to her, fearing he might die on the operating table.[16]

Queen Alexandra could hardly refuse a written request from her husband. With reluctance she allowed the king's mistress to be admitted to the king's private suite. When Alice curtseyed low, the Queen greeted her coldly and observed, 'I'm sure you had a good influence on him.'

Queen Alexandra positioned herself as far away as possible from her husband's mistress and gazed out of the window so she did not have to look at Alice holding her husband's hand and whispering to him.

In Mrs Keppel's 'sanitised' version of events, as related by her daughter Sonia in her book *Edwardian Daughter* – the title cleverly chosen to suggest Sonia Keppel could have royal parentage – the Queen sent for her in a gesture of friendship to say goodbye to the King. The story Alice put out was that the dying king asked his wife and his mistress to kiss each other 'as a token of their friendship'. According to courtiers who were present, this was purely an invention by Alice. Senior Buckingham Palace courtier Lord Esher and royal physician Sir Francis Laking related very different versions of the King's deathbed in which Mrs Keppel appears in a far less favourable light as distinctly avaricious.

Sir Francis Laking agreed with Lord Esher's account that the king was comatose and unable to recognise Mrs Keppel. As his condition worsened, Sir Francis administered a fatal injection of morphine. This practice, now regarded as euthanasia, was carried out so that news of the King's death could appear in the morning papers.

Once Edward VII was pronounced dead, Queen Alexandra remained calm and dignified. In contrast, Mrs Keppel lost control, sobbing and laughing hysterically.[17]

Lord Esher felt that Mrs Keppel's hysterics were caused by the realisation she would not receive the gift of money promised by the monarch, which in 1911, represented a small fortune. Between sobs and bursts of manic laughter, Alice cried out, 'I never did any harm – what is to become of me?'

Queen Alexandra finally had enough of the histrionics of her husband's mistress. Her iron control snapped, and she ordered Lord Esher

16 Stanley Weintraub, *Edward the Caresser*, Free Press, New York, 2001, p394.

17 *Ibid.*, p 394, cites eyewitness accounts of royal physician Sir Francis Laking and Lord Esher, who both insisted that Edward VII was comatose so did not recognise Mrs Keppel.

to, 'Get *that woman* out of here'.[18]

Sonia Keppel's book omits Alice's hysterical outburst. Undoubtedly, Alice had been genuinely fond of Edward VII, the lover who had given her large sums of money and beautiful jewels and made her life very pleasant. Edward VII knew that his heir, the future George V, hated his mistress and feared that once he was dead, Alice would be ostracised by the new king and his pious wife, Queen Mary, and relegated to a social limbo. At the reading of Edward VII's will, it was revealed that the monarch *had* left Mrs Keppel a large bequest (the wits called it 'Mrs Keppel's wages of sin').

This bequest angered George V, who was convinced Mrs Keppel had already received quite enough jewels and money from his father. The new king and queen banned Alice from Buckingham Palace and prevented her from signing the condolence book for the late king.

Alice, now aged forty-one, had been her family's sole provider. Taking stock of her situation, she realised that remaining in London was going to be difficult for her socially. The new king detested her, regarding her as an evil woman whose relationship with his father had caused great pain to his beloved mother.

Nevertheless, Alice was allowed a private viewing of the king at his lying in state to pay her last respects to her lover.

The wedding of Camilla's grandmother

Violet Keppel, Alice's elder daughter, and Sonia Keppel, Camilla's grandmother, were very different in personality. It was believed they had different fathers. Violet had been fathered by Alice's first lover, now Lord Grimthorpe, and Sonia had either been fathered by the king or by George Keppel. Alice feared that if it was exposed, Violet's scandalous lesbian relationship with fellow author Vita Sackville-West could damage Sonia's chances of a happy marriage. She used her money to arrange a marriage of convenience for Violet to an army officer wounded in the Great War who was unaware of his bride's love for Vita. To seal the bargain, she bought Violet and Denis Trefusis a country cottage, so they could live in rural seclusion and write books.

Alice's main preoccupation became how to arrange 'a good marriage' for Sonia, and to do this, Sonia needed to be presented to Queen Mary at Buckingham Palace and have a London Season to meet eligible young men.

As Alice was still blacklisted at Buckingham Palace, a titled friend

---

18 Theo Aronson, *The King in Love, Edward VII's Mistresses*, London, 1989, claims Sir Francis Laking led Mrs Keppel away from the dead King.

agreed to present Sonia at court. However, Mrs Keppel was allowed to accompany her youngest daughter to Buckingham Palace. Aware she was the subject of gossip and innuendo as the late King's mistress, Alice defiantly wore a magnificent diamond necklace once owned by Queen Marie Antoinette to boost her confidence.

Sonia's coming-out season was deemed a great success. By the end of the season, she had received a proposal of marriage from the Hon Roland Cubitt, heir to the wealthy Lord Ashcombe. He had inherited a very profitable building company founded by his ancestor Tom Cubitt, a well-known builder of elegant mansions in Belgravia including Eaton Square where Diana's grandmother lived as did Diana's elderly confidante Lady Elsa Bowker. Tom Cubitt had also built rows of elegant terrace houses on the Duke of Bedford's estate in Bloomsbury.

Sonia's husband, Roly Cubitt, would eventually inherit a title, a country estate and a profitable construction company.

However, Lord Ashcombe was far from happy that his heir wanted to marry the daughter of Edward VII's mistress. He was surprised to find he was expected to negotiate a marriage settlement with Mrs Keppel, rather than with her husband. As an astute businessman, it did not take Lord Ashcombe long to realise that Mrs Keppel had the money in this marriage.

Alice proved to be as shrewd a negotiator as she was a bridge player. She named a large sum she was prepared to settle on her favourite daughter, smiled disarmingly at Lord Ashcombe and invited him to match it.

Unnerved by having to negotiate with the mistress of the late king, Lord Ashcombe agreed. After offering a great deal more money than he had originally intended and signing the settlement, Lord Ashcombe told Mrs Keppel that he hoped such an expensive marriage would endure.

'My dear Lord Ashcombe,' replied Alice in her low husky voice, 'neither you nor I can legislate for the future.'[19]

On 17 November 1920, the Hon Roland Cubitt married Miss Sonia Keppel at the Guards Chapel, Wellington Barracks. [20]

Half a century later, history would repeat itself. Sonia's granddaughter, Camilla Shand, married Major Andrew Parker Bowles in the Guards Chapel. Camilla anchored her veil with the diamond tiara that Sonia Keppel had worn at her wedding. When the king died, to escape from gossip, Alice and her obliging husband left London for Florence. Using money bequeathed to her by the late king and her own stock market earnings, Alice was able to purchase the Villa dell'Ombrellino at

---

19 Sonia Keppel, *Edwardian Daughter*, p199.

20 *The Tatler and Bystander*, December 1920.

Bellosguardo, which had a superb view over Florence from its terrace.[21]

Alice renovated the Villa Ombrellino, invested the rest of her money in French and Italian banks and made frequent trips to London. She and George based themselves at the Ritz in Piccadilly where Alice became known as 'the Queen of the Ritz'.

Villa Ombrellino, lived in by Camilla's great-grandmother, Mrs Alice Keppel and her husband. (Private collection)

The Keppels were dining at the Ritz during the Abdication Crisis when Edward VIII made his abdication speech over the radio. Alice was overheard by Janet Flanner (foreign correspondent for the *New Yorker*) to say disapprovingly, 'Things were done far better in my day.'

In August 1939, just before the start of World War Two, the Keppels returned to England for the coming-out-ball of their granddaughter, Rosalind Cubitt (Camilla's mother) and this girl would grow up in comfort thanks to Cubitt money. Rosalind married Camilla's father, Major Bruce Shand, a twice-decorated war hero.

Alice's last visit to the Villa dell'Ombrellino took place in 1947, the year Sonia and her philandering husband divorced. Under their divorce settlement, as the innocent party, Sonia kept Hall Place, her beautiful home at East Meon near Petersfield and a large house in London's Hyde Park Gardens near the home of Sir Winston and Lady Churchill. In July of the same year, Sonia's daughter, the Hon Mrs Rosalind Shand, gave birth to a

21 The street address of Villa dell'Ombrellino is Piazza di Bellosguardo, 11-50124 Florence. For more details see http://www.villadellombrellino.it

blonde baby girl named Camilla Rosemary Shand.

On learning she had cirrhosis of the liver, Alice decided she would prefer to end her life at the Villa dell'Ombrellino. She died there on 11 September 1947, aged seventy-eight. Her husband died soon after, and they were buried side by side in the English cemetery in Florence. Sonia never remarried, unlike her former husband who had three more marriages and two divorces.

Camilla's grandmother was devoted to her charities and was awarded an OBE for her work on behalf of the St John's Ambulance Service. Baroness Sonia Ashcombe died on 16 August 1986 leaving her fortune to be shared by her grandchildren. To Camilla, she bequeathed a quarter of a million pounds, which in 1986, was a considerable fortune.

A happy country childhood

Camilla Rosemary Shand was born in King's College Hospital in London on 17 July 1947, two years after the end of World War Two. She was given her middle name of Rosemary after her wealthy maternal grandmother, whose ex-husband being awarded a barony, was now Baroness Sonia Rosemary Ashcombe.

Camilla's father, Major Bruce Shand, had served with distinction in France and North Africa before he was taken prisoner by the Germans. In 1945, on his return to civilian life, Major Shand, who won the Military Cross for bravery twice, married the Hon Rosalind Cubitt, a former debutante. The marriage was a very happy one with no money worries, and Bruce Shand became a partner in a Mayfair wine merchants.

Camilla's parents owned a house in East Sussex, where her father was invited to become joint Master of Foxhounds of the Southdown Hunt. A gentleman of the old school, with an upright military bearing, charm and good manners, Camilla's father was later honoured by being created Deputy Lord Lieutenant of Sussex.

Camilla's paternal grandfather, Philip Morton Shand, was a highly intelligent man who gained a degree in history from Cambridge and spoke fluent French and German. He fought in World War One and later wrote books on architecture, wine and food. His sexual appetite was voracious: he had four wives, three divorces and countless mistresses.

Philip Morton Shand passed his intelligence to his son, Bruce, but showed little interest in him after divorcing Bruce's mother. Aged three at the time of his parents' divorce, Bruce Shand would not see his father for another fifteen years.

Bruce's mother, Edith Marguerite Harrington, married again, and she and her new husband raised Camilla's father and took him with them to live in the United States. Later Bruce was sent to England to be educated at Rugby and Sandhurst Military College where, as a young lieutenant, he was able to indulge in fox-hunting and polo.

During World War Two, Camilla's father fought bravely in France and Africa and was awarded the Military Cross twice, although out of modesty, he did not mention the medals when writing his autobiography.

Bruce Shand was wounded by the Germans and spent the rest of the war as a prisoner and, thanks to Red Cross parcels of books for prisoners-of-war, became extremely well read. Bruce was determined his children, Camilla, Mark and Annabel, would have the sense of security that had been missing from his own childhood and succeeded[22]

The money she inherited from Alice Keppel and Baroness Ashcombe and her share of her mother's Cubitt inheritance, ensured Camilla would never need to work for her living. She was able to enjoy a lively social life as well as owning and maintaining thoroughbred horses and hunters. Her skill with horses and her interest in polo aroused the interest of Prince Charles when he was introduced to her by their mutual friend, Lucia de Santa Cruz, in her apartment in London in 1971. Lucia and Camilla had apartments in the same block in Cundy Street, near Victoria Station. She was Catholic and would marry a Catholic but felt that Charles who had no regular girlfriend would get on well with her friend who shared his love of horses and country pursuits and loved reading and discussing books as Prince Charles did (in fact all the things that Lady Diana disliked were what Charles and Camilla had in common).

Unlike that of Lady Diana Spencer, Camilla's childhood had been happy and secure with two loving parents. She inherited the high IQ of her father and paternal grandfather and their love of books. Her father read aloud to her each night from classics of English literature to ensure she became a keen reader.

Camilla was sent to a primary school named Dumbrells after its founder, which was located in a run-down building in the small village of Ditchling, three miles from the Shand's country home. In summer, little Camilla walked to school accompanied by her nanny, but in the cold of winter was driven there by her father. The school building had no central heating and was freezing in winter. Pupils were made to take cold showers after indulging in sporting activities, even in mid-winter.[23]

---

22 Tom Corby, Obituary, 'Major Bruce Shand, Camilla's father', *The Guardian*, 22 June 2006. The obituary of Camilla's father states that he lived with his mother and stepfather and did not see his father again until he was eighteen.

23 Gyles Brandreth, *Charles and Camilla, Portrait of a Love Affair*, pp196–197

Camilla was a resilient child who thrived under the harsh conditions. In the post-war period, Camilla, Mark and Annabel Shand were loved but not spoiled. Their father insisted they take care of their pet dogs and ponies to give them a sense of responsibility.

Camilla joined her local pony club, went camping with the club and won prizes for horsemanship. Encouraged by her father, Camilla became a fearless horsewoman.

In 1957, Camilla Shand, known to her friends as 'Milla', was sent to Queen's Gate School for Girls, at 131 and 133 Queen's Gate, within easy walking distance of a family home in Kensington bought by her mother, so she did not have to attend a boarding school.[24] This all-female private school advised prospective parents that the school emphasised 'the importance of good manners and social skills' as the girls were being trained for marriage and motherhood.

Like her brother, Milla Shand had a wild streak and broke school rules by flirting with boys and smoking cigarettes (rather than pot). The Shand children were good looking, intelligent and amusing and had a wide circle of friends.

Milla Shand knew she would inherit money so never bothered to work hard at school, concentrating on sporting activities. She left Queen's Gate School with only one 'O' level. She received an allowance from her parents and knew she would inherit part of the Cubitt fortune from her grandmother, Baroness Sonia Ashcombe, who lived near her Sussex home.

Camilla's brother, Mark, inherited his share of the Cubitt building fortune held for him in a trust. After being expelled from boarding school, Mark was sent to Australia to 'jackeroo' on a cattle station and then returned to England via India. He purchased Tara, an emaciated elephant covered in sores and rode her eight hundred miles (one thousand, three hundred kilometres) across India, aided by friends and wrote an award-winning book called *Travels With My Elephant*. The success of this book and money from his trust fund made it possible for Mark to pursue a life of travel and adventure with exploits like meeting Dyak head-hunters and crossing the Andes on horseback.

Like her brother, Camilla had an unconventional side to her nature and was proud, rather than ashamed, of Alice Keppel's success as a royal mistress.

---

24 *London A to Z Street Atlas, Geographer's Map Company* spells Queen's Gate with an apostrophe but both spellings are correct.

'Quite the sexiest girl I ever met' [25]

Camilla competed successfully in gymkhanas and horse shows as a member of the Southdown Pony Club and, with the blessing of her father, joined the local hunt. She attended parties, barbecues and barn dances with a group of young men who, like her, enjoyed the thrill of riding fast in pursuit of foxes. This wild group was led by Johnny Scott, son of a local Sussex landowner, Sir Walter Scott, and the boys teased and tormented any girls who rode to hounds with them. Camilla was the only girl brave enough to stand up for herself. She won their respect as she could outride them and jump fences better than they could.

'The boys with whom we went hunting respected Camilla for her horsemanship,' wrote another unconventional young woman, Clarissa Dickson Wright, the star of the popular television series *Two Fat Ladies*.

In her memoir, *Spilling the Beans*, Clarissa described Camilla as 'a tomboy, happier with boys than girls'.[26] She claimed that Camilla awed even the toughest boys with her skill at managing horses, dogs and ferrets. Clarissa admired Camilla Shand for her horsemanship and her courage out hunting and described her as 'quite the sexiest girl I ever met'.

At sixteen, Miss Shand had blue eyes, shoulder-length brown hair and a curvaceous figure. She left school to attend Mon Fertile, an expensive Swiss finishing school, where she spent a year learning to speak French. She also acquired social skills, including how to run a large household and the art of giving successful dinner parties.

The confident *sportif* Camilla enjoyed skiing and skating, made many friends and enjoyed her year in Switzerland. In this, she was the total opposite of shy young Lady Diana who hated her Swiss finishing school and begged to be allowed to leave and return home. Another result of a happy year in Switzerland was that Camilla became a good cook, as her son Tom, a celebrated food writer, confirms.

At eighteen, Camilla made a brief trip home to see her family before spending a year in Paris attending classes in French language and culture at an establishment under the auspices of London University. Camilla, young and full of life, found Paris exciting and very different from life in a stuffy English girl's school.

---

25 Clarissa Dickson Wright, *Spilling the Beans,* Hodder and Stoughton, London, 2007 quote by the author.

26 *Spilling the Beans,* pp 48–50. Clarissa Dickson Wright, daughter of Arthur Dickson Wright, the famous surgeon, was the first female barrister in London. Following the death of her mother and the man she loved, she began drinking heavily. In her memoir Clarissa admitted that success on television in the popular cookery program, *Two Fat Ladies,* helped her to sober up.

Doing the 1965 London debutante season

On her return to London, Camilla's mother took her to buy ball gowns, cocktail dresses and stiletto heels suitable for the parties and dances she would attend when taking part in the 1965 debutante season.

Camilla's debut cocktail party was scheduled for the evening of Thursday, 25 March 1965 near the commencement of the round of parties and dances which would last from late spring until the end of July. Camilla was one of three hundred and eleven girls making their debut that year, all of them experiencing their first taste of freedom. Bringing out a daughter was an expensive business and could cost parents as much as one hundred and twenty thousand pounds should they fund the kind of grand coming-out ball that Frances Shand Kydd gave her eldest daughter, Lady Sarah Spencer.

In the Edwardian era and up to World War Two, debutantes who were not engaged to be married by the end of the London Season were made to feel they had failed.

But slowly the idea was gaining ground that it was unwise to rush into marriage at seventeen or eighteen. In Camilla's time, 'doing the season' was a good way for girls meet a wide selection of young men and get to know what they wanted in a husband before they married.

Camilla's mother, Rosemary Shand, met other debutante mothers at coffee mornings or tea parties in private homes. They compiled a list of titled, wealthy bachelors to invite to parties and dances. Known as 'debs delights', once these upper-crust young men were on 'The List' they would receive invitations to scores of parties and dances. Ambitious mothers prayed their daughters would attract the attention of young men whose career prospects and inheritances had been assessed before they were placed on 'The List.'

In the days of Camilla's mother and grandmother, the virginity of debutantes was guarded by elderly chaperones. By 1965, the contraceptive pill was available for unmarried girls from broadminded doctors. The highlight of Camilla's London Season was not a presentation at Buckingham Palace, as Prince Philip had persuaded the Queen these were outdated by an evening at Queen Charlotte's Ball, after which proceeds were donated to charities. Debutantes wearing white ball gowns and gloves made their curtseys to a gigantic birthday cake rather than to the Queen!

Instead of a ball, Camilla had a coming-out cocktail party with dancing allowed later on in the evening. Her mother invited one hundred and fifty guests and held her daughter's party in a mews house at 30

Pavilion Road, owned by society caterers, Searcy's. They provided the food and drink and cleared up afterwards. Pavilion Road is a narrow street composed of former mews houses which runs parallel to the red brick residences and offices that line Sloane Street.[27]

A photograph taken inside 30 Pavilion Road shows Camilla standing beside her mother receiving their guests, smiling nervously. She wears a black cocktail dress which, at the age of eighteen, she probably felt gave her an air of sophistication rather than the long white dresses worn by debutantes a generation earlier.

Unlike the head of silver blonde hair that distinguishes the Duchess of Cornwall today, in her debutante year, Camilla's hair was light brown. For her party, she wore it drawn back with a droopy fringe that highlighted her blue eyes. Camilla chose a pair of chandelier drop earrings, so large they looked like costume jewellery rather than the small pearl earrings favoured by most debutantes.

Betty Kenward, author of the social column 'Jennifer's Diary' in *The Tatler*, described Camilla as 'attractive' and the party as 'successful'. Kenward added that Camilla's parents were 'in attendance all the time and the party ended at 11 p.m.' Contrary to what has been written about the party, the society caterers did not allow wild parties on their premises and their well-trained staff ensured exuberant young guests behaved themselves.

In *Camilla, Her True Story*, author Caroline Graham claimed Camilla wore 'a lovely white dress' at her party, but the photos clearly show her wearing a black cocktail dress with a black chiffon overlay.

Graham's unnamed source claimed everyone at the party got tipsy and that Camilla behaved coarsely, telling bawdy jokes and flirting with all the men in the room. It is unlikely a daughter of the Lord Lieutenant of an English county would have behaved 'coarsely' in public, but this claim was later used by Camilla's enemies to imply she was a fast, young woman with a fondness for drink and drugs.

Camilla's coming-out party was not wild, and there were no hard drugs. In 1965, ecstasy and marijuana were not yet freely available, and party behaviour was considerably more decorous than today. Camilla's party ended an hour before midnight with Searcy's staff in attendance as well as Camilla's parents and a few married friends.

Although she lacked the stunning beauty of Alice Keppel, Camilla had charm, a shapely figure, a good bust, an engaging personality and that

---

27 The author was living at Number 112 Pavilion Road when Camilla's debutante party took place at Number 30. She attended several debutante parties there, which were far from wild.

indefinable something known as sex appeal. Over the next few years, Camilla would lose her distinctly unflattering fringe and, like the much younger Lady Diana Spencer, improve her looks by lightening her hair.

Most of the 'debs delights' Camilla had danced with in her debutante year had attended Eton. Her first escort was Kevin Burke, the nineteen-year-old son of Sir Aubrey Burke, an aircraft tycoon and grandson of a baronet, who had the good manners Eton was believed to impart.

According to the celebrated gossip columnist Nigel Dempster who wrote for the *Daily Express* in the 1960s before moving to the *Daily Mail*, Camilla lost her virginity to Kevin Burke during the first weeks of the London Season – though how Nigel Dempster knew this remains a mystery. He was married to the daughter of a duke and, clearly, had good connections, so someone must have confided in him. Kevin Burke had no need of money so was not likely to have betrayed Camilla for the traditional thirty pieces of silver.

The young men who danced with Camilla during her debutante year liked 'Milla Shand', as did her fellow debs. Kevin Burke claimed to author and Member of Parliament Gyles Brandreth that he and Camilla had a very happy year together as Camilla 'was always amusing company'.[28]

Camilla's other Old Etonian admirer was the extremely handsome Rupert Hambro, whose father headed Hambro's Bank and the pair of them were photographed together at dances looking happy and relaxed.

Rupert Hambro later claimed that Camilla had been 'a charming, intelligent and amusing dance partner'. Kevin Burke, Camilla's regular escort that season told Taki, author of the High Life column in *The Spectator,* he had been Camilla's first lover. And he admitted to author Gyles Brandreth that, at the end of her debutante season, Camilla 'ditched' him for Andrew Parker Bowles.

Prince Charles, a shy sixteen-year-old, was working hard for his A Level exams at a boarding school at Gordonstoun, situated in a remote area of the north of Scotland. Charles was very shy and not interested in the debutante balls and cocktail parties that the extroverted Camilla was attending. as part of the excitement of her debutante season. She was 18 months older than Charles, had spent a year alone in Paris and was far more mature and sophisticated as girls always mature before boys. They would not meet for another six years in 1971 when Charles had left Cambridge University and gained more self-confidence. The idea of the two of them having an affair unnoticed when he was an immature schoolboy and Camilla a sophisticated debutante is ridiculous. Charles was

---

28 Gyles Brandreth, *op. cit*, p151.

watched by the press, even going into a pub and having a cherry brandy caused a stir in the press let alone meeting a debutante and having an affair managed to escape notice.[29]

Prince Charles and Camilla are well documented by several sources as being introduced in 1971 not 1965. The introduction was made by their mutual friend, Lucia de Santa Cruz, the daughter of the former Chilean Ambassador to London. Lucia and Camilla were living in the same apartment block, and Lucia thought Charles and Camilla would get on well together. In 1965, Camilla was having the time of her life in London and that summer met the sophisticated debutante escort, Captain Andrew Parker Bowles and fell for him.

Camilla was launched into a British society in 1965 on the cusp of social change. Within a few years, the debutante season had changed dramatically. The sons of the seriously wealthy and of dukes and earls who in the past would have featured on 'The List', were instead following the Beatles to Kathmandu and spending their time in a happy drug induced haze.

As England became more democratic and the 'stately home set' no longer ran everything, so the importance of the London Season diminished. Andrew Parker Bowles' parents were close friends of the Queen Mother and Queen Elizabeth II due to a shared interest in horseracing, which enabled Andrew to bridge both worlds with ease and be seen as highly eligible by both Protestant and Catholic mothers. His skill on the polo field, plus the fact he had the money to participate in this costly sport, his good looks and good manners made him popular. Andrew was a

---

29 The claim by British born Australian Simon Dorante-Day on the television programme *Sunrise* and in *New Idea* that he is the love child of Charles and Camilla and hence Prince Harry's half-brother is impossible. Simon Day has stated on several occasions his birth certificate bears the date 5 April, 1966 six years **before** Charles and Camilla actually met in London in 1971 introduced by Lucia de Santa Cruz, a diplomat's daughter who I met in the 1960s. I sympathise with anyone trying to find birth parents which is a harrowing experience. But no one can be pregnant for six years retrospectively. In 1966 Camilla was a debutante photographed many times enjoying herself at debutante balls and cocktail parties and certainly not pregnant. Prince Charles was a shy schoolboy studying for A Levels at Gordonstoun, a strict boarding school 500 miles away in the far north of Scotland. Charles was young for his age while Camilla was mature and he would later have a semester at Geelong Grammar School, attend university and mature. Mr Day's kind grandmother was probably trying to cushion the blow to her adopted grandson by inventing a fairy story of being royal to comfort him as adoption is very stressful for any child to acknowledge. *New Idea* has encouraged Mr Day to believe he is related to royalty and have published his open letter to Prince Harry, claiming him as his half-brother, and can be accused of seeking increased sales by doing so. The Queen, Camilla and Prince Harry deal with fake news by remaining silent. Attempts to warp history should not be made for profit when dates and facts make this story impossible.

particular favourite of the Queen Mother, who had known him since he was a child.

When Camilla made her debut, the double standard prevailed. Girls were meant to go to the altar as virgins, but young men could have multiple sexual partners, and no one thought any the worse of them. No one told girls to sow their wild oats.

By the end of the season, Camilla was head over heels in love with Captain Andrew Parker Bowles, a wealthy twenty-seven-year-old with a string of titled girlfriends and no intention of marrying any of them for a long time. Andrew's regiment, the Blues and Royals, were part of the Queen's Household Guards. Camilla was dazzled by Andrew, even though she knew he played the field and dated many other girls. Andrew and Camilla's on-off sexual relationship would continue for the next five years, while she hoped in vain that he might propose. But Andrew preferred dating titled girls.

His mother, Dame Anne Parker Bowles, DCVO, came from one of England's oldest Catholic families, and his maternal grandfather was the multi-millionaire racehorse owner Sir Humphrey de Trafford. Andrew and his parents were frequent guests at Birkhall, the Queen Mother's private residence on the Balmoral estate. Andrew was attracted by Camilla's bubbly personality, her earthy sense of humour and her passion for horses and fox-hunting.

Several of Camilla's friends claimed that Andrew treated Camilla badly, refusing to commit, although she was devoted to him. But she was young, head over heels in love and prepared to put up with the fact that Andrew was dating other women. Her mother, with her background of the scandal of Alice Keppel, did not fawn after titles like Andrew, and she was worried that Andrew was just using Camilla and would eventually marry an aristocratic girl with a title.

In search of less parental supervision and with a private income of her own, Camilla left the comfort of the families' South Kensington home to share a very basic two-bedroom apartment in Cundy Street near Victoria Station, which although no architectural marvel, was handy for buses and the London Underground. Camilla lacked a title, but her father was a much-decorated war hero, and her mother had a large private income. Camilla shared the rented apartment with Lady Moyra Campbell, the daughter of a duke.

Lucia de Santa Cruz, a friend of Prince Charles from his years at Cambridge, lived upstairs in the same building in Cundy Street. Her father, the former Chilean Ambassador to Britain, had left London and Lucia missed her family. Camilla, with her customary kindness, invited Lucia home for Christmas and made her welcome.

When Moyra Campbell left Camilla's apartment to get married, she was replaced by attractive Virginia Carrington who would eventually marry Camilla's philandering divorced uncle, Harry Cubitt. So at Cundy Street in 1971, rather than at a polo match as the tabloids claimed Lucia introduced Camilla to her old friend Prince Charles.

Lucia and Camilla's other flatmates were fond of Camilla and found her even-tempered and easy to live with. Virginia described Camilla as 'warm-hearted, dependable and good fun to be with, and so nice that her untidiness did not matter'.

Not everyone agreed. An elderly visitor to Camilla's apartment was shocked by the piles of clothes everywhere and described Miss Shand as 'a total slob who dropped her clothes on the bedroom floor and never picked them up'.

In love with Andrew, Camilla spent the occasional night in his apartment in Portobello Road, Notting Hill. However, hopes that their affair might lead to an engagement were dashed when, early one morning, Camilla arrived unexpectedly at Andrew's apartment and discovered her lover having breakfast with a young woman who was naked, apart from the fact that she was wearing Andrew's pyjama jacket. On seeing Camilla his female visitor fled into the bathroom and locked the door.

While most girls would have created an angry scene or burst into tears, Camilla kept calm, made a few scathing remarks about Andrew's behaviour and the other girl's appearance, turned on her heel and departed.

It was *finis* to the relationship as far as Camilla was concerned. Andrew then started dating young Princess Anne, but as a Catholic, could not marry her. It had later been claimed that out of pique, this led to Camilla having a passionate affair with Prince Charles.

Unlike Camilla's happy childhood, Charles always felt that he had had been treated badly by his stern father who did his best to toughen him up.

When his sensitive son turned nine, Prince Philip sent him to board at Cheam Preparatory School, where Charles was teased about his protruding ears and bullied relentlessly by older boys. (Why his ears were never pinned back on doctor's advice from an early age, as is done with most children with this problem, remains a mystery.)

At Cheam Prep School, Charles' classmates were middle class rather than aristocratic and did not want to be known as 'sucking up' to the heir to the throne. To avoid being bullied themselves, they supported the sadists who conducted a relentless bullying campaign against Prince Charles. Charles longed to return to Nanny Mabel Anderson and her 'haven of security' in the nursery. But it was too late, Nanny Anderson was now caring for the young Prince Andrew.

As Charles grew older, the bullying increased. Aged thirteen, still shy and introverted, Charles was sent to Gordonstoun, a tough all-male boarding school in the north of Scotland attended by his father, although the Queen Mother would have preferred him to have attended Eton College which was just across the Thames from the Windsor Castle.

Charles was out of the frying pan and into the fire. In another effort to toughen him up, his father sent him to a Spartan boarding school which resembled a boot camp rather than to Eton, the boarding school traditionally attended by the sons of the aristocracy. Prince Philip, having endured a bleak and miserable childhood after his father was exiled to Paris in disgrace, was looked after by Mountbatten relatives in England. With no money of his own but by hard work and talent, Prince Phillip achieved academic and sporting success at Gordonstoun, and feeling his son had life far too easy, demanded Charles equal his sporting and academic success.

Once again, the Prince of Wales was bullied mercilessly at a time when bullying at Gordonstoun went unchecked, and resident staff turned a blind eye as sadistic bullies stuck younger boys' heads down the lavatory and brutalised them in a variety of ways. On one occasion, the bullies hung Charles upside down from an upstairs window, and if they had dropped him, he could have been paralysed or killed.

To his credit, Charles did not 'sneak' on those who bullied him but stoically endured a tough time which, coupled with his conflict with his father, affected him badly.

Believing he was doing the right thing to raise a resilient future king, Prince Philip, refused to listen to Charles' anguished requests to move to a different school.

Charles' grandmother worried about her sensitive grandson and confided to her close friend, Lady Ruth Fermoy, Diana's grandmother, that Charles was a 'troubled soul', aware that Prince Philip resented anyone who questioned his authority. Princess Margaret was also aware that her nephew lacked self-confidence and described him as 'needy', The Queen Mother ensured that in term time Charles spent weekends with her at Birkhall, her home on the Balmoral estate, near Gordonstoun.

Fortunately for Prince Charles, Gordonstoun had an inspiring art teacher who developed in this sensitive, young man a love of drawing and painting. Charles also took part in school plays, enjoying playing the roles of princes or kings in various Shakespearian productions. Eventually, much to his surprise, he was made Head of School.

The happiest time in his school career began in February 1966 when, at seventeen, he was put on a plane for Australia to attend Timbertop, the bush camp of the prestigious Geelong Grammar School, Australia's equivalent to Eton. Unlike Gordonstoun, Charles found that at Geelong Grammar he was accepted on his own merits and the friendship of his Australian classmates gave him a sense of confidence and self-worth. He loved the freedom of bush life at Timbertop Camp and made good friends there.

Mr Garnett, Geelong Grammar's headmaster, later described Charles as 'a friendly, intelligent boy with a good sense of humour, someone who by no means has an easy task ahead of him.'[30]

Prince Charles would later claim that his six months in Australia had been 'the most wonderful period of my life'.

One pleasant experience was at a school dance where met a teenage girl from a wealthy Melbourne family named Dale Harper. The shy prince admired the blonde self-confident Dale for exactly the same reasons he would later be attracted to the blonde self-confident Camilla Shand. But in the 1960s in Australia when he met Dale, Charles was not living among hippies but in a strictly supervised school environment, and their relationship was purely platonic.

After a very happy time at Timbertop, Charles returned to London with a tan and greatly increased self-confidence. However, Prince Philip still worried his son was far too sensitive, never gave him the praise Charles yearned for and continued to demand a great deal from his heir.

Even worse was the fact that Prince Philip often criticised and humiliated his son in front of his staff, as Jonathan Dimbleby recorded in his biography, *The Prince of Wales*.

At the age of eighteen, Charles managed to acquire the necessary qualifications to enrol at Cambridge. He was the first member of the British royal family to achieve this.

At Trinity College, he studied archaeology and anthropology and took part in university amateur dramatics. Prince Charles, unlike his fellow students, had a valet to care for his clothes. He usually wore a navy blazer, a hand-tailored shirt and well-pressed grey flannel trousers rather than jeans and a rumpled T-shirt like the rest of the students. Showing how times have changed, in contrast to his father, Prince William when attending St Andrew's University decades later, wore a rumpled T-shirt and jeans like the other students.

Prince Charles after leaving Cambridge initially found public

30 Cited in Philip W Pike, *The Royal Presence in Australia*, Royal Publishing, Adelaide, 1986.

speaking difficult. When comfortable and relaxed among friends, Charles could be witty in a self-deprecating way. But on a public platform or in front of cameras, his body language revealed how stressful he found the experience as he nervously clenched and unclenched his hands and fiddled with his cuffs.

For the shy, introverted prince, life changed for the better after he was introduced to Camilla Shand. Fifteen months older than Charles, she was more worldly and sexually experienced, and their affectionate relationship gave him a great deal of self-confidence.

CHAPTER FIVE

Camilla's two separate affairs with Prince Charles

Sow your wild oats before marriage and then marry a sweet-natured virginal girl. Lord Louis Mountbatten, great-uncle and godfather to Prince Charles.

Such a blissful, peaceful and mutually happy relationship. Prince Charles talking about his time with Camilla in a letter to Lord Louis Mountbatten.

When she first met Prince Charles, dark-haired Lucia de Santa Cruz had been employed as a research assistant to the Master of Trinity College, Cambridge. One of her duties was to make the shy prince feel welcome at Trinity and to introduce him to suitable friends. She and Prince Charles became fond of each other, but as the future Defender of the Anglican Faith, Charles knew it was impossible for him to marry a Catholic, so any serious relationship was out of the question.

After she left Cambridge and rented an apartment in Cundy Street, in the same block of apartments as Camilla, Lucia enjoyed going to the theatre with Charles, who still had no regular girlfriend. She was convinced that Camilla and Charles would get on well, as they had many similar interests, aware that Andrew was having an affair with Princess Anne.

In 1971, Lucia decided to introduce her friend after staying at Camilla's home for several weekends and getting to know her well. Lucia felt Andrew had not treated her friend very well and that she and Prince Charles had many shared interests including a love of horses, hunting, polo, fishing and reading. Lucia introduced him to Camilla, and she was right. Their attraction was immediate and electric.

He asked Camilla for a date, and their friendship turned to love. The shy, introverted twenty-one-year-old Prince of Wales, struggling with the fact that his parents were remote and his father constantly expected too much of him, found consolation in his first serious love affair with the confident twenty-two-year-old Camilla.

Camilla, who shared Charles' love of reading as well as horses, hunting and parties, still on occasions saw her former boyfriend, the recently promoted Major Andrew Parker Bowles who was part of the same polo team as Prince Charles.

Camilla had a streak of daring in her character that appealed to the Prince of Wales who, in an effort to impress his father, tested his courage on the hunting field and playing polo, both of which can be a dangerous sport.[31] Camilla won Charles' admiration for her excellent horsemanship, her lack of fear jumping her horse over high fences, her quick wit and easy-going nature. She was his first real love and trusted confidante in a period when most girls were married in their early twenties.

Her mother worried that Camilla would not be acceptable as a wife of the Prince of Wales, although her social skills were a great deal better than his.

On their first date, according to protocol, Camilla had to address the Prince of Wales as 'Sir' while he called her by her Christian name. But with the bubbly, extroverted Camilla, this situation did not last long, and they were soon on first name terms.

For their important first date, Charles took Camilla to Annabel's, the exclusive members-only nightclub in Berkeley Square run by Mark Birley and his wife Lady Annabel Birley, the unconventional daughter of the eighth Lord Londonderry. Annabel's was a favoured meeting place for affluent members of high society, many of whom were related or knew each other from school. The décor resembled an English country house complete with oil paintings on the walls. I remember evenings at Annabel's with Lady Annabel Birley as hostess, and it was like attending a well-organised private party.[32]

On their first night out together, Charles and Camilla were given a cosy, quiet table and found they had a similar sense of humour. As they danced cheek-to-cheek, aided by the music and dim lighting, Prince Charles relaxed and found that with Camilla he was able to talk about a wide range of topics. Camilla made intelligent and sensitive comments, and at the end of a very enjoyable evening, Prince Charles drove Camilla back to her apartment and kissed her goodnight.

Later, it was here in this untidy apartment that Charles and Camilla spent the first of many nights together, which Charles would later tell his biographer Jonathan Dimbleby had been their 'blissfully happy love affair'.

'Charles has always liked older women,' one of his friends revealed, 'because he feels relaxed with them.'[33]

---

31 Vere Davidge, the husband of my school friend, Philippa, who lived near the Spenders of Althorp, was killed going over a jump on the hunting field, and several of my school friends had bad accidents while out hunting.

32 The Hon. Nancy Mitford observed that once they have borne the heir, aristocratic women are often flagrantly unfaithful. Diana's friend Lady Annabel Goldsmith admitted that in the final years of her marriage to Mark Birley she was having an affair with the wealthy financier Jimmy Goldsmith, by whom she had two children before her divorce, but none of her friends seemed upset by these extra-marital couplings.

33 Cited by Gyles Brandreth, *op. cit*.

And in this particular case, not only was Camilla sixteen months older than the Prince of Wales, but he found himself able to relax when he was with her. Camilla taught him a great deal about sex and women,

Prince Charles realised he could trust Camilla completely, aware that no matter what he told her, she would never reveal a word of what he had said. And in later life when harassed by journalists, Camilla always remained silent and has never once spoken publicly about her relationship with Prince Charles and rarely gives interviews to journalists.

⁂

Even when Charles turned twenty-one, Prince Philip continued to be critical of his son, fearing he was still too 'soft' to make a good king. His father told Charles most of his ideas were stupid and unless he 'pulled his finger out', he would never amount to anything.

Stung by his father's scorn, Charles tried even harder to win Prince Philip's approval, but without much success. No matter how hard he tried, his father always pushed the bar higher. Charles learned to fly planes and helicopters, took risks in polo matches, jumped the highest fences out hunting and competed in point-to-point races, in which amateur riders had been known to break their necks but rarely received the approval he craved from his father.

Camilla's loving support helped Charles through this difficult period adjusting to his role as a perpetual king in waiting. Prince Charles was happy to have an attractive and sexy girlfriend who was easy-going and loving. Unlike many titled girls, Camilla was not demanding. With a private income to support her, she had no need to work for a living and only took occasional temporary jobs for pocket money, so was always happy to fit in with Prince of Wales' busy schedule.

Unlike Lady Diana Spencer, who only pretended to like the pastimes that gave Charles pleasure – fishing, riding, fox-hunting, sketching, painting and attending the opera, Camilla genuinely loved them. As her father encouraged her to read widely from an early age, she was well read and enjoyed reading the same books as Charles and discussing them with him.

Camilla was not only intelligent, but fun to be with and exceptionally skilful in the way she boosted the prince's ego which had been battered by his father's constant criticism.

One of Camilla's strengths is the fact that she is an excellent listener and a very unselfish.

As a breeder of racehorses, the Queen Mother was extremely knowledgeable about bloodlines and was also interested in royal history.

She knew that Camilla's great-grandmother had been the mistress of Edward VII, which counted against her, as did the fact that several of her wealthy Cubitt uncles led wild lives with multiple divorces.

On occasions, Charles and Camilla met Andrew and Princess Anne when they went dancing at Annabel's and even found they were seated at the same table at this exclusive nightclub. Although Camilla was still attracted to Andrew, her previous experience with him had made her wary.

In contrast to Andrew's philandering, Camilla valued the fact that Charles was completely faithful to her. In those days, Charles was lean and muscular as well as having the glamour and presence that royalty imparts. His sleek sports car, good haircut and tailoring added to his image of a young and virile prince. The magic of the words 'Your Royal Highness' meant waiters and *maitre d's* automatically gave the Prince of Wales and Camilla the best tables in restaurants, and the royal box at West End theatres and at Covent Garden. Camilla enjoyed the envy of other girls when she and Prince Charles were driving in his Aston Martin or dancing cheek-to-cheek at Annabel's.

Charles valued the fact that Camilla remained calm in a crisis and never resorted to tears to get her own way, and the physical side of their relationship was good.

Being in love meant that the Prince of Wales was prepared to overlook the fact Camilla was a heavy smoker, though he disapproved of smoking. On the hunting field, Camilla, wearing a smart black jacket with her hair tucked under a black velvet riding hat did not photograph well and these photos made her look stern. However, at hunt balls Camilla looked stunning in off-the-shoulder evening gowns cut low to reveal her magnificent cleavage, which drew admiring glances from men.

For eighteen months, Charles spent most of his available free time with Camilla and their love deepened. She enjoyed watching him play polo and could talk knowledgeably about the game. They often spent weekends with Lord Mountbatten at his country estate near Romsey on the edge of the New Forest.

Charles felt he had found his 'soul mate' and told Lord Mountbatten that he was 'blissfully happy'. This alarmed his godfather, who had plans for Charles to marry his granddaughter, Lady Amanda Knatchbull who, eight years younger than Charles, was still at school. Lord Mountbatten advised Charles to gain sexual experience before marriage but that he must follow centuries of tradition and marry a titled virgin.

Charles told Camilla he loved her but never mentioned marriage, aware that his parents would not approve of his choice. The Queen's approval and that of her Privy Council was vital should the heir to the throne wish to marry. Calling themselves the 'two Cs', they rode, swam and danced together, went sketching and enjoyed reading the same books and discussing them. They shared the same off-beat sense of humour and loved *The Goon Show*, the irreverent 1950s radio series starring Spike Milligan, Peter Sellers, Harry Secombe and Michael Bentine playing characters like Major Bloodnok and Grytpype-Thynne.

To avoid press photographers, Charles sometimes met Camilla at Hall Place, the secluded country home of her grandmother, Baroness Sonia Ashcombe. When staying there, Camilla made little effort to dress up. On one occasion, just before Prince Charles arrived, the zip on Camilla's jeans broke. With no time to stitch them, she held them together with a safety pin. The fact she had done this scandalised her grandmother, a lady accustomed to dressing in her best before meeting royalty, and Baroness Ashcombe criticised her granddaughter for dressing so inappropriately when Prince Charles was arriving for tea. Camilla shrugged and replied that he had already seen whatever there was to see, so she was not bothered.

Raised in a different era, Baroness Ashcombe was horrified to realise that her granddaughter was in a sexual relationship with the heir to the throne, knowing she would be considered unsuitable to be his bride. There was the added complication that Baroness Ashcombe, the former Sonia Keppel, was rumoured to be the illegitimate daughter of Edward VII. If this rumour were true, it meant Charles and Camilla were distant cousins, so were they to defy the ancient precepts about marrying titled virgins, these old scandals would still resurface and cause problems.

The Abdication Crisis of 1936 had shaken the House of Windsor to its foundations and had resulted in the Queen Mother, who had been badly damaged by it, being apprehensive about Camilla Shand. Charles knew that his duty was to wed a titled Protestant virgin.

But in the early 1970s, there were no unattached Protestant princesses of the right age for him. The *Royal Marriages Act 1772* laid down that all members of the royal family needed the monarch's permission to marry, so there were very good reasons why Prince Charles did not ask Camilla Shand to wait for him before he went away to sea for almost eight months.

Marriage advice to Prince Charles

Lord Louis Mountbatten, the great-uncle and godfather of Prince Charles, had married the wealthy socialite Edwina Ashley. The main inducement to marry Edwina for the cash-strapped former Prince of the House of Battenburg was her fortune. However, his marriage to the highly sexed heiress had not been a success in the bedroom. Lord Mountbatten would later admit to close friends 'Edwina and I spent all our married lives getting into other people's beds.'[34]

The domineering Lady Edwina Mountbatten had sizzling affairs with playboys and Negro jazz musicians before falling in love with Indian leader Pandit Jawaharlal Nehru. For political reasons, Mountbatten was forced to tolerate this love affair, and blamed his sexual inexperience for his dysfunctional marriage.

He did not want Prince Charles to make the same mistake and advised his godson to 'sow his wild oats' before marriage. Mountbatten felt that Camilla's stable character and sexual experience made her an ideal 'fill-in' girlfriend for Charles. He continued to invite the pair of them to Broadlands, his secluded country estate near Romsey in Hampshire.

Charles' godfather, who he regarded as a surrogate father, became worried once he realised that Charles was deeply in love with Camilla. What Mountbatten had recommended as a sexual 'fling' with a nice girl was now getting out of hand. It has been alleged that, as a former Admiral of the Fleet, Mountbatten had arranged for Charles to undertake a long tour of duty to the West Indies as part of their independence celebrations in order to separate the lovers, hoping Charles' love for a girl with no title and a 'past' would fade if enough distance were placed between them.[35]

Years later, Mountbatten's daughter Lady Pamela Mountbatten defended her father to author Gyles Brandreth claiming several senior Buckingham Palace courtiers had regarded Camilla as a most unsuitable wife for the heir to the throne and they had expressed this view to Charles.

In January 1973, Prince Charles, as a junior naval officer, obeyed orders and departed for an eight-month tour of duty aboard HMS *Minerva*. Before leaving England, he said nothing about getting engaged to Camilla, aware that his tour of duty in the West Indies was an extended one.

Camilla's mother and grandmother must have realised that the dice were weighted against Camilla marrying the heir to the throne and if she wanted a husband and children, she must look elsewhere. At twenty-five, many of her contemporaries were married and starting families.

Camilla must have been disappointed at Charles' departure for the West Indies without mentioning the word 'marriage' but aware of the precepts for virginity and blue blood that governed marriage to a senior member of the royal family, precepts with which she did not comply.

Stories in social pages and gossip columns referring to Camilla as the

---

34 Gyles Brandreth, *op. cit.* A witty, well-connected author had questions he did not dare to ask Camilla, now Duchess of Cornwall.

35 This explanation, first propounded by Sarah Bradford in *Diana* (Penguin, London, 2006), seems likely but was denied by some loyal Mountbatten descendants.

'constant companion of the Prince of Wales' had made her more desirable to Major Andrew Parker Bowles. Now in his early thirties, he had spent years doing what Lord Mountbatten had recommended Charles to do and 'sow wild oats'. Now his formidable mother was urging him to settle down, and as a Catholic, believed marriage must include children.

At this juncture, having ceased dating Princess Anne, Andrew Parker Bowles met Camilla at a polo match. He was reminded of her intelligence, her pleasant easy-going personality and sense of humour. They slipped back into their former intimacy and after more dates, Andrew, feeling it was time he started a family, proposed marriage.

Prince Charles leans back on to railings as he chats with Camilla Parker Bowles during a break in a polo game at Windsor Great Park ©Mirrorpix

Having known and loved him for years, even though his infidelities had often made her very unhappy, and aware that Charles could not offer her a wedding ring, Camilla, now in her mid-twenties with most of her friends happily married, accepted Andrew's proposal. It was agreed children of the marriage would be raised as Catholics, but any male children could attend Eton.

Camilla at this stage believed marriage would stop Andrew chasing other women (an illusion as it turned out). Marrying a handsome old flame who was wealthy, well-connected, a descendant of the sixth Earl of

Macclesfield was an attractive alternative to marrying the younger and less confident heir to the throne. Camilla also knew that marrying Prince Charles and becoming Princess of Wales would entail a regimented life of royal duties, stifling protocol and overseas tours. And now that planes were replacing the royal yacht, air travel to Commonwealth countries would be a nightmare for someone like her who suffered from fear of flying.

Camilla's parents were relieved to be told of her engagement, but her mother worried that after leading a life devoted to seducing young women and then abandoning them if Andrew could settle down and become a faithful husband.

'Can a leopard change its spots?' Mrs Shand asked her daughter rhetorically and Camilla thought it possible but later realised she had been wrong.

Major and Mrs Shand formally announced their eldest daughter's engagement in *The Times* on 15 March 1973.

Camilla's mother started planning a white wedding with a large reception at St James's Palace, provided through the auspices of the Queen Mother, a good friend of Andrew's parents She must have been very relieved marriage would end what she saw as an unsuitable romance between Camilla and her grandson.

Meanwhile, on board HMS *Minerva*, Prince Charles was missing Camilla a great deal and reproached himself for not asking permission to marry her before he left England although he had feared the answer would be negative.

It has been claimed that Prince Charles had decided to write to Camilla asking her to marry him, provided his mother could be persuaded to give her consent. Aware of the enormity of what he was asking, and the requirements demanded of royal brides, Charles vacillated. But before he could write to Camilla, he saw an airmail issue of *The Times* announcing Camilla's engagement to Major Andrew Parker Bowles.

En route to the West Indies, the broken-hearted Prince of Wales locked himself in his cabin for two days and nights and refused to emerge for meals, aware there was nothing he could do to avert Camilla's marriage to his polo-playing friend.

Camilla Shand & Major Andrew Parker Bowles

The Parker Bowles-Shand wedding took place on 4 July 1973 at the Guards Chapel, Wellington Barracks, London where her parents had married. The elegant reception was held at St James's Palace, with over 800 invited guests including the Queen, the Queen Mother, Princess Margaret and Princess Anne.

Camilla's white tulle dress with a three metre train was designed by Bellville Sassoon, the trendy Knightsbridge designer. Her veil was anchored with her grandmother's beautiful diamond tiara. Andrew was handsome in morning dress, and the page boys wore miniature versions of the bridegroom's military uniform. Camilla was twenty-five approaching her twenty-sixth birthday, and Andrew was thirty-three but looked younger.

Prince Charles sent the couple a handsome wedding present and a letter of apology, regretting he had to attend the Independence Day celebrations in Nassau as the Queen's official representative.

Mutual friends were convinced Charles could have requested special permission to attend but was too upset to do so.

As a former page boy at the wedding of Queen Elizabeth, a protégé of the Queen Mother Major Andrew Parker Bowles had been given permission to hold his wedding reception at St James's Palace.

The honeymoon was spent at the villa of family friends in the South of France. Camilla sent postcards to Prince Charles and other friends, telling them that the weather was marvellous, they were enjoying themselves and were very happy.

Major and Mrs Parker Bowles were affluent newlyweds who could afford to buy Bolehyde Manor near Chippenham in Wiltshire. This spacious country house had paddocks and stables for Camilla's horses.

Camilla, a country girl at heart, was happy in baggy old sweaters and jeans mucking out the stables. Andrew spent the week in London living with his brother-in-law Nic Paravicini in Camilla's former Cundy Street apartment while on duty with the Household Cavalry dating other women but always came home to Bolehyde Manor at weekends. With time on her hands, Camilla started to create what would become a beautiful garden and enjoyed furnishing and decorating her new home with its mellow stone walls.

Thanks to time spent in France and at her Swiss finishing school, Camilla knew how to give interesting dinner parties and serve good food. From her father, she knew a great deal about which wines to serve and was helped in her role of hostess by the services of a live-in married couple.

The Parker Bowles had both agreed that they would not subject their children to the constant displacement experienced by many military families and their children. No matter where in the British Empire Andrew was posted, Camilla would remain at Bolehyde Manor, their Wiltshire home on the edge of the village of Allington with its 200 acres of land, her beloved horses and her dogs, an ideal place to bring up the children they planned to have.

Once Camilla was safely married to alpha-male Andrew, the Queen Mother was happy to have them as house guests at Birkhall, her home on the Balmoral estate. A lover of dogs and horses, Camilla fitted perfectly into the Balmoral way of life consisting of shooting parties, fishing for trout, hill-walking and deer stalking.

On his return from naval service, Prince Charles managed to hide his disappointment over the loss of Camilla and date other girls including briefly Lady Sarah Spencer, Diana's elder sister.

Having always liked Andrew, Charles slipped easily into the role of an old friend of the couple. He became a favourite member of the Parker Bowles 'set', which consisted of wealthy hunting, shooting and polo-playing friends with large country houses, wives and young children.

Prince Charles became a frequent house guest at Bolehyde Manor after his team played polo matches in Wiltshire and always enjoyed Camilla's amusing dinner parties. Camilla knew she had a special place in the prince's heart, but for both of them, the romance was over: maintaining a close friendship was what mattered. There were long phone conversations in which he asked her opinion on many topics. She and Andrew stayed at Sandringham and Balmoral or attended the Queen Mother's lavish parties at Royal Lodge in Windsor Great Park.

Charles was dating a variety of girls, some marriageable, others less so according to the unwritten rules that governed royal relationships in the 1970s. Just as Camilla's younger brother Mark sometimes asked her for advice about his girlfriends, Charles consulted Camilla about the titled girls he was dating and whether they would make suitable wives.

A year into their marriage in December, Camilla and Andrew's first child was born. Prince Charles agreed to become Tom's godfather with the christening held at the Guard's Chapel where Andrew and Camilla had married.

And so, the prince's godson's birthday and pre-Christmas celebrations became additional reasons for the Prince of Wales to drive to Bolehyde Manor in his sports car to visit the Parker Bowles. Sometimes Charles accepted invitations to go fox-hunting with the Duke of Beaufort's private pack of hounds over parts of Gloucestershire and Wiltshire owned by the Duke, and he saw Camilla on these occasions.

Fox-hunting was the dangerous but exciting sport Camilla and Charles both enjoyed from October until March while Andrew preferred shooting. In summer, Andrew played polo on the same team as Charles and they were the best of friends. The trio attended many of the same social events including the social highlight of the hunting set, the Beaufort

Hunt Ball, where vast quantities of wine were consumed, and Camilla was often photographed in glamorous evening dresses.

Kanga: Charles' Australian girlfriend

Dale, the Australian with the dazzling smile and curvaceous figure, was the daughter of a very wealthy Melbourne publishing tycoon. She claimed Charles had christened her 'Kanga', though later her husband claimed he had done this. As a child, Dale had suffered from Perthes disease, which affected one hip and the bones of one leg which meant she had spent part of her childhood in leg irons. In her teens, her condition stabilised, and Dale was able to attend boarding school, gain a university degree and enjoy life. She had a similar warm and outgoing personality to Camilla, and like her rival, Dale realised that Charles was shy and insecure, and her admiration flattered him and boosted his ego.

Charles and Kanga met very briefly when he was at Geelong Grammar. When Charles met Dale again, she was working in the London office of the *Australian Women's Weekly*. Her lively personality and quick intelligence meant she would soon be head-hunted for the public relations department of Qantas, and she and Charles had a brief but sizzling affair.

One of Charles' sporting friends, Lord Anthony Tryon, a fellow fishing enthusiast, met Dale and was as captivated by her looks and *joie de vivre* as Charles had been. Lord Anthony was a merchant banker at Lazards whose father had held the post of Keeper of the Royal Privy Purse, and he and Charles moved in the same circles. Dale had initially entertained hopes that her *amitie amoureuse* and dalliance with Prince Charles might lead to an engagement. All too soon she became aware that although her father was wealthy, like Camilla, she lacked the necessary blue blood to become Princess of Wales.

By now Prince Charles had become very fond of the bubbly, energetic Kanga describing her as 'the only woman who really understands me'.

This annoyed Camilla, who prided herself on being the only woman who *really* understood Prince Charles.

The difference between Dale and Camilla was that Camilla never talked to the press. In contrast, Dale, with a background in journalism and public relations, enjoyed hinting to journalists that she was on intimate terms with the heir to the throne, something Camilla never did. However, friends of the royal family talk to the press at their peril and soon Prince Charles ceased dating 'Kanga' Harper.

Aware her royal romance was over, Dale was planning to return to her family in Australia when tall, good-looking Lord Anthony Tryon said he loved her. He proposed, and Dale accepted.

With permission from the Queen, the wedding of Miss Dale Harper and Lord Anthony Tryon took place in 1973 at the Chapel Royal at St James's Palace.

Having overcome her childhood illness, Dale possessed boundless energy and self-confidence. She resolved that with her father's money and her head for business they would work hard and try to buy back her husband's former ancestral home, the old manor at Great Durnford. Prince Charles now became a welcome guest on trips to the Tyrons' fishing lodge in Iceland and agreed to become godfather to their first child.

Tabloid journalists hinted, without a shred of evidence, that the prince was the father of Dale's son, who was named Charles after his godfather. This was unpleasant for all concerned. Prince Charles had been overseas when the Tryons' first baby was conceived, but this did not prevent unkind gossip, which Dale and her husband ignored. Lord and Lady Tryon were invited to Birkhall when Charles was there staying with his grandmother, and the three of them enjoyed fishing for trout in the River Dee together.

Realising there was a market for clothes that were easy to pack in what was now the new era of cheap air travel, Lady Tryon became the London agent for a firm selling uncrushable one-size dresses which suited women with a busy lifestyle. What these dresses needed was clever marketing, which Dale was able to supply. She soon took over the business, renamed it 'Kanga Fashions' and broadened the range of designs. Through Lord Tryons' hard work at his merchant bank and Dale's skilful publicity for Kanga Fashions, the couple eventually made enough money to repurchase Lord Tryon's ancestral home. Dale became a success in the fashion world as well as raising their four children.

She found it easy to obtain additional publicity for Kanga Fashions by insinuating to journalists that she and Prince Charles were more than just good friends, and then refusing to deny the subsequent stories in the press although the sexual side of their relationship was over well before her marriage. However, gossip columnists continued to insist that Dale was 'consoling' Charles when he visited the Tryons' family home.

Living in a beautiful part of Wiltshire and enjoying life with her children, Camilla was nevertheless aware her husband still had a wandering eye and was chasing other women, although as a Catholic, he had no intention of leaving her or the little son he adored. But from the gossip of regimental wives and other friends, Camilla learned about her husband's extra-marital activities which hurt her deeply, although Andrew's 'flings' never seemed to last very long.

Camilla hid the fact that she was hurt by her husband's infidelities and would joke with Charles about her husband's London girlfriends when the Prince of Wales drove down to Bolehyde Manor to see her and his godson. Meanwhile Andrew's military career was progressing, and increasingly important overseas postings took him away from home for long periods. Camilla refrained from asking awkward questions, and she was luckier than many army wives in having a private income and a permanent home instead of living in army accommodation. At weekends when Andrew returned to Bolehyde Manor, the Parker Bowles were hoping for a second child.

In 1978, Camilla had a baby daughter named Laura, and although it had been agreed the children would be raised as Catholics, Tom had his name down for Eton.

Charles still played polo and continued to drive his sports car to Bolehyde Manor to see Camilla, bringing presents for the children and asking her opinion about various girls he was dating, and did she consider they would make suitable wives.

Andrew was promoted in rank and work often took him further afield. The unspoken bargain in this unconventional marriage was that Andrew would not take any of his 'flings' seriously or acquire a permanent mistress. Camilla concentrated her energies on raising happy children, running her home, creating a beautiful garden and painting, a hobby she enjoyed. While Andrew was away, Camilla had the support of her younger sister Annabel, now married, and a wide circle of friends because Camilla has always been good at attracting and keeping friends.

Living at Buckingham Palace, now in his late twenties, Charles worked hard setting up various charitable schemes under the umbrella of his Prince's Trust. He improved conditions in his Duchy of Cornwall properties and for the farmers whose land he owned. He was still under pressure from his family and the press to marry and give the nation an heir.

Prince Charles' search for a titled virginal bride

The Queen Mother knew that a Princess of Wales with a baby would arouse increased interest in the royal family just as it had done when Princess Elizabeth and Princess Margaret were young. Charles had brief affairs with young women but still had to find one who would make a suitable wife. Titled girls seen as suitable had boyfriends or interesting careers and were not interested in a life of endless royal duties and stultifying protocol.

Camilla was keen on the idea of Charles marrying Lady Jane

Wellesley, daughter of the eighth Duke of Wellington, whom she believed had the brains and breeding to become an excellent consort. Charles had been a guest at the Duke of Wellington's estate in Spain and liked her family. Lady Jane was working at the BBC, was fond of Charles and appreciated his sincerity and his kindness. Like Lord Mountbatten's granddaughter Lady Amanda Knatchbull of whom he was also very fond, Lady Jane Wellesley had seen enough of the royal goldfish bowl to know that she did not want to swim in it.

Charles found Lady Jane very attractive and an interesting, intelligent companion, and proposed. Tactfully, she let him know that she preferred her career as a BBC film producer but wanted to remain friends.

Another candidate for the role of Princess of Wales was Sabrina Guinness, the daughter of James Guinness, an English member of the wealthy brewing family, who was a merchant banker rather than a brewer.[36]

Prince Charles, intrigued by Sabrina's good looks and her personality, invited her to stay at Balmoral. Tabloid editors had christened Sabrina 'The It Girl' for her close friendships with film stars like Jack Nicholson and Ryan O'Neal, and Charles found her intriguingly different from the usual run of debutantes. Unfortunately, Prince Philip had read lurid press accounts about Sabrina Guinness and her friendship with pop stars known for imbibing banned substances, so was prejudiced against Sabrina before she arrived at Balmoral.

She was nervous about meeting the Queen and Prince Philip and made a fatal *faux pas*. The Queen had not yet arrived, and as no one indicated where Sabrina should sit, she chose a chair Queen Victoria had always used that was traditionally reserved for the Queen. Sabrina was very embarrassed when Prince Philip gruffly ordered her to vacate it. This *faux pas* and press reports about Sabrina's wilder friends in the entertainment world ensured she received the thumbs down as a future Princess of Wales. However, Sabrina went on to have a stellar career, founded her own television station and become a multi-millionaire in her own right at a relatively young age.

Another tall blonde who had the looks, elegance and personality to become Princess of Wales was Davina Sheffield, the granddaughter of Lord McGowan and a sister-in-law of the Duchess of Beaufort who Prince Charles knew because he went fox-hunting with the Duke of Beaufort. Charles was attracted to Davina who was beautiful, intelligent, and compassionate and had many of the qualities he admired in Camilla.

---

[36] The Guinness dynasty produced Lord Iveagh, the noted philanthropist who bequeathed Kenwood House on Hampstead Heath to the people of London to enjoy its garden and his magnificent collection of art and antiques.

Davina gained the approval of the Queen and Prince Philip after being invited to lunch with them at Windsor Castle. She seemed happy to spend the afternoon watching Prince Charles play polo, another acid test for a royal wife, and tabloid journalists began following Davina Sheffield like hawks after a rabbit.

The sister-in-law of the Duchess of Beaufort was then invited to spend a weekend at Balmoral where she watched Prince Charles and Prince Philip shooting pheasant and stalking stags and gained the royal seal of approval for being 'just the right type of girl'. Davina had a titled grandfather and no previous liaisons as far as anyone knew. A former debutante, she had done the standard round of parties and dances, but rather than spend her time hunting foxes and frequenting Mayfair nightclubs, she had volunteered to work in war-torn Vietnam.

Davina was a humanitarian who had spent a year working in a Saigon orphanage and experienced the horrors of war. She only returned from Vietnam due to tragic family circumstances after her mother was murdered by two mentally disturbed men while burgling her home. Prince Charles, always kind to friends in need, provided comfort at this tragic time in Davina's life, and they became fond of each other.

Everything was going well with the couple until Davina's former boyfriend revealed to a journalist that he and Davina had spent months living together in a country cottage just before she left for Vietnam. The former boyfriend misguidedly believed his comments were 'off the record' and would not be published which was naïve of him in a world where salacious royal stories were in hot demand.

The fact that Davina Sheffield had shared a cottage with a lover became a juicy story for the tabloids. It was ridiculous that, despite her sterling record of public service and only one previous love affair, Davina was deemed unsuited to marry a prince who had been sleeping around for years – an example of the double standard for males and females.

And so, with genuine regret, Prince Charles ended his promising relationship with the sweet-natured Davina. A young woman with beauty and brains, she soon announced her engagement to a highly eligible man.

At an earlier stage, the petite brunette Lady Angela Neville, daughter of Lord Rupert Neville, who was a goddaughter of the Queen, was considered as a suitable royal wife. A sensible young woman, Lady Angela had built a successful career as an art consultant. She worked from her Chelsea home, purchasing paintings at auction from Sotheby's and Christie's or private vendors, researching their provenance and reselling them profitably to Arab sheiks and wealthy Australian collectors, including

Alan Bond.[37]

Intellectually, Lady Angela would have been an ideal companion for Prince Charles, but the tedium of royal life had little appeal for this clever young woman enjoying the excitement of the international art world. She did not fancy the stultifying boredom of royal duties and would eventually marry her business partner Billy Keating.

Prince Charles' relationship with his father continued to be difficult. Prince Philip constantly reminded his son he was approaching thirty and it was his duty to marry very soon. Charles stalled for time, claiming he could only marry a girl he found physically attractive who was a 'companion of his heart and soul', remembering how happy he had been with Camilla who he saw as the perfect companion.

Meanwhile, the press continued to describe the Prince of Wales as Britain's most eligible bachelor and continued speculating how long it would be before he did his duty by marrying and producing an heir.

In 1979, aged thirty, Britain's most eligible bachelor was still single. Many years earlier he had confided to Camilla that he would be married by this time, but his thirtieth year came and went, and he was no nearer to finding a suitable wife.

Photos of the dashing Prince of Wales in naval uniform, playing polo, skiing, sailing or dancing with a variety of young women were constantly in the tabloids and *The Tatler*. Any girl the Prince of Wales was alleged to be dating fuelled a furore of press speculation, and she would be pursued relentlessly by the paparazzi.

Charles dated scores of young women in the period after Camilla married Andrew, which he later described as his 'footloose' years. The Queen Mother, worried about Charles, compiled lists of possible brides for her favourite grandson which featured Lady Caroline Fane, Lady Caroline Percy, Lady Bettina Lindsay and Lady Henrietta St George, but none of them fancied royal life. Lady Lenora Grosvenor, sister of the Duke of Westminster, would have been suitable, but in 1975, Lenora married the Queen's handsome cousin, the talented photographer, Lord Patrick Lichfield.

On one of his Australian tours, Charles visited Sydney's Bondi Beach, where attractive young women pursued him into the surf.

---

[37] During the art boom of the 1990s Lady Angela invited the author to her Chelsea home seeking information about the artist who accompanied Charles Darwin on the Beagle's voyage from Montevideo to Valparaiso. She had bought Van Gogh's *Irises* for around $30 million for Australian entrepreneur Alan Bond, which, after allegations the full price ha not been settled with Sotheby's is now in the Getty Museum and the story is in Susanna de Vries, *Impressionists Revealed, Masterpieces and Collectors*, 1992.

Years later, the Prince of Wales confessed to Jonathan Dimbleby that he had behaved badly with several of his dates when living in his bachelor apartment at Buckingham Palace. After getting what he wanted, he did not drive the girl home or ask her to stay the night but merely rang a taxi to take her home.

'Dearest Janet' and a possible love child

An attractive blonde English girl with whom the Prince of Wales had a happy uncomplicated relationship was the divorced Janet Jenkins, who was employed as a receptionist at the British High Commission in Montreal.

Early in the relationship, Prince Charles wrote to Janet after spending the night with her in a hotel, 'my new private secretary is horrified by the idea of ladies in hotel rooms during foreign visits…I shall have to get married as soon as possible and then all these people might relax a little.' Many of his letters to Janet were signed 'love and a vast hug.'

Although Janet Jenkins came from a modest background, she was an intelligent, perceptive young woman whose company Charles enjoyed. She used to return to Britain on holiday to see relatives, visited Prince Charles and spent the night with him at Buckingham Palace or at Sandringham.

Janet claimed they wrote to each other regularly, but both knew their relationship could never become serious as Janet lacked a title and was divorced. While Princess Diana claimed on her 'Secrets tapes' that Prince Charles was a 'lack-lustre lover', Janet told the *National Enquirer*, 'I found Charles to be a wonderful lover'.

What Charles called his 'special relationship' with Janet was through chatty letters and occasional meetings. Like Camilla Parker Bowles, Janet was a sympathetic listener to whom Charles felt he could unburden his problems with no risk she would talk to the press.

In one of his letter addressed to 'Dearest Janet' when he was still single, Charles confided that he was worried about making the right decision in choosing a wife and admitted that if he didn't make the right decision, 'the consequences would be dire'. And he was right. Forced into an arranged marriage to please his family and the nation he was still in love with Camilla and had almost nothing in common with the young aristocrat everyone thought he should marry.

He told Janet that there were no Protestant princesses of the right age available to marry and so his quest for a suitable bride among the British aristocracy must continue.

He and Janet continued writing for many years and he confided his unhappiness to her calling his marriage was 'a Greek tragedy, so awful and so extraordinary that very few people who haven't been witnesses [to it] would believe it.' Charles used an identical phrase in a letter to Nancy Reagan dated 21 June 1982.

Two years later in 1984, the year of Prince Harry's birth Janet Jenkins gave birth to a son named Jason who is said to bear some resemblance to Prince Charles. When Jason was born Janet was married to a Canadian whose name she is careful never to mention.

The scandal-mongering *Globe* magazine and the equally sensationalist *New Idea* ran a story in which Janet allegedly told *Globe* that 'at the time neither of us used birth control or any other protection. It was just before AIDS and we just didn't think about it.'

Their affair ended in July 1992 after Janet spent a weekend with Charles at Highgrove.

Globe magazine asked Janet whether Charles was the father of her son Jason, born in the same year as Prince Harry, and Janet told them, 'It's nobody's business but my own.'

What Charles did not foresee was that decades later his affectionate chatty letters to Janet, (written between 1976 and 1980), would end up in the hands of a celebrity agency and be offered on eBay where they sold for twenty thousand pounds stirling.

Janet Jenkins claimed that she did not receive any money for the letters and loaned them to a celebrity agency believing they were to be exhibited in a museum. The question is, who received the money for the letters? If Janet Jenkins was as fond of Prince Charles as she claimed why loan his intimate letters to an exhibition? If she needed money, why not explain the position to Prince Charles, known for his generosity to friends and ask for financial help and give his letters back rather than betray a friend?

New Idea printed photographs of Prince William and Jason, side by side claiming, 'Monarchy in Crisis' and Janet's Jenkins son might be able to take precedence over Prince William. *Right Royal Bastards,* the standard reference work by Burke's Peerage, claims that royal bastards have never been able to inherit.[38]

⁂

The murder of Mountbatten by the IRA hurt Prince Charles deeply. He had regarded Mountbatten as his surrogate father and was devoted to him. Charles' his sense of loss was devastating. He was on a fishing trip in

---

[38] Peter Beauclerk Dewar and Roger Powell. *Right Royal Bastards,* Burke's Peerage, New York 2006, page xvi.

Iceland with Lord and Lady Tryon when he heard the dreadful news and was stunned by the enormity of what had happened.

Charles could not image life without Mountbatten. He flew back to London to see his parents at Buckingham Palace who were shocked by the news, then drove down to Wiltshire to see Camilla in search of solace.

Warm-hearted Camilla had always been good at comforting friends and siblings in times of trouble, providing hugs, a gin and tonic and time to talk to those in need. Camilla's heart went out to Charles at this terrible time. Perhaps he broke down and cried? Who could blame him after the shock and the loss of those he loved in such a horrible way? Charles and Camilla ended up in each other's arms and renewed their former close relationship.

Prince Charles began staying overnight at Bolehyde Manor when Andrew was absent on regimental duties. Loyal friends were sympathetic, aware Camilla was good for Charles in his distress. They knew that Andrew was an unfaithful husband and that being with Charles made Camilla happy. Andrew could scarcely object, given his own infidelities but divorce was not a possibility as they loved their children, and they got on well when they were together.

During the early part of 1980, Charles and Camilla sometimes spent the night in the stately homes of friends, whose high walls provided protection from the telephoto lenses of the paparazzi.

To throw the press off the scent and make his family think he was still looking for a wife, Charles continued to date unmarried girls, but without a great deal of enthusiasm. He was aware that one day he would have to marry but put it at the back of his mind as his emotions were once again concentrated on his soul mate, Camilla.

To please his godfather, Charles had between 1974 and 1980 seen quite a lot of Mountbatten's granddaughter, Lady Amanda Knatchbull, but theirs was a close friendship rather than a romance.

The young woman who interested Charles because, like Camilla, she was a brilliant rider was Anna Wallace, the attractive daughter of a major Scottish landowner who he had met out hunting. Anna's courage and skill on the hunting field reminded Charles of Camilla at the same age. Charles knew she had another boyfriend, but she was a useful screen to invite to society balls where he wanted to spend time with Camilla who attended the same functions.

When his grandmother suggested that young Lady Diana Spencer would make him an ideal wife, Charles responded that Diana was very sweet but far too young for him to make him the kind of companionate wife he wanted.

However, the Queen Mother and Lady Fermoy were not going to abandon their marriage plans for Lady Diana that easily.

The Queen Mother and Prince Philip were united in their determination to get Charles away from Camilla Parker Bowles and find him a suitably aristocratic and virginal wife – no easy task in the era of the contraceptive pill.

Meanwhile, the newly promoted Lieutenant Colonel Andrew Parker Bowles was posted to Rhodesia as Senior Military Liaison Officer to the British Governor, Lord Christopher Soames, before the British colony celebrated independence. Society gossip claimed that in Rhodesia Andrew was spending a lot of time with a daughter of Lord Christopher Soames, a sister of Charles' good friend, Nicholas Soames.

While Andrew was serving in Rhodesia, Camilla made only one quick visit to her husband, aware and hurt he was involved with another woman.

The Queen Mother's eightieth birthday fell in August 1980. Charles knew that Andrew would return from Rhodesia for a celebration ball to be held at Windsor Castle and that Camilla would accompany him and invited Anna Wallace to attend as his partner. She had already been invited to spend a weekend at Balmoral and believed she had passed the 'wife' test from the Queen and Prince Philip.

James Whitaker, always keen for a royal story, was already describing the fiery Anna, nicknamed 'Whiplash Wallace' for her skills on the hunting field, as a possible Princess of Wales.

The Queen Mother's birthday ball took place on a warm summer night. Camilla wore a low-cut dress which revealed her magnificent cleavage. She felt jealous of Anna Wallace and demonstrated her hold over her royal lover by encouraging Charles to dance cheek-to-cheek and embrace her on the dance floor. By this display of affection, Camilla was showing Anna Wallace that if she were to marry Charles, it would not be easy to get rid of her.

Happy to be with the woman he adored, Charles forgot Anna and spent the evening kissing Camilla and nuzzling her hair.

Andrew Parker Bowles, back from Rhodesia for the ball and involved elsewhere was not perturbed by the fact that his wife and Prince Charles were locked in a passionate embrace on the dance floor. His thoughts were elsewhere, and he may have felt flattered by the fact that the future king found his wife attractive.

Eventually, Anna Wallace, a sophisticated twenty-five-year-old had quite enough of sitting and watching Charles and Camilla dancing and embracing. When Charles returned to the table, she was overheard to say, 'Never ignore me like that again. No one treats me like that, not even you.'

When she heard what had transpired at the ball, the Queen Mother was upset that Charles had revealed his passion for Mrs Parker Bowles in front of many people.

Later that month, Prince Charles and Lieutenant Colonel and Mrs Parker Bowles were guests at the Cirencester Polo Club Ball held on Earl Bathurst's estate. Once more, Charles invited Anna Wallace as his partner, aware that Camilla would be there. Their host, Earl Bathurst, was seated at their table and saw Camilla and Charles behaving as they had done at the Queen Mother's eightieth birthday ball, dancing cheek-to-cheek and kissing passionately.

A concerned friend drew Andrew Parker Bowles' attention to the dance floor. Without raising an eyebrow, he replied, 'His Royal Highness is very fond of my wife. And she appears to be fond of him!'[39] Eventually, Charles and Camilla disappeared into the garden for a long time and reappeared with grass stains on their clothes.

By now, Anna Wallace had had quite enough. She borrowed a car from her hostess and left the ball in a rage, saying she had never been treated so badly in her life and vowed it would not happen again. A few weeks later, Anna announced her engagement to Johnny Fermor-Hesketh, a relative of Lord Hesketh, and married him.

Charles' valet, Ken Stronach, soon proved to be disloyal. For a handsome fee, Stronach confided to a *News of the World* journalist he had had difficulty removing the evidence of the grass stains from the Prince of Wales' evening clothes. Stronach would soon leave Prince Charles' service considerably wealthier after talking to the press.

When news of Charles and Camilla's behaviour at the Cirencester Polo Club Ball reached Buckingham Palace, the Queen and the Queen Mother were not amused. Camilla, already code-named 'The Problem', was now seen as a real danger and the Queen gave orders Mrs Parker Bowles was to be declared *persona non grata* in all royal residences, although her husband continued to be a welcome guest at the Queen Mother's various residences, and Andrew sometimes escorted the Queen Mother to various race meetings.

Senior royals found Prince Charles' renewed infatuation with a married woman disturbing with its echoes of Edward VIII and Mrs Wallis Simpson. The Abdication Crisis still haunted the royal family, and they had had no intention of letting anything similar happen again.

Camilla's parents were unhappy about her renewed love affair with

---

39 'HRH is very fond of my wife' was first cited in Anthony Holden, *Charles: A Biography*, Bantam Press, London, 1998, p139. Anthony Holden would become a close friend of Lady Jane Wellesley, daughter of the Duke of Wellington.

Prince Charles. They feared it could affect her marriage, her children and Andrew's career prospects. Baroness Sonia Ashcombe was also worried about her granddaughter, aware of the dangers to Camilla's reputation. She did not want her to become another Mrs Keppel.

Worry over Charles' passion for Camilla led the Queen Mother and Lady Fermoy to draw up a shortlist of suitable royal brides with Lady Diana heading it. They both hoped it might be possible to make Charles see what a suitable wife Lady Diana Spencer would make. The fact Diana had had a troubled, motherless childhood which had made her insecure and highly emotional was not mentioned by the Queen Mother's close friend, Lady Fermoy. The ambitious Lady Fermoy, keen to promote the marriage of her granddaughter to the heir to the throne, kept quiet about Diana's emotional problems, her exam failures at school and the fact that she was now working as a house cleaner to Lady Sarah, her elder sister.

A Prince buys a country house & needs a wife

For several years, Charles, independently wealthy from his Duchy of Cornwall revenues, had wanted to buy a country residence rather than living in a cramped bachelor suite at Buckingham Palace in the shadow of his parents.

Prince Charles inspected many large country houses for sale but rejected them, wanting something smaller and easier to run without a battalion of servants and with a home farm attached to the main house.

Eventually, the Prince of Wales was shown an estate called Highgrove in Wiltshire, near Andrew and Camilla's home. It featured an early Georgian house with a plain façade and a garden.

The estate was owned by Maurice Macmillan, son of a former Prime Minister. Both the house and garden needed a great deal of restoration, but Charles liked the home farm that went with the house as well as the surrounding countryside. He asked Camilla to view Highgrove with him and give an opinion on it. Camilla saw the potential in the house and felt it would be possible with hard work to create a magnificent garden. She advised Charles that the price was good, the house and garden could be made very attractive and he should buy Highgrove.

Trusting Camilla's judgement, the Prince of Wales took her advice and contracts were exchanged in July 1980. The run-down house had nine bedrooms, four reception rooms, accommodation for staff and stabling for horses and was surrounded by five hundred acres of farmland. Best of all from the lovers' point of view, Highgrove House was secluded and within easy driving distance of Camilla's home.

Highgrove as it was when Prince Charles purchased it.

Camilla relished the chance of renovating a neglected garden. They pruned and removed overgrown shrubs and planned beautiful walks, arbours and flowerbeds capable of being enjoyed without the use of pesticides. Highgrove would be a series of different gardens and the results were satisfying to both of them. Camilla and Charles were back on their former footing, best friends as well as lovers, happy to be able to meet frequently.

Camilla was aware of the family pressure on her lover to marry as soon as possible and produce an heir. She realised he owed this duty to his family and the nation and they must break off their renewed affair before he married to give his marriage every chance to work. But until that time came, she and Charles seized every opportunity of happiness in their re-ignited love affair.

CHAPTER SIX

Diana: courtship and a semi-arranged marriage

The youngest Spencer girl was a sweet little thing, quiet, passive, obedient. Richard Parker Bowles, Camilla's brother-in-law.

Charles has gone back to his lady and I don't know how to deal with it. Princess Diana to her security guard, Ken Wharfe.

Young Lady Diana Spencer collected news clippings and press photos of the Prince of Wales, but was ignorant of the fact that Charles had renewed his passionate affair with Mrs Camilla Parker Bowles.

Diana's grandmother, Lady Ruth Fermoy, and the Queen Mother were still trying to persuade Prince Charles to marry Lady Diana. Clearly Diana's grandmother, who enjoyed court gossip, was not about to tell Diana that her rival for Charles' affections was Camilla, and she would not find this out until much later.

Diana and her sisters knew that the ultimate test for a royal wife was an invitation to spend a weekend at Balmoral or Windsor Castle, where candidates to be the next Princess of Wales were under strict observation and assessed for suitability by the Queen and Prince Philip.

Ever since his childhood, Balmoral had been Prince Charles' favourite holiday destination. This nineteenth century copy of a medieval castle built for Queen Victoria in 1852 was situated amid magnificent scenery in the Scottish Highlands near Aberdeen where Prince Albert, Queen Victoria's husband, had instituted the sport of deer stalking. This became a favourite pastime at Balmoral and often ended with a magnificent stag being killed. Had she known this in advance, Diana would have been appalled, as she hated blood sports.

Charles had spent his summer holidays from school and some weekend breaks from his boot camp boarding school at Balmoral with beloved grandmother at Birkhall on the Balmoral estate or with his parents at Balmoral Castle.

Birkhall, one of two Scotttish homes of the late Queen Mother which now belongs to Prince Charles is an attractive two-storey residence with a conical tower in the centre and dormer windows. The shy insecure young prince who was bullied at Gordonstoun and by his stern father felt happy and secure here with his beloved grandmother.

At seventeen, having failed to achieve her ambition to join a ballet company, Diana was working as a house cleaner for her sister, Lady Sarah.

After so much friction at home, Diana was happy to be away from Althorp.

Frances, although rarely in London, was worried, not wanting her youngest daughter to be seen as a 'Mrs Mop' for hire by all and sundry. Her mother paid for Diana to take a course in French cookery, hoping her problem daughter might be able to support herself cooking dinner parties for wealthy married school friends. Diana, who liked housework and ironing, did not gain the same pleasure from cooking. What she did enjoy was eating the rich sauces and desserts produced in class. As a result, Diana gained several kilos but found that losing them was difficult.

Deciding she preferred working with children to cooking, Diana took a poorly paid job as a nanny in Wimbledon. Lacking a car, she travelled to and from work on the underground but disliked strap-hanging in a crowded train. Diana obtained a better paid job as a nanny with a wealthy American family in elegant Belgravia, only a short bus ride from her mother's apartment.

Patrick Robertson, the nine-month-old American boy Diana was paid to care for, soon adored her. Diana's duties were to feed Patrick, take him for walks, play with him and do his washing and ironing. As Diana never discussed her private life, her American employer had no idea that shy 'Miss Spencer' had a title or that her father owned a stately home.[40] For major expenses, like dentistry, she relied on money from her mother.

Diana's sister Lady Sarah was about to announce her engagement to former Guards Officer Neil McCorquodale who farmed in the north of England. Working for Savills, the estate agent, Sarah found the perfect apartment for her mother to buy so that Diana had a place of her own at last on the fourth floor of a block called Coleherne Court.

The apartment complex had been built in the Edwardian era and consisted of three separate blocks with a private garden to the rear, situated in a quiet street called The Little Boltons.

Number 60 Coleherne Court lay within walking distance of South Kensington tube station and was only two bus stops away from Harrods and Harvey Nicholls (Harvey Nicks to Sloane Rangers), where she spent her free time window-shopping. Her mother told Diana that if she was still single once she came of age at twenty-one, she would put the title deeds in Diana's name.[41] Frances was generous with her money, and as Diana had passed her driving test with flying colours, Frances gave her youngest

[40] For the full story of Diana's employment with the Robertson family see Tina Brown, *The Diana Chronicles*, Doubleday, New York, 2007 pp69–72.

[41] Frances Shand Kydd planned to transfer the title deeds of Number 60 Coleherne Court to Diana after her youngest daughter turned 21. She paid £150,000 for the apartment, which soared in value and fetched over a million pounds when Frances sold it to a Japanese buyer.

daughter a bright red Mini Metro for her eighteenth birthday. Diana loved this car and the fact that she was able to park in the street in front of her apartment.

In July 1979, moving into Coleherne Court, decorating it and buying furniture, meant that for the first time in her life Diana was truly happy. She became a very different person to the moody, miserable teenager who had fought with her stepmother at Althorp. At Coleherne Court, she was having fun with her friends and, as she described it, 'laughed her head off'. Sharing the apartment with her were Carolyn Pride, Diana's friend from West Heath, Anne Bolton and Virginia Pitman.

The entrance to Coleherne Court, the Chelsea apartment where Diana lived with her girlfriends before her marriage. (Photo Jake de Vries)

Lady Diana had her own bedroom with her favourite stuffed animals at the end of her bed and her favourite photos pinned to the walls, including those of Prince Charles. A well-organised girl, she proved highly competent in her new role of landlady and, as such, had the largest bedroom. Diana collected rent from the other three girls, paid the rates and the electricity bills, drew up a roster of household duties and did the largest share of the housework herself. Unselfishly she took on the thankless jobs no one else wanted, such as cleaning the oven and emptying the Hoover bag. The friends took turns to go downstairs and bring in the morning milk, in those days delivered to the main entrance by the milkman.

In the 1970s, girls like Diana and her flatmates were known as Sloane Rangers. Many of them had pleasant, undemanding jobs as receptionists or secretaries in art galleries, fashion magazines or on the front desk of Sotheby's or Christie's.

Diana enjoyed flirting and described herself as being 'careful to keep myself tidy for marriage'. In Sloane Ranger language, this meant she was determined to remain a virgin until she went to the altar. Some male friends thought this because Diana was afraid of sex.

The Coleherne Court girls, being young and attractive, had plenty of male friends. They enjoyed going to local pubs or inexpensive restaurants or bistros in groups with young men whose families they knew, most of whom at been at Eton or Sandhurst together. They enjoyed playing childish practical jokes, such as telephoning anyone listed in the phone directory under the name 'Lyon' and asking, 'How's life in the London zoo?' before dropping the phone in fits of giggles.

Diana discovered she preferred living in the centre of London to rural life surrounded by the hunting-shooting set, who she found as boring as her mother had done decades earlier.

The well-connected young men who squired the Coleherne Court girls grew in number as they gave more and more parties, and met members of Lloyds, junior stockbrokers or junior officers in smart cavalry regiments. Several of the young men had been given expensive sports cars by wealthy parents and drove the girls to picturesque pubs like the Grenadier in a mews close to Hyde Park Corner, the Antelope in Eaton Terrace or the Nag's Head in Kinnerton Street, before dining in Chelsea bistros lit by candles stuck in Chianti bottles.

Special treats for birthdays were rich cakes that Diana loved and she bought at the French pastry shop on the corner of Montpelier Street opposite Harrods. Diana used to talk about losing weight but never stuck to any diet for very long, and her unsuccessful attempt at dieting became a joke among her friends. James Gilbey nicknamed Diana 'Squidgy' because she was plump and cuddly.

As her father was still recovering from a brain hemorrhage, Diana rarely returned to Althorp which she no longer saw as home because her stepmother ruled the roost. Mohamed Al Fayed had become a friend of her father and stepmother and given Raine a seat on the Harrods' board, and Diana had met him at several charity events that Raine organised.

By the time she turned eighteen, Diana was curvaceous in all the right places. Her mother paid for her daughter to have a skiing holiday in the French Alps with a group of Sloane Ranger girls and former Etonians.

On holiday, Diana enjoyed herself but had no romances. She met the recently qualified Dr James Colthurst, son of an Anglo-Irish peer who would become a good friend, as was James Gilbey, a handsome, car-mad young man whose family became very wealthy brewing Gilbey's gin. When they returned to London at Coleherne Court, discussing a certain restaurant, James Gilbey casually suggested he and Diana should dine there, and she accepted.

However, Gilbey forgot their arrangement and wined and dined a more sexually available girl. Diana, dressed in her best, waited outside the selected restaurant for over an hour and was mortified when James Gilbey failed to appear. A tearful Diana returned to Coleherne Court and told her flatmates what had happened. They took revenge on her behalf, went out late that night and covered Gilbey's precious sports car with a paste made of eggs and flour that by morning had set solid.

Diana's love of children secured her a job as a part-time child care assistant at the Young England Kindergarten in Pimlico – a combined nursery school and day care centre for upper-crust children run by two former West Heath girls. Lady Diana played with the children, taught them finger painting and used what she had learned at Madame Vacani's dance academy to give the children dancing lessons.

⁂

Lady Fermoy made certain that Diana received invitations to musical evenings at Clarence House. Diana wore her prettiest dresses and put mascara on her eyelashes, but Prince Charles still paid no attention to her. Lady Fermoy had not told the Queen Mother about Diana's fear of horses and her dislike of blood sports, aware these conflicted with Prince Charles' favoured pastimes – hunting, shooting, polo and reading. Neither did she tell Diana about Prince Charles' relationship with Mrs Parker Bowles.

Charles and Diana both liked music but had very different tastes. Diana liked Chopin and Rachmaninov and played some of their compositions; she also enjoyed listening to Dire Straits on her Sony Walkman and dancing along to their music.

In contrast, the Prince of Wales detested all pop music and enjoyed

Mahler, Berlioz and Bach. He also enjoyed the zany humour of *The Goon Show*, and books on philosophy, psychology, architecture, history and the preservation of the environment.

Diana shopped at chain stores and the Kensington High Street branch of Laura Ashley, selecting demure blouses with pie-frill collars, flower-printed skirts in pastel colours and flat shoes in an attempt to minimise her height.

The Queen Mother repeatedly assured her grandson that Lady Diana Spencer would make an ideal wife and excellent mother but received no response as Charles was obsessed by Camilla.

The next step in the Queen Mother and Lady Fermoy's campaign was for the Queen to ask Earl Spencer if his daughter could visit Balmoral for the weekend. The Parker Bowles were to stay at Birkhall, with the Queen Mother as Andrew was back on leave from Rhodesia. Camilla realised that for Lady Diana to receive an invitation from the Queen meant she must be a contender for the role of Princess of Wales, even though Charles had shown so little interest in her.

At Charles' suggestion, Camilla invited the prince and Lady Diana to stay at Bolehyde Manor for the weekend. As a married woman, Camilla was to act as Diana's chaperone so the formalities would be observed. In hindsight, it seems ironic that the prince's mistress was acting as chaperone for the girl to whom his family were trying to marry him.

Diana did not realise the deep waters into which she was being drawn. What did surprise her was that Mrs Parker Bowles knew so much about Prince Charles' activities and likes and dislikes.

When finally they were alone, Charles told Camilla that his family approved of Lady Diana as a future princess. However, Charles was angry that no one seemed to think of his feelings in something as important as marriage. He agreed Diana was sweet but could not see a giggly teenager as a soul mate or imagine spending the rest of his life with her. Could one marry and then grow to love someone was the question he asked himself as this had happened to some Princes of Wales in the past.

To Camilla, the shy Lady Diana seemed unlikely to be a threat to her and Charles remaining friends after the wedding. Camilla badly underestimated Diana and did not realise how deeply in love Diana was with her 'Prince Charming' or how determined she was that her husband would adore her and her alone.

⁂

Charles realised Lady Diana was from a totally different generation who spoke and thought differently to him and Camilla. To close friends, he wondered whether such a relationship could work.

Approaching the age of thirty-two, Charles realised he had to make a decision about a wife soon but was worried by making a lifelong commitment to a nineteen-year-old with whom he seemed to have very little in common.

Camilla, feeling she was doing the right thing, advised Charles that that he should propose before anyone else started dating Lady Diana, a warning echoed by his father. By now, Camilla was having second thoughts about her own marriage and trying to make it work. Nine years earlier, she had returned to the previously unfaithful Andrew thinking he would change once he married, but that had not been the case.

Her parents advised Camilla to give her marriage another chance and end this renewed affair with Prince Charles.

On 3 May 1980, at the Queen Mother's request, Lady Ruth Fermoy organised pre-concert drinks and tickets for a group, which included Lady Diana and Prince Charles, to attend a performance of *Verdi's* Requiem at the Royal Albert Hall. *Verdi's* Requiem enthralled Diana and would remain one of her favourite pieces of music.

At the buffet supper that followed, the Prince of Wales had a few quick words with Diana and, to please his grandmother arranged for Diana to be included in an invitation to visit Balmoral with Lady Jane Fellowes and her husband Robert, under the pretext that Lady Jane needed help with Laura, her new baby. Diana, who adored children, would be an ideal guest. This was an opportunity to demonstrate to Prince Charles what a good mother she would make.

Privately, Camilla told her brother-in-law, Richard Parker Bowles, that she thought young Lady Diana Spencer was 'gormless', an antiquated Scottish word meaning 'stupid, foolish or dim' and regarded Lady Diana as 'a sweet little thing, shy, quiet, passive and obedient, so how could she possibly be any trouble?'[42]

But under that protective layer of sweetness and smiles, Lady Diana was tougher than Camilla had realised. Her motherless childhood deprived of affection n adolescence spent fighting with her stepmother had given Diana a strong will and a vocabulary of swear words not usually found among princesses. Given this background, it was highly unlikely that Lady Diana would remain 'shy, quiet, passive and obedient' for very long.

---

[42] Richard Parker Bowles, *Executive PA Magazine*, 25 November 1995.

'If it wasn't for bloody polo, all this wouldn't have happened'

This remark by Lady Diana, using her favourite swear word, referred to an invitation she received in the summer of 1980 to a polo weekend at the home of the de Pass family, friends of the royal family. Strings were being pulled by an increasingly desperate Queen Mother, backed by Lady Fermoy, to place Diana in the path of Prince Charles so she could flirt with him.

Lady Philippa de Pass was a lady-in-waiting to the Queen, and Lady Philippa's son had been asked to invite Diana to join their weekend house party at New Grove, their eighteenth-century home near Petworth. Prince Charles was to be the guest of honour, along with several members of his polo team. House guests were to drive to Cowdray Park, watch Prince Charles and his team play their match and then drive back to Petworth for an informal barbecue at New Grove where, as set up by the Queen Mother, Charles was seated beside the young Diana.

Polo held little attraction for Diana, who was still afraid of horses. Having watched several polo matches, she was not keen on watching another. But the thought of meeting 'Prince Charming' in less formal surroundings than Clarence House was worth the boredom of watching polo. Worried that she could once again become tongue-tied with nerves, Diana carefully rehearsed what she would say to the Prince of Wales at the barbecue. Fearing he would have forgotten she was Lady Sarah's younger sister and not remember her name, Diana wore a large 'D' on a slender gold chain round her neck, a birthday present from her classmates at West Heath, one of the few pieces of jewellery that she owned.

On that fateful Saturday afternoon, the guests, including Diana, drove to Cowdray Park and cheered themselves hoarse as Prince Charles' team won the match. James Whitaker was also present. He described Diana spending most of her time playing with a friend's baby rather than watching the match.

At the barbecue, Prince Charles was skilfully manipulated into sitting on a bale of hay beside Lady Diana as they ate their barbecued steaks and salad. Diana could not help blushing as she spoke to the Prince of Wales who protocol insisted she address as 'Sir' while he called her by her first name.

Having prepared herself for what she saw as an opportunity to make a good impression, Diana told 'Sir' how much she sympathised with him over the murder of his great-uncle, Lord Mountbatten, which was an unusual approach at a party, but aroused Charles' interest.

Lady Diana added that she had watched him on television attending

Lord Mountbatten's funeral and that 'her heart bled for him' as he looked so lonely. Greatly daring, she added, 'Sir, you clearly needed someone to look after you.'

Diana had no way of knowing that Camilla had been 'looking after' Charles extremely well. But Diana's sweetness and solicitude touched a chord with Charles, and he now saw her as an attractive young woman who was sympathetic and understanding.

According to Sabrina Guinness, who was also a guest at the barbecue, Diana (who on the tape she made for Andrew Morton claimed how shy she had been at the barbecue) clearly overcame her shyness quickly, giggled and flirted with Prince Charles and ended the evening by sitting on his knee.

Charmed by Diana who seemed so jolly and uncomplicated, Charles kissed her on the cheek to which she responded warmly by kissing him back. He later admitted having qualms about having kissed Lady Diana, as she seemed so young and innocent – aware that Camilla was also at the barbecue, he may have felt guilty about kissing Diana.

Many years later, Diana would remember that fateful polo weekend and exclaim angrily, 'If it hadn't been for bloody polo and that barbecue, all this wouldn't have happened!'

Having stayed the night with the de Pass family, early on Sunday afternoon, Charles casually asked Diana if she would like a lift back to London in his Aston Martin, his standard ploy for seducing girls. Keen not to be seen as 'available', Diana cleverly replied that leaving the house party early would be rude, aware from her readings of Mills and Boon and Barbara Cartland romances that insisting she was not an 'easy' target for seduction would make her more desirable.

Charles said goodbye with a vague promise of an invitation to Balmoral for Diana to watch the Braemar Games, which coincided with the start of the grouse-shooting season. Being refused had piqued his interest. Both Scottish grandmothers were overjoyed when they heard what had transpired.

Back in Wiltshire, the more Camilla saw and heard about shy Lady Diana, the keener she became on a marriage that would present no threat to her influence over the heir to the throne.

What worried her was that the press might discover their clandestine affair. James Whitaker seemed to have eyes and ears everywhere. Camilla had no wish to be exposed as a royal mistress. She was reaching the conclusion that, for the sake of her children, she needed to give her unfaithful husband and her marriage another chance.

Charles must have been aware that if he were to please his family and court Lady Diana seriously, he must tell her the truth about his sexual relationship with Camilla.

However, Diana was still lost in a romantic dream. She failed to realise that what she was being offered was an arranged marriage to a prince who thought she was very sweet and hoped he could grow to love her.

From house cleaner to royal guest at Balmoral

In the late summer of 1980, Diana's visit to Balmoral to attend the Braemar Games was organised by the Queen Mother and Lady Fermoy.

Balmoral Castle at the time of Diana's visit (Private collection)

Diana and her elder sister, Lady Jane Fellowes, her husband and their baby were invited to a house party at the Queen Mother's home, Birkhall on the Balmoral estate. This visit had been carefully planned by the two grandmothers to enable the Queen and Prince Philip to 'vet' Lady Diana at close quarters.

This visit was a test, and Diana knew it. She confessed her feelings on videotapes years later, admitting 'I was terrified, shitting bricks, as I wanted to get it *right*.'

And Diana did get it *right*. With her good manners, youthful charm and the right clothes – corduroy trousers and a thick sweater for long walks with Charles, and long dresses to change into for dinner – Diana won the approval of the Queen and Prince Philip. She seemed like a very sweet bride for their eldest son.

Balmoral was the place the royal family loved most, where they could relax away from the world on their annual summer holiday, with traditions created by Queen Victoria with six pipers playing the bagpipes from 6 a.m. each morning to wake the royal family, rain or shine.

Despite chilling rain with the occasional burst of sunshine, Diana took long walks through the heather with Patti Palmer-Tomkinson, the wife of one of Charles' skiing friends. Diana was keen to be seen as an ideal bride for Charles, a jolly, no-nonsense, country girl. She laughed when caught in a heavy rainstorm that soaked both of them to the skin. Back in her room in a separate lodge, with stuffed deer heads with glass eyes on the walls (which she found macabre), Diana dried her hair and changed her clothes to have tea with the royal family.

At teatime and dinner, she hung on Prince Charles' every word and laughed politely at family jokes, many of which she did not understand, and spoke very little.

The next day the sun shone, and photos were taken of Diana and Charles together before the Prince of Wales announced he was going fishing. This was not Diana's idea of an amusing afternoon. However, she sat on the river bank watching Charles who wore high rubber boots called waders as he stood thigh-deep in cold water. The Prince of Wales concentrated on his favourite sport and took it for granted that Diana, with her background of country house life, was enjoying herself. Diana did not want to disillusion him. This was the big chance for the girl who had worked as a house cleaner for her sister to become a princess and make her siblings respect her.

Through binoculars, Diana saw James Whitaker and his photographer skulking in the undergrowth on the opposite bank. Diana proved to be smarter than anyone had believed. Turning her back so Whitaker could not photograph her face, she delved into her leather tote bag for her powder compact and observed the gossip writer in her mirror. All Whitaker saw was a flash of light from the tree against which Lady Diana was leaning, and realised with a shock that she was observing him. Clearly, Lady Sarah's younger sister was not nearly as dumb as Whittaker had believed when he found her so boring at Lady Jane's wedding that he couldn't be bothered to talk to her.

Diana claimed to love being at Balmoral, but years later during a row with her husband, she admitted she hated the place and anything to do with fishing, shooting or polo. Among the Windsors, this was tantamount to treason. When Kate Middleton was given the Balmoral test before she married Prince William, she had to join a hunting party where a stag was stalked; not only did she have to watch the poor beast being killed, but following tradition she had to be 'blooded' or dabbed on the cheek with the blood of the dead stag and look as if she was enjoying herself.

Fortunately, Diana did not have to endure this – she would have regarded it as a hideous ordeal. Diana adored Prince Charles but was still in awe of him and still calling him 'Sir.' She was determined to get Prince Charles to propose and become the Princess of Wales and, like someone in a fairy story, live happily ever after.

Dinner table conversations with the royal party bored Diana as they eagerly discussed stalking stags, shooting game birds, fishing and breeding racehorses. Any discussion of killing animals always upset Diana, but as a well-mannered guest, she was careful not to show her distaste for blood sports. Aware she was being appraised, Diana was at pains to appear enthusiastic about everything at Balmoral. As there was no one of her own age to talk to, and Prince Charles was seated some distance away from her, Diana had to spend meals listening and saying very little.

In the early 1980s, television was still banned at Balmoral. At night after a formal black-tie dinner, guests were entertained by Princess Margaret singing hit tunes from old musicals, accompanying herself on the piano, a glass of champagne at her elbow.

On the first night of the house party this was amusing, but on subsequent evenings Diana was bored. Princess Margaret resembled Prince Charles in expecting guests to do as she wanted. For reasons of protocol, none of them could retire to bed until the Queen's sister was tired. This was not Diana's idea of an enjoyable evening, and there was little chance for her to have heart-to-heart talks with the Prince of Wales.

Prince Philip liked the idea of a pretty girl descended from Stuart monarchs joining the royal family. Earlier in the week he had privately urged his son to propose soon. If he did not act now he might miss his chance and someone else would court the delectable Lady Diana.

Prince Charles, cautious by nature, was still vacillating. Later he told his biographer Jonathan Dimbleby he was worried by Diana's immaturity and was unwilling to commit himself until he knew her a great deal better.

Nevertheless, having been rejected as a husband by several aristocratic young women, Charles was flattered that a pretty girl like Lady Diana hung on his every word and laughed at his jokes. He began to have second thoughts about this admiring, young girl.

James Whitaker and his photographer were still stalking Lady Diana, convinced they were onto a good story. Whitaker watched the young Spencer girl leave Balmoral in a chauffeur-driven car to catch the afternoon plane from Aberdeen to London. He observed that she had been given two male escorts, one of them in army uniform. Whitaker and his photographer followed the chauffeur-driven car to what was then an extremely small airport at Aberdeen before oil was discovered in Scotland.

With a shock, the journalist realised that one of Lady Diana's escorts was Prince Charles' equerry and close friend the Hon Nicholas Soames while the tall man in uniform beside her was Lieutenant Colonel Andrew Parker Bowles of the Household Cavalry. There had to be a reason for this VIP treatment of a young girl.

The journalist watched the trio pass through airport security. When an official asked to see what was inside Lady Diana's tote bag, she produced a suede jewel case. She blushed with embarrassment when the search revealed only a single item of jewellery in her jewel case, a thin gold chain holding the gold 'D' that she had worn each night at dinner.

Whitaker suspected that, in spite of her youth, Lady Diana Spencer was the hot favourite to marry the heir to the throne.

The paparazzi believed they were onto a good story and sat outside Coleherne Court following Lady Diana everywhere, making her life difficult, as she lacked a detective or a protection officer to fend them off. Charles felt guilty that Diana was being harassed by the press because her name was being linked to his. However, he felt he was being rushed into making a decision before he was ready and was annoyed. He remained distant from Diana, who was puzzled.

⁂

Back in London, Prince Charles still dithered about proposing to Lady Diana although the press continued to write about her as the perfect royal bride.

After Diana's trip north to Balmoral, journalists besieged Coleherne Court, hoping to get an in-depth story on her. One press photographer rented the vacant apartment opposite Lady Diana's so he could photograph Diana and her friends from its windows. Another stood beside the milkman when Diana went down to fetch the morning milk at the front door. Diana felt harassed, with no detectives or bodyguards to protect her. Camera lenses were thrust in her face day after day as she left her apartment.

Members of the paparazzi approached Diana in the street demanding to know if Prince Charles had proposed and even went through her garbage bin looking for evidence. Diana felt her privacy had been invaded, yet still, Charles made no move. He did not phone and had not told her he loved her.

In the privacy of her bedroom, Diana wept. Her old insecurities returned, and she felt no one loved her because she was unlovable, and her parents had always preferred her brother. She felt it was her fault that Prince Charles had not declared his hand and proposed. Once again, she was a failure.

Charles continued to be cautious, aware that in his position divorce would be impossible. Diana seemed to be very sweet and photographers loved her and followed her around like a film star, and has mentioned, he did feel sorry for her because she lacked police protection or a press attaché to fend off the paparazzi.

Lady Diana was smart when chased by the media and soon realised she could evade photographers and journalists by rushing out of the main door of Coleherne Court, climbing into her little red Metro and roaring away into the traffic.

The Queen Mother was delighted that at last her grandson was taking some notice of 'that sweet young Spencer girl'.

In October 1980, Charles and Diana were again invited to a house party at Birkhall.

Once more they were rarely alone, but this time, Diana was not nearly as nervous as on her previous visit. There was more fishing in the River Dee, and the Queen Mother donned waders and joined in. Charles and his father and other male guests went out with the guns. Charles continued to dither about whether to propose, to the annoyance of his father.

Lady Fermoy behaved like a character in a Jane Austen novel, claiming that if the Prince of Wales did not propose soon, Diana's chances of marrying anyone else were ruined.

Camilla knew that once her lover became engaged, it would be the end of the physical side of their relationship but perhaps took comfort from the allegation that Prince Philip had told his son if his marriage did not work out after five years, he could take a mistress.

At Clarence House, the Queen Mother and Lady Fermoy agreed it was unfortunate that Lady Diana was taller than the Prince of Wales, but as long as she wore flat shoes, there would be no problem. They fondly imagined Prince Charles would always be the centre of attention, so Diana's shyness would not be a problem either.

In November 1980, the *Sunday Mirror* published a story that the Prince of Wales had been joined by a mysterious blonde on the royal train when it was parked in a deserted rail siding at Staverton in Wiltshire. The train had luxurious sleeping compartments that made it an ideal meeting place for lovers. The *Sunday Mirror* wrongly identified the blonde on the royal train as Lady Diana Spencer, rumoured to be a hot favourite to become Princess of Wales. Other sources identified the mysterious blonde climbing into the empty royal train as Mrs Parker Bowles but did not print this for fear of legal action.

Both Lady Diana and her father were shown the story. Earl Spencer was furious that Diana's reputation was being trashed and wrote a letter of complaint to the paper's editor, as did Frances Shand Kydd.

Jonathan Dimbleby records that in a note to his son Prince Philip demanded that Charles propose to Lady Diana or stop seeing her. Charles bitterly resented his father's efforts to pressure him into marriage and carried his father's letter around with him and showed it to close friends as proof his father was bullying him.

To Diana, desperate for contact with Charles, he always seemed to be busy with official functions or off to play polo. However, he did spend one weekend with her when they stayed with the Parker Bowles. To protect her reputation, Diana had to be chaperoned by a married woman as though they were living in the days of Queen Victoria, and this task fell to Camilla. The arrangement whereby the prince's mistress chaperoned his virginal girlfriend was ironic, but Diana was still unaware of the real situation.

Charles seemed perfectly happy as a bachelor with all his wants catered to. However, he told friends and family that he knew he must marry to 'do the right thing for the country and his family'. He admitted this to his close friend Nicholas Soames who replied that he did not see Lady Diana as a suitable wife. Neither did Lord Mountbatten's son-in-law, Norton Knatchbull and his wife, Lady Penny Romsey. The three of them believed that Lady Diana and Prince Charles had far too little in common for a marriage between them to work. Lady Penny thought that Diana was in love with the fairytale concept of being a princess without any idea of the responsibilities attached the job.

Diana's mother and the Romseys believed the immature Lady Diana was in love with the image of 'Prince Charming' rather than with the real life, serious-minded workaholic prince. She ignored the fact that Prince Charles was concerned with preserving the environment, finding a meaning to life, studying psychology and comparative religions and enjoyed solitude in the Kalahari Desert with his friend, Laurens van der Post.

On a rare visit to London, Frances Shand Kydd tried to warn Diana against the marriage, telling her that the Windsors had a very different outlook on life to the way her daughter had been brought up. In fact, she was correct as, with no mother, Diana's upbringing had been haphazard and undisciplined.

Diana continued to view Prince Charles through rose-tinted glasses convinced that, as his wife, if she provided him with a male heir, he would love her forever. The prospect of dazzling her family by becoming Princess of Wales was irresistible.

The press continued to urge the Prince of Wales to declare his intentions to the girl they christened 'Shy Di' from her habit of blushing and peering at them from under her fringe. Charles, still feeling he was being forced into an arranged marriage, dug in his heels and refused to propose, worried by Diana's immaturity and lack of education and interest in reading anything but romantic novels.

Diana, having seen what had happened to her sister, Lady Sarah, after she spoke to James Whitaker, refused to speak to the press. Eventually, in desperation Diana granted an interview to Philip Taverner of the Press Association. Knowing this would be read by Charles' staff, she told the journalist, 'I'd like to marry soon, I don't think nineteen is too young. It all depends on the person one marries.'

Diana had chosen her words carefully, hoping they might encourage Charles to propose, assuring him that in her eyes their thirteen-year age gap was not significant.

Diana was helped when a sexy photograph of her with young children appeared in the press. A photographer had asked permission to photograph her with two of her young charges at the Young England Child Care Centre. Diana, who always enjoyed being photographed, agreed. She was caught on camera, backlit by the afternoon sun, wearing a diaphanous summer skirt without a petticoat, which made her long slim legs even more appealing under the gauzy material.

When Diana saw her photo, she was mortified. However, Prince Charles and most of the male population of Great Britain found her photograph alluring. Journalists swarmed around the front entrance to Coleherne Court trying to interview Lady Diana, who fled to her little red car and drove away at top speed.

With her mother far away in Scotland, Diana needed advice from someone more mature than her school friends, who were agog with excitement about her royal romance. She did not trust her stepmother and wished her grandmother, Lady Cynthia, was still alive.

She telephoned her grandmother's friend Lady Elsa Bowker now widowed and residing in Belgravia. Tearfully, she confessed to the sympathetic Lady Bowker how much she longed for Charles to propose. Diana said to her, 'Prince Charles is the love of my life, but I'm not worthy of him.'

Lady Bowker did her best to soothe and comfort Diana, who had lost confidence in herself and was back in one of her nobody loves me moods.

Christmas 1980 was far from merry for Diana. She spent it at Althorp with the stepmother she hated and her ailing father. Among several bones of contention was that Raine had sold antique dealers valuable first editions from Althorp's library and a pair of solid gold wine coolers worth a million pounds at greatly reduced prices. The opinion in the antique trade was they would have fetched double that amount at auction. But Raine insisted that she was saving the family's reputation, and no one must know that they were short of ready cash to maintain and redecorate Althorp.

The atmosphere at Althorp was poisonous. Raine's stepchildren believed she was frittering away their heritage and spending money she earned from Spencer heirlooms on buying stupid, vulgar things.

Still worried about Diana, Lady Bowker telephoned Althorp and spoke to Raine who told her that her stepdaughter was walking around the garden in floods of tears. Prince Charles had sent her a formal Christmas card but no flowers or written message inside.

By now Diana's self-esteem, always low, was ebbing fast. She was convinced she was so stupid that Charles could never love her, blaming herself for the situation. The only thing from which she could derive any comfort was on that last visit to the Parker Bowles; at one of the few moments she and Charles were alone, he had muttered the words 'everyone' thought they should marry.

Lady Bowker tried to cheer Diana up by pointing out that Charles had finally mentioned the word marriage. Diana replied this was scarcely a proposal.

New Year's Eve 1980 was even worse for Diana than Christmas. Prince Charles, still agonising over whether to please his family and propose, did not ring Diana.

Without an invitation to join Charles at Sandringham and unable to bear more arguments with her stepmother, Diana accepted an invitation to spend New Year's Eve with Princess Margaret and her sophisticated friends, drinking champagne in Margaret's apartment at Kensington Palace. The Queen's sister, whose divorce from Tony Armstrong-Jones was something she wanted to forget, performed her usual routine of songs at the piano and drank far too much champagne.[43]

When Diana complained that the paparazzi were hounding her, Princess Margaret was not sympathetic as Diana's situation highlighted the fact that the divorced Margaret was no longer of interest to the press.

---

[43] Princess Margaret married Tony Armstrong-Jones in 1960. Tony had attended Eton and was considered a member of the Establishment as his mother held the title of Anne, Countess of Rosse, as a result of her second marriage (when Tony was only five) to the Earl of Rosse, and he grew up at Bir Castle in Ireland. He was created Earl of Snowdon when he married, but retained a bohemian attitude to marriage and sired several love children.

By mid-January 1981, Prince Philip was so irritated by his heir's delays that he demanded (as in his earlier note) Charles propose immediately or 'stop seeing the little Spencer girl'. Philip, never one to mince his words, added that if Charles did not marry soon, the public would believe he was gay. He ended by ordering his son to, 'Just hurry up and get on with it,' then turned on his heel and walked away.

Charles consulted Camilla before taking such an important step. She reassured her lover that marrying Lady Diana Spencer was 'the right thing to do' and that she would always be there for him. This seemed to have been the deciding factor for Charles, and reluctantly he decided to propose to Lady Diana.

Diana would later claim that Camilla telephoned, advising that Prince Charles would be making a formal proposal 'very soon'. Diana found it odd that her chaperone knew so much about the workings of Prince Charles' mind but took comfort from the fact that in romantic novels she loved, the path to the altar was never easy for the heroine. But Diana still failed to realise that Prince Charles' deepest emotions were reserved for Camilla.

Prince Charles followed his usual pattern and took off with friends on a Swiss skiing holiday but did not invite Diana to join them, which depressed her still further, as years earlier, Lady Sarah had joined Charles on a ski holiday.

Years later, when making videotapes about her marriage, Diana stated that at this period she had only been alone with Prince Charles on thirteen occasions and was still addressing him as 'Sir'.

A royal engagement at last

Finally, Prince Charles, tanned from his skiing holiday in Switzerland, telephoned Diana and thrilled her by asking her to meet him at Windsor Castle at 5 p.m. on Friday, 6 February 1981 as he had something to ask her. The date and time had been arranged to suit Charles, who was playing polo that afternoon in Windsor Great Park. He had not thought to send a car to collect Diana, and it was Friday, she had to drive to Windsor through heavy traffic as cars were streaming out of London for the weekend.

Fortunately, Diana was familiar with the route, her father and brother having attended Eton, which was very close to Windsor. Just before the appointed hour of five o'clock, Diana drove her red Metro down Windsor High Street, turned left under the arch leading to the forecourt of Windsor Castle, gave her name to the guard on duty and was shown to a reserved parking area.

A nervous Lady Diana was escorted through awe-inspiring reception rooms with enormously painted ceilings showing the apotheosis of the House of Hanover-Windsor, heading to the former nursery quarters where the Prince of Wales was waiting for her.

His former nursery seemed an odd setting to propose marriage, but presumably, Charles felt secure there. According to the taped account Diana gave Andrew Morton, Prince Charles asked Diana to sit down and told her he had missed her while he was in Switzerland. In a short formal speech without mentioning the word 'love', the heir to the throne asked Diana to marry him. Charles had been raised to hide his emotions, and this occasion was no exception. Or perhaps he was just being honest and felt this was how he should present it to Diana, a marriage where it was hoped love might grow after having children?

Diana was disappointed by Prince Charles' lack of passion. It was nothing like the romantic proposals described in novels by Barbara Cartland, but she was thrilled that 'Prince Charming' had finally proposed and giggled nervously as Charles informed her that one day she would be Queen of England.

Years later, recounting the event for Andrew Morton's book, Diana insisted that a small voice inside her head told her she would never be queen.

However, she replied to Charles' proposal with genuine emotion. 'I love you so much,' Diana said and meant it.

'Whatever love means,' Charles replied, in a cryptic phrase he was to make famous in a subsequent televised interview.

Prince Charles told Diana she could choose an engagement ring later as a personal gift from his mother. They kissed briefly and said goodbye and Charles went to phone the Queen and give her the news.

Feeling happy and relieved, Diana drove back to London at top speed to see her mother who had just arrived from Scotland. She broke the good news to her mother and brother and asked her mother for help in choosing her trousseau as she had no money of her own.

According to a royal biographer, Sarah Bradford, Diana's brother Charles recalled Diana bubbling with happiness.[44] She was convinced that as the wife of Prince Charles her life would be wonderful.

Diana's ailing father was thrilled when she phoned him and told him she was engaged. The Coleherne Court girls were beside themselves with excitement and hugged Diana, yelling with joy. Later they all drove around London in her little red car to celebrate, unlike most engagements where

---

44 Andrew Morton, *op. cit.*, p34, repeated with additions in Sarah Bradford's *Diana*, Penguin/Viking, London, 2006, pp 74-75.

the couple celebrates together.

Charles felt there were bound to be difficulties due to the thirteen-year difference in their ages and Diana's limited education. He would later tell his biographer Jonathan Dimbleby that although he had not loved Diana when he proposed, he did what he believed to be his duty and that love would follow when they had children and shared interests.

Diana's sister, Lady Jane, now part of royal circles, was pleased for her younger sister but wondered how she would be able to cope with the stresses of royal life. Diana had no such worries. In love with Charles, presumably still unaware of his obsession with Camilla, Diana did not foresee any difficulties.

When told that Prince Charles and Lady Diana were engaged, the Queen and the rest of the royal family were delighted and relieved. Lady Diana fulfilled the criteria that had governed the selection of royal brides for centuries. Charles had fulfilled his duty to the House of Windsor and his country.

For reasons never revealed, the engagement was kept secret for a fortnight. Diana chose her engagement ring – an enormous sapphire surrounded by eighteen diamonds set in gold– from a tray sent over by Garrards, the crown jewellers. It was a personal gift from the Queen to show her approval of the marriage of her son to the daughter of Earl Spencer, a family friend.

Westminster Abbey, where Diana's mother and members of the royal family married, would not be the venue for Diana. Charles wanted his wedding to take place in St Paul's Cathedral, as the acoustics were better for the music that he wanted. The New Zealand opera singer Kiri Te Kanawa had agreed to give a solo performance, and many more guests could be accommodated in St Paul's. The teenage Diana had no say in the choice of venue or in most of the wedding arrangements.

The engagement of the heir to the throne was announced on 24 February 1981 at a press conference at Buckingham Palace. Headlines that 'the Golden Couple' were to marry delighted the public who were thrilled at the idea of a royal wedding. Amid all the euphoria, stock market prices soared, and millions of wedding souvenirs were produced.

After so much plotting on behalf of her granddaughter, Lady Fermoy was annoyed that Diana did not come in person to thank her. However, she was thrilled to think her 'problem' granddaughter would one day be Queen of Great Britain.

To show her pleasure at the success of their plans, at the suggestion of the Queen Mother, Lady Ruth Fermoy was created a Commander of the Royal Victorian Order, given for 'devoted service to the royal family'.

(Lady Fermoy told everyone she was thrilled by the engagement, but years later, when the marriage was in trouble, Diana's grandmother changed her tune and insisted she had been against it from the start. Not everyone believed her.)

For her first television interview, Diana relied on her mother to help her buy a suitable outfit, as she still had no income of her own. Frances came down from Scotland and took her youngest daughter to the Knightsbridge couturier Belinda Belleville, where they were confronted by a snooty *vendeuse* who ignored them, unaware that the tall teenager waiting nervously to be served was to marry the heir to the throne.

Frances was annoyed and swept Diana off to Harrods Ladies Dress Department with its long mirrors and respectful assistants. After much agonising, they decided on a blue wool suit to be worn with a blue and white silk blouse with a pussy-cat bow at the neck. Later Diana admitted she had not liked the blue outfit very much and it had been her mother's choice.

Looking at herself in the mirror on the morning before her first television interview, Diana was worried that the short boxy jacket made her look chubby, the word she had hated when Charles had first used it.

'Whatever "in love" means'

Feeling nervous, Diana faced her first television interview in the garden behind Buckingham Palace. To make matters worse, a few days earlier Charles had put his arm around her waist and whispered, 'Getting a bit chubby, aren't we?' For the insecure Diana, this remark made her terrified that her fiancé no longer found her attractive.

When the interviewer asked Prince Charles how he felt about getting married, Charles replied he was 'delighted and frankly amazed that Diana is brave enough to take me on'.

Asked were they in love, Diana blushed, looked down at her feet in embarrassment and replied softly, 'Yes, of course.'

When it was Charles' turn to answer the same question, he shocked viewers by replying, 'Whatever "in love" means.'

Diana found this a strange reply. She blushed, rolled her eyes and said nothing.

To save the situation, Prince Charles added hastily that they were 'two very happy people'. Diana agreed but admitted later to friends that her fiancé's bald statement, 'Whatever "in love" means,' had shocked her.

BBC TV organised a second interview, this time with Angela Rippon, who asked the couple what interests they shared. Among those Diana cited were fishing and watching polo – two things she loathed, but she would rather have died than admit the truth.

Meanwhile, Prince Charles, who disliked being interviewed or discussing his emotions in public, fiddled with his cuffs to cover his embarrassment and terminated the interview.

During their five-month engagement, Prince Charles was often away on royal duties or playing polo. The couple spoke on the phone, but not nearly as often as Diana would have liked. As Prince Charles always seemed to be busy, they still did not spend a great deal of time in each other's company.

When they did spend a weekend together, it was invariably at the country house of the Parker Bowles, where Camilla continued to act as chaperone for the bride-to-be and the couple were rarely alone. On these occasions, Camilla told Diana a great deal about Charles' likes and dislikes in food as well as other things the older woman felt Diana should know.

Diana began to feel uncomfortable at the interest Camilla was showing in her relationship with Charles. Diana knew that Charles had had plenty of women as lovers and slowly the idea began to dawn that Camilla could have been one of them. From then on, she started wondering if their close relationship could be more than pure friendship. In the romantic scenario Diana had constructed in her head about her fairytale romance, this was impossible, but now she was not so sure. Alone in her bedroom, she devoured boxes of chocolates trying to work out what link there could be between Camilla and her fiancé and why Camilla knew so much more about him than she did. She consoled herself by thinking about the honeymoon when they would have time at sea for long heart-to-heart chats.

Wedding plans but little time with each other

Diana had her portrait painted by Bryan Organ and broke with tradition when she chose to be portrayed in a collarless white shirt, black waistcoat and trousers, seated in front of the doorway of a stately home, a reminder of her ancient lineage. The portrait completed, Diana flew to Australia to stay with her mother at the Shand Kydd sheep property, near Yass in New South Wales.

Diana's mother had been loaned a beach house at Mollymook on the coast where over the next ten days mother and daughter drew up a list of guests they wanted to invite to the wedding. Diana loved the heat of Australia, adored swimming in warm water and relaxing on the sandy beach while preparing to face the biggest challenge of her nineteen years.

Charles and Diana each remembered her three weeks' stay in Australia differently. Diana claimed that she had been upset because her fiancé rarely telephoned her. Charles, involved with his public appearances and working for his charities, insisted he had called Diana frequently.[45]

Diana's mother worried that Lady Fermoy had pushed too hard for this marriage, which could be a disaster for her overly-emotional daughter. Diana had no idea of the kind of life she would lead as a member of a family trained to show no emotion in public. Clearly, there was a long way to go before this mismatched couple achieved a rapport.

Frances believed there was too wide an age gap and too many differences in personality for her daughter's marriage to work.

Diana refused to listen to her mother's concerns and was optimistic about her future, aware that Charles did not love her as she loved him but convinced he would love her once she gave him a male heir. In a strange way, Diana was repeating the role of her mother who had been married off at eighteen, too young to know what she really wanted in life. Frances had been married to provide a male heir for the Althorp estate just as Diana knew that her role was to provide Charles with a son.

Due to the media now surrounding Coleherne Court and the lack of security, it was decided that Diana should move temporarily to Clarence House, home of the Queen Mother, before moving into a suite at Buckingham Palace. Clarence House was surrounded by security guards from Scotland Yard and high iron railings, so Diana would be shielded from the photographers and television cameras that dogged her footsteps every time she stepped out into the street.

The Kensington Palace apartment that Charles and Diana were to occupy was still being renovated, as was their country residence, Highgrove House in Gloucestershire. By now, Diana had realised that one of the attractions of Highgrove was that it was only eleven kilometres away from the home of the Parker Bowles and was becoming suspicious of Camilla's interest in her marriage.

Before leaving Coleherne Court with her suitcases and the row of stuffed animals that sat at the end of her bed, Diana wrote her flatmates a farewell note, telling them she would miss them. She added poignantly, 'For God's sake ring me up – I'm going to need it.'

On the tape she made for Andrew Morton, Diana claimed her husband was not there to welcome her on her arrival at Clarence House, where she was 'pushed into the fire like a sacrificial lamb'. But, in reality witnesses confirm Prince Charles *was* there to welcome her.

---

[45] Max Riddington and Gavin Nadal, *op. cit.*

Reliable sources show Diana was given a welcome dinner at Clarence House by the Queen Mother, supported by Lady Ruth Fermoy. Both grandmothers wanted to make Diana feel welcome and ensure the success of the marriage they had championed. But wanting to be seen as a victim, Diana omitted this from her taped account of that evening which was given to Andrew Morton for his book. When feeling loved by Charles, Diana showed the affectionate side of her personality. In the period before the wedding, royal watchers who observed the two of them together thought they seemed to be fond of each other. But below the surface lurked hidden tensions and fears about this marriage on both sides.

In the days that followed, Charles, the workaholic prince, was busy and Diana missed her girlfriends and Coleherne Court badly. When, finally, she moved into her suite of rooms at Buckingham Palace, she found them chilly and unfriendly.

Everyone assumed that as Earl Spencer had been equerry to King George VI and Queen Elizabeth, Lady Diana must be accustomed to large dinner parties and formal banquets. Lady Fermoy had given the royal family no hint that Diana's childhood had been unusual or that she hated large formal dinner parties, which reminded her of life with her stepmother. In contrast, meals at 60 Coleherne Court had been jolly and companionable rather than formal, and this was the kind of life that Diana enjoyed.

The rooms that had been prepared for Diana at Buckingham Palace were on the former nursery floor overlooking the Mall. Immured there, Diana had very little contact with anyone her own age. The immature nineteen-year-old found herself surrounded by courtiers much older than herself. At Kensington Palace, she was introduced to members of the royal family who each had their own apartments and were jealous of each other's privileges. This was not the warm, loving extended family into which Diana had hoped to marry. Unlike Kate Middleton, who before her wedding to Prince William had the emotional support of her parents and her sister, Diana did not have family support.

Lady Sarah, recently married, was living far away from London and Lady Jane Fellowes, wife of the secretary to the Queen, was living in a house in the grounds of Kensington Palace and was kept very busy looking after an active toddler and her hardworking husband. Diana's mother Frances was mainly in Scotland where her second marriage was under stress, and her father was still in poor health after his cerebral hemorrhage, and Diana refused to ask for help from her detested stepmother. Rather than being a comfort, Earl Spencer, in poor health, was a source of worry for Diana, concerned whether he would be well enough to walk her up the long aisle of St Paul's Cathedral.

Wedding bells for a Princess

The guest list for Lady Diana's wedding was enormous. Many foreign royals and Commonwealth prime ministers had to be invited, as well as British dignitaries and close friends of the royal family, which was intimidating for Diana.

For their part, the Coleherne Court girls felt intimidated by the strict security measures they had to undergo in order to visit Diana at Buckingham Palace. Diana wrote them another note saying they needed to phone before they came to visit her so she could clear them with security in advance. There was a complicated procedure for them to follow with protocol, a walk across a courtyard and down miles of passages. They did join her for a couple of lunch parties, but none of the girls were invited to stay the night and keep Diana company.

Occasionally, the sisters lunched together. Lady Jane helped Lady Diana become familiar with royal routines, although the official position of Jane's husband tended to separate rather than unite the sisters. It seems Diana's elder sister may not have been allowed to mention the exact nature of the relationship between Camilla and Prince Charles to Diana. The full story has never been revealed, but had she done so, history may have been different. When Diana mentioned Mrs Parker Bowles to anyone at the palace, they were evasive in their replies. With her mother far away in Scotland, Diana had no one she could trust enough to confide her fears about her new role and what part Camilla might play in it.

One of her protection officers from Scotland Yard pointed out to Diana that the days of her freedom were nearly over. Her future would be dominated by routine, duty and protocol, which was daunting for someone so young and so nervous. On the days when she was feeling positive, Diana was determined to do her best to be a success in her new role as Princess of Wales to show Charles how much she loved him. But there were bad days when she worried whether she was good enough to be Princess of Wales and whether she would be able to cope with the stress of an enormous televised wedding.

The Queen kindly assigned Lady Susan Hussey, one of her senior ladies-in-waiting to help Diana get to know the intricacies of royal etiquette and rank, protocol and who took precedence on formal occasions. Initially, Diana welcomed Lady Susan Hussey's induction course but soon started to distrust the older woman. Lady Susan had known Prince Charles since he was a child, which roused Diana's jealousy; being fiercely possessive of anyone she loved she felt that Lady Susan was too close to her fiancé.

Diana became convinced the older woman was in love with Charles, which was absurd. Lady Susan had known the Prince of Wales since his childhood and was fond of him, but that was all. Diana's jealousy of anyone close to her fiancé led her to ignore Lady Susan's advice. The situation known in psychiatry as transference took place and Diana transferred her possessive feelings about her father and the jealousy of her stepmother to *anyone* to whom Charles gave his time and attention which would become a big problem in their marriage.

Lady Diana and Prince Charles both wanted love, reassurance and praise. Both of them had suffered difficult childhoods despite the trappings of privilege, and both wanted more comfort and attention than their marriage partner could provide.

When Charles was a baby and up to the age of three before his mother became Queen, she was able to spend a great deal of time with him, and like most young mothers, was besotted by her first baby. But as a very conscientious Queen, she dedicated herself to the task and made long trips to Commonwealth countries on the royal yacht with her husband leaving Charles to depend on Nanny Mabel for love and comfort. Before the days of jet aircraft, they made very long tours by sea on the royal yacht *Britannia*.

Her televised wedding was to take place in July 1981. However, with the builders way behind on preparing her London apartment and country residence, Diana was under pressure. She continued to lose weight, yet she was gorging sweet food for her anxiety. Fearing she would put on weight, she forced herself to vomit. She had to choose outfits for many different official events without the help of her mother, who was still in Scotland, or a fashion advisor.

Leading up to the royal wedding, when Diana needed support and advice from her mother, Frances Shand Kydd made only one brief visit to London to attend Diana's first fitting for her wedding dress. It was made in the workshop of the Emmanuels, a couple of young designers selected by Diana who had never designed for a royal wedding before.

As the bride, Diana knew the secrecy that had to surround the design of her wedding dress. (It was later disclosed that she had spent over two million pounds on clothes in her bridal year.) Diana, unsure of her taste and with no background in fashion, bought many designer clothes, some of them not at all suitable. Only after her wedding did she receive expert advice from editors at *Vogue* magazine and became a fashion icon.

With the help of her mother's interior decorator Dudley Poplak, Diana was kept busy planning the décor of their apartment at Kensington Palace; her fiancé had given her a free hand and an unlimited budget. The apartment needed extensive electrical work and new plumbing before they could move in. Diana was to have her own sitting room, for which she had chosen feminine tones of pink and blue. Charles would have his own study with a kennel for an elderly and incontinent Labrador that the houseproud Diana would have preferred to have been kept at Highgrove, but Charles refused to be parted from his beloved gun dog.

Diana brought with her the row of stuffed animals that always sat at the end of her bed, which she had cuddled for comfort when her mother disappeared from her life. She was determined these stuffed animals would sit at the end of her double bed when she was married. At heart, she was still the unwanted child cuddling her stuffed animals instead of the mother who had left her when she was only six.

Accustomed to the palatial splendour of Althorp, Diana was not impressed by the dilapidated and rather severe Highgrove House. The garden needed a great deal of work, and its design was being planned by Camilla and Prince Charles and two elderly gardening enthusiasts. They aimed to turn it into an environmentally friendly and beautiful garden. Alterations to their Kensington Palace apartment were foremost in Diana's mind and decorating Highgrove House was low on her list of priorities. She was aware that Camilla had helped Charles chose Highgrove because it lay in Beaufort Hunt territory and was very near the home of the Parker Bowles.

The royal wedding was to be televised and watched by millions of viewers around the world.

Diana felt lonely and isolated at Buckingham Palace with no friends her own age at the palace, and she had to attend wedding dress fittings alone after her mother had returned to Scotland. Due to binge eating of comfort foods and vomiting to keep her weight down, she was losing kilos. This meant that the Emmanuels had to keep altering her wedding dress, another source of stress for Diana and for the designers as this was their first royal commission.

Diana could not turn to her father for comfort as he was in poor health and she refused to consult Raine, her stepmother. Her mother had returned to her remote island off the Scottish coast and a second marriage which was disintegrating. Her grandmother, Lady Fermoy, architect of this semi-arranged marriage was not someone in whom Diana wanted to confide.

At Buckingham Palace, no one seemed to have much time for the future Princess of Wales.

Courtiers and other staff were busy with their duties, and Diana discovered there was a great deal of rivalry between the different offices. Diana's lonely induction into the royal family was vastly different to the comforting one provided for Kate Middleton as the fiancée of Prince

William. Kate had her family with her while she was preparing for her wedding. While in the same situation, Meghan Markle lived with Prince Harry in his cottage in Kensington Palace. Alone at Buckingham Palace and missing all the schoolgirl banter and jokes at Coleherne Court, Diana behaved as she had done at Althorp, gossiping with the staff in the servant's hall. She was surprised and hurt to find that at Buckingham Palace the staff did not see her as a friend and want to gossip with her.

When Diana visited the staff sitting room at Buckingham Palace and introduced herself, the staff were shocked to see her there. A senior staff member warned Lady Diana she should not be below stairs eating cake with 'the likes of us but remain upstairs, learning how to be a princess'.

Feeling humiliated by his rebuke, Diana left the staff sitting room on the verge of tears. Alone in the privacy of her chilly bedroom, she sobbed her heart out, feeling lonely and unsure of herself. Her loneliness only increased her fears she might make a terrible mistake at her wedding in St Paul's Cathedral, which would be recorded by the television cameras and relayed to millions of viewers around the world.

Another problem was the slowness of the building trade, and the alterations to their Kensington Palace apartment and Highgrove House were way behind schedule – and, in fact, after the wedding nothing was ready for them and they were forced to spend the first six months of their marriage in the cramped surroundings of Charles' bachelor apartment at Buckingham Palace. This was a spectacularly inept piece of administration on the part of those who looked after royal building contracts.

Before the wedding, Prince Charles had a full programme of engagements which he assured his fiancée he could not cancel, and Diana soon discovered that Charles was a workaholic (something Camilla would eventually discover). Whatever free time Prince Charles had was reserved for his favourite 'horsey' pastimes – playing polo or racing his steeplechaser, Allibar.

The differences in their personalities were becoming apparent. Charles was in his thirties and loved the countryside and rural pursuits, while Diana was a naïve teenager on the threshold of adulthood discovering the pleasures of life in the centre of London. Charles loved hunting, shooting and fishing and enjoyed family holidays at Balmoral in the wet and windy north of Scotland; Diana liked the heat of Mediterranean beaches and would come to love holidays in the West Indies. This couple were poles apart in their likes and dislikes.

When Diana and Charles spent weekends in Wiltshire as guests of Lieutenant Colonel Parker Bowles and his wife, Camilla succeeded in making Diana feel uncomfortable at the dinner parties she hosted to celebrate the engagement. Her guests were all much older than Diana and were friends of Charles'. Horses, polo, shooting and their private jokes about their sporting lives and people she did not know made Diana feel excluded.

In the limited time they had together, Charles was becoming aware how little he and Diana had in common. The things that interested him seemed to bore her. As his wife, she would be expected to entertain visiting heads of state and know something about their countries. Charles found it disturbing that his fiancée had no idea where many Commonwealth countries were situated or anything about their political systems and problems. Diana had no wish to read the official briefings that would help her to understand these and other important issues.

Prince Charles preferred mature women like Camilla and Lady Jane Wellesley (who had remained a good friend to him and Camilla) who were well-educated, sophisticated and well-read. What interested him at that time were the mystical writings of his guru and friend, Laurens van der Post, who shared the Prince's concerns over the degradation of the environment. A dinner party to introduce Laurens van der Post to Lady Diana was not a success. The elderly guru did not impress Diana, and she had very little to say to him as she did not understand what he was talking about.

For Diana, adapting to royal life was not easy. Although she had lived at Sandringham and played with Prince Andrew as a toddler, she did not feel at ease in a world ruled by protocol and formal events. Diana could be witty and amusing when she was relaxed, but in the formal atmosphere of Buckingham Palace, she felt unsure of herself.

While Prince Charles was away on a royal tour, Diana received a note from Camilla, delivered to Buckingham Palace, inviting her to a 'girls lunch' at a smart London restaurant. Diana accepted but never forgot that meal as Camilla casually asked whether she intended to take up fox-hunting once she moved to Highgrove.

Diana confessed she was afraid of horses so would not be going hunting. Camilla seemed relieved by this news, a reaction which puzzled Diana. Years later, Camilla strongly denied that she had had an ulterior motive with this question, but the damage had been done, and Diana was now wary of the friendliness of Mrs Parker Bowles.

The day before Charles was to depart for Australia on a five-week tour, Diana, who as a six-year-old had listened at doors hoping to glean information about her vanished mother, now listened to phone conversations of her fiancé and claimed to have heard Prince Charles on the phone to Camilla telling her, 'Of course I'll always love you'.

For an insecure girl in love, this was a nightmare and led to a row between the couple.

On the following day when Prince Charles was due to fly to Australia, Diana accompanied him to London airport in a chauffeur-driven car. CCTV cameras recorded Charles giving Diana a quick peck on the cheek rather than a passionate kiss before climbing the gangway and disappearing into the plane without a backward glance at his fiancée. Diana returned alone to the waiting limousine in tears. She was driven back to her chilly rooms in Buckingham Palace where the central heating was turned down low, as the Queen and Prince Philip practised economies in their heating bills. With three enormous residencies to heat and maintain, they did not wish to spend more than they had to – unlike Charles and the Queen Mother who believed in living in the lap of luxury surrounded by well-trained staff without worrying about the expense.

Pre-wedding doubts on both sides

On videotapes Diana made years later (known as 'The Secrets Tapes'), she confessed she had often rebuffed Charles' moves at physical contact before their marriage. Having fended off sexual advances for several years, she described her sexual response to Charles as 'Big F' (referring to being frigid).

According to Catherine Meyer, author of *Charles, Heart of a King*, an unauthorised biography of Prince Charles, he was also having doubts about this marriage and told a close friend just before the wedding, 'I can't go through with it, I can't do it.' Meyer, a journalist with *Time* magazine, insisted Charles was worried that Lady Diana was not the jolly teenager he imagined her to be but a very vulnerable, insecure girl. But Prince Charles' strong code of honour and sense of duty would not allow him to back out of the wedding.

By now, Diana had been given a desk of her own in Michael Colbourne's office. He was Charles' personal secretary, a down-to-earth fatherly individual who was dealing with the thousands of letters of congratulation, invitations and requests sent to the Prince of Wales and his fiancée. Diana could not type and insisted on handwriting notes thanking those who had sent wedding gifts that particularly appealed to her.

Diana sorted through a pile of recent letters and gifts and came across a blue box with the name of a Bond Street jeweller embossed in gold. Assuming Charles had bought her a present, Diana could not resist opening it. Inside the silk-lined box, she found a solid gold bracelet with a blue enamel disc engraved with the initials 'GF' and a card addressed to Camilla awaiting Prince Charles' signature.

Diana reckoned these initials stood for Girl Friday, the subject of many jokes at the Parker Bowles' dinner parties as Camilla had spent a few days working as a Girl Friday for a firm of Mayfair interior decorators before being fired for arriving late for work. The other alternative was that GF stood for 'Gladys' and 'Fred', two characters from *The Goon Show* radio programme that Charles and Camilla found hilarious and Diana found very boring.

Reading the card addressed to Camilla and seeing the expensive bracelet, sparked a jealous scene during which Charles told Diana she was being ridiculous. Why shouldn't he send Camilla a farewell gift?

Diana retorted why didn't he ask the jewellers to send the gift direct. Was he going to give it to Camilla in person?

When Charles admitted he had planned to do this, his response sparked more jealous recriminations from Diana.

Worry about the televised ceremony and anxiety about Camilla's closeness to her fiancé made Diana's bulimia worse. She described herself as being 'as sick as a parrot' after gorging on comfort foods like bowls of ice-cream and chocolate followed by self-induced vomiting. The televised rehearsal for the ceremony was a disaster, and at one point, Diana, thinking about Camilla, was in tears. So, the BBC felt it was kinder to store the footage and not to show it.

Filled with foreboding about her marriage, Diana visited Lady Jane at Old Barracks House in the grounds of Kensington Palace and found both her sisters having lunch there. A tearful Diana told them that in view of what she knew about Mrs Parker Bowles, she could not go through with the wedding. 'I can't do this. I can't marry him,' she sobbed, almost identical to the words that Prince Charles had told his friend.

However, instead of the sympathy and support Diana had expected, she was shocked when her sisters told her, 'Your face is on the tea towels, you can't chicken out. You *have* to go through with it.'

Lady Sarah and Lady Jane were right. It was far too late to call the whole thing off. Millions of wedding souvenirs had been made and a small fortune spent on scaffolding and street decorations. Distinguished guests were arriving from all over the world, and many were already on the plane to London.

Diana tried to assert some control over her wedding day by having Camilla and Lady Dale Tryon, excluded from the post-wedding lunch (confusingly referred to as 'the wedding breakfast').

From gossip relayed by friends, Diana was convinced that Lady Tryon had once filled the same role in Charles' life as Camilla, which was why Camilla disliked her.

Charles refused Diana's request to withdraw the invitations to the post-wedding lunch which had been sent to the Parker Bowles' and Lord and Lady Tryon. He told Diana she was being ridiculous, and his affair with Camilla was definitely over. He had given her his word, and it was disloyal of her to doubt him.

Andrew and Camilla were two of his best friends, and they had to be invited, as did Lord and Lady Tryon. The Tryons had shown him hospitality at their Knightsbridge house and their Icelandic fishing lodge and had given them a beautiful watercolour as a wedding present. He had been staying with the Tryons at their fishing lodge when he learned of the death of Lord Mountbatten when they had been extremely kind to him, and he would never forget this.

In spite of Diana's tearful protests, Charles refused to discuss the matter further. Her only success lay in banning her hated stepmother and Raine's mother, Barbara Cartland, from the wedding breakfast.

On the night before the wedding, Lady Fermoy and the Queen Mother dined together. For reasons never explained, Diana dined with her sister, Lady Jane, in a separate room at Clarence House.

Charles wanting to reassure his nervous bride, sent an equerry to her with a velvet-lined box containing a gold signet ring engraved with the Prince of Wales' crest and a handwritten note saying, *'When you come up the aisle tomorrow I'll be there waiting for you. Just look them in the eye and knock them dead!'*[46] What the note did not contain was the magic phrase 'I love you', the words Diana had longed for 'Prince Charming' to say when he had proposed to her.

On the eve of the royal wedding, firework displays took place all over Britain. Everyone seemed thrilled about the royal wedding except the anxious bride and groom.

'A fairytale wedding' – The Archbishop of Canterbury

Diana was to be led up the long aisle of St Paul's Cathedral by her elderly, ailing father. To overcome her nerves, Diana reminded herself that she was a Spencer, a family known for their courage and determination.

In hindsight, it seems amazing that the shy twenty-year-old, riddled with doubt about her husband's feelings for her could rise above it and become the star of a televised wedding ceremony and win the hearts of millions of television viewers all over the world.

On 29 July 1981, the slender young girl in the fairytale dress walked

[46] Cited in Sarah Bradford, *op. cit.* and Sally Bedell Smith, *op. cit.*, p116.

up the aisle on the arm of her proud but frail father. She wore a billowing dress of silk organza created by a pair of young designers new to royal events rather than an established royal couturier like Norman Hartnell, the choice of designer being the only decision Diana was allowed to make.

Her gown was ivory silk organza with a wide crinoline skirt embroidered with 10,000 seed pearls. The dress had a sweetheart neckline and enormous puffed sleeves, which made Diana's arms look very thin. Worry and bulimic vomiting had made Diana lose so much weight that the magnificent dress at times appeared to overwhelm the young bride with yards of ivory coloured silk.

Diana's dress was a young girl's vision of what a princess should look like when she married Prince Charming. Lady Diana, conscious of the fact that she was a descendant of a great English dynasty, had rejected the offer to borrow one of the Windsor tiaras. Instead, she chose to anchor her bridal veil with the delicate diamond and pearl tiara made for the wedding of Diana's grandmother, Countess Cynthia Spencer. This was a subtle way of emphasising Diana's descent from the Stuart kings who ruled England long before George I of the Hanover-Windsor dynasty arrived from Germany and pointed out that the Spencers were English to the core and proud of their heritage.

The future Princess of Wales, former school drop-out, failed ballet dancer, house cleaner, nanny and kindergarten assistant, was driven through the City of London in a fairytale glass coach to St Paul's Cathedral with an escort from the Household Cavalry. As a senior member of the official escort, Lieutenant Colonel Parker Bowles rode beside Diana's coach in an elegant scarlet uniform covered in gold braid. The presence of Camilla's husband was scarcely reassuring. It demonstrated how securely the Parker Bowles were ensconced in royal favour and how difficult it would be for Diana to dislodge them.

Despite her youth and inexperience, Diana carried herself with dignity and poise confronted by hundreds of popping flashbulbs on her arrival at St Paul's Cathedral. The Emmanuels, inexperienced in designing for royal occasions, had not taken into account the difficulty of getting a large hooped crinoline skirt in and out of the narrow door of the royal coach. Helped by her bridesmaids, Diana managed to manoeuvre her wide skirt and long train through the door of the state coach and walked up the steep flight of steps covered in red carpet leading to the magnificent doors of St Paul's Cathedral.

Diana walked slowly down the long aisle holding her father's arm, carefully supporting him so he would not stumble. She was reversing the normal pattern whereby the father of the bride supports his daughter. She caught a glimpse of Camilla Parker Bowles in a pale grey dress and matching hat, with her young son, Tom, Prince Charles' godson, standing beside her on the seat of their pew. Diana's heart lurched, but she continued up the aisle under the gaze of the assembled guests and a battery of television cameras.

At the altar, Diana joined Charles, handsome in full dress naval uniform and medals. To herself, she claimed, 'As I approached the altar, I thought I was the luckiest girl in the world.'[47]

She felt a surge of love for the handsome prince she was about to marry, and her fears disappeared as she remembered Charles' heart-warming message telling her to 'look them in the eye and knock them dead'. During the ceremony, Diana gave her responses to Dr Robert Runcie, Archbishop of Canterbury, clearly and calmly. She made only one tiny mistake when repeating her new husband's long list of Christian names. But by then none of the viewers cared. The beauty, youth and vulnerability of Diana, Princess of Wales, had won the hearts of millions of television viewers. In his sermon, the Archbishop of Canterbury claimed they were participating in a fairytale wedding, and at that moment, the newly created Princess Diana believed it to be true.

After the ceremony, the newlyweds rode in the open state carriage back to Buckingham Palace through streets lined with cheering crowds. The gilded carriage clattered over the paving stones in the front court of Buckingham Palace and halted at the imposing portico to let Diana descend from the coach, once again aided by her young bridesmaids.

The schedule allowed the new Princess of Wales time to freshen up and relax with her young bridesmaids before she had to face the ordeal of the enormous crowds waiting to cheer the newlyweds.

Prince Charles, with his young bride beside him, stepped onto the Buckingham Palace balcony. Following tradition, the entire royal family appeared on the balcony to face cheering crowds, many of whom were waving small Union Jacks.

As Prince Charles kissed his bride, the crowd roared its approval. Millions of television viewers had tears in their eyes. Her worries about the ceremony over, Diana felt happy at last, her fears about Mrs Parker Bowles temporarily forgotten.

---

[47] Sally Bedell Smith, *op. cit.*, cites an extract from the Settelen tapes made in 1992.

Prince Charles and Princess Diana stand on the balcony of Buckingham Palace in London, following their wedding at St. Pauls Cathedral, June 29, 1981. © REUTERS/Stringer

CHAPTER SEVEN

Diana: a wonderful mother consoled by lovers

Being a princess isn't all it's cracked up to be. The worst day of my life was realising Charles had gone back to Camilla. Princess Diana to Lady Elsa Bowker.

She is a very unhappy girl facing situations she finds difficult to deal with…dosed with anti-depressants and sleeping drugs. Her troubles are emotional, not pathological. Letter dated 5 February 1983 from Dr Alan McGlashan to author Laurens van der Post after Sir James Batten, the Queen's physician, and Dr Michael Pale, the psychiatrist of St Bartholomew's, had both seen Diana. Both claimed the Princess of Wales was suffering from an undiagnosed mental illness which was later queried by the psychiatrist with whom my late husband had worked, the distinguished Professor Sir Martin Roth. – The Mail on Sunday, 24 Sep 2017 - Ian Gallagher and Barbara Jones

The honeymoon of the Prince and Princess of Wales was a curious blend of pleasure cruise and official royal tour. They had a couple of days rest at Broadlands, near Romsey, the secluded handsome country house me of the Mountbatten family on the edge of the New Forest.

Broadlands, home of Lord Mountbatten (Private collection)

And then the newly wed couple flew to Gibraltar, a British enclave and boarded the royal yacht *Britannia.*

On their honeymoon, Charles and Diana cruised around the Mediterranean and as far as the coast of North Africa aboard the royal yacht *Britannia* which was larger than most cruise vessels with twenty-one officers and two hundred and fifty-six crew aboard. This meant the vessel was unable to dock at the smaller and more picturesque ports on the French Riviera that Diana had hoped to visit on her honeymoon.

H.M.S. Britannia

It seems Diana's introduction to marriage and sex had not been like the accounts in the romantic novels she read so avidly. Having spent much of their engagement apart, Diana had hoped the honeymoon cruise would draw them closer.

But this did not happen. Prince Charles was still tired after the hectic lead-up to the wedding and the ceremony and happy to stay in their suite and read. According to Diana her husband had brought with him seven books by his friend and guru, Laurens van der Post, a disciple of Carl Jung and several works by the Swiss psychiatrist who had been a disciple of Freud.

Determined to introduce Diana to the work of Jung, Charles gave her a copy of a hefty volume by the Swiss psychiatrist and asked for her opinion on Jung's theory on dreams, which Jung regarded as a way of communicating with what he called 'the collective unconscious'. Charles wanted to discuss Jung's philosophies while Diana shuddered inwardly at the idea of doing this on honeymoon and told her husband Jung did not interest her.

Charles was disappointed, having assumed his wife would read the books he read, and they would discuss them together as he and Camilla used to do when on holiday together.

At lunch served in their suite, Charles insisted on reading aloud key passages from Jung. Diana was uninterested in reading what she called 'heavy books' on honeymoon so they spent most of the day apart. Diana still a teenager, swam in the pool, worked on her tan and flirted a little with the ship's officers.

When not reading the works of Jung and van der Post, Charles, a talented artist when they were close to the coast made a series of sketches in water colour, delighted to have the time for his favourite hobby as being a workaholic in London he was always busy.

Unlike Camilla Diana was not interested in sketching and annoyed her husband did not seem to want to spend time talking to her or swimming and lying in the sun with her. Was he thinking about Camilla? Angry that he might be phoning Camilla on the ship to shore phone finding a pile of finished water colours in their suite, she tore them in pieces, something Diana never mentioned on the video tapes she made years later about the stages in the breakdown of their marriage.

Dinner on the royal yacht was a black-tie affair for the royal couple, with the captain and his senior officers.

Diana would have preferred to have dined with her husband in romantic waterfront restaurants rather than entertaining foreign dignitaries. Haunted by jealousy of Camilla she even dreamed about the woman she regarded as her rival for her husband's love.

Officials at the Foreign Office and Buckingham Palace who had planned this cruise aboard the royal yacht saw it as a chance to enhance British prestige and introduce the Prince and Princess of Wales to foreign and Commonwealth prime ministers as it cost an enormous amount of money to send the royal yacht overseas.

Dinner invitations had been sent by Foreign Office staff to foreign royalty, prime ministers and politicians at most of the ports where the *Britannia* called. These invited guests had to be formally entertained by the Prince and Princess of Wales, and dinner table conversations included political and environmental issues in which Charles was knowledgeable and Diana revealed her total ignorance so stayed mute.

The teenage princess wore attractive new dresses from her trousseau and looked sweet but was totally out of her depth and longed for the meal to end. Several official guests observed that the Princess of Wales was very attractive but difficult to talk with very limited conversation.

Frances Shand Kydd, Diana's mother, had foreseen this would be a problem due to her youngest daughter's lack of general knowledge. She had specifically warned Diana against marrying into the royal family, telling her she would dislike the formality of royal life. But Diana was headstrong and believed that being a princess would make her happy and she refused to take advice.

When she and Charles were planning joint future engagements, two photos of Camilla fell out of her husband's diary and fluttered to the floor. The fact that Charles was insensitive enough to bring photos of Camilla, his former mistress, with him on honeymoon shattered Diana emotionally. The little girl who believed that her parents had never loved her was convinced her husband did not love her and had broken his promise not to contact Camilla and was phoning her from the royal yacht.

At this stage, Charles was determined to make his arranged marriage work. But the fact he had brought photos of Camilla with him in his diary upset Diana, just as it would upset most newly-married wives.

To make matters worse, as the newly wed couple were changing for dinner, Diana saw Charles struggling to insert a pair of gold cuff links into his evening shirt. The links were engraved with entwined Cs; clearly a present from Camilla.

Diana burst into sobs and confronted Charles about his feelings for Camilla, convinced they were in constant touch. The Prince of Wales was angry that his word was being doubted and left their cabin, slamming the door behind him.

Alone in their suite Diana consoled herself by eating ice-cream and vomiting, which gave her some comfort. When she telephoned the cabin steward to order more ice-cream, it was assumed her order included a portion for her husband, so a double portion was delivered, and Diana ate the lot. Fearing she would put on weight and Charles would find her repulsive, she made herself vomit into the toilet bowl. Diana's bulimia which had begun at Buckingham Palace due to pre-wedding nerves was not going away and was getting worse.

By the end of their disappointing honeymoon on the royal yacht Diana was vomiting three or four times a day and had lost a great deal of weight and the couple had the first of many bitter arguments. For some time her husband was unaware of Diana's gorging of food in secret and bulimic vomiting as at that time bulimia was a relatively rare psychiatric syndrome.[48] Charles did not understand what was happening and Diana was not going to tell him as she was ashamed of her bulimia. But he realised that his wife was totally unlike any member of his family and was

---

48 Andrew Morton, *op. cit.*, and subsequent editions.

distressed by her frequent bouts of crying but hoped this just post-wedding tiredness and it would pass.

However there were happy moments when Diana forgot about Camilla and the couple held hands and the crew felt they were in love. On the sandy beach on the tranquil Greek island of Ithaca the crew organised an evening barbecue for the couple and at the end of the cruise there was a farewell concert by the crew which they both enjoyed.

After two weeks aboard the SS *Britannia,* the newlyweds flew north to Aberdeen where a chauffeur drove them to chilly Balmoral Castle for the second part of their honeymoon. The Prince of Wales could have afforded to hire a villa in the sun, which Diana would have loved. Instead he followed family tradition and the newly weds joined his family for their annual summer holiday staying at a small lodge on the Balmoral estate and eating occasional meals with the Queen and Prince Philip and other family members.

No matter how wet and windy the weather, males in the royal family indulged in their love of blood sports. Diana was familiar with shooting parties as her father had held them at Althorp. Like her mother, she hated blood sports, the traditional pastimes of the British aristocracy and the royal family.

The second part of the royal honeymoon was an unmitigated disaster. After a few days accompanying Diana on long walks through the heather, Charles grew restless. He left his new wife alone to join his father shooting grouse or went stalking deer with his friend, Norton Romsey, son-in-law of Lord Mountbatten.

On other days he went fishing in the River Dee, up to his thighs in cold water. As Charles' fiancée, Diana had been happy to sit beside him while he fished but had hoped that on their honeymoon, they would do interesting things together and have really long talks. When she protested at being left alone, they spent a few more days walking and lying side by side in the heather, but even then, Charles brought with him a volume of Jung and read extracts to his young wife.

As on Diana's previous visits, each night Princess Margaret took charge of the entertainment. A selfish woman trying to forget her failed marriage, she kept members of the party up late, playing favourite tunes from old musicals on the piano and drinking copious amounts of champagne. She and Charles expected their guests to do all the things they enjoyed. No one had thought to invite any of Diana's young friends, and she was bored at meals with no one of her own age to talk to so stayed silent.

During their second week at Balmoral, Diana was desperately lonely as Charles went out with the guns or spent the whole day fishing. She started missing meals, finding it hard to make small talk with her in-laws.

Conversations at breakfast revolved around the weather and the day's plans for shooting game birds. Dinner conversations were an ordeal for her, dominated by tales of success or near misses with the guns or interminable discussions as to who had caught the biggest fish. Diana behaved as she had done at dinner parties at Althorp when bored by her stepmother's friends: she sat at the dining table wearing headphones, listening to tapes on her Sony Walkman. No one had ever behaved like this in front of the Queen. Her Majesty made no comment. Diana felt lost and lonely. At Althorp, she had made friends with the staff and enjoyed gossiping with them in the staff quarters being fed slices of cake by the friendly cook who was married to the butler.

At Balmoral and Buckingham Palace, the staff did not welcome her to their quarters. Having recently been a house cleaner, nanny and kindergarten assistant, she was embarrassed when people curtseyed to her and called her Your Royal Highness. All this coupled with brooding over Camilla and whether Charles still loved her, made it hard for Diana to sleep. Four weeks of bulimic vomiting on the royal yacht and at Balmoral had resulted in a noticeable drop in her weight and a loss of potassium and calcium which affected her brain causing violent mood swings. She had lost her flattering tan and was looking pale and gaunt.

While Charles was enjoying himself, outside in all weathers, shooting, fishing and deer stalking with Lord Romsey, Diana remained alone in their bedroom. Realising that Camilla still had an extraordinary hold over her husband, Diana came up with a solution. She told Charles that if he really loved her, he should arrange with his mother for Lieutenant Colonel Parker Bowles to be given an important post overseas, with the stipulation Camilla must accompany him.

When Charles refused to consider what Diana regarded as a reasonable request, she reacted with tears. Years later, Diana said she had realised that even on their honeymoon Charles was telephoning Camilla and discussing his marriage. Charles denied this was true and claimed that his wife was obsessed with Camilla. He had given his word that his affair was over and that he had every intention of keeping this promise. He was annoyed that Diana was making their lives miserable with what he regarded as unfounded jealousy.

This made no difference. Diana feared that he was phoning Camilla and discussing the fact that he was disappointed in their sex life.

By now Charles and Diana had moved out of Balmoral Castle and into Craigowan Lodge. Diana complained bitterly whenever he went shooting. Charles rang his Private Secretary Michael Colbourne and asked him to catch a train to Aberdeen so that he could go deer stalking for the day with Norton Romsey without any more rows as he knew she liked Michael Colbourne. Diana's childhood separation anxiety resurfaced, and she paced around the room kicking the furniture and ranting about how much she hated Balmoral.

Diana's severe weight loss worried the Queen. The Queen Mother, practical as ever, wondered whether Diana would be able to bear a child – the whole purpose of this arranged marriage. Diana was so unhappy at Balmoral and the weather was so bad that they cut short the second leg of the honeymoon and returned to Buckingham Palace to find that the builders were still working on their apartment at Kensington Palace and Highgrove was still not ready for them either, so they had to continue to stay in cramped quarters at the palace.

Prince and Princess of Wales at Swansea during their tour of Wales 1st October 1981. © Mirrorpix.

When Diana and Charles made their official tour of Wales, Diana had lost so much weight that wearing a formal evening dress it was easy to see that her arms were now stick thin.

Journalist James Whitaker was ordered to obtain an interview with the Princess of Wales. As he was young and persuasive, Diana chose to ignore the fact that he had caused trouble for her sister Sarah and agreed to give him an interview. She was guarded in what she told him, but he observed her hand-span waist and emaciated arms and thought to himself that losing weight had made Diana's face much prettier.

During the royal couple's tour of Wales, a blustery wind was accompanied by rain or sleet. The Princess of Wales wore a two-piece wool suit and no overcoat so the crowds could see her better. She was often drenched or chilled to the bone but, wanting to impress her husband, did not complain.

Diana hoped to present a glamorous but more approachable image of royalty and win the approval of the public and the love of her husband. She was a great success with young children, stooping low to talk to them, accepting little bunches of wildflowers, thanking them and addressing some of the children by name. They adored her, and her informal approach was the beginning of her enormous popularity as 'the people's princess'.

Diana talked to elderly people, holding their hands or patting them on the shoulder while she spoke to them, as Miss Stevens had taught her. No member of the royal family had ever responded in this way, being content to drive around and wave gloved hands at cheering crowds. The Welsh public seemed thrilled with their new Princess of Wales. Diana had struck her first blow in what would become a campaign to modernise the royal family.

Prince Charles was surprised at his wife's popularity, as she knew next to nothing about Wales. Since his induction as Prince of Wales, Charles had become an expert on Welsh history and was proud of the fact. But Diana's interest in people, the naturalness of her approach and her beauty fascinated the Welsh crowds. They did not care that the beautiful princess knew little about Welsh history.

On their return London, it was apparent that in spite of eating well and devouring numerous bars of chocolate to sustain her between meals, Diana had lost even more weight. Her vomiting which she kept secret from her husband by running the bathroom taps while she was doing this, had an effect on her brain, increased her sense of inadequacy and her anxiety despite the fact she had been such a success in Wales. She felt angry her husband had not appreciated what a huge effort she had made to please him, and how hard it had been to overcome her natural shyness.

As part of a mental process known to psychiatrists as 'transference', in Diana's mind, Camilla had replaced her hated stepmother who she regarded as having 'stolen' her father's love from her. No matter how hard Diana tried, she felt she and her husband would never be totally compatible, as Charles was with Camilla.

Once her pregnancy was confirmed, Diana's sense of helplessness over Camilla, her secret bulimic vomiting and the side effects of the Valium which she had been prescribed to help her sleep, caused mood swings, with bursts of rage followed by tears. Prince Charles found it difficult to cope with his emotionally volatile wife, raised as he had been in a family whose members were careful to cry behind closed doors.

In February 1982, five months pregnant and happy about this, with Charles acting as a dutiful husband, his young wife felt happier and gained weight. Diana was rewarded for this with the kind of beach vacation she had longed for on her honeymoon. For reasons of privacy British royalty rarely stay in hotels.

This second honeymoon was spent in the private villa of relatives of the late Lord Mountbatten on the beautiful island of Eleuthera in the West Indies. Diana acquired a flattering tan, and she and Charles were photographed enjoying themselves on the beach and looking happy together. It seemed as if 'the Golden Couple', as the press called them, might yet make a success of their marriage.

Meanwhile, carpenters, electricians and painters beavered away to finish the couple's Kensington Palace apartment so it would be ready for them on their return to London. The move to Kensington Palace went well, and hundreds of wedding presents were finally unpacked by their staff.

Diana bought Charles gifts of silk ties and slip-on shoes to modernise what she called his old-fashioned wardrobe, and Charles was pleased. However, Stephen Barry, the gay valet who normally advised the Prince of Wales on his wardrobe, was annoyed and made snide comments about Diana. The situation became unpleasant, and eventually, Diana insisted the valet be fired. To keep the peace, Charles gave in and did so.

With Major Parker Bowles as a member of Charles' polo team, the royal couple met Andrew and Camilla at polo matches and post-match parties. They also attended Camilla and Andrew's house-warming party to celebrate their move from Bolehyde Manor to Middlewick House. Their new house was even closer to Highgrove, which Charles now regarded as his primary residence.

Diana preferred London and their Kensington apartment which she had decorated as she wanted and disliked Camilla's involvement in planning the garden at Highgrove. The fact that Camilla was now nearer than ever to Highgrove upset Diana, convinced that her husband and Camilla were using their love of fox-hunting as an excuse to meet without her being present.

Another problem was that neither Charles nor the Buckingham Palace mandarins who organised the schedules for Diana's public appearances gave her the credit she felt she deserved. It was difficult for her to undertake royal duties while suffering from morning sickness, and she deserved praise for continuing her public appearances, smiling and waving by her husband's side while feeling ill. But no praise was forthcoming.

Many years later, Diana would confess to Dr James Colthurst, a supportive friend she first met on that ski party when she was only eighteen, that her marital relations were infrequent, usually once every three weeks. (Ken Stronach, Charles' replacement valet would confirm this.) It seemed that these were more of a duty than a pleasure to both of them.

Diana's jealousy of Camilla continued. Staying for a weekend at Althorp to visit Diana's ailing father, the Prince and Princess of Wales had a bitter argument which ended in a stand-up fight in their bedroom during which Diana attacked her husband with her fists.

One of the domestic staff heard the sound of breaking glass and what sounded like splintering wood, but were afraid to interfere. According to journalists Nigel Dempster and Peter Evans in a book, aptly titled *Behind Closed Doors,* the member of staff who cleaned the couple's bedroom the following day discovered a shattered antique mirror as well as a broken window and a leg snapped off a valuable antique chair.

Charles was mystified that his wife seemed to have two different personalities – sweet and loving in public but, when stressed and jealous, turning into a raging virago when they were alone.

While staying with her royal in-laws at Sandringham or Balmoral, Valium soothed Diana and helped her sleep, but the stress of being in a place she did not like where blood sports occupied most of the day intensified her mood swings. Diana had seen several doctors who had been unable to discover what was wrong and like most bulimics she was not going to reveal her shameful secret. (Recent studies in the *American Journal of Psychology* and in *Science Now* suggest eating disorders have a genetic basis. Diana's mother suffered an eating disorder but so little was known about them that Diana's sufferings were made worse)

For her first Christmas at Balmoral, Diana purchased expensive cashmere sweaters for her in-laws. Neither her husband nor anyone in his office had thought to warn her that the royal family give each other inexpensive utilitarian presents under twenty pounds. Compared to the simple or joke gifts exchanged by the Windsors, Diana's lavish gifts looked excessive and made her embarrassed and angry with Charles for not warning her how the royal family behaved.

Just as she had done at her stepmother's dinner parties, Diana found making polite conversation with strangers difficult. Watching her husband shooting, going out riding with the Queen or fishing were not pastimes Diana wished to share. So, during her pregnancy, when at Sandringham, she spent a great deal of time alone in her bedroom, just as she had done on her Balmoral honeymoon.

A cry for help and the birth of an heir

Diana knew she must produce an heir for the House of Windsor and like the Queen Mother was aware that the birth of a healthy boy would delight the public and hoped that a baby would draw her and her husband closer.

During her pregnancy, Diana was expected to accompany her husband to various functions. The many formal dinners that Charles and Diana were obliged to attend were an ordeal, attended by Privy Councillors, senior ministers and other public figures. Diana found it impossible to join in serious conversations due to her lack of general knowledge. Terrified of saying the wrong thing and looking foolish, she remained silent and felt miserable.

His wife's lack of general knowledge continued to astound Charles, and her total ignorance of the world and current issues made him wince. When talking to foreign presidents or prime ministers, it was clear that Diana had not the faintest idea about their countries and had not read the briefings prepared for her by Charles' staff. The meetings went well if the distinguished foreign visitor had brought his wife, as the Princess of Wales would happily talk to her about babies and children.

In his diary Roy Strong, the Director of the Victoria and Albert Museum, later recorded that Princess Michael of Kent had told him in confidence that due to Diana's many mood swings, staff were leaving, and claimed that the royal couple 'were often pulling in opposite directions'.[49]

Matters came to a head in January 1982, three months into Diana's pregnancy. Spending Christmas at Sandringham House with her husband and her in-laws, Diana tripped on a stair rod and fell. Later Diana would claim to Andrew Morton that she had thrown herself down the stairs in a suicide attempt. This was clearly an exaggeration as Diana would never have done anything to injure her much-wanted baby. In reality, all she had done was trip, fall down a single step and hurt her ankle. She converted her fall into a suicide attempt in order to draw attention to what she felt was the misery of her marriage.

---

[49] Roy Strong, Diary, entry for May 1984

The Queen witnessed Diana's fall on the stairs. She and Prince Charles were worried it could have affected Diana's baby and summoned the royal gynaecologist, Sir George Pinker.

Sir George made a car journey in bad weather from London to Norfolk to see the pregnant princess. His opinion was that, although Princess Diana had suffered some bruising, the foetus was uninjured.[50] Prince Charles did not go out riding immediately afterwards, as Diana later claimed, but stayed with his wife all that evening. The next day he organised a picnic and took her to the Norfolk coast, still trying to do everything possible to make their marriage work. His wife's changing moods, alternating between depression and elation, were hard for Charles to take. He missed the stability of his previous relationship with Camilla and talked to her on the phone a great deal.

It was traditional for royal wives to give birth in their bedrooms, rather than among their subjects in a hospital frequented by the public. The Princess of Wales was a modern woman and insisted Sir George Pinker, as the royal obstetrician, deliver her baby at St Mary's Hospital, Paddington, a London teaching hospital.

On 21 June 1982, at St Mary's Hospital, Paddington, Sir George Pinker attended Princess Diana and delivered a healthy baby after a long and difficult labour lasting sixteen hours.

In June 1982, large crowds stood patiently waiting for the Princess of Wales and little Prince William outside the Lindo Wing of St Mary's Hospital. Diana appeared wearing a green and white spotted smock with knee-high white pressure stockings. She stood proudly beside her husband and showed the little prince to the waiting crowd before she and Prince Charles were driven away by a chauffeur.

Following Prince William's birth, the nation rejoiced. However, Princess Diana was suffering from post-natal depression which hit her very hard. Diana later admitted to author Andrew Morton she was in a very dark place and the depression continued for a long time, she glossed over the full details of her mental state when making tapes to send to Andrew Morton but for the new mother it was a worrying time. Diana dropped thirty pounds or almost fourteen kilograms in weight due to her renewed bulimic vomiting.

The Queen and the Queen Mother were very worried about Diana, as was Prince Charles. Diana's mood swings were fierce in their intensity not helped by the side effects of Valium and her binge eating and vomiting.

Charles was alarmed at the way that the jolly country girl he thought

---

[50] Obituary of Sir George Pinker, CVO, KCVO, *Daily Telegraph,* 1 May 2007.

he was marrying had turned into a moody and introverted young woman bursting into sobs and having panic attacks whenever he left her to make speeches or work in his office in St James's Palace.

Diana's unhappiness had brought on a reversion to her previous pattern of what is now known by psychologists as 'childhood separation anxiety' caused originally by the loss of her mother. As a child, after her mother left her, her fear of being abandoned by those she loved was such that Diana threw wild tantrums or sobbing fits in an effort to emotionally blackmail her father into staying at home with her. Now under stress, her childhood behaviour returned and she repeated the pattern with her husband in an effort to manipulate him as she had done with her father. Diana was still very young and very stressed by the changes in her life and the fear her husband did not love her. She burst into tears or threw tantrums and hated him leaving her.[51] She was particularly upset when he went to play polo which she said she found very boring so did not want to watch any more games.

The Queen Mother saw Diana as a problem and Diana started to dislike her. Diana's rapid weight loss worried the Queen as well as Prince Charles and it was decided to send her to Sir John Batten, the royal physician who first saw her when she lost so much weight on her honeymoon. Tests he had run showed Diana's rapid weight loss was not due to cancer, often a precipitant of sudden weight loss. Diana like most bulimics was embarrassed by her vomiting behaviour and in denial about it.

Sir John Batten referred the Princess of Wales to Dr Michael Pare, Head of Psychiatry at St Bartholomew's Hospital in the City of London, but he lacked the expertise of Sir Martin Roth who had been consulted by several members of the royal family.

The fact that her daughter-in-law was talking about committing suicide alarmed the Queen who insisted she saw her own physician, Sir John Batten to check that she did not have any underlying physical illness like cancer. He was puzzled by Diana who managed to hide her bulimia from him. Professor Sir Martin Roth, for whom my late husband worked as Senior Registrar on his research team, was President of the Royal College of Psychiatrists. For many years he had seen members of the royal family suffering from depression for which Sir Martin was the acknowledged expert. He knew of Dr Pare's report as this was an affair of national importance if the woman expected to give birth to a future king had a mental illness that could affect the mental health of her children. However,

---

51 A detailed disclosure of this and Michael Colbourne's witnessing of Diana's behaviour is given by Penny Junor in her biography *The Duchess* by Penny Junor published by William Collins in 2017.

Sir Martin doubted Dr Pare's opinion.

Sir John Batten and Dr Michael Pare, head of psychiatry at Barts Hospital had written reports claiming that the Princess of Wales had a rare form of mental illness which could be dangerous to her unborn children. Sir Martin felt they were unused to dealing with royalty and were overawed by it. Their concern seemed to lie more with the survival of the House of Windsor than with what was clearly clinical depression of a young woman trying to cope with the stress of a new role, a new marriage, pregnancy and motherhood. It was all too much for a shy girl who felt inadequate, isolated and alone. It was unfortunate that Sir Martin, a brilliant clinician, was unable to treat Diana since he had moved to Cambridge.

The late Sir Martin Roth, President of the Royal College of Psychiatrists when my late husband worked for him, was consulted by several members of the royal family and was greatly admired by all those who worked for him. (Private collection)

Sir Martin felt Dr Pare and Sir John Batten were panicking unduly. Sir Martin was now heading a new department of Clinical Psychiatry at Cambridge, and it was not feasible to see his former patients in London let alone take on new ones. He suggested that a psychiatrist who lived near Buckingham Palace should go there as often as needed and make regular calls.

As a brilliant clinician and neurologist as well as one of the world's leading psychiatrists, Sir Martin would have asked the right questions, interviewed household staff and learned that while Diana was losing weight each week, she was devouring bowls of custard and tubs of ice cream. He then would have discovered that she was hiding the fact she was bulimic. But this did not happen until after four years of misery and anxiety for Diana when she made a remarkable recovery.

A letter recently discovered by the biographer of analyst Dr Alan McGlashan written to author Laurence van der Post, reveals that Dr Michael Pare, was terrified that the Princess of Wales might carry out her threats to commit suicide and he would be blamed. With such a famous patient, he could not risk admitting her to the psychiatric wing of St Bartholomew's (Bart's) Hospital to monitor if she was taking the antidepressants and Valium he had prescribed. Should the Princess of Wales commit suicide while under his clinical responsible, his career would be ruined. Sir Martin recommended a younger psychiatrist he knew who lived near Buckingham Palace should, see the Princess of Wales every morning and evening to discuss what was troubling her and check she was taking the antidepressants and Valium prescribed. But Valium must only be a short-term measure until other less addictive drugs became effective. It was now known the drug had severe side effects as indeed would bulimia, as continual vomiting strips the brain of essential chemicals.

Prince Charles, having received the report that Diana had a dangerous but previously unknown mental disorder, was worried. On the advice of his friend, the author Laurens van der Post, he took the depressed and very anxious Diana to the elderly analyst Dr McGlashan hoping he could cure her.

But Diana was not an ideal client for analysis. Dr McGlashan also failed to discover Diana was bulimic and the constant vomiting was depriving her brain of essential minerals like potassium and several vitamins which alter brain chemistry. Over eight sessions, McGlashan attempted to analyse Diana's nightmares and realised she was obsessed by jealousy of Camilla and refused to believe she and Charles were not seeing each other. It had become what psychiatrists call an *idée fixe*.

Prince Charles was impressed by Dr McGlashan who was an interpreter of the theories of Jung. Charles was also fascinated by the Jungian analysis, and he consulted Dr McGlashan over the next fourteen years. His problems were caused by his lonely childhood behind palace walls and a difficult relationship with his father. Both Princess Diana and Prince Charles were needy and lonely due to difficult childhoods. Both of them needed a sympathetic spouse who would devote a great deal of time to them. The tragedy of their mismatched marriage was that neither of them could give the other the support and sympathy they needed.

Dr McGlashan's letter, published in full in the *Daily Mail* in 2017 by royal columnist Richard Kay, reveals the troubled state of mind of the princess at this time.

But none of her doctors, including Dr Michael Linnett who accompanied the Prince and Princess of Wales on royal tours, asked the right questions and discovered the sweet comfort foods on which Diana was binge eating and then vomiting, so her bulimia went undiagnosed for a few more years. Only then did Diana's former school friend Carolyn Pride threaten to tell the press unless she accepted treatment from eating disorders specialist Dr Maurice Liversedge.

Fortunately, once Diana's depression lifted, parenthood drew them closer together. Prince Charles became a frequent visitor to the nursery and became a devoted 'hands-on' father. He changed nappies and enjoyed feeding baby William and playing with him.

The Royal Australian tour of 1983

In March 1983, the young Prince and Princess of Wales were scheduled to undertake a long tour of Australia and New Zealand, but Diana was reluctant to go if it meant leaving her baby son behind for many weeks. She was still struggling with bulimia but finally agreed to undertake the tour, but only on condition that little Prince William accompany them. Diana was supported in her wish to do this by the then Australian Prime Minister Malcolm Fraser as no member of the royal family had ever brought babies on royal tours before.

On the long flight to Australia, Prince Charles was horrified to discover that his wife did not know that Canberra was its capital city. Prince Charles' laughed at her for not knowing the name of Canberra or any details about Australia which she had visited when staying with her mother at Mollymook before their wedding. This upset Diana, always sensitive about her lack of education and qualifications, and another row followed. He was quite right to point it out, as it would cause big problems in the early stages of the marriage when Diana was so immature.

After landing at Alice Springs and posing for photographs in the warm tropical air which Diana initially enjoyed, she and Prince Charles left William and his nanny, Barbara Barnes, with family friends on a sheep station in New South Wales. At intervals, she and Charles travelled there and spent time with their nine-month-old son, making certain that Prince William's childhood would be different to that of his father who had been left for long periods in the nursery at Buckingham Palace while his parents were making state visits to Commonwealth countries on the royal yacht.

The 1983 Australian tour was a huge success for Diana, but not for Prince Charles. In Sydney and Brisbane record crowds lined the streets to catch a glimpse of the young Princess of Wales. Diana was feted wherever she went. Young girls screamed with excitement as she passed them or groaned with disappointment if they discovered they were on the wrong side of the street to see her. Remarks like 'Oh it's only Big Ears!' did little for Charles' self-esteem.

Having attended Geelong Grammar School, Charles felt a special affinity with Australia and Australians and was mortified that all the excitement aroused by the royal visit was for his wife.

Diana had imagined that after the birth of William interest in her would die away. Instead, 'Di-mania' was increasing and Prince Charles did not appreciate being upstaged by his wife. She was supposed to be the supporting act, not the star of the show.

Immediately after their Australian visit, came a second and shorter state visit to Canada, which was ill-timed. The royal couple were exhausted and jet-lagged from their Australian visit, and Diana was unhappy because she had to leave her baby in London. Success with the crowds boosted Diana's self-confidence but made Charles resent her popularity. While he worked hard on his various speeches, Diana was far too terrified to speak in public. But people were thrilled to meet her, deluged her with flowers, asked questions about little William and conveyed their good wishes.

Diana and Charles at the Melbourne Cup, 1985 (both photos, Australian Information Services)

With her talent for talking to hospital patients and those who were disabled, photos of Diana were on front pages of magazines and newspapers everywhere. The tabloids tried to turn the Princess of Wales into a blend of Florence Nightingale, Mother Teresa and Marilyn Monroe. Editors competed for the latest cover photos of Princess Diana, aware they would double or treble the circulation of their publications.

All this praise and adulation was not easy for Prince Charles to accept. No matter how much background reading he did and how well-prepared his speeches, the press ignored him and the charities for which he was raising money and concentrated on the dress Diana was wearing or her latest hairstyle.

By now Diana had totally changed her image, aided by advice from a fashion editor at *Vogue.* She no longer wore gauche fashions, hats with large drooping feathers and frilly-neck blouses. On this tour, the new-look Princess Diana favoured sleek, elegant clothes selected for her by leading fashion experts for their clear colours and clean lines. She had taken deportment lessons and now stood tall and proud like a fashion model instead of hanging her head to minimise her height aware she was taller than Prince Charles, a fact he did not appreciate.

Between making public appearances all over Britain, Prince Charles and Princess Diana, still deemed 'the Golden Couple', were much in demand for European goodwill visits. The British Government realised that the presence of the elegant, beautiful young Princess of Wales helped boost exports for

British fashion houses and British luxury goods. Diana had developed her own special magic. She did not need to utter a word or know anything about the history of the places she visited with her husband. All she had to do was wear beautiful clothes and smile, and crowds went wild for her. She was a bigger celebrity than any Hollywood star.

Diana's enormous popularity meant she and her husband were made to take long and exhausting tours of Europe and North and South America as well as Japan and India, and jet-lag and fatigue affected Diana, who hated leaving her infant son with a nanny. Her sudden outbursts of rage followed by tears of exhaustion were intensified by the Valium she had been prescribed to help her sleep, and her volatile moods caused more matrimonial rows.

Diana was addicted to Valium to help her sleep and to the adoration of the crowds. She enjoyed being known as 'the people's princess' which made the girl who had felt unloved feel loved at last. In front of crowds, the couple were all smiles, but behind the scenes, the 'Golden Couple' argued fiercely, disagreeing about everything from what music to play on the car radio to where to spend their holidays. She and Charles had totally different friends. Charles' married landowning and polo-playing friends bored his young wife while he found her girlfriends immature and frivolous.

Despite so much marital discord, and even though they rarely had sex, Diana fell pregnant again. She knew that having produced 'the heir' she was expected to produce a 'spare' as insurance.

On 15 September 1984, Prince Harry was born. Diana's husband demonstrated the rift in the marriage by making only a brief visit to the Lindo Wing of St Mary's Hospital. In contrast, when Prince William was born, Charles had sat patiently beside his wife through her long and difficult labour.

The fact her husband left her alone during another long and difficult labour greatly upset Diana, as did her husband's unfortunate comment that their second son had 'rust-coloured hair'.

In fact, many of the Spencers had red hair. A portrait of the 'Red Earl' which hangs at Althorp shows him with red hair and a red beard, and this genetic inheritance appeared in Diana's brother and her elder sister Lady Sarah.

Much later there would be ridiculous allegations that Harry's father was red-headed Captain James Hewitt, but he and Diana had not even met when Harry was conceived. It is alleged that DNA tests revealed this was impossible and Hewitt has finally admitted that this is impossible but large numbers of people still believe it. For years, Harry's paternity was the most widely asked question of royal biographers.

Prince Harry's birth and her husband's disappointing reaction to his arrival marked a low point in Diana's marriage. Charles spent very little time with his wife in the hospital, and he left her with the excuse his team needed him for an important polo match.

Diana, exhausted after giving birth, was upset that her husband ignored her pleas to stay longer and did not congratulate her sufficiently for fulfilling her duty as a royal wife and producing a second heir.

'From that moment something inside me died,' Diana told Lady Bowker, who she now regarded as a surrogate mother. Diana's own mother did make the effort to leave Scotland for Harry's christening. Like a lioness defending her cub, Frances defended her daughter when Prince Charles tactlessly expressed his disappointment that Diana had not given him a daughter.

Frances, remembering her horribly disabled baby who had died soon after birth, turned on Charles in a rage. Royalty are seldom criticised, but Frances told the Prince of Wales he was arrogant, selfish and spoiled. He should be delighted Diana had given him such a handsome, healthy boy.

Frances's words caused more rows between the Prince and Princess of Wales, even after Diana's mother had left for Scotland and her new one-story luxury home she had bought on the island of Seil.[52]

By now Frances was trying to overcome her depression over her failing love match to Peter Shand Kydd, and it helped she had converted to Catholicism. She filled the void in her life by opening a gift shop on Seil and donating the proceeds to the widows of local fishermen and funding groups of disabled people to take pilgrimages to Lourdes and even accompanying some of them herself.

These charitable activities meant Diana's mother was rarely in London at a time when her youngest daughter badly needed her support with a new baby and an absentee husband. With no mother on hand, Diana turned to two mature women to advise and comfort her: society hostess Lady Annabel Goldsmith, now divorced from Mark Birley and married to wealthy financier Jimmy Goldsmith; and the cosmopolitan but childless Lady Elsa Bowker, whom Diana first met at Althorp with her grandmother Countess Cynthia Spencer.

---

52 After her marriage break up Frances bought herself a small but luxurious residence that had been built by Kenneth McKellar, a wealthy Scottish folk singer but her final years would be sad ones in which she immersed herself in charity work for the poverty-stricken fishing community of the remote Isle of Seil.

Diana: The world's most photographed woman

In spite of bitter arguments with her husband, Diana still wanted to make her marriage work for the sake of their sons and to fulfil her dream of a happy family life. She longed for a baby daughter to complete their family, but Charles, tired of constant fights and dramas, was not interested in having more children.

For Diana, the new mother, maintaining her role as an international beauty took time and plenty of money. Thanks to a personal hairdresser, her hair always looked perfect; she wore very high heels to show off her long slim legs and dressed in clothes that looked wonderful in photos. She had become the most photographed woman in the world, adored by millions who loved reading about her. Women's magazines promoted Diana as a model mother, aware that photos of the Princess of Wales on their covers would double or triple their sales.

Diana only had to appear at a fundraising function, and the crowd were wild. Charles' hard work was largely ignored by newspapers, but a photo of Diana with a sick child was front page news. Diana was virtually ignored by her husband, who spent his time working hard for his Prince's Trust, playing polo or fox-hunting. So, she derived comfort from scouring the press for photos of herself, cutting them out and placing them in large albums. Soon she could not keep up and paid an international agency to do this for her and send the press clippings to her.

Although her celebrity reassured the former 'unwanted child' of her appeal, what Diana wanted most was a happy family life and her husband's undivided attention. To Diana, her husband's absences were proof he had resumed his affair with Camilla.

Prince Charles only admitted his unhappiness to close friends. Before his marriage, whenever he had wanted to discuss his problems, Camilla had listened, sympathised and offered practical advice. In contrast, Diana was absorbed in her children, maintaining her weight and remaining 'the world's most beautiful and alluring woman', as several women's magazines now called her. She made new friends, magazine and fashion editors, hip designers and media celebrities like the witty Clive James, who adored her.

Charles felt trapped in a marriage made to please his father and grandmother, and from which he could see no escape. Camilla, worried about her former lover, was aware that her support was necessary, or he could become depressed. His reaction to a wife who was temperamental and could be difficult was to go away with his mentor Laurens van der Post to the Kalahari Desert or retreat to Scotland.

Always possessive when he was there, Diana lashed out at her husband, demanding that he stop seeing or telephoning Camilla. Charles retorted that he hardly ever saw Camilla alone, only with friends or with her husband. She was not his mistress but a good friend who he trusted completely. It was foolish of Diana to resent this.

In one of their many bitter rows, in a blind rage, Diana admitted she hated everything her husband loved – holidays with his parents at Balmoral and Sandringham, polo and living at Highgrove, which had become linked in her mind with the ubiquitous Mrs Parker Bowles. It was Camilla who had chosen Highgrove with Charles because it was near her home. She had helped regenerate the gardens, and it was Camilla who shared a love of horses and dogs with Charles.

Diana had insisted that Charles get rid of Harvey his ancient Labrador and former gun dog who had a place for his basket in their Kensington Palace apartment. She said the dog was unhygienic and that he had to go and although it hurt Charles very much to give him away he did this to please his wife.

While the Princess of Wales enjoyed her life at Kensington Palace and the delights of shopping in Knightsbridge stores, in his free time from royal duties, Charles wanted to relax at Highgrove where he was implementing organic farming practices. He loved country life, horses and dogs, but Diana was still afraid of horses and had little affinity for dogs. Their incompatibility was total.

Charles continued fox-hunting with the Duke of Beaufort's pack often hunting on the same days as Camilla, but at this stage, they were merely platonic friends. The fact that Charles met his former mistress, even though many others were present, upset Diana even more than his solitary pastimes like fishing and reading. Diana, still in her twenties, wanted to dance at discos with friends from Coleherne Court days. But Charles had done this in his twenties with Camilla and other young women, and he was no longer interested.

Charles' valet Ken Stronach would eventually reveal, in return for a large fee, that before Harry's birth the royal couple slept apart and had little contact with each other.

Eventually, Rupert Murdoch's *News of the World* scandal sheet published a transcript of Ken Stronach's revelations, in which the disloyal valet betrayed his employer. He had confirmed that Camilla and Charles had resumed their love affair just before the birth of Prince Harry.[53] Other friends stated their reunion took place after Harry's birth.

---

53 Interview with valet Ken Stronach, *News of the World*, 15 January 1995.

Years later on television, Charles defended himself saying the reunion took place because he felt the marriage had 'broken down irretrievably'. If Prince Philip's remark about taking a mistress if the arranged marriage failed had influenced his decision, it will never be known. But no doubt, as he knew from his study of history, so many royal ancestors with mistresses (as shown in the table at the start of the book) had convinced the Prince of Wales he was merely following royal tradition rather than breaking the seventh commandment.

But Diana did not feel the marriage was totally broken. She wanted to repair the damage for the sake of their sons and still longed for that baby daughter to complete their family. Charles, tired of constant fights, repeated he was not interested in having more children. But in the meantime, they were the Golden Couple with countless engagements to fulfil.

A trip to Washington was good for British prestige, and Charles discovered an affinity with Nancy Regan who was not nearly as kooky as her detractors claimed. He found he could talk to her while Diana, wearing a svelte off-the-shoulder evening gown, was photographed dancing with John Travolta amid rapturous applause from fellow guests who paid scant attention to Charles. Photos of the dancing celebrities were flashed around the world's television stations. Diana, the failed dance student, was now an icon of ballroom dancing from her performance in the White House.

The fact that the once 'shy Di' was now an international celebrity did not go down well at Clarence House. The Queen Mother regarded Diana as being far too popular for her own good and too fond of courting the tabloids. This was not what royalty was meant to be about.

Still jealous of Camilla and desperate for another child, Diana tried to rekindle her husband's sexual interest by providing him with a surprise for his thirty-seventh birthday.

She spent days with the ballet dancer Wayne Sleep rehearsing a sexy dance routine for a gala performance at a Covent Garden benefit concert which raised funds for charity. Dancers sang, and singers danced, and participants and the audience enjoyed it.

Diana wore a slinky frock of silver satin with a tulip skirt that swirled around her as she danced. Her dance routine, after much practice, had attained professional standard. The Princess of Wales was thrilled to receive huge applause and eight curtain calls.

But instead of being impressed by her talent as Diana had hoped, her husband was embarrassed at seeing his wife on stage. Alone in private, he accused her of 'cavorting on stage with a ballet dancer' and considered Diana's misguided attempt to win him back, highly unsuitable for the wife of a future king. Her birthday surprise for her husband had fallen flat. It demonstrated how little Diana understood Charles and the vast gulf that separated them.

Four years after their fairytale wedding at St Paul's, the marriage was at crisis point. Charles was at a loss as to how to deal with Diana's surges of anger and moods of deep despair, her jealous outbursts and tantrums caused by her bulimia which was no longer a secret between them and Charles found the idea of his wife throwing up her food revolting.

Even more divisive was the fact Charles resented his wife's popularity, which he believed eclipsed the hard work he put into his Prince's Trust which he ran to help young people from disadvantaged backgrounds achieve their potential.

Diana retaliated by demanding Charles sell Highgrove and buy a country estate further away from Camilla's home. They drove north to inspect Belton House, a stately home for sale in Lincolnshire. Having grown up accustomed to the grandeur of Georgian architecture of Althorp, Diana liked this magnificent residence. But Charles claimed Belton House would be too expensive to run and was too far away from London and the Duchy of Cornwall to be suitable.

Since they were virtually leading separate lives, Diana took on more engagements on behalf of her many charities. The hardworking Princess employed nannies to look after her children, but Diana insisted on taking her boys to nursery school, and she accompanied them whenever she had no commitments. And they loved being with her as well as her goodnight kisses and hugs – the embraces she had longed for as a child.

Diana was careful to schedule royal duties, so she was always there when her boys came home. Thanks to her, her sons were now enrolled for Eton where she hoped they would not be bullied as Charles had been at Gordonstoun and would lead as normal a life as was possible for princes with friends of their own age.

Camilla's grandmother, the daughter of Alice Keppel, had died in 1986 leaving Camilla a substantial legacy. This and Andrew's money had enabled the Parker Bowles to sell Bolehyde Manor which needed extensive renovations and buy an estate of five hundred acres which contained Middlewick House, an eighteenth-century Wiltshire stone manor with landscaped gardens. Diana was dismayed that Middlewick House was even closer to Highgrove than their former home. She resented having to accompany Charles to the Parker Bowles' housewarming party along with the rest of Charles and Andrew's polo team.

Princess Diana takes Prince William & Prince Harry to Wetherby 1989
Off to school for new term (MirrorPix)

Charles resumes his love affair with Camilla

Charles was gloomy about the future and often short-tempered. He was also depressed and tired of Diana's constant jealousy of Camilla when he had broken off his relationship with her just before his marriage and stuck to his promise.

Lady Susan Hussey, a senior lady-in-waiting to the Queen, had known Charles since he was a child. She spent the evening before the wedding with him when he did not have a traditional stag night like Prince Andrew, and she had done her best to persuade him that this arranged marriage might still work.

Now seeing Charles depressed and miserable and fearing he might become suicidal, Lady Susan Hussey felt protective of him and contacted Camilla, the only person who could help him. She advised Camilla of the gravity of the situation asking her to contact Charles. And so, Diana's fears that Charles would return to Camilla became a self-fulfilling prophecy.

Initially, Charles made long phone calls to Camilla telling her about his unhappiness and how he could not understand Diana and several royal doctors felt she was suffering from some rare mental complaint which made her throw terrible tantrums, but which disappeared when she was with crowds who adored her. She was like certain actors and actresses who crave the admiration of the crowd like a drug.

Charles went back to driving to Wiltshire, ostensibly to see his godson, and felt happy and relaxed at being reunited with Camilla.

Seated in her large comfortable kitchen with a glass of good wine in front of him, the Prince of Wales received sympathy and good advice. Sometimes, Major and Mrs Parker Bowles were dinner guests at Highgrove, or Camilla would visit the house by herself.

Originally, to please Diana, Charles had abandoned grouse shooting and deer stalking at Balmoral which angered the royal family as they felt she was turning him against them. Now Charles went shooting with Andrew on his new estate.

Charles spent long holidays at Balmoral Castle or at Birkhall with his grandmother.

At the official opening of Expo 1986 in Vancouver, the media ignored Prince Charles' speech and concentrated on the fact that the Princess of Wales had fainted. Diana was now vomiting after every meal, and unfortunately, her husband wrongly believed her fainting was a publicity stunt to draw attention to herself and told her she should have fainted away from the public which left her hurt and furious and provoked still more bitter arguments.

By the end of 1987, the Prince and Princess of Wales were leading totally separate lives. He stayed at Highgrove where Camilla was often a guest, while Diana's base was their apartment at Kensington Palace. But aware of the fact that royalty were meant to provide an example to their subjects, they were careful to keep up the appearance of a happy couple in public.

Friends of Prince Charles and the Parker Bowles were made aware that Camilla and Charles had resumed their former love affair at a large party in June 1987 to celebrate the marriage of the young Marquess of Worcester. Diana spent the evening dancing with Philip Dunne and a few other young men she knew from her Coleherne Court days. She did not know that while she was enjoying herself dancing and flirting, Charles and Camilla had disappeared hand in hand and were absent for several hours.

That summer, Camilla joined Charles in Italy for a short sketching and painting holiday. Diana bitterly hurt, remained at Kensington Palace with their sons in August with nowhere with sufficient security for them to go.[54]

---

54 Gyles Brandreth, *op. cit.*, p 249.

From September 1987, Charles spent five weeks at Balmoral and Diana and the boys joined him for two weeks before returning south. As usual, Diana's bulimia was always at its worst at Balmoral where she was unhappy hating the blood sports that the royal family enjoyed, the chilly weather and everything about the place she had once sworn to Charles she loved.

Now that marital relations with her philandering husband who had betrayed her with so many other women was over, Camilla slipped back happily into her former role with Prince Charles, the man she knew would never betray her. She and Charles met in the stately homes of friends like the Duke and Duchess of Devonshire. At Chatsworth and similar walled country houses safe from prying eyes, Charles and Camilla were happy to be together just like Alice Keppel and her Prince of Wales.

By travelling separately, they avoided detection, and before or after Charles' official commitments managed to spend short holidays together in Italy. Planning their love trysts gave an added frisson to the time they spent in each other's company.

To fill the emotional vacuum in her life, Diana did more charity work and became fond of her avuncular protection officer, Barry Mannakee. Many years later, she admitted on what she called her 'Secrets videotapes', that she loved Mannakee, seeing him as a father figure. It upset her that Charles had her security guard sent back to Scotland Yard accusing him of 'over-familiarity'.

The following year, Diana was very distressed when Barry Mannakee was killed in a motorcycle accident. Her distress was intensified by Charles' decision to inform her of Mannakee's death just before the made a joint public appearance at the Cannes Film Festival which threw her completely.

Diana was convinced her protection officer had been murdered by MI6 and later spent considerable time and money trying to contact him through a spiritualist. She claimed on her 'Secrets videotapes' made with the assistance of her voice coach, Peter Settelin, that the affair was never consummated, and she saw Mannakee purely as a surrogate father in whom she could confide her distress over the failure of her marriage.

Fun-loving Fergie, future Duchess of York

Diana had met the effervescent red-headed Sarah Ferguson, known as Fergie, through Fergie's father who was employed as polo manager. Major Ronald Ferguson, was employed as a polo manager by Prince Charles. In the status-conscious world of the Windsors, the daughter of a polo manager would not normally have been admitted to their inner circle of aristocrats had it not been for the friendship formed between Fergie and

Diana, Princess of Wales.

In her autobiography *My Story,* Fergie described herself as Diana's best friend, but this was a relatively short-term friendship. They were totally different in character, but the fact that both girls had been abandoned by their mothers in childhood formed a bond between them.

Like Camilla, Fergie had attended Queen's Gate Secretarial College. But while Camilla had worked as a secretary-cum-Girl Friday. occasionally for fun when it suited her, Fergie needed money and had worked as a secretary in public relations and later in publishing – areas that would help her become a prolific author of adult and children's books when her marriage broke down.

Then Fergie became the live-in mistress of racing driver Paddy MacNally who had no intention of marrying her. She spent her winters at McNally's ski chalet in the expensive ski resort of Verbier organising house parties for her lover. Aware that Fergie loved skiing, Diana invited her to join Prince Charles and his friends in a chalet party in Switzerland. Fergie shone on the ski slopes and made the house party laugh with plenty of jokes and funny stories.

Back in England, Diana introduced Fergie to Prince Andrew. They were both loud and boisterous, sharing a bawdy sense of humour and a love of practical jokes. They bonded immediately and fell for each other, 'Randy Andy' declared his love for Fergie at a house party at Sandringham. As it seemed unlikely that Prince Andrew, the second son of the Queen, would become king, it was agreed that in spite of Fergie's past and her lack of a title, she could marry the Queen's favourite child. The Queen found Sarah Ferguson amusing and enjoyed going riding with her.

And so, Miss Sarah Ferguson and Prince Andrew, Duke of York, were married in Westminster Abbey on 23 July 1986. She became Her Royal Highness the Duchess of York. Before the wedding, Fergie encouraged Diana to join her in a crazy prank. They were to dress up as policewomen and gate crash Andrew's stag party, something totally out of character for Diana.

After the marriage of the Duke and Duchess of York, Andrew had only his relatively modest income as a naval officer and Fergie had extravagant tastes, so the Queen gave the newlyweds a large sum of money and they built themselves a luxurious 'McMansion' named Sunninghill Park. Fergie enjoyed spending large sums on garish clothes, fad diets, dubious therapists, claiming she needed to do this to cheer herself up as Andrew was away for a large part of the year on naval service.

Fergie was responsible for urging Diana to seek advice from an astrologer and assorted therapists who arrived at Kensington Palace with New Age ideas and crystal balls promising to help Diana relax. The

Duchess of York employed a 'mind-body' therapist called Stephen Twigg who specialised in deep massage and digestive problems and recommended him to Diana. Stephen Twigg later claimed he had cured Diana's bulimia, but the cure was only temporary, and her bulimic vomiting returned as soon as she was under stress.

Other therapists treated Diana for her back pain, and Fergie introduced her to a new form of weight loss therapy – colonic irrigation, which washed out the bowel and removed faeces but provided only a temporary weight loss.

Like Diana, the Duchess of York suffered criticism of her behaviour from officials at Buckingham Palace. The stress saw food-loving Fergie's weight rise to one hundred kilograms (two hundred and twenty pounds), and the press ridiculed her as 'the Duchess of Pork'.

Diet pills and possibly Prozac® also made Fergie behave in ways that were far from royal. She and Andrew were lavish spenders, always in need of cash. They spent far more than Andrew earned, and in order to make money, they let themselves be photographed by *Hello* magazine relaxing in their mansion. This annoyed the Queen and Palace officials who regarded this kind of cash for exposure as vulgar.

Diana's first lover

Diana was still haunted by her childhood fear of horses. But she was aware that riding and polo played an important role in royal life and wanted her sons to learn to ride well. She engaged a handsome, red-headed riding instructor, Captain James Hewitt, a polo-playing Guards Officer with a muscular figure and red hair. They were introduced when Captain Hewitt was the staff officer responsible for royal ceremonies at the time of Andrew and Fergie's wedding (a fact which made the James Hewitt as Harry's father theory ridiculous).

Captain Hewitt taught the athletic young princes to ride well and became a good friend of the lonely princess. He was good for her, made her laugh and enjoy herself. His evident admiration gave her confidence to overcome this childhood fear of horses. Diana knew her long legs looked good in jodhpurs and high boots and her attentive instructor, two years younger than herself, helped her to conquer her fear of horses.

James Hewitt's mother owned stables near Exeter, but he was at ease moving among aristocrats in court circles. Their romance was facilitated by the fact Captain Hewitt's army quarters at Knightsbridge Barracks were conveniently close to Kensington Palace.

The Princess of Wales took advantage of her husband's long absence on a royal tour on the yacht *Britannia* to see a great deal of James Hewitt. And she invited him to dine with her in her apartment at Kensington Palace. After dinner, Diana led him into her bedroom, and their affair began. According to Hewitt, when making love, Diana showed few signs of guilt, claiming that since her husband was having sex with Camilla, 'What is good for the goose is good for the gander'.

Although claiming that she wanted another child by her husband, Diana was on the contraceptive pill so was not worried about having a child by her lover. She did not take the affair with Hewitt very seriously and began it as a form of revenge on her husband for returning to Camilla, hoping that his passion for Mrs Parker Bowles would fade as time wore on.

'I was with Diana because she needed me,' Hewitt recalled. 'I could have been for her what Camilla has become for Charles.' But this never happened. James Hewitt described Diana as calm and controlled in public, but behind the scenes having violent mood swings, alternating between anger and despair at her husband's behaviour, which had hurt her deeply.[55]

On their visits to the cottage of Hewett's mother in Devon, Hewett noticed that Diana ate large quantities of ice-cream and chocolate biscuits and wondered why she did not put on weight.

Eventually, Diana plucked up the courage to tell her lover about her 'secret illness', fearing he would find it as repulsive as her husband and break off their relationship. However, James Hewitt was deeply in love with Diana. He read everything he could about bulimia and told Diana he still loved her and wanted to help her. She was relieved as this was such a contrast to her husband's reaction who, on the rare occasions when they ate together, would mock her saying, 'What a pity all this good food will come up again.'

Diana expressed her gratitude to James Hewitt for accepting her bulimia with expensive gifts, including a complete wardrobe of expensive clothes. They met on most Fridays for lunch in Diana's favourite restaurant, The San Lorenzo, in Beauchamp Place, Knightsbridge where the owner claimed to be psychic, became a friend and encouraged the relationship. Diana and Hewett used to drive to Devon and spend the weekend with his mother riding horses and watching television. Carolyn Pride, Diana's great friend from West Heath and Coleherne Court, was sworn to secrecy and on one occasion spent a weekend in Devon with them.

In the spring of 1987, Captain Hewitt was promoted to the rank of Acting Major and posted to a barracks near Windsor Castle. Whenever

---

55 The rows between Diana and Charles were described by Anna Pasternak in her book *Princess in Love*, Signet Publications, London, 1995, giving details of the affair between James Hewitt and Princess Diana.

Charles was away, Diana and Hewitt met at Kensington Palace or at Highgrove. Staff in both residences felt awkward about the situation, just as they did when Prince Charles and Camilla stayed at Highgrove when Diana was absent.

Diana's sense of duty was still strong, and she completed a large number of public engagements, including numerous visits to hospitals and clinics and entered the controversial area of treatment for patients with AIDS.

In April 1987, Diana opened the Broderip Ward at London's Middlesex Hospital, Britain's first AIDS ward. She was photographed shaking hands with patients and did this without wearing gloves, highlighting that this condition could not be transmitted by contact, which was important because many people feared that AIDS could be caught by merely touching a sufferer. Diana did her best to educate the public that this was not true.

Aware AIDS suffers were being victimised, Diana was later photographed embracing an AIDS patient. Her participation in this campaign was not received well by her in-laws, who felt royalty were not meant to involve themselves in anything controversial. Diana did not care. She forgot her own problems by helping others for which she was termed the 'caring princess' and was the first celebrity in Britain to reach out to AIDS sufferers.

In 1988, Diana undertook a gruelling schedule of two hundred and fifty public engagements, which compared favourably with the one hundred and fifty-three engagements performed by Sarah, Duchess of York, in the same period. As her reputation as a humanitarian grew, Diana's friendship with Fergie cooled. The Duchess of York came into open conflict with officials at Buckingham Palace, one of whom called her 'Vulgar, vulgar, vulgar' for her less than royal behaviour and poor taste in clothes.

After Fergie's father, Major Ronald Ferguson, was caught by the paparazzi leaving a London massage parlour, Diana felt it was wise to distance herself from the wife of Prince Andrew determined the word 'vulgar' would never be applied to her.

In fact, it never could. The Princess of Wales was always beautifully dressed, and in public, her manners were faultless –although in arguments with her husband, her language would deteriorate. Diana's strong sense of duty made her behave impeccably in public even when she was very tired, and her kindness to those she visited in hospitals and hospices was legendary. She would often stay much longer than the itinerary called for talking to certain patients and made visits unannounced to some hospital wards and wrote letters of consolation to patients with whom she had developed a rapport.

⁂

Diana's 'secret disease'

In January 1988, Charles and Diana flew to Sydney to take part in Australia's Bicentennial celebrations. As always, Diana wore attractive outfits and was adored by the crowds. Charles felt jealous and humiliated when huge crowds held up banners proclaiming 'Di, we love you' and chanting her name over and over again outside the Sydney Opera House.

Diana scored another victory over her husband in Melbourne where, having bothered to learn the words of the Australian national anthem, she sang them, which Charles was unable to do. In a Melbourne concert hall, Charles played the cello to applause from music lovers. But once again he was outshone by his Diana, who gave an impromptu but superb rendering of a difficult Rachmaninov concerto without sheet music and was applauded enthusiastically.

Back in Britain, things went from bad to worse.

Her blistering rows with her husband affected Diana so badly that her bulimia which she had been able to limit to her visits to Balmoral and Sandringham returned with a vengeance in London.

Soon the tabloids were describing Diana as 'painfully thin to the point of gauntness'. The once fresh-faced princess now wore a great deal of pancake make-up to hide the fact her complexion was deteriorating as constant vomiting meant that she was not receiving the vitamins and minerals contained in a normal diet.

Diana's school friend, Carolyn Pride, now Mrs Bartholomew, became very worried about Diana's weight loss and her emotional state. She had read up about bulimia and warned Diana that vomiting and frequent purging with laxatives were draining her system of vitamins essential for brain function and healthy skin.

Carolyn threatened to call a press conference and reveal the truth unless Diana saw Dr Maurice Lipsedge, a psychiatrist specialising in eating disorders. (Many years earlier he had successfully treated Diana's mother and her sister Lady Sarah for anorexia since eating disorders tend to run in families.)

Diana deeply ashamed of her behaviour had hidden her own eating disorder from her family and wanted them and her friends to believe her marriage was a success. Carolyn was one of her few friends to know the truth behind the smiling façade.

Her school friend's threat to tell the media terrified Diana, who feared that her popularity with the public would vanish, which along with her beloved boys were the things that kept her going.

She contacted Dr Maurice Lipsedge, and he realised this was serious. Unlike Dr Pare, he did not think she had some rare syndrome. He knew what she had and reached out to her and helped her. Dr Lipsedge arrived at Buckingham Palace, asked if she had tried to commit suicide, listened to Diana, understood her problems and gave her advice on eating a sensible diet.

As Dr Pare and Sir Martin Roth had agreed over the phone, the psychiatric hospital option was impossible for Princess Diana, whose image was now so well-known it was feared her identity would be revealed. Tabloid journalists had large sums of money at their disposal to bribe poorly paid cleaning staff and kitchen staff in private clinics to provide them with salacious stories about the rich and famous in psychiatric clinics.

Dr Lipsedge came frequently to Kensington Palace and treated Diana with behavioural conditioning and insisted she exercise every day as an alternative means of weight control rather than self-induced vomiting. Diana was grateful and followed his advice, and after some time she had her eating disorder under control.

Nevertheless, old habits die hard. Diana would later claim that her cravings for sweet foods and her bulimia would return in times of severe stress when she had to visit Balmoral or Sandringham.

In mid-November 1988, Charles and Diana attended a ball at Buckingham Palace for her husband's fortieth birthday. Naturally, the Parker Bowles were among the three hundred invited guests. Charles spent most of the evening dancing with Camilla. Diana managed to sneak James Hewitt into the ball. Looking radiant, Diana danced with many partners and enjoyed herself, but she only gave James Hewitt one dance, which made him unhappy.

Ken Wharfe, the loyal protection officer provided to Diana by Scotland Yard, felt that while Hewitt was besotted by the princess, she did not really love him and was using this affair with him as a way to revenge herself on her husband.

The Queen and Prince Philip were aware their son's marriage was in trouble. Although the Queen liked Andrew Parker Bowles, she strongly disapproved of Camilla as Charles' mistress (although Andrew Parker Bowles successful philandering when in London during the week was well-known in polo-playing and royal circles.

The Queen was alleged to have told several of her ladies-in-waiting, 'I wish Mrs Parker Bowles would go away and leave Charles alone.'

In 1989, Diana's affair with James Hewitt was interrupted when he was posted to Germany. Always possessive about those to whom she was close, Diana was annoyed to think that James Hewitt was leaving her when she needed him. She ignored the fact that her lover had to obey orders like all army officers and accompany his regiment wherever it was posted.

Diana's childhood 'separation anxiety' had never entirely disappeared, and she regarded this separation due to Captain Hewitt's posting to Germany as a lack of loyalty on his part. Childishly, she revenged herself on him for leaving her and refused to answer his phone calls or his letters.

However, all was forgotten when he returned from serving with his regiment as part of the British Army of the Rhine in Germany. They enjoyed a passionate reconciliation when Captain Hewitt returned. But then in 1991, Diana felt betrayed once again when her lover was sent in command of a tank to join the Gulf War. This time she realised he could not avoid his posting and having been promoted to Acting Major, Hewitt was risking his life on active service, so Diana did write to her lover. Carried away by patriotism, she watched scenes from the Gulf War every night on television, hoping to catch a glimpse of Major Hewitt in his tank. But her strong possessive streak meant she could not forgive her lover for leaving her, and subconsciously she held this against him.

On Major Hewitt's return to London, tanned, fit and still in love, instead of the romantic reunion he was expecting, Diana ended their affair by refusing to take his calls. As Diana could not or would not explain her feelings, Hewitt was upset and hurt at the abrupt way she ended their affair, and as a result, failed the exams he needed to pass to become a Major. The colonel of his regiment, aware of the scandal surrounding Hewitt as the lover of the Princess of Wales, used his exam failure to end Hewitt's army career.

This was a disaster as he had no private income. Diana's ex-lover became involved in a couple of business schemes that went wrong and she heard he was about to publish a book called *Love and War* containing a guarded account of his affair with her and this upset her badly.

As well as ending a five-year relationship with her lover, Diana also ended friendships with several female friends very abruptly by refusing to answer their calls and changing her mobile phone number. She claimed the friends had shown lack of loyalty, and she refused to answer their letters. As a result, they were hurt when she cut them ruthlessly out of her life.

While previous princesses of Wales had tolerated infidelity in their husbands, Diana was a modern woman with very different expectations of marriage. Remembering her mother's misery over losing her children, she did not want a divorce, and for the sake of her sons was prepared to maintain the façade of a happy marriage. She wanted her sons to have a more normal childhood than the lonely bullied years Prince Charles had endured.

Diana braved criticism from her in-laws and took William and Harry to hospitals as well as to amusement parks and to Disneyland to give them an insight into the lives of ordinary people which she felt had been missing from her husband's isolated childhood.

Confronting Camilla & wooing the media

Early in 1989, Diana attended a birthday party in a beautiful house at Ham, near Richmond, hosted by the wealthy Sir James and Lady Annabel Goldsmith, in honour of Annabel Elliot, Camilla's sister. Her husband objected to Diana's wish to attend the party aware Camilla would be there. Diana insisted on attending, accompanied by her bodyguard, aware this was an ideal opportunity to confront her hated rival.

The Prince and Princess of Wales split up on arriving at the party. Eventually, Diana found Camilla sitting on a sofa beside Charles in the children's playroom in the basement of Lady Annabel's home.

Seeing Charles and Camilla together and Diana trembling with rage, Ken Wharfe made an excuse and left the room, as did Prince Charles. This left Diana facing her rival at long last. She told Camilla that she was not an idiot, she knew the pair of them were having an affair and that she was inconvenient to both of them.

Camilla retorted that Diana had everything: money, a husband, two healthy sons and 'all the men in the room' were in love with her. What more did she want?

The answer was obvious. Diana wanted a husband who loved her and her alone. Thinking how foolish she had been to enter into an arranged marriage with a man obsessed by another woman and thinking of all her ancestors' arranged marriages, Diana exclaimed sadly to a friend, 'With our family history you'd think I'd have seen it coming.'[56]

The sad thing is that Diana had not 'seen it coming' when she agreed to marry Prince Charles. She had hoped her love would vanquish Camilla, not only because she was younger and prettier but because she had given her husband an heir.

The truth was humiliating. Charles had never loved her as he loved Camilla. And he never would.

---

56 Gyles Brandreth's book, *op. cit.*, ends with Camilla and Charles' marriage in 2005, but provides an interesting account of Camilla's life up to that date.

Diana's moods alternated between despair and rage that the husband she adored had deceived her, and her dependency on Valium made her mood swings worse. She was determined to win what the media would refer to as 'The War of the Wales' by making friends with powerful editors and high-profile journalists, charming them with her wit now that she was no longer shy. Diana had found her stride and was able to manipulate the media more cleverly than most royal spin doctors.

Diana had developed her own way of dealing with the media. She would pose for photographers with a patient attached to the piece of equipment one of her charities was trying to raise money for. She would listen intently as patients told her about their lives and their illnesses while being photographed, aware that photos of her doing this made an appealing 'hook' on which tabloid journalists could hang a story.

The media savvy Princess had taken the time to learn how the media worked and how they had to cope with deadlines for their copy and photos. She made it easy for journalists to write stories and would pose happily for the photos they needed to accompany the story.

What really annoyed Diana was the fact that no one in the extended royal household praised her work for hospitals and various other charities. In the 1980s and early 1990s, touching hospital patients and sitting on their beds were not considered 'royal.' Protocol demanded members of the royal family remain aloof from those who were in pain or dying. A more sympathetic approach to illness and suffering was one of Diana's legacies to the British monarchy.

Winning the 'War of the Wales'

Although the Prince and Princess of Wales were living separate lives, they did their best to keep up the appearance of a happy marriage. In this way, the truth about their failed marriage was kept from the public in order to preserve the image of the royal family maintaining family values.

Should Charles have an appointment in London early in the morning, he stayed overnight at St James's Palace and drove there alone. He no longer stayed overnight at Kensington Palace and used Highgrove as his headquarters. Diana's popularity had become a thorn in Charles' side. He felt sidelined when she was around and was tired of being photographed standing in the background while his wife was the focus of attention. Years later, Diana's Private Secretary, Patrick Jephson, would reveal in *Shadows of a Princess* how the Prince and Princess of Wales tried to upstage each other, with Diana more adept at this manoeuvre than her husband.

Prince Charles was depressed at the way the marriage made to please his family had turned out but found some relief from his problems through intense physical activity such as polo.

In the summer of June 1990, the Prince of Wales suffered a serious accident while playing at Cirencester. Charles lost his balance while making a shot and fell between two polo ponies. His right arm was badly damaged when one of the ponies kicked him, and he was rushed to hospital.

Diana visited her husband in hospital and drove him back to Highgrove, feeling that Charles needed her and this was an ideal time for a reconciliation. However, Diana's offer to look after her husband at Highgrove was rebuffed. Charles, in great pain, made it abundantly clear he did not want his wife around and wanted to be nursed by Camilla.

According to Paul Burrell, working as a footman at Highgrove, Princess Diana felt rejected, humiliated and unwanted. She stayed at Highgrove House for an hour then fled back to London in tears.[57]

Camilla arrived soon after Diana departed, summoned by a phone call from Charles. During her lover's convalescence, she was in regular attendance but was careful not to stay overnight. She and Charles ate together, listened to music and discussed books and enjoyed each other's company. A full-time physiotherapist was employed to supervise his exercise regime. It took several months before the damaged arm healed sufficiently for him to be able to use it without pain.

In her memoirs, Wendy Berry, housekeeper at Highgrove, described Prince Charles greeting Camilla by 'taking her by the hand and kissing her on the lips'.[58] She recorded that when Camilla visited Highgrove, ashtrays overflowed with cigarette butts; at that time Camilla was virtually a chain smoker. Charles, a non-smoker who detested the smell of tobacco, put up with her heavy smoking, which could be seen as proof of his love.

Charles had previously complained of being overshadowed by his glamorous wife, and now she gave him cause to do so.

'Hell hath no fury like a woman scorned', runs the proverb. Whenever the heir to the throne undertook an important engagement or made a significant speech, Diana managed to steal the limelight with a new hairdo or a speech on issues dealing with health and welfare. Diana used her celebrity, her beauty and her charisma to promote good causes and also to upstage Charles and deflect attention from the husband who she felt had betrayed her with another woman – an older and less attractive woman at that.

---

57 Related in Paul Burrell, *A Royal Duty*, London 2003.

58 Wendy Berry, *The Housekeeper's Diary*, New York, 1995.

The book that stunned the nation

Diana, Her True Story by Andrew Morton was compiled from tapes made by Princess Diana. Aided by Dr James Colthurst, Morton claimed that the well written narrative was quite rightly an authoritative biography but could not say that Diana was the main contributor.

There was no way Diana, who had failed 'O' level English, could write a book on the topic of her failed marriage or be interviewed at length by Andrew Morton. Dr James Colthurst, her old friend from Coleherne Court days, asked her questions and taped the answers. He passed the tapes in secret to Andrew Morton, an ambitious young journalist with a degree in history. Morton had already written about Diana when he worked as a reporter on a small paper called *The Star.*

The idea of the tapes originated when James Colthurst, who regularly played squash with Andrew Morton, told him he knew of a good subject for a biography. The subject could not be interviewed, but Morton could receive the story on tape.

Told the identity of the mysterious 'royal personage', Morton became excited at the idea of this biography and contacted Michael O'Mara, an enterprising American publisher working in London. O'Mara realised he was being offered a potential bestseller and agreed to publish Diana's story.

In June 1992, Diana broke the tradition that royal wives remained silent and exposed her anguish over the sham her marriage had become in Morton's book which entered the bestseller lists in Britain, America and many Commonwealth countries. Diana's decision to tell the story as she saw it, not always correctly but with emotion, triggered a train of events which ironically would end in the divorce she had not wanted.

To protect herself from accusations she had cooperated with Andrew Morton, Diana used Dr James Colthurst, a medically qualified Old Etonian as her go-between delivering the tapes he helped her to make.

Young and happily married, Dr Colthurst had been genuinely worried about Diana, who he had met years earlier when on a ski party in Switzerland and wanted to help her. In 1991, in his spare time, Dr Colthurst asked Diana questions which she did her best to answer on tape. Her answers revealed her husband's relationship with Camilla, Diana's problems with bulimia, and her attempts at self-harm. Repeating the behaviour of her childhood, wanting to be loved by those who read the book, Diana's tapes included some embellishments and 'tall tales' guaranteed to arouse sympathy, and at this stage, they were believed.

Michael O'Mara was cautious after reading Morton's typescript and demanded proof that Charles and Camilla really were lovers before committing money to the project.

Diana managed to find revealing letters from Camilla to Prince Charles after riffling through his briefcase when they were staying with her in-laws at Balmoral and Charles was out shooting. The 'purloined' letters were shown to the publisher, who was satisfied, and Diana replaced them. O'Mara went ahead with publication of Morton's book.

In the spring of 1992, *Diana: Her True Story* appeared in bookshops. Some journalists were jealous, aware it was a bestseller in the making. Others claimed it was a total fabrication and Andrew Morton was a hack journalist ignoring the fact Morton had a degree in history from Sussex University and had already written a book on Kensington Palace.

In fact, much of the book was based on Diana's own words, turned skilfully into a narrative with background information added by the author and colour photos provided by Princess Diana herself.

Initially, the hardback edition sold slowly, deemed too incredible to be true. It only became a bestseller after *The Times* serialised it. The first instalment was published on Saturday, 7 June 1992. Sales boomed, and a paperback edition went on to sell five million copies worldwide, turning Andrew Morton into Britain's wealthiest journalist and enraging the occupants of Buckingham Palace.

Diana had been thrilled that her side of the story would be published. She hoped that the Queen would read Morton's book and understand her hurt and anger that no one had warned her about Camilla's affair with Charles before she agreed to marry him. Adding insult to injury was the fact that Andrew Parker Bowles remained a favourite of the royal family while his wife was making Diana's life miserable.

While Morton's book was at the printers, Diana confessed to Lord Peter Palumbo, a property tycoon with media experience, that the book was taken from tapes which she had provided. Lord Palumbo and his wife were horrified by her admission. They warned Diana that she could be in trouble and must not admit to anyone that she had provided any information for Morton's book.

Diana took fright, and when the book appeared in the shops told her brother-in-law Robert Fellowes and other officials of the royal household she had absolutely nothing to do with the book. A convincing liar since childhood, Diana claimed the information and photographs had been provided by 'good friends', and they had talked to Morton without her knowledge.

Andrew Morton did his best to protect Diana by backing up her story. On the tapes given to Morton, Diana revealed the depth of her anger and humiliation over Camilla's hold on her husband. She confessed that her marriage had been unhappy, that she had attempted suicide (an exaggeration, but she had been very depressed). She did 'self-harm', making small cuts to her wrists and arms. This psychiatric disorder, known as 'cutting behaviour', was relatively unknown at that time, although today psychiatrists encounter it frequently among disturbed teenagers who, like Diana, are convinced that suffering physical pain can counter mental anguish.

Morton's book depicted Diana as a devoted mother locked in a loveless union with a callous, unfaithful husband who she still loved as he was the father of her much-loved sons. Princess Diana insisted on tape that she did not know until a few days before her wedding that Camilla Parker Bowles was her husband's mistress.

To the discomfort of Charles and Camilla, Morton's book focused the spotlight on Diana's disastrous marriage as well as on Camilla Parker Bowles, the 'other woman' in this royal love triangle.[59] Prince Charles was questioned by a journalist who accosted him in the street when the badly flustered prince muttered something to the effect that Andrew Morton's book was 'Fiction, pure fiction' before fleeing to his car.

The press office at Buckingham Palace, led by Press Secretary Dickie Arbiter, did their best to defend Prince Charles. Arbiter had glimpsed the bitterness between the erstwhile 'Golden Couple' on a trip to Seville. He liked Diana but suspected that she was 'being economical with the truth' and was the main source of the information given to Morton.[60]

Everyone suffered from Morton's book. Morton's office was broken into, and papers were stolen, he received death threats and was threatened with being horsewhipped by an irascible colonel in the Household Brigade. Diana was now regarded as dangerous by Buckingham Palace. The public saw Charles as weak and cruel which may have been true later on in the marriage, but at the beginning, he had tried very hard to understand his wife but with a limited understanding of female psychology. Charles had bravely refused to believe the royal physician and Dr Pare when they told him Diana had a serious mental illness and he had taken her to Dr McGlashan who had stated that in his opinion this was not true though Diana would continue to be plagued by rumours of madness by her detractors.

Camilla, now seen as 'the scarlet woman' was deluged with hate mail and her home besieged by the media. At one point she was filmed crawling through a shrubbery to avoid journalists who had surrounded her marital

---

59 Diana claimed on her 'Secrets Tapes' that she had begged Charles to give up Camilla for the sake of their sons.

60 Andrew Morton, *op. cit.*, and Dickie Arbiter, *On Duty with the Queen*, Blink Publishing, 2013.

home. Eventually, Camilla sought refuge in Wales with a relative of her husband.

Diana was questioned by her brother-in-law, Sir Robert Fellowes, in his role as Private Secretary to the Queen. Diana swore that she had nothing to do with the book (a lie) and had never met Morton (true). She insisted that 'good friends' had talked to Morton without her knowledge. Prince Philip was no fool and suspected Diana had cooperated with Morton when he questioned her. Diana, playing the innocent, admitted that a school friend may have talked to Morton without her knowledge.

Prince Philip suspected Diana was lying. He saw photographs of Diana greeting Carolyn Bartholomew affectionately on the doorstep of her London home and regarded them as evidence Diana was not upset by the incident and had gone there to thank Carolyn rather than to reprimand her. Sir Robert Fellowes, believing Diana had deceived him, offered his resignation to the Queen, which was refused.

Camilla feared the effect of Morton's book on the Prince of Wales, and it damaged his image badly. It was clear Diana was a lonely and unhappy wife, no longer prepared to do her part to support the illusion of a happy marriage.

After losing over a stone in weight, Camilla fled from Wales with her younger sister Annabel to Venice's luxurious Hotel Cipriani, located on an island in the Venetian lagoon. I visited this beautiful hotel, accessible only by boat, years later.

I learned that Camilla, wearing dark glasses, spent her time sketching in the beautiful garden and eating in the open-air restaurant on the terrace of the Cipriani, one of the world's most luxurious hideaways.

Back in London, Camilla was cornered by journalists but always well prepared with the media, the only comment she was prepared to make was that she had not read it [Morton's book] but 'I plan to read it later'.

⁂

By now the unthinkable had happened and royal marriages were snapping like twigs. Princess Anne and Mark Phillips divorced in 1992 due to his infidelity. In March 1992, Prince Andrew and 'Fergie', Duchess of York, agreed to separate in their troubled marriage, with Prince Andrew often away.

Soon after the birth of Princess Eugenie in 1991, Fergie went on holiday to Morocco with the handsome Steve Wyatt, son of a Texan oil baron with business interests of his own. Wyatt paid for Fergie to stay in New York's luxurious Plaza Athénée Hotel. In another strange coincidence when doing the research for my book, *Impressionists Revealed, Masterpieces and Collectors,* I couriered a very valuable Renoir which was illustrated in the book to New York and stayed in the same room that Fergie had at this hotel where the security is so excellent that all the staff know your name the moment you cross the threshold. The manager told me that Fergie did so much shopping they had to put extra cupboards into her room.

Fergie's affair with Wyatt continued when he came to London. Fergie was ordered to end the affair by Buckingham Palace and did so, but unfortunately, there were repercussions. Wyatt left very revealing photos of Fergie in a cupboard of his London hotel bedroom. This and the affair with 'the financial advisor' led to the Yorks separating.

Princess Diana had been warned off Fergie by her admirer, John Gilbey. At the time of her separation from Andrew, Fergie had tried to persuade Diana to leave the royal family with her. Although she was jealous of Camilla, Diana had no wish for a divorce as this would mean separation from her beloved boys, so she distanced herself from her former 'best friend'.

After her affair with Steve Wyatt ended, Fergie took up with another American, John Bryan, a financial advisor who had volunteered to help the debt-ridden Yorks get their finances back on track. The pair embarked on a wild rollercoaster ride of expensive living which left John Bryan bankrupt and Fergie with a mammoth overdraft. In August 1992, nude photos of the Duchess having her toes sucked by her financial advisor while on holiday in the South of France were published on the front pages of the Sunday tabloids when Fergie was staying at Balmoral where Prince Philip saw them and expressed his opinion of Fergie in forceful terms.

After a scandal-prone marriage lasting five years, Andrew and Fergie would finally divorce in 1996. Despite her adulterous affairs and dubious money-making schemes like the 'cash for access' scandal for a businessman to meet Prince Andrew when he was a trade envoy to the Middle East and its exposure by a journalist masquerading as a businessman, the divorced couple remained friends and raised their daughters, Princess Beatrice and Princess Eugenie, together.[61]

Perhaps Andrew felt guilty that Fergie's divorce settlement had been so modest. He asked one of his wealthy friends to help pay off Fergie's debts, with the assistance of her earnings from Weight Watchers, and when

---

[61] Princess Beatrice attended St George's Ascot, the author's old school and, in spite of being dyslexic, managed to become head girl and gain entrance to university. As a concerned parent Fergie, Duchess of York was briefly made a member of the Board of Governors after she and Prince Andrew donated money towards building a new theatre wing (money presumably provided by the Queen.)

she was in England, she lived in her former husband's home. Today the Yorks jointly own a ski chalet at Verbier worth thirteen million pounds, amid allegations that some dodgy friends of Andrew's contributed. However, it is alleged that the Queen paid Fergie's half-share in order to provide a holiday home for her beloved granddaughters.

Diana greatly admired the Queen but was annoyed she did not do more to help when she visited the Queen to advise her of her distress over Camilla re-entering Charles' life. In Morton's book and on her 'Secrets' tapes, Diana claimed her mother-in-law replied, 'Charles is hopeless.'

However, this may not be the actual words as when Diana was upset, she was prone to exaggeration. However, it is known that the Queen refused to become involved in matrimonial disputes among her children after the failures of the marriage of Princess Anne followed by the failure of the marriage of Prince Andrew and the Duchess of York.

⁂

Diana: Her True Story by Andrew Morton brought the problems in what was now shown to be a sham marriage to public attention.

The first impulse of the Queen and Prince Philip was to try and salvage the marriage for the sake of William and Harry, who were ten and eight years old, respectively. While the royal family was staying at Windsor Castle for Royal Ascot week, the Queen and Prince Philip talked privately to Charles and Diana about Morton's book, calling it the most serious royal scandal since the Abdication Crisis of the 1930s.

Prince Philip did his best to save his heir's disintegrating marriage. In letters to Diana, he did not defend his son's conduct but suggested Diana examine her behaviour. He reminded Diana of the difficulties posed by her post-natal depression as well as her outbursts of jealous rage which had upset Charles. They had both been at fault and should try to heal the breach for the sake of their children.

According to the *Sunday Times*, the Queen was led to believe that the couple would try to resolve their differences, and a six-month cooling-off period was suggested.

At the insistence of the Queen, a 'honeymoon cruise' was hurriedly arranged for Prince Charles and Princess Diana on a luxurious yacht owned by John Latsis, the Greek shipping tycoon. It was a bizarre honeymoon: the couple refused to share a bed and ate at separate times. Charles read and sketched while Diana practised her high diving from the deck and enjoyed water-skiing behind the yacht's tender. The breach between them seemed irreparable: things could only get worse.

On 28 June, the *Sunday Times* published an article called 'The Case for Charles', claiming the Prince of Wales had requested his friends keep a 'dignified silence' which prevented them from revealing the difficult behaviour and mood swings of Princess Diana that they had witnessed.

The Prince of Wales decided his wife had helped Andrew Morton with his book after Diana refused to sign a legal statement, prepared by his Private Secretary, Richard Aylard, condemning 'inaccuracies and distortions' in Andrew Morton's account of her marriage. The knowledge made him very angry that Diana had lied to everyone about it.

In 1992, the Queen's *annus horribilis,* Diana revealed the depth of her humiliation over her husband's preference for Mrs Parker Bowles in a bugged telephone conversation with James Gilbey. It had been recorded two years earlier, in 1989, and not published until now.

Spending New Year's Eve alone in her bedroom at Sandringham House, Diana confessed her misery to Gilbey, an old friend from Coleherne Court days who was briefly her lover. She told him she nearly burst into tears in front of her in-laws at lunch, thinking about Park House and remembering how happy she had been there before her mother left home. Diana admitted to James Gilbey how badly the failure of her marriage had affected her.

What was evident was that James Gilbey, the young man who once stood her up for another more available girl, was now in love with Diana, calling her by her teenage nickname, 'Squidgy', from the days when she had been plump.

It was a strange situation. On New Year's Eve 1989, Diana, the world's most glamorous and photographed woman had refused to join her husband and her parents-in-law to see in the New Year and had spent the evening alone.

In her long and often tearful conversation with her ardent admirer, she told James Gilbey she feared she might be pregnant. Gilbey reassured her that he had taken steps to ensure this would not occur. What Diana did not know was that this call was being recorded illegally and years later would be broadcast to the world in an attempt to embarrass her.

On tape, Diana mentioned her previous lover, Captain James Hewitt, saying that she had bought Hewitt new clothes and dressed him from head to foot…'He cost me quite a bit,' she observed.

For two and a half years this tape recording lay hidden, like a ticking time bomb. In August 1992, the transcript, which would be known as 'Squidgygate', was released and picked up by the *National Enquirer,* an American scandal sheet, who published it word for word.

CHAPTER EIGHT

'Camillagate' – Diana furious & Camilla divorced

I'd suffer anything for you. That's the strength of love. Camilla to Prince Charles, taken from the 'Camillagate' transcript.

Once the curtain sheltering the doings of royalty is pulled back, the public will no longer venerate the monarchy. Tom Paine (1737–1809), author and political figure.

In January 1993, Rupert Murdoch's Australian family magazine, *New Idea* included the full transcript of this erotic bedtime conversation between Prince Charles and his mistress. Like Diana's 'Squidgygate' conversation with James Gilbey, it had been illegally recorded three years earlier on 17 December 1989 and stored away by persons unknown.

The phone conversation between Camilla and Prince Charles was first broadcast in the middle of the night and picked by ham radio enthusiasts.[62] The tape recording was christened 'Camillagate' by the media, associating it with the 1970 American scandal over the tape recordings which ended the presidency of Richard Nixon. The taped conversation revealed clearly what Buckingham Palace spin doctors had desperately tried to hide for so long: that Prince Charles was committing adultery with a married mistress.

Interestingly enough, the authenticity of this tape was never questioned by Buckingham Palace, and the identity of those who recorded it remains unknown. But the 'Camillagate' scandal ended the marriage of the Prince and Princess of Wales, and the marriage of Camilla and Andrew Parker Bowles.

It has been suggested it may have been recorded by M15 when monitoring the prince's calls due to fears of an IRA attack on members of the royal family and been stolen and broadcast over radio frequencies three years later.

On the night of 18 December 1989, Prince Charles was a guest of the elderly widow of the Duke of Westminster at her stately home. Before going to bed, Charles phoned Camilla at her family home, aware that her husband was away organising his army unit which was providing emergency ambulance services during a strike of ambulance drivers.

Clearly, there were problems in the Parker Bowles 'open' marriage. At one point in their conversation, Camilla described her husband as 'looking like an angry stoat', and added 'Pray God, Andrew won't be here until Thursday!'

---

62 The first published 'Camillagate' tape had its own website.

Camilla comes across in this conversation as the ideal mistress, another Alice Keppel, clever at flattering the ego of a depressed prince. She repeatedly told the Prince of Wales how clever he was, how she loved him and assured him she needed sex with him 'all the week, all the time'.

Prince Charles responded enthusiastically to this. He joked about becoming a tampon inside his mistress, to which she responded by laughing and replying, 'You are a complete idiot! What a wonderful idea!'

The press fuelled public outrage at the sexual frankness of their conversation, even questioning the Prince of Wales's fitness to rule.

More than twenty years later, with more relaxed attitudes to sexuality, Prince Charles' comments no longer appear as outrageous as they did in the late twentieth century as phone sex no longer has the same power to shock.

Their raunchy sex talk was in fact only a small part of a very long and more serious conversation between the lovers. Charles had just read Camilla a long extract from his latest speech on the not very exciting topic of rebuilding communities. Camilla praised her lover extravagantly, clearly trying to bolster his confidence. She repeatedly told him what a good brain he had and begged him to send her the draft of his latest speech.

Camilla's enemies claimed her flattery was blatant. Her friends claimed she was doing her best to soothe Charles' damaged ego because he was hurt that the public clearly preferred his wife.

Camilla told Charles he was 'underestimating himself' and reassured him not once but twice how special he was. She insisted 'You're a clever old thing with an awfully good brain lurking there…I love you, and I'm proud of you. I'd suffer anything for you. That's love.' In a touching assertion, Camilla tells him that loving him is 'as easy as falling off a chair'.

Charles responded to his mistress by saying 'Your biggest achievement is loving me!' This seemingly arrogant reply raised the hackles of many female listeners and the reference to the Prince of Wales becoming a tampon shocked them.

In fairness to Prince Charles, he may have meant something different. Despair and depression are often allied to low self-esteem. Only Camilla and the prince's closest friends knew how depressed this difficult marriage had made him. His friends would later claim Camilla's love and psychological support had prevented him having a nervous breakdown as Diana's moods and constant demands had become impossible.

In a particularly poignant part of the conversation, Charles thanked Camilla for her loyalty to him and acknowledged the 'indignities and calumnies' she had suffered for him. They concluded by repeating over and over again how much they loved each other. Ignoring the sexual content, this was a loving conversation between two people who knew each other very well and wanted to be together but were prevented from doing so.

Advised by a member of her staff that she had to know about 'Camillagate', early in the New Year of 1993 Diana listened to the tape and read the transcript published in the press. She was hurt and angry at the confirmation of what she had suspected for years. It was one of the worst moments of her entire life.

Unlike Charles, who had only married to please his parents, Diana had gone into this marriage because she loved and admired him.

Hearing the father of her children tell Camilla how passionately he loved her when her own sex life with Charles had been infrequent and she had been unable to revive it, as Charles had rejected her, Diana felt humiliated. She had desperately wanted her marriage to be a success. She had only taken Hewitt and Gilbey as what her security guard referred to as 'revenge fucks' and had never been serious about them.

Diana, the little girl denied the love of her mother who had done spiteful things to nannies who upset her, was now hell-bent on revenge however she could get it. She was angry with the royal family who she considered responsible for her misery.

In her view, they had not tried very hard to remedy the situation; the Queen had a rule never to interfere in her children's marriages. Diana was also hurt that couples she had entertained to dinner as friends, and who had attended her wedding, had been deceiving her.[63] It was the last coffin nail in what was a failed marriage.

The publication of the tape was intriguing. Dulcie Boling, the Sydney editor of Rupert Murdoch's magazine *New Idea,* was embroiled in a circulation war with her arch-rival Nene King, editor of Woman's Day owned by media magnate Kerry Packer.

The normally discreet Boling realised the 'Camillagate' conversation was dynamite and would raise the circulation of *New Idea* to new heights. So, she bought the tape and gave the go-ahead to print the sexually explicit transcript, justifying her decision on the grounds of 'the public's right to know' what the Prince of Wales and his married mistress were doing.

The transcript of the bugged or hacked conversation between Charles and Camilla appeared in print in Australia in January 1993 in *New Idea.* Boling was rewarded when sales of *New Idea* doubled overnight. An additional five thousand copies were flown to London and copies sold for an exorbitant price on news stands there.

---

63 The names and addresses of willing friends happy to deceive Princess Diana are detailed in Gyles Brandreth's comprehensive biography, *op. cit.,* pp258–264, which ends with Camilla's marriage to Charles.

Soaring sales figures reassured Murdoch that Dulcie Boling had made a smart decision to buy the tape. Buckingham Palace did not question the tape's veracity, and Prince Charles wisely declined to make any comment and hid away at Highgrove House, appalled at what had happened.

Enormous damage had been done to his reputation which would take him years to live down. Back in 1993, London's *Sunday Mirror* justified publication of a private phone conversation by claiming it was now in the public domain as the story had been published in Australia. This Murdoch paper published the transcript of Camilla and Charles' bedtime conversation on Sunday, 17 January 1993, and it caused a sensation. Nothing similar had been published about royalty – not even in the days of Wallis Simpson, and no one had managed to record their bedtime conversations.

'I wish Mrs Parker Bowles would go away and leave Charles alone'

Following publication of the 'Camillagate' tape, the Queen told a good friend that Mrs Parker Bowles was a 'very wicked woman who hung onto Charles,' adding, 'I wish she would go away and leave Charles alone.'

The Queen gave orders that Mrs Parker Bowles be banned from entering Buckingham Palace and all other royal residences. 'Camillagate' ended any chance of the Prince and Princess of Wales reconciling.

When Camilla read the transcript of her intimate conversation, she was horrified. The grounds of Middlewick House were besieged by photographers with telephoto lenses, determined to obtain a photo of the lady of the manor who, it was now clear, was the mistress of the Prince of Wales.

The press even questioned Charles' fitness to become king. 'Sex Tape Could Cost Charles His Throne' ran the headline when the *Sunday Sun* published the 'Camillagate' transcript in full. It also featured on the Internet with its own website.

Opinion polls revealed that Prince Charles' approval rating was in free fall. Tom Paine's remark about the public no longer respecting royalty once the curtain was pulled back had come true.

Camilla was mocked on an American TV chat show – Mick Jagger, no model of marital fidelity himself, appeared on screen offering a tampon on a silver platter to an actress representing Camilla.

In hindsight, it is clear that publication of the 'Camillagate' transcript occurred at an unfortunate time for the monarchy. The public had had enough of the antics of Prince Andrew and Fergie and was annoyed by more royals behaving badly.

More worrying constitutionally was the fact several Members of Parliament declared that Prince Charles should not become king as he could not be taken seriously as Defender of the Faith of the Church of England since he was breaking one of the Ten Commandments. Talk-back radio shows received calls demanding the succession leapfrog Charles in favour of Prince William. Letters to newspapers expressed the same view. But as Prime Minister John Major observed, 'Time changes everything.'

Prince Charles went into hiding at Sandringham to avoid journalists. He emerged later that month to fulfil speaking engagements to be met by cries of 'Shame!' and 'You're a complete disgrace!'

Camilla remained at her country house, grateful for Middlewick House's five hundred acres of meadows and woods, which provided some protection from the paparazzi. She was distressed about the damage she had inflicted on her teenage children, her parents and her husband. Brigadier Andrew Parker Bowles, in a gallant attempt at damage control, stated 'all was well' between him and his wife. Few people believed him.

Tom Parker Bowles, a clever young man in his last year at Eton, took his final exams with results that could have been better if it were not for the scandal surrounding his mother. Laura Parker Bowles was only fourteen, and both teenagers had to face the ordeal of returning to boarding school with the scandal a hot topic among their school friends. Princes William and Harry, being at primary school, were shielded from much of the scandal.

The tabloid press reported that outraged housewives at the Chippenham branch of Sainsbury's supermarket had yelled insults at Camilla. One TV channel showed footage of a woman they claimed was Camilla, running from the supermarket to a parked car after being hit by bread rolls thrown by outraged shoppers. However, Camilla's friend, the well-known author Jilly Cooper, insisted the TV clip had been staged with actors.

The only member of the royal family to emerge unscathed from this debacle was Diana. Women who had heard her conversation with John Gilbey on the 'Squidgygate' tape were outraged by the sexy conversations on the 'Camillagate' tape and Charles' admission that he was Camilla's lover. They sympathised with Diana's troubles, loved her for her vulnerability and forgave her for having taken James Hewitt as her lover as she said she had loved him and he let her down.

Many of the pro-Diana faction failed to grasp that Gilbey had also been Diana's lover, as revealed by his assurances that Diana must not worry as she could not get pregnant by him so that minefield was avoided.

⁂

As winter turned to spring, the storm of outrage swirling around Mrs Parker Bowles and the Prince and Princess of Wales abated. Camilla turned to reading and gardening for comfort. She and her husband put on a show of marital accord and behaved as though nothing had happened. With aristocratic aplomb, they were photographed walking arm in arm at the wedding of a friend's daughter chatting amicably.

Towards the end of that summer, Camilla went on a tour of India with two female friends. When asked about his wife, the newly-promoted Brigadier Andrew Parker Bowles staunchly replied that 'Camilla is all right. Everything is all right between us.'

Andrew's younger brother Simon loyally declared, 'Both Andrew and Camilla have said they will never divorce and, while the relationship is rather eccentric, it appears to work'.[64]

For the rest of 1993, Camilla's husband and Buckingham Palace spin doctors continued to insist that both marriages were intact, but in reality, Brigadier Parker Bowles had asked for a divorce. He was having a serious affair with Mrs Rosemary Pitman, the divorced wife of a fellow polo player, which would end in their marriage.

But as his relationship with Camilla had always been amicable, he and Rosemary Pitman had agreed to wait until Tom and Laura – Camilla and Andrew Parker Bowles' children – had left school before he divorced and remarried.

Meanwhile, Prince Charles and Princess Diana continued to carry out their public engagements, arriving separately and departing in separate cars. Charles, although humiliated and depressed, went doggedly about his duties, determined to redeem himself through hard work.

In an attempt to win back public sympathy, Prince Charles agreed to cooperate with the journalist and broadcaster Jonathan Dimbleby who having written Charles' biography had been allowed to make a television interview about his work with his charities and his ideas on conservation. This broadcast would become another disaster for Charles, who was unaware of the tricks resorted to by television interviewers in search of high ratings and increased sales for their books.

Jonathan Dimbleby's book, *The Prince of Wales: a biography*, was published in 1994 to coincide with the silver anniversary of Charles' investiture as Prince of Wales. As well as the book, Dimbleby presented a two-and-a-half-hour documentary about the prince. It incorporated a

---

64 Cited by Gyles Brandreth, *op. cit.*, p278, source not provided.

television interview with the hardworking heir to the throne allegedly to ask him to discuss his work with his charities.

Prince Charles unwisely trusted his biographer and regarded him as a friend. He had given Dimbleby extensive access to his personal correspondence and papers, so much so that the Queen became alarmed and insisted her son demand the return of confidential state papers.

Prince Charles was aware of the damage done to his reputation and only agreed to a televised interview after being assured it would only feature his work for his various charities. It was agreed it must not deal with his marriage and private life.

Trusting that this agreement would be adhered to, Prince Charles hoped that by telling his side of the story he would mitigate the damage inflicted by 'Camillagate', Andrew Morton's book and Diana's televised BBC interview with Martin Bashir on the *Panorama* programme, in which she told the sad story of her marriage from her point of view.

Prince Charles and an aide, who had previously worked for Diana, prepared replies designed to show him in a favourable light. They rehearsed replies that Prince Charles could make to questions he was likely to be asked by Dimbleby.

'It's so difficult to know how to play the media,' said Prince Charles to Dimbleby before the interview admitting, 'I'm not very good at being a performing monkey.'[65] It was the understatement of the century.

Two centuries earlier, the Republican writer Tom Paine had made adverse comments on the sexual excesses of the spendthrift Prince Regent who ruled as George IV and his four younger brothers who refused to make arranged marriages, took mistresses and fathered at least a dozen royal bastards. This distressed their pious father, George III, who had no legitimate grandson after the death of the much-loved little Prince Charlotte.

Tom Paine made his memorable statement aware that a great deal of information about the marriages and adulteries of the royal family was kept from the public and wrote how, 'Once the curtain sheltering the doings of royalty is pulled back, the public will no longer venerate the monarchy'.

Tom Paine's sheltering curtain was yanked open by the 'Camillagate' scandal and by Jonathan Dimbleby's interview with Prince Charles, which went to air on 29 June 1994 on Britain's ITV network. His press officers failed to warn Prince Charles of the dangers inherent in a 'live' television interview, in which unlisted questions could easily be sprung on the

---

65 This story first reported in Canada by Bruce Wallace in *Macleans Magazine*, Canada's only weekly current affairs periodical, dated 11 July 1984, but the source of the quote was not cited.

person being interviewed.

Jonathan Dimbleby wanted to promote his forthcoming biography of Prince Charles and needed sensational revelations to ensure sales of his book would skyrocket. He ignored the agreement made with the prince's office and, in the middle of the interview, asked the prince if he had been faithful to Princess Diana.

Prince Charles fell headlong into the trap and was caught.

The Queen and Prince Philip waited with trepidation for the interview with Charles to be broadcast. It was a matter of principle with them not to discuss their private affairs in public (a policy Camilla has always followed).

Charles' parents and his mistress, situated hundreds of miles apart, watched with dismay as this Prince of Wales who prides himself on telling the truth became the first member of the House of Windsor to confess in public he had committed adultery.[66] Charles was certainly not the first adulterous prince in the scandal-ridden British royal family, but his predecessors had kept quiet about their many adulteries, which I documented as part of my research for *Royal Mistresses of the House of Hanover-Windsor.* at time hardly able to believe what certain documents and letters revealed of the sexual exploits of the priapic George IV and Edward VII.

Prince Charles made his admission of adultery in front of an audience of millions. Replying to Dimbleby's question about a possible separation from Diana, Charles became flustered and gave a confused reply: 'Well, obviously, I don't recommend it [separation] to anyone. Obviously, I would much rather it hadn't happened.'

Dimbleby countered with: 'Separations on the whole do lead to divorce. Do you intend to divorce?'

Charles scented danger, became even more nervous, and made a second rambling answer: 'Well, I don't think you'd really expect me to tell you what was in my mind! I mean, that sort of question, you know, is very much for the future, and if it happens, then it'll happen. And, anyway, it's something which I think is very personal and private between my wife and myself.'

The Prince of Wales's discomfiture was obvious to viewers. Dimbleby continued his relentless probing, doing precisely what he had agreed beforehand he would not do and did his best to force Charles to name Mrs Parker Bowles, saying, 'The most damaging charge made in relation to your marriage is that you were, because of your relationship with Camilla

---

66 Jonathan Dimbleby, *op. cit.*

Parker Bowles, from the beginning, persistently unfaithful to your wife which caused a [marriage] breakdown.'

Prince Charles became even more flustered but could not refuse to answer without appearing shifty and evasive. He attempted to explain himself but made things worse by naming Mrs Parker Bowles: 'The trouble is, you see, that these things are so personal, it's difficult to know how to talk about them in front of everybody. And all I can say is that there is no truth in much of this speculation. Mrs Parker Bowles is a great friend of mine. And she has been a friend for a very long time and, along with a lot of other friends, will continue to be a friend for a very long time. I think most people probably would realise that when marriages break down…it is your friends who are the most important and helpful and understanding and encouraging. Otherwise, you would go stark raving mad.'

This remark about going mad suggested that Charles was under a great deal of pressure.

Ruthlessly Dimbleby continued asking, 'Did you try to be faithful and honourable to your wife when you took on the vow of marriage?'

Prince Charles was now so stressed he made the damaging ungrammatical admission, 'Yes, until it [the marriage] became irretrievably broken down, us both having tried.'

Dimbleby realised he had the Prince of Wales on a toasting fork and proceeded to grill him slowly. 'Do you now expect this issue to go away?'

Prince Charles doggedly persevered to try to explain his position, clearly upset at being put on the spot and that his interviewer had not honoured the agreement, the only reason he had agreed to appear on the programme.

Charles made another rambling admission of adultery ending by saying wistfully 'It would be nice if it could be over and done with.'

Jonathan Dimbleby knew that this hot topic would never be 'over and done with' but he had done what he wanted, trapped Prince Charles into admitting adultery and ensured his biography would sell like the proverbial hotcakes. But damage had been inflicted on the Prince of Wales, his sons and on the Parker Bowles' children by naming Camilla in public.

In Britain, amazed viewers in pubs choked on their beer. Elderly maiden ladies who had loved the Prince of Wales since he was a little boy with neatly brushed hair, were shocked by it.

After reviewing a tape recording of this disastrous interview, Prince Charles flew into a rage and blamed his Private Secretary and Treasurer Richard Aylard who 'by mutual decision', left his service.

Viewing the interview in her sitting room at Kensington Palace, Diana was delighted to think how embarrassed Camilla must be after being named on television.

Dimbleby's book, *The Prince of Wales: a biography*, would prove humiliating for Diana; in it, Prince Charles claimed that he had never been in love with his wife although during their second honeymoon on Eleuthera and at Balmoral during their first press interview this did not seem to be the case.

Charles shocked readers even more by blaming his parents for his miserable childhood, a statement that distressed his parents. This was probably a result of hours spent with the analyst Dr Alan McGlashan, as in analysis and therapy-speak, parents are usually blamed. Charles claimed he had been deprived of love as a child, as his mother was often away on long overseas tours and absent for three of his earliest birthdays. He described his father as harsh and bullying and claimed the Duke of Edinburgh had forced him into marrying Diana to give the country an heir which were strong words, but he did have a point.

A member of Diana's staff claimed that the Princess of Wales became so angry watching the television interview that she expressed the hope a vital male portion of Charles' anatomy would shrivel up. But she felt vindicated by her husband's admission of adultery and was keen to present her side of the story to the public.

Princess Diana knew she lacked the skills to present her narrative in book form so decided to make a series of videotapes telling her story with the aid of a speech therapist.

To limit the damage the Prince of Wales had inflicted on himself, Prime Minister John Major's office found it necessary to deny reports that the Prince and Princess of Wales were contemplating divorce. Prince Charles was hoping divorce would be possible but did not like to be the one to say so.

As a result of being cited as Charles' mistress, Camilla received an avalanche of hate mail, and her phone rang hot.

Her husband's younger brother Simon was critical of Charles: 'Prince Charles does not have our sympathy…You can't go back and blame your upbringing or your parents, particularly if you are a member of the royal family.'

After being publicly humiliated, Lieutenant Colonel Andrew Parker Bowles asked his wife for a divorce. He had intended to wait until their children left school. But he had had a long liaison with the divorced Mrs Rosemary Pitman, and now wished to marry her.

By joint agreement, Brigadier and Mrs Parker Bowles filed for divorce in December 1994 and sought a divorce on the grounds that they had been separated for three years. Unlike the Prince and Princess of Wales, the

Parker Bowles did not air their dirty linen in public. They maintained a friendly relationship and the welfare of their children was paramount to both of them.

A dignified statement released on 10 January 1995 by their solicitor announced,

> *The decision to seek an end to our marriage was taken jointly and is a private matter. As we have no expectation our privacy will be respected, we issue this statement in the hope that it will ensure that our family and friends are saved from harassment.*

Camilla in limbo and Charles in the spotlight

Hopes that media interest in the failing royal marriage and Prince Charles' relationship with Camilla would diminish ended after Ken Stronach – Prince Charles' valet for the past fifteen years – decided to sell his story to the highest bidder, which was Rupert Murdoch's scandal sheet the *News of the World.*

Stronach, never fond of Diana, was disillusioned that his employer seemed happy to talk to the media, which was contrary to the rules for royal household staff. He decided to sell his story for money but later panicked and tried to retract. It was too late. His eye-witness account of the breakdown of the royal marriage appeared under the lurid headline: 'Charles Bedded Camilla as Diana Slept Upstairs'.

His valet revealed that the Prince of Wales had moved out of the marital bedroom following the conception of Prince Harry, not after his birth, as sometimes stated. The headline to Stronach's story in the *News of the World* inferred that Diana was living at Highgrove House when Charles was sleeping with Camilla, which was untrue.

Wendy Berry, the housekeeper at Highgrove, stated categorically that Camilla was often at Highgrove House during the day when Diana was absent, but she did not spend the night there and did not attempt to run the house or interfere with Highgrove staff, as Mrs Simpson had done at Fort Belvedere.

The Queen consulted the Prime Minister and the Archbishop of Canterbury, who both urged Charles to renounce Camilla for the good of the monarchy. The Prince of Wales retorted that his relationship with Camilla was 'non-negotiable.'

After her divorce, Camilla kept her married name of Parker Bowles and remained living in Wiltshire, but Middlewick House had to be sold and the money from the sale shared between them. With her high status 'open' marriage shattered, Camilla was humiliated and left in limbo. At times Diana felt sorry for Camilla observing she had lost a great deal and gained nothing.

Camilla's father, the widowed Major Bruce Shand, requested a meeting with the Prince of Wales to ask Charles what he planned to do about the untenable situation in which he had placed his daughter by naming her on television. Prince Charles assured Major Shand that he would not abandon Camilla but later issued a statement promising, 'I will never remarry,' no doubt designed to placate the hierarchy of the Church of England.

With money from her divorce settlement, Camilla purchased Ray Mill House near the picturesque village of Laycock. It was within easy driving distance of Highgrove. The Georgian manor house with extensive grounds cost eight hundred and fifty thousand pounds. Camilla moved in with horses, dogs, children – and her father, though he would later go to live with Camilla's married sister.

Prince Charles had made no firm commitment to Camilla beyond stating on television she would always be his 'good friend'. Camilla suffered a heavy financial loss when two syndicates failed in which she had invested inherited money. Consequently, she was advised by those who had her best interests at heart that she should buy a large house on acreage which would prove expensive to run. This would mean that Charles, with his very large income from the Duchy of Cornwall, would need to give financial help to the woman whose reputation he had ruined. Friends claimed Charles had to be made to feel responsible for his mistress. He meanwhile had given all his investments and borrowed from a bank to pay the seventeen million pounds that Diana was asking as her divorce settlement, down from the original twenty-two million pounds. Diana had learned a lesson from her mother: in any divorce, do not be the one to leave the matrimonial home.

Once Charles started providing financial assistance, Camilla regarded her role as his mistress as a full-time job. She signalled that she was the new woman in Charles' life by stabling her favourite hunter at Highgrove that was to be looked after by the grooms there employed by Charles. A member of Charles' staff did her grocery shopping in a local supermarket, paid for by the prince and delivered to her at Ray Mill.

As the Prince of Wales, Charles could not be seen with his mistress in public, so he and Camilla resumed the same pattern as they had previously, spending time together at various stately homes belonging to close friends, where high walls ensured protection from prying eyes and the long-range lenses of the press.

CHAPTER NINE

Princess Diana alone at Kensington Palace

I'm going to cut a very different path from everyone else... I would hope my husband would go away with his lady... and leave me and the children to carry the Wales name until William ascends the throne. Princess Diana, 1992.

Stand by for a mood swing, boys! Diana to her Private Secretary Patrick Jephson aware her staff had been suffering from her volatile moods during the stormy period before her divorce.

While Charles was being consoled, cosseted and supported by Camilla at Clarence House, Diana was living alone at Kensington Palace. The Queen and Prince Philip were deeply shocked by what they saw as Diana's disloyalty in cooperating with Andrew Morton.

In an interview with the feuding couple, the Queen suggested 'a cooling-off period' of six months before making any decision about their future. Charles and Diana should remain living apart carefully before deciding to divorce, which would deeply affect their children.

A meeting of the Prince and Princess of Wales was convened by lawyers to discuss the terms of a legal separation. The meeting was a stormy one, with tears and angry recriminations from Diana.

Diana was not the only one having problems. For the Queen, 1992 was, she claimed, her *annus horribilis*. In March, the separation of Andrew and Fergie was announced, and in April, Princess Anne divorced Captain Mark Phillips amid rumours of an ex-nuptial child in New Zealand.

In June, *Diana, Her True Story* was published revealing Prince Charles' affair with Camilla Parker Bowles in great detail. On 24 August, publication of the transcript of 'Squidgygate', an illegally recorded conversation between Diana and her admirer James Gilbey appeared in *The Sun*. The article and long extracts from their conversation were headlined with a quote from Diana claiming, 'My Life is Torture'. *The Sun* was able to publish the transcript without legal problems as the transcript had already appeared in the *National Enquirer* in America. The bugged conversation between James Gilbey and Diana had taken place two years earlier when Diana was staying with her in-laws at Sandringham on New Year's Eve, fourteen days after the Prince of Wales had his sexually revealing conversation with Camilla, known as Camillagate.

Gilbey always denied he was in a romance with Diana but called Diana 'darling' more than fifty times in their phone conversation. He assured her frequently that he loved her and added reassuringly that she could not get pregnant by him as he had taken precautions.

Prince Philip was enraged by a recorded phone conversation from Sandringham House. In it, Diana had called her in-laws 'this fucking family' claiming they were ungrateful for everything she had done to raise their popularity. He demanded a meeting with his son and daughter-in-law and vented his rage on a sullen Diana. Charles remained silent, as usual awed by his tall imposing father. Prince Philip, as hot-tempered as Diana, eventually realised he had gone too far.

Worried about his grandsons, he attempted to restore good relations. In a letter to Diana, he asked her how it was possible that Charles could forsake her for Camilla, who was older and not nearly as good looking. He implored his daughter-in-law to 'patch things up' for the good of their children and the future of the House of Windsor.[67]

At the insistence of the Queen, the feuding Prince and Princess of Wales made a joint visit to Korea in November 1992, presented by royal spin doctors as a 'togetherness tour' but which only served to highlight their estrangement.

The Prince and Princess of Wales hated being together. They travelled in separate areas of the plane, each of them had their own suite on separate floors of the same hotel and only ate together when journalists were present. At times they looked so miserable a journalist as a joke called them 'The Glums' – a very miserable couple made famous by a popular BBC radio show.

Their brief tour of India was not a success in promoting the desired image of a happy couple. Before departing, Diana told Ken Wharfe, her protection officer, she would no longer 'pander to Prince Charles' every wish' on this Indian tour and added, 'Why the hell should I?'[68]

Prince Charles, on an earlier visit to India as a bachelor, sat in front of the Taj Mahal (a monument to married love, built by Indian potentate to his dead wife) and promised the media that one day he would return with a wife that he loved.

Now with his arranged marriage failing and remembering that promise with some embarrassment, Prince Charles had no wish to revisit the Taj Mahal with his wife. Tactfully, he announced he had had to attend a meeting of business leaders in Bangalore over 1,000 miles from the Taj

---

67 Tina Brown records this in *The Diana Chronicles*, pp338–346, drawing on sources from British and American newspapers and personal interviews. A doctor who treated Diana who was a colleague of my late husband discussed this with me but for professional reasons cannot be named here.

68 Ken Wharfe *Closely Guarded Secrets*, Michael O'Mara, London, 2002.

Mahal and was unable to reschedule it.

Diana proved how clever she had become at manipulating the media to her own advantage. She outsmarted her husband by visiting the Taj Mahal alone, sitting on the same bench that Charles had been photographed on and encouraging photographers to take photos of her looking sad and pensive.

When a journalist asked Diana what she thought of the tomb built by a mogul ruler as a tribute to his adored wife, Diana replied, with a catch in her throat, 'I feel it's a healing experience.'

Puzzled, the reporter asked the Princess to explain.

'Work it out for yourself!', Diana retorted.

Diana, with her skill at using visual symbols to make a statement, knew she had given journalists a golden opportunity to discuss problems in her marriage.

While she was doing this, the Buckingham Palace Press Office, headed by Dickie Arbiter, were claiming what a happy marriage the royal couple enjoyed. The Prince and Princess of Wales were to meet up in the ancient city of Jaipur, where Charles was to play in a polo match, and Diana was to award the prizes. Diana announced she was tired, had had quite enough of polo to last her a lifetime and had no intention of going to Jaipur.

The tactful Press Officer Dickie Arbiter and the director of the royal tour pleaded with Diana to go to Jaipur, explaining that if she did not show up, it would offend their Indian hosts. As Diana had a strong sense of duty, they managed to convince her to go to Jaipur to watch her husband playing polo, the game she resented her husband devoting his time to rather than spending it with her which had initially caused such friction in the marriage. During the match, Charles shot several goals, received his prize, a large silver cup, from his wife, turned his back and walked away. Then, realising he had omitted the standard kiss on the cheek for his wife, and photographers were waiting for it, he dutifully headed back and tried to kiss Diana on the cheek. At the last moment, Diana deliberately turned her head away, and the Prince of Wales was caught on camera, clumsily kissing his wife on her ear which made him look stupid, as Diana knew it would.

That evening, the Prince and Princess went their separate ways once more. Charles flew to Nepal, while Diana went to Calcutta to visit Mother Teresa.

The feuding couple were booked to return to Britain on the same plane but sat far apart in a reserved area out of sight of other passengers, preserving the illusion that they were happily married.

On 13 November 1992, a transcript of the 'Camillagate' tape was published by London's *Daily Mirror.* The sexual content damaged the reputations of both Charles and Camilla.

Again, acutely embarrassed, Charles sought refuge with his grandmother in Scotland. Meanwhile, everyone was talking about Prince Charles' sexual fantasies and the frankness with which they discussed their sex life as they had no idea they were being illegally recorded and what was a very private conversation would be broadcast worldwide.

The Prince of Wales talked wildly to close friends and family of leaving England and moving to Tuscany with Camilla or committing suicide. The fact Charles had mentioned suicide alarmed the Queen Mother aware the failure of this popular marriage was blamed on him and had made him depressed.[69] The Queen Mother remembered the suicide of Crown Prince Rudolf of Austria (heir to Emperor Franz Josef) and his mistress Mary Vetsera at the imperial hunting lodge at Mayerling and realised such a thing could happen again.[70]

One result of the furore was that Camilla and Charles could not risk meeting, and his only consolation was telephoning her. Her love and her sense of humour were what kept him from falling into the black hole of depression which Diana was experiencing.

The separation of Diana & Charles announced

The following month on 9 December 1992 as rumours circulated around Whitehall, Prime Minister John Major told the House of Commons: 'The Prince and Princess of Wales are separating.' He added reassuringly, 'Their Royal Highnesses have no plans to divorce. They will carry out separate public engagements but attend family occasions and national events together.' No further explanation was provided about the eleven years of a high-profile marriage designed to produce an heir which had failed so completely.

Under the circumstances, Diana refused to spend Christmas and New Year at Sandringham and stayed with her brother the new Earl and his wife at Althorp. Diana was angry that Charles had only sent her a token Christmas present as her spies told her he had given Camilla an expensive

---

69 The tragedy of Mayerling or double suicide is alleged to have been caused by the fact the dissolute Prince Rudolph had been diagnosed with syphilis. Before the discovery of antibiotics, syphilis was fatal and led to a horrible death.

70 This royal suicide is no longer seen as a love pact and it is reckoned Crown Prince Rudolf shot himself having had syphilis, at that time an incurable disease leading to a slow and painful death and his emotional young mistress had insisted on dying with him, so it was nothing at all like Prince Charles and Camilla's situation.

diamond necklace.

Prince William and Prince Harry spent Christmas with their father at Sandringham.

In a bid to keep the peace, Prince Philip wrote to Diana admitting that his son's behaviour with Mrs Parker Bowles was wrong and once again he expressed surprise that Charles could prefer Camilla to Diana. Prince Philip hoped Charles and Diana would remain married, live apart without acrimony and continue their royal duties. This was what Diana wanted, as she found the idea of divorce repugnant, fearing a divorce judge could deny her any access or limited custody of her beloved boys as had happened with her mother. She felt herself to be the victimised outsider, convinced that the royal family would try to limit her access to her sons.

Diana's emotions were in turmoil. Like most people involved in a separation or a divorce, there were times when she hated her husband and was glad their marriage was over and moments when she missed Charles, believed she still loved him and yearned for a happy family life with a husband and children.

But it was too late for a reconciliation. Camilla was in the middle of an amicable divorce from Andrew and firmly entrenched in Charles' life. He had quite enough of a beautiful but volatile wife who seemed to enjoy eclipsing him on their public appearances and would throw up her latest meal if upset. He wanted a relationship that was calm, stable and supportive, the kind of relationship he had with Camilla.

Prince Charles did not hate Diana and for many years would continue to worry about her. But having been talked into marrying her against his better judgement, he felt he had paid a high price for doing his duty as a Prince of Wales.

In the eyes of the public, he was completely to blame. But most people had no idea that Charles had loved Camilla long before he was urged to marry Diana, and regarded Camilla as a Jezebel who had broken up a devoted marriage. But the truth was somewhat different and more complex.

It was agreed the terms of the princely couple's separation were to be clarified in a legal document and sent to both parties. Diana was advised by her elderly financial advisor, Joseph Sanders, that he needed details of her income and expenditure to send to her husband's lawyers so an appropriate sum of money for her maintenance could be worked out.

As Joseph Sanders compiled a statement of Diana's finances, the accountant was worried to learn how little the Princess of Wales actually owned after almost a decade of marriage to the heir to the throne. The valuable jewels Diana wore at state banquets and first nights and her apartment at Kensington Palace were the property of the Crown.

All Princess Diana actually possessed were a few pieces of jewellery received as presents, a collection of designer clothes, her car and furniture from 60 Coleherne Court stored at Highgrove House which was now the home of Charles and Camilla.

Diana had no qualifications and few job skills, so Sanders felt avuncular about the now fatherless Princess and that he had to protect her interests.

Prince Charles had always been a generous provider. Diana's clothes and personal grooming amounted to over several thousand pounds each month, as spending large sums on designer clothes and a personal hairdresser and a masseuse had been considered necessary for her to fulfil her royal role.

Diana's only personal source of income came from her share of the lease of Spencer House in St James's Place, Piccadilly, to Lord Rothschild – an income shared with her siblings. Lord Rothschild had organised the funding for expensive renovations to this palatial house where Diana had never lived. Palatial Spencer House had been restored to its former glory and once again was a showpiece of Regency architecture and leased to the British Government who used it to entertain foreign prime ministers and presidents.[71]

When Diana's mother had bought the apartment at 60 Coleherne Court, she promised Diana that if she was still unmarried by the time she was twenty-one, she could take over the title deeds.

A few years earlier, convinced that her youngest daughter would not need the apartment anymore now she was married, Frances decided to sell Number 60 Coleherne Court to a Japanese investor for over a million pounds sterling – more than an eighty per cent profit on its original purchase price as the fact that Princess Diana had lived there as a single girl added a premium to the price.

Lawyers for the Crown wanted Diana to move to a smaller apartment in Kensington Palace. She refused, claiming her sons needed continuity in their lives and must remain in their familiar surroundings.

At times, Diana, like the proverbial bird in a gilded cage was admired by millions and feted at charity functions, film premieres and ballet first nights while spending her evenings alone. When not at charity functions or first nights, she sat alone on the sofa watching East Enders and other 'soapies' on television, eating her calorie-counted dinner from a tray.

Diana redecorated a few rooms in her apartment, and she hung framed cartoons of her husband in the guest lavatory. Showing her

---

71 At the time of writing it can be viewed in a small guided groups on selected Sundays see www.spencerhouse. on payment of a fee.

mischievous sense of humour, Diana carefully selected cartons to frame that emphasised Charles' large ears or showed him talking to his plants.

A removal truck arrived at Kensington Palace with instructions to take the matrimonial bed and other items belonging to Prince Charles to Highgrove. Charles also wanted a few water colours of his Hanoverian ancestors and some family silver.

Diana made certain that her Kensington Palace apartment was stripped of evidence that Charles had ever lived there. Meanwhile, at Highgrove, Charles ordered the staff to remove *anything* that reminded him of Diana. So, she and Lady Sarah drove there to collect the few pieces of furniture stored there from Coleherne Court.

At Kensington Palace, assorted therapists gave the Princess of Wales deep massage and heat treatment to ease her back pain, and Diana enjoyed visits from aromatherapists and spiritual healers, including an Irish nurse-turned-acupuncturist named Oonagh Shanley-Toffolo. Regarding her therapists as friends, Diana often paid them with unwanted gifts received when she spoke in public. This did not please all of them, some would have preferred cash, and so a few of them for high fees sold stories about Diana to the press which upset the Princess.

The astrologers came up with strange predictions. One assured Diana that Charles would never become king, another predicted he would die in a plane crash. A third predicted the prince's demise in a skiing accident. The astrologers, in whom Diana believed implicitly, claimed to be able to foretell the future. It was therefore unfortunate that none of them warned the Princess of Wales against entering a road tunnel in Paris in a black Mercedes with her seat belt unfastened.

Diana had never enjoyed formal entertaining and did not intend to start now. A butler employed by Prince Charles transferred his loyalties and went to work across the courtyard for Princess Margaret and was replaced by a footman from Buckingham Palace named Paul Burrell. Diana found him useful and called him 'Mr Fix It.'

The secretarial staff distrusted Burrell, alleging he listened at doors to private conversations and nicknamed him 'Mrs Danvers', after the creepy housekeeper who spied on the young second wife in *Rebecca*, Daphne de Maurier's most famous novel. Paul Burrell was genuinely concerned about his employer but was also gleaning every bit of information possible so he could write his own book about Diana to fund his retirement.

To stop the feeling of loneliness, Diana became a mobile phone junkie. Each evening when not watching television she would chat away happily for hours to favourite therapists or friends on one or other of her four cell phones.

Diana's personal hairdresser arrived at Kensington Palace every morning to blow-dry her hair, now blonde and cut very short, which enhanced the colour of those mesmerising blue eyes.

A manicurist came each week to deal with Diana's nails now that the days of her nervous nail-biting as a motherless child were over and varnished her nails a delicate shade of pale pink. Diana wore very little make-up, which she applied herself rather than use a make-up artist – unless she was having an important photo shoot.

Diana's well-run office in St James's Palace resembled an advertising agency, with large blow-up photos of herself on the walls. She joked that 'Brand Diana' was on display to those who discussed her promotions for the many charities she supported loyally and efficiently.

At times, Diana suffered from bouts of rage towards Camilla for her role in the breakdown of her marriage. Close friends tried to comfort the Princess by reminding her that Camilla was a heavy smoker. It was known that Prince Charles hated the smell of tobacco, so life at Highgrove would not all be rosy and Charles, known for being obsessively neat, would find it hard to live with a woman known to be extremely untidy.

At Kensington Palace, Diana's personal staff included Patrick Jephson, her Private Secretary, who dealt with requests for public appearances and other official tasks. She trusted Jephson enough to make him the executor of her will but would soon fall out with him. Anne Beckwith-Smith as Diana's lady-in-waiting dealt with Diana's personal affairs and accompanied her to functions when required, but neither Patrick or Anne lived on the premises. Diana had a female PA named Victoria Mendham who in an angry moment Diana fired leaving Mendham with hefty bills acquired in Diana's service. Charles always generous settled the bills for Miss Mendham feeling she had been badly treated by his wife.

During the day, Diana had the company of a band of constantly changing young media assistants, several of whom were fired by Diana who was planting favourable stories about herself in the media.

Diana also employed a part-time cook, as she still did not enjoy cooking, and a cleaning lady. But in the evenings, all her staff went home, and when the boys were away at Ludgrove Prep School or with their father, Diana was lonely and watched television with her dinner eaten in front of the set. At her insistence, William and Harry had been enrolled for Eton College, near Windsor, the school attended by Diana's brother, her father and many of the young men she had known in her Coleherne Court days.[72]

Diana loved it when her sons stayed with her during their holidays

---

72 For details see https://en.wikipedia.org/wiki/Eton_College.

and planned activities they would enjoy together. In the evenings, her beloved boys sat on the sofa beside her watching their favourite television programmes. She was sad she only had them for half their holidays, and they spent the rest with Prince Charles who, though he did not receive credit for this in the press, was a supportive father.

Diana, the celebrity princess, enjoyed flying to America for public appearances, meeting pop singers and Hollywood stars who supported the causes she did. Her close friend Lucia Flecha de Lima was living in Washington where her husband was the ambassador, and Diana enjoyed spending time there with Lucia.

What Diana disliked was the fact she was guarded and followed around the clock by protection officers from Scotland Yard's Royal Protection Squad. She believed they were being used by her enemies at Buckingham Palace to spy on her in case she took a lover. Should Prince Charles decide to divorce her, her protection officers would be made to supply evidence against her and she feared that a divorce judge would limit her access to her adored sons.

Diana feared her phones were bugged, as although relatively unknown, this practice was widespread. Journalists from the *News of the World* routinely bugged and hacked the cell phones of celebrities and sports stars.[73]

Diana twice insisted on having her rooms swept for bugs, but none were found. Prince Charles' staff unkindly mocked her suspicions and claimed it showed that the Princess of Wales was paranoid or mentally unbalanced.

Between 1992 and 1993, Diana made a second series of tapes – this time using a video camera. Their production was overseen by actor-turned-voice-coach Peter Settelen. On what Diana called her 'Secrets Tapes' (really videotapes) she admitted that, after the birth of Prince Harry, she had been desperate to have a baby girl, but Charles refused sex with her. She revealed she had gone to Harrods and bought sexy underwear to try and lure Charles back to her bed, but he had merely laughed at her and said she looked ridiculous.

At one point on the 'Secrets Videotapes', Diana added the accusation that the royal family had wanted to her to marry Charles in order to use her as a 'baby-factory'.[74]

---

[73] This practice went unnoticed until messages were hacked from the cell phone of a murdered schoolgirl named Milly Dowler and resulted in media magnate Rupert Murdoch closing down the *News of the World*, a newspaper whose journalists had hounded Diana.

[74] Valium, one of a group of drugs known as benzodiazepines, was discovered in the 1960s in America. The pharmaceutical company who developed and manufactured Valium complied

Mood swings, isolation & marriage problems

Professor Malcolm Lader, a colleague of Professor Sir Martin Roth and regarded as a world expert on benzodiazepine addiction, had written widely on the topic in the late 1980s and 1990s warning general practitioners and the public in a series of publications that although Valium was an excellent drug to ease anxiety and help patients sleep on a short-term basis, a patient taking Valium for more than a few months could become addicted and exposed to its harmful side effects such as severe mood swings, which have damaged or broken many marriages.

In Diana's case, Valium originally prescribed by psychiatrist Dr Michael Pare, helped her sleep but may have increased the frequency and severity of her mood swings[75]

In 1991, hospital records showed Diana suffering one of her panic attacks when placed inside a large drum for an MRI scan to investigate her persistent back pain. She asked to be given two Valium tablets, but it took several hours until the Princess was calm enough to be given the scan.

By 1992, Diana and Lady Fermoy were no longer on speaking terms. Diana could not forgive her grandmother for withholding the fact that Camilla and Prince Charles were lovers before encouraging her to hope she could marry Prince Charles. In revenge, Lady Fermoy told close friends including the Queen Mother that Diana had known this all along and was 'two-faced' and 'a consummate actress'. Diana's mother, married off at eighteen to a much older man, had never been enthusiastic about a royal marriage for Diana, warning her that the Windsors had a very different sense of humour to the Spencers and a very different lifestyle.

Frances had grown up at Park House on the Sandringham estate where her parents were close friends of George VI and his wife (now the Queen Mother). She knew the royal family enjoyed rugged outdoor sports in all weathers and a fondness for shooting game birds, fishing and deer stalking, and Diana did not enjoy them and thought shooting little birds

---

with regulations and tested their drug on animals prior to releasing it for human consumption. But animal testing did not reveal the side effects in humans. Subsequent studies showed the pleasurable effects of Valium caused dependency and addiction after as little as four weeks. Side effects vary from person to person, and have been recorded by Emeritus Professor Malcolm Lader of the University of London in 'Benzodiazepines revisited: will we ever learn?' *Addiction*, Volume 106, Issue 12, pages 2086–2109, December 2011.

75 Interview by the author of general practitioners Dr Gillian Cameron and Dr John de Vries (the latter a clinical teacher of general practitioners) in April-May 2014. They both stated they would not prescribe Valium for more than six weeks for these reasons. Confirmed by information on http://www.valiumaddictionhelp.com and http://www.dependency.net/learn/valium/

and deer stalking was cruel. It was ironic that in view of so much grief and agony over her absentee mother in childhood, Princess Diana would now become estranged from Frances Shand Kydd.

⁂

It was agreed that since Diana refused to agree to a divorce, a Deed of Separation would be drawn up by lawyers, outlining terms and conditions for a legal separation for the Prince and Princess of Wales. While this legal separation was being negotiated, and fearing she would be made to divorce, Diana wanted some advice from her mother who had gone through two divorces.

Deeply upset by the fact that Peter Shand Kydd had left her for an elegant and much younger French woman working for a champagne importer in London, and facing a second divorce, Frances neglected her health and ate poorly so that even a small amount of alcohol affected her.

Diana, who drank very little, was convinced that her mother was drinking too much as Frances lost her licence for driving over the legal limit, but friends on the Isle of Seil said she drank relatively little. Diana had a different opinion of the situation and claimed it was impossible to telephone her mother after six o'clock because she could not have a sensible discussion with her.

Diana had, it seemed, never told her siblings about her bulimia as she wanted them to see her as a success.

Once she felt William was mature enough to handle it, Diana took him to The Passage, a Catholic support centre for the homeless in Westminster, to see the grimmer aspects of life that royalty never normally encountered. Diana wanted her eldest son to see all sides of life, and this has helped make Prince William a well-rounded character.

She claimed that her sons – her 'love bugs' as she called them – were the love of her life.

After their separation when it was her turn to spend a weekend with their sons, Diana took 'her' beloved boys to movies, amusement parks and football matches. Remembering her motherless childhood, and how much she missed her mother's hugs and kisses, she hugged and kissed her boys constantly to show them she loved them.

Battling bulimia, the 'shameful friend'

Diana was urged by her former school friend Carolyn Pride, now Mrs Bartholomew who was worried about what was happening to Diana to seek treatment from a doctor who specialised in eating disorders. Fearing Diana could damage her health by constant vomiting, Carolyn threatened to tell the press about Diana's bulimia unless she sought treatment from Dr Lipsedge who specialised in treating eating disorders and saw patients at Guy's Hospital as well as at his rooms.

Dr Lipsedge had successfully treated Lady Sarah Spencer for anorexia a few years earlier, and initially, he saw the Princess of Wales at her home (so she would not be recognised by other patients) after her former school friend Carolyn Pride had threatened to tell the press about her bulimia.

Dr Lipsedge treated Diana with behavioural therapy and gave very practical advice like telling her to exercise more and take up jogging and put Diana on what was then a new anti-depressant called Prozac®.

One side effect of Prozac® is insomnia, so at that time it was often prescribed in conjunction with Valium® to combat sleeping problems, so Diana continued taking Valium®.

In addition to radically changing Diana's diet, he taught her to keep her weight down with exercise rather than self-induced vomiting and warned her against the crazy weight loss treatments of some therapists she had attempted without much success.

As a result, Diana became keen on visiting a gymnasium to control her weight and started work on improving her posture to address her lower back problems. Princess Diana had a long period free of bulimia thanks to Dr Lipsedge, but later relapsed and consulted Susi Orbach, the celebrated psychoanalyst and author of *Fat is a Feminist Issue*, who had managed to cure her own bulimia and treated others with her methods.

Diana attended treatment sessions at Susi Orbach's North London home and was doing well. But someone tipped off the media with the date and time of her next appointment, and when Diana next drove to Orbach's home, the paparazzi were waiting for her. They swarmed around her car, shoving lenses into Diana's face through the open window and insulting her with foul language, reducing her to tears. This was deliberately cruel. The paparazzi desperate for money knew a photo of Diana in tears fetched far more money than a photo in which she was smiling.

Clearly, it was impossible for the Princess of Wales to attend Susi Orbach's home clinic, and the well-known psychoanalyst was too busy to travel from Hampstead to Kensington Palace, so Diana ended her treatment with Orbach.

However, she stuck to the advice of Dr Lipsedge, and exercise became a necessary ritual and only when very stressed when staying with her royal in-laws at Sandringham and Balmoral would her bulimia briefly return, but at other times it was under control.

Hurtful allegations and broken friendships

Hoping to speak in public on topics that would benefit the charities of which she was a patron, from 1992 onwards Diana took coaching from an actor-turned-voice-coach named Peter Settelen. She paid him to work with her at Kensington Palace on breathing exercises and voice projection and produced what Diana called 'The Secrets Tapes'. These were videotapes on which Diana recorded details about her early life and her failed marriage, adding information withheld from the Andrew Morton tapes made by Dr Colthurst many years earlier. The Secrets Tapes were shown worldwide on the 20th anniversary of her death which inflamed public sentiment against Camilla and Charles.

Princess Diana became skilful at telling her own story with a few embellishments to make her look better. Prince Charles allowed Jonathan Dimbleby to tell his story which was not a great success from his point of view.

After a year of private voice coaching, at last Diana felt she had overcome her nerves and was able to speak with confidence in public, which had been impossible in the early years of her marriage. And so, after eleven years as the silent partner in their marriage, she became an excellent speaker on behalf of causes in which she believed. In April 1993, Diana was finally able to confront her demons and speak about eating disorders to an audience of doctors and nurses. Her knowledge of the topic astonished her listeners, most of whom had no idea that the Princess of Wales had suffered from bulimia, but Diana was still too ashamed of her 'secret disease' to admit she suffered from what she called a 'shameful friend'.

With her newly acquired speaking skills, Diana made an excellent speech on drug and alcohol abuse to assist a charity called Turning Point, citing the cases of drug abuse she had seen during her visits to the Catholic homelessness centre The Passage. Once again, Diana spoke from the heart, and her speech was applauded.

In June 1993, Diana again spoke out in public about women suffering from depression and becoming addicted to antidepressants. Conscious of her dependence on Valium, which may have contributed to her severe mood swings, she described the 'haze of loneliness and desperation that turns women into anxious zombies addicted to antidepressants, tranquilisers and sleeping pills'. She still did not mention that she was trying to break her own dependence on this addictive drug or her own struggles with bulimia.

She took advice from influential friends, upset by rumours she was mentally unstable (citing the findings of Sir James Batten, royal physician and Dr Michael Pare, who replaced Professor Sir Martin Roth as royal psychiatrist). It was hinted she had borderline personality disorder (now reclassified as emotional personality disorder) and should divorce on these grounds. There were suggestions that, like Anne of Cleves, divorced wife of Henry VIII, she should be sidelined and given a house far away from London, something Diana would have hated.

Diana's friends advised her that her best course of action was to make speeches about mental health and joke about her alleged madness, and for once, the headstrong Princess of Wales listened to sound advice.

Making a speech to doctors and nurses at a London teaching hospital, Diana used the potent weapon of ridicule. She told her audience they might have heard rumours that 'men in white coats were coming to take me away'. There was a sharp intake of breath, as her listeners were shocked by her words. Diana added one of her beautiful smiles as she explained she was sorry to disappoint those who had spread lies about her, but she was 'just fine'.

Many in the audience had read Andrew Morton's book detailing the misery of Diana's marriage and her husband's relationship with Camilla Parker Bowles, convinced she *had* been badly treated by the royal family. At the end of her speech, Diana received a standing ovation.

Diana was now under great stress. In November 1993, she showed enormous courage by visiting a troubled part of Northern Ireland to attend a Remembrance Day service at Enniskillen, a dangerous area where many British soldiers had been killed or maimed by IRA bombs or marksmen. Civilians suspected of being informers had been kidnapped and killed, and their bodies were never found.

Diana dared to enter the danger zone, aware it could make her a target for an IRA bullet or a bomb as she spoke about dealing racial and religious problems and did it superbly well.

The Princess of Wales wanted a refuge from the paparazzi who pursued her, and she hoped to find a quiet country retreat where, without the need for bodyguards, she and her sons could spend a holiday, and William and Harry could go shooting together – the sport they and their father enjoyed, and she disliked. She asked her brother (now the ninth Earl Spencer) if she could rent the Palladian style Gardener's House at Althorp. He initially agreed but then fearing an onslaught of paparazzi descending on him as the house lay near the boundary fence of Althorp, refused.

Bitterly hurt by her brother's decision, Diana refused to consider alternative accommodation on the family estate and stopped all communications with him.

After ten years of a turbulent marriage filled with rows and physical fights behind palace walls, Diana was no longer the shy, tongue-tied girl who had married her 'Prince Charming', hoping he would adore her and devote all his time to her. She failed to realise she had married a workaholic in love with the woman he should have been allowed to marry years before he met her.

Unlimited funds from Prince Charles to spend on clothes and beauty treatments meant Diana had acquired great elegance, and what one observer called 'the classical beauty of a Greek statue'. She had changed the image of royalty as well as becoming greatly loved for her informal approach to meeting the public.

Before Princess Diana, royal women like Queen Mary and the Queen Mother wore flowery hats and flowing dresses with long white gloves and drove around waving to a distant public.

Diana was different. She did walkabouts and chatted to people about their children and what they were watching on television, topics they could relate to. She wore well-tailored casual clothes that suited her tall, lean figure. She could look magnificent in a formal ball gown and a tiara or a plain white T-shirt under a linen blazer with well-cut designer jeans that showed off her long, slim legs. A shorter haircut and blonde highlights made Diana look 'cool' to young people, and she was admired for the down-to-earth way she comforted the sick. In short, she had her own very special magic, and the public adored her.

Opinion polls voted Princess Diana, the most popular member of the royal family, but this immense popularity rang alarm bells at Buckingham Palace. Diana had made powerful enemies among the 'Establishment' Old Guard, who feared she was leading royalty into a new era of celebrity they did not appreciate.

In her working life, Diana had always called Patrick Jephson 'my rock'. He wrote many of her speeches, and she leaned on him for support when criticised. Jephson provided her with wise advice, but to his annoyance as a headstrong young princess she often ignored wise advice and did the opposite.

As her relationship with Prince Charles became so difficult, they could hardly bear to be on the same platform but protocol meant outwardly they had to maintain the charade of a happy married couple.

Patrick Jephson was Diana's fourth Private Secretary, as she was not easy to work because of her mood swings and she also fired a female P.A.

She also broke off her relationship with her faithful long-term friend and confidante Dr James Colthurst, a brilliant young radiologist who had given up his time to act as her intermediary with Andrew Morton. He supported her emotionally for many years, often against the advice of his wife who felt Diana did not realise what a busy life her husband led when she asked him to do things for her or railed against Prince Charles to him.

In a friendly phone call, Dr Colthurst attempted to warn Diana that it might be wise if she did not visit Prince William so often on weekdays at Eton College to confide her problems to her son.

Dr Colthurst who had also attended Eton tried to explain gently to Diana that other parents did not behave like this and they limited visits to weekends. He feared Prince William could be teased about being 'a mother's boy' and was too young to be burdened by his mother's intimate confidences.[76]

Diana was furious at being told the truth. Enraged by his words, Diana forgot how much Dr Colthurst had done for her out of the kindness of his heart. And as her contact with Andrew Morton, her biographer, Dr Colthurst had spent a long time helping her record her first set of tapes and took them personally to Andrew Morton so her story could be told. He had written some of her speeches and been a wonderful friend and advisor in times of trouble. But Diana, headstrong as always, ignored all he had done for her, and refused to take his phone calls and did the same with school friends she accused of being disloyal. This behaviour was largely due to the fact the chemical balance of her mind was disturbed by the lack of essential vitamins and minerals caused by continual vomiting of her food in order to remain slim and elegant.

This was a sad period in Diana's life. Feeling lonely with Prince William and Prince Harry at school, her secret bulimic vomiting became worse. She felt a failure as a royal wife being unable to make her husband love her.

She was desperate enough to attempt to fill the void in her life by stealing someone else's husband, a handsome man with three children, doing her best to break up his marriage. Diana was not thinking clearly. Having an illicit love affair with a married man was grounds for Charles to divorce Diana for adultery, and it could be used against her in court to show she was not a good mother. In her role as princess, she was expected to set an example to the public, so a divorce for unavoidable breakdown of the marriage was preferable to one of adultery.

Charles also felt that divorce was a better solution for their boys than continual arguments over whose turn it was to have custody of their sons during the holidays. Diana often changed her mind at the last moment and would upset schedules made many months in advance.

---

76 For the full story see Tina Brown, *op. cit*.

CHAPTER TEN

Diana – sadness and a possible phantom pregnancy?

Never again will anybody accuse the Princess of Wales of being as thick as a plank. Brian Hoey, *People Magazine*, July 1996.

Diana's shrewd financial adviser, fearing she might be divorced, worried about her lack of financial resources. He estimated Prince Charles was worth at least two hundred million pounds in assets, and the annual revenue from his Duchy of Cornwall estates amounted to some ten million pounds. He felt Prince Charles should be asked to pay his wife serious money for maintenance or, if they divorced, should make Diana a substantial financial settlement worth many millions.

In contrast to the formidable wealth of Prince Charles, his younger brother Prince Andrew had only his relatively modest salary as a naval officer. Since Andrew and Fergie were big spenders they depended on additional funding from the Queen and always seemed to be in need of money.

During 1993, Fergie had to move out of 'South York', the luxurious Sunningdale mansion built with money from the Queen. Fergie, lacking funds, rented a relatively modest house while her divorce settlement was being negotiated.

At this juncture, Diana paid a visit to her sister-in-law and was horrified to learn that Fergie's debts amounted to millions and her proposed divorce settlement would be relatively small. Like Diana, Fergie had no savings but managed to put a brave face on her disgrace, claiming she would pay off her debts by writing books and working as a spokesperson for Weight Watchers.[77]

Diana's visit to Fergie had been a revelation. As the mother of a future king, Diana was determined not to be treated like the Duchess of York and to obtain a more favourable settlement whether for a separation or a divorce.

On the advice of Joseph Sanders, Diana engaged the legal firm of Mishcon de Reya to act for her in negotiations with Prince Charles' lawyers. Anthony Julius, Diana's canny young legal advisor, advised her to obtain a bank loan, warning that legal fees could reach a sizeable sum if

[77] The Duchess of York was reduced to resorting to 'cash for access schemes' targeting businessmen hoping to do business in the Arab World where Prince Andrew's official position gave him excellent contacts. She was taped by a journalist masquerading as a businessman asking him for thousands of pounds for an introduction to Prince Andrew.

negotiations were protracted.

Diana was summoned to Buckingham Palace to discuss the situation where Prince Philip now tried to bully her into doing what he wanted, warning her that should her lawyers raise difficulties he could have her title removed.

Prince Philip did not succeed in frightening Diana. Earl Spencer, her father had explained that the Spencers had been ennobled under the Tudors and were English through and thorough whereas some members of ancient families used to refer to Prince Philip as 'Phil the Greek' and Diana when angry with her father-in-law called him 'Stavros'.

'My title is a lot older than yours, Philip,' retorted the daughter of fifteen generations of Spencers. 'I had it before I married Charles. It can't be taken away.'

Prince Philip was referring to the 'Her Royal Highness' prefix, which ensured minor royals had to curtsey to Diana. Her spirited reply was a subtle dig at Prince Philip, whose mother, Princess Alice of Battenberg, was German. When she was angry with the Windsors, Diana would always refer to them as 'The Germans'. She was determined that William would become a very English king and disliked things about the Windsors she regarded as being German influenced.

Through lawyers, Prince Charles confirmed he was prepared to be very generous provided his wife agreed to a divorce rather than a legal separation. Diana was horrified by the word 'divorce', unable to forget the judge who had banned her mother making contact with her children. She had no intention of letting history repeat itself with her sons.

When Prince Charles attempted to discuss terms for a divorce settlement, Diana burst into tears and left the room, slamming the door behind her. In desperation, Prince Charles asked his tactful art dealer friend Oliver Hoare to act as mediator, hoping Hoare could persuade Diana that divorce was the best solution for both of them.

Oliver Hoare was what was once known in certain circles as a 'hunk' with a well-toned body, attractive features and brown eyes. Although not born to great wealth, he had attended Eton, studied at the Sorbonne and spent a long time in the Middle East, where he mingled with a wild crowd. After returning to Europe in 1976, he married Diane de Waldner, the attractive daughter of Baroness de Waldner from one of France's wealthiest 'old money' families. Eventually, he headed the Islamic Department of Christie's auctioneers in King Street, Mayfair. Money from Oliver Hoare's wife and David Sulzberger of the *New York Times* dynasty enabled him to set up a gallery in Eccleston Street, Belgravia specialising in rare Islamic antiquities.

Among Oliver Hoare's wealthy clients were Queen Noor of Jordan, the Sultan of Brunei, and Asil Nadir, an elderly Turkish textile tycoon who owned a London fashion house, textile factories in Turkey and mansions in both Istanbul and Mayfair. Oliver became friends with the textile magnate and his young wife, Ayesha Gul, a former beauty queen turned film star. As Ayesha's marriage to the elderly Nadir was unhappy, she and Oliver Hoare became lovers.

The Turkish tycoon sought and obtained a divorce just as his business empire was collapsing. Warned that the Fraud Squad were about to arrest him, Nadir fled to Cyprus. Ayesha had hoped Oliver Hoare would divorce his wife and marry her and was very angry to learn this would not be the case.

Diane de Waldner Hoare was a wealthy sophisticated Frenchwoman who had already seen off several female rivals hanging around her handsome husband and had no intention of losing him, and the couple adored their three children.[78]

Oliver Hoare was one of very few friends of Prince Charles' whom Diana liked. In order to convince Diana that divorce would be a better solution to their problems, Hoare lunched with the Princess of Wales on several occasions and did his best to charm her into accepting the idea.

Diana, lonely and hurt, was intrigued by the handsome art dealer and paid frequent visits to Hoare's Ahuan Gallery at 16 Eccleston Street, Belgravia, allegedly to borrow books about Islam, but in reality, to talk to the owner. One thing led to another, and they became lovers. Ken Wharfe, Diana's detective-bodyguard from Scotland Yard's Royal Protection Squad, admitted in his memoir *Closely Guarded Secrets* that he had helped the Princess smuggle Hoare into Kensington Palace in the boot of Diana's car. Diana hoped that Princess Margaret, whose windows overlooked the entrance to Diana's apartment, would not spot Oliver Hoare and report to Buckingham Palace that often Hoare stayed overnight, departing early the next morning.[79]

Wharfe cordially disliked Hoare, thinking him very selfish. On one occasion, Diana's protection officer was woken by the shrill sound of a

---

78 Diana's affair with Oliver Hoare appears in Sarah Bradford, *op. cit.*, pp 238–241 and Tina Brown *op. cit.*, 2007, pp 365–389. The first British mention of Diana being pregnant by Oliver Hoare was made by Rebecca English in the *Daily Mail* http://www.dailymail.co.uk/news/article-328819/Diana-secrets-abortion.html. Rebecca English had seen the full story in the American edition of Lady Colin Campbell's book *The Real Diana*, Arcadia Books, 2013 and spoke to Sanders' widow. According to Lady Colin Campbell, Diana agreed to let her write her biography and gave her several interviews but, realising she could not control what would be written, did not continue with the project, worried what Lady Colin Campbell might say. Oliver Hoare declined to be interviewed by Rebecca English or anyone else.

79 Ken Wharfe *op. cit.*

smoke alarm and found a semi-naked (presumably post-coital) Hoare smoking a cigar in the hall of Diana's apartment – Diana disliked cigar smoke.

Oliver Hoare seemed oblivious of the fact that the noise made by the smoke alarm was loud enough to have woken Princess Margaret and Diana's other neighbours, the Duke and Duchess of Kent. Fearing Diana's apartment was on fire they might have come to investigate.

Wharfe was alarmed by Hoare's increasing influence on Princess Diana and what he considered his reckless behaviour in jeopardising the reputation of the Princess of Wales during negotiations with Prince Charles.

In October 1993, after Hoare and Diana had been intimate for almost a year, Hoare moved out of his marital home in Tregunter Road to stay with a male friend in Pimlico for a few months, possibly at the request of his wife while he sorted himself out. Their trial separation encouraged Diana to think Oliver was serious about starting a new life with her. Diana was in love – eating properly and exercising every morning, glowing with happiness.

Princess Diana with her two sons on holiday in Austria in November 1993.
© Mirrorpix

At the start of the Christmas 1993 school holidays, Diana took Prince William and Prince Harry to Lech, a ski resort in Vorarlberg, Austria, where they skied together and took long sleigh rides. On one occasion, escaping from Wharfe's supervision, allegedly to meet Oliver Hoare, also on a skiing holiday at the resort, Diana recklessly jumped from a balcony into a deep snow drift, risking breaking a limb.

On her return to London, as a proof of her love, Diana gave Oliver Hoare her late father's solid gold cufflinks engraved with the Spencer Crest. She cherished the unrealistic idea that the two of them would start a new life together somewhere in Europe and start a second family.

Lady Colin Campbell in her book *The Real Diana* indicated that Diana refused to listen to Joseph Sanders when he warned her that Oliver Hoare was merely enjoying a mid-life fling. Although he talked about it and may even have believed it initially, Oliver would never actually leave his wife and the three children he loved. Lady Bowker, a worldly woman wishing to protect Diana, knew the Hoares because they and her late husband, Sir James Bowker, KCMG and a British Ambassador in Turkey, were interested in antiquities.

Oliver Hoare escorted Diana to a party given by Lady Bowker, and then the two women met up for a heart-to-heart since Lady Bowker had been like a surrogate grandmother to Diana when she was a child.

Diana confided to her that she was in love with Oliver Hoare, who was hoping to obtain a divorce and marry her, so she was happy to divorce Prince Charles. Lady Bowker, in her eighties, had a great deal of experience of the ways of the world and wondered how she could break it gently to Diana that Oliver Hoare was devoted to his wife and owed his very pleasant lifestyle and his gallery to her money. He might have had a brief affair with Diana and talked about leaving his very attractive wife and the three children he adored but would not actually do it. Diana was the one who would be hurt.

But Diana did not want to hear this and was convinced she had found her soul mate in Oliver Hoare and that he would divorce and marry her.

In August 1994, in return for the proverbial thirty pieces of silver, Hoare's chauffeur, Barry Hodge, revealed details about his employer's love affair with Princess Diana to the *News of the World*. Hodge alleged one of Hoare's Turkish business associates had loaned his employer a handsome waterfront villa overlooking the waters of the Bosporus so he and Diana could enjoy a romantic holiday safe from the lenses of the paparazzi.

According to the talkative Hodge, during his employer's two-year affair with Princess Diana, Oliver Hoare borrowed a luxury yacht and crew from a friend so they could cruise along the Turkish coast, a romantic holiday when Oliver had plenty of time to devote to Diana, which made her happy. They discussed buying a house together in Italy or Turkey and living there. Like the naïve Ayesha Gul Nadir, Diana also believed Oliver Hoare would leave his wealthy wife and children for her.

Barry Hodge related to the *News of the World* a fight between Oliver Hoare and Diana one evening during their four-year affair when he collected the Princess from Kensington Palace to take her to Chelsea restaurant in Chelsea for a quiet dinner with Hoare. His employer apologised to Diana that he would have to return home immediately after dinner as his wife was away and Olivia, his teenage daughter was ill, so he promised to spend the rest of the evening with her as Diane his wife was worried about Olivia.

This upset Diana, brought down to earth by the reminder that the man she hoped would leave his wife and marry her saw himself as having family responsibilities. Her rage, despair and misery ended in a heated argument. As the glass partition that separated the front from the rear of the limousine was closed, it was impossible for those in the front of the car to hear the exact words. But what was clear was that the Princess of Wales was furious her lover was following his wife's instructions, rather than thinking about *her*.

At the traffic lights linking Sloane Street with Sloane Square, the car slowed a halt at a red light. Princess Diana, tears streaming down her face, opened the rear door, jumped out among the traffic and fled into the night not seeming to care that people might recognise her.[80]

Scotland Yard protection officer Ken Wharfe recorded how he, Oliver Hoare and his chauffeur spent hours searching for Diana and found her sitting on a park bench near Kensington Palace, sobbing hysterically.

Lady Colin Campbell in *The Real Diana* suggested (without medical evidence) that Diana's hysterics were due to the fact that she was pregnant with Hoare's baby. The author claimed Anita, Joseph Sanders' widow, told her that Joseph Sanders had offered to provide an alibi for Diana while she had an abortion.[81] Sanders would tell the press that Diana was staying at his home for a few days, so he could summarise her financial situation for the lawyers who were drawing up the Deed of Separation.

In 2004, Lady Colin Campbell claimed that Diana was so distraught that she had to abort Oliver Hoare's baby. During her four-year affair with Hoare, Diana had often said she had always wanted a little girl but could

---

80 The story of Diana leaping out of Hoare's car in tears is in Ken Wharfe *op. cit.*, and related by Barry Hodge, Hoare's chauffeur, to a journalist from the *News of the World*, August 1994.

81 Lady Colin Campbell, *op. cit.*, only mentions Diana's pregnancy and abortion in the American edition of her book.

not bear her sons to know about the pregnancy. It is far more likely that the princess was suffering from what was merely a phantom pregnancy.

Rosa Monckton, a close friend of Diana in her final years, told the *Paget Inquiry* that Princess Diana was meticulous about taking the contraceptive pill every evening before she went to bed. Her subsequent lover, Dr Hasnat Khan, also confirmed that Diana took the pill every night in his written statement to the *Paget Inquiry,* countering the claim of Mohamed Al Fayed that Diana had been pregnant by Dodi at the time of her death.

Lady Elsa Bowker, loyal confidante and friend

Very telling in this context is the story Lady Bowker related that the day after Diana's hysterical outburst with Hoare, the Princess of Wales paid her a surprise visit. Lady Bowker had been shopping at Harrods and returned home to Number 3 Eaton Place to find a distraught Diana sitting on the stone steps sobbing hysterically.

Diana had both arms wrapped around her body and was rocking back and forth, a characteristic gesture of those in deep distress. Between sobs, she insisted, 'I'm destroyed, I'm destroyed.'

Once again as the Princess of Wales did not seem to care if passers-by recognised her, Lady Bowker helped the weeping young woman to her feet, ushered her inside and persuaded her to lie down. She sat beside Diana, holding her hand, while Diana sobbed inconsolably. It took more than an hour before Diana was calm enough to tell Lady Bowker about the break-up of her love affair with Oliver Hoare.[82] This depth of grief does suggest it could have been caused by a phantom pregnancy.

Lady Bowker, worried that the distraught princess might try to harm herself, accompanied her in a taxi and saw her installed in her apartment in Kensington Palace.

Hoare's chauffeur, Hodge, continued to reveal snippets of information to the *News of the World.*

On Sunday 21 August 1994, in an article headed 'Princess Di's Cranky Calls to Married Tycoon', the paper claimed that Diana had phoned the Hoare residence as often as twenty times a day over a long period – a total

---

82 When discussing this incident with me, Lady Bowker was careful not to confirm whether or not Diana had been pregnant. Under British law to procure an abortion two registered doctors each have to sign a form confirming the mental or physical health of the pregnant woman would be harmed by having a child. There is no evidence from doctors' records to support Lady Colin Campbell's theory, but this would of course be a closely guarded secret in any medical practice.

of more than 300 calls. Barry Hodge told the *News of the World* that his employer had hidden from Diana's frantic telephone calls in his 'quiet room', where the art dealer retreated to study sale catalogues or antiquities he had purchased before placing them in his gallery.

If Oliver Hoare's wife Diane picked up the phone and said her husband was unavailable, she received a torrent of abuse from a female voice she recognised as that of the Princess. Often, she heard the sound of sobbing before the phone went dead.

Unwilling to expose the story of her husband's infidelity with Princess Diana, Mrs Hoare made an official complaint to the Metropolitan Police. She concocted a tactful story, telling them her husband had been threatened by Muslim terrorists who had made more than 300 'heavy breather' calls to their residence.

Biographer Sally Bedell Smith in *Diana, In Search of Herself,* claimed Oliver Hoare had become alarmed and tried without success to stop his wife from reporting Diana's 'nuisance calls' to the police[83]

The *News of the World* confirmed that police had placed a trace on the Hoares' phone. Additional calls had been traced to offices rented by the Princess of Wales at Kensington Palace and from one of Diana's four cell phones.

Lady Colin Campbell claimed Diana always called the Hoare residence from public phone boxes wearing gloves so the police could not identify her from fingerprints.

To counteract Barry Hodge's damaging comments that she was 'a phone pest' (Diana was making nuisance calls to Camilla also threatening she had sent men to kill her) Diana gave a story to handsome young journalist Richard Kay hoping he would defend her reputation.

In an article in the *Daily Mail* titled 'What Have I Done to Deserve This?', Richard Kay claimed that the Metropolitan Police had learned Oliver Hoare had been receiving nuisance calls from a boy at his son's school, so would not be prosecuting.

Diana must have hoped this would be the end of the matter. But worse was to come.

In the first week of September 1994, journalists and photographers surrounded the Hoares' mansion in Tregunter Road after learning that the Princess of Wales had defied a request from the Diplomatic Protection Department of the Metropolitan Police that she cease contacting the residence of Mr and Mrs Hoare.

Diana had been so upset that she chose to ignore police warnings and

---

83 Sally Bedell Smith *op. cit.*

made more nuisance calls from phone boxes but, due to her royal status, she was never charged by the police.

The truth died with Oliver Hoare in 2018. He had managed to remain silent during the furore over Diana's hundreds of desperate phone calls to his marital home. The staggering number of her tearful phone calls lend credence to what Lady Bowker hinted, namely that the Princess was pregnant or suffering a phantom pregnancy, as Diana realised her lover would never leave his wife. She must have worried about the effect on her beloved boys, still far too young to deal with the situation. Fearing the outcome of her own divorce and that Ken Wharfe's weekly reports to Scotland Yard contained evidence Hoare had often spent the night with her at Kensington Palace which could be used against her, things became fraught. Eventually Wharfe resigned and unfairly Diana became known as 'a phone-pest' by her enemies.

Diana unwisely decided to dispense with the trained protection officers supplied by Scotland Yard when the Queen removed her HRH status. Diana said she was tired of being followed around and wanted privacy. As a result, detectives provided by the Royal Protection Force of Scotland Yard were removed unless Prince William and Prince Harry were staying with their mother at Kensington Palace.

In February 1995, Richard Kay published Diana's version of the story writing 'Diana views Hoare as a pretty spineless creature since his failure to help her over the nuisance calls business...He is more besotted with her than she is with him,' which of course saved face for Diana, as she did not want to have the fact she had been deceived made public.

Oliver Hoare remained with his wife and refused offers from various newspapers to tell his story. Lady Bowker later told me he had returned Diana's gift of her father's solid gold cufflinks to Lady Bowker's home from where they were collected by Diana's butler, Paul Burrell.

For Diana, the return of a gift was loaded with emotional significance – allegedly her most precious possession – and signalled the end of an affair which had spun out of control and caused her enormous grief. (Earl Spencer's crested gold cufflinks subsequently made another appearance as Diana would eventually present them to her final lover, Dodi Fayed.)

Diana was now under more stress as she had heard rumours that James Hewitt was attempting to sell love letters she had sent him during their five-year affair. Legally, the letters were Diana's copyright and, fearing legal action, no newspaper editor would buy them. Diana heard rumours that Hewitt, in debt after making unwise business investments once he left the army, was telling his story to a journalist who planned a 'kiss-and-tell' account of their affair. Hewitt's story, related to journalist Anna Pasternak, appeared in 1994 under the title *Princess in Love*.[84]

In an interesting twist to this tale, the *Treason Act* of 1351 was still in force under which any man who had sex with the wife of the heir to the throne could be beheaded. It seems unlikely James Hewitt believed he could be prosecuted for treason when he retained the services of the well-known Australian barrister Geoffrey Robertson. Hewitt believed Diana's accusations that Barry Mannakee, her detective-cum-bodyguard, had been murdered by the British Secret Service[85]

Accused of being a 'love rat' and fearing MI6 might be after him, Hewitt hid in the attic of his barrister's London home, according to Geoffrey Robertson's wife, author Kathy Lette.

When short of money, Hewitt hinted he was the father of Prince Harry, conveniently forgetting he had not met Diana until several years after Harry's birth. (In 2017 after a heart attack and possibly a DNA test, he admitted he was not Harry's father.)

Criticism from Lady Fermoy

After reading Andrew Morton's book, Lady Fermoy wrote to Diana expressing her disapproval of the way she had cast doubts on Prince Charles' ability to rule. Lady Fermoy confided to Robert Runcie, Archbishop of Canterbury, who had married Diana and Charles, that her youngest granddaughter was 'an actress and a schemer'.[86]

As a result of these and other unpleasant comments, Diana had a bitter argument with Lady Fermoy. She ordered a staff member to show her grandmother out of her Kensington Palace apartment and vowed never to speak to her again.

It showed the forgiving side of Diana's nature that when she learned her grandmother did not have long to live and aware that Lady Fermoy's only son, Lord Edmund Burke Roche (her uncle who had sworn on oath to Prince Philip she was a virgin) had committed suicide, Diana showed compassion and visited her grandmother at her Eaton Square home before

---

84 Allegedly, Hewitt earned £300,000 from shared royalties under an agreement with Pasternak who, before committing write the book, wisely insisted on seeing the original love letters as proof that Hewitt's story was true.

85 Diana admitted her love for Barry Mannakee on the Peter Settelen videotapes, recorded between September 1992 and 1993.

86 Sally Bedell Smith, *op. cit.* p140, claims Diana's mood swings and rages were caused by Borderline Personality Disorder, with no evidence from psychiatrists and ignoring the fact that medical literature contains sad cases of thousands of women who have experienced severe mood swings from Valium dependency who, like Diana, were prescribed the addictive drug by doctors.

Lady Fermoy's death in July 1993, but her daughter, Frances, refused to do this.

On 15 July 1993, Diana, her siblings and Prince Charles attended Lady Fermoy's funeral at St Margaret's Church, King's Lynn where Lord Maurice Fermoy was buried. Diana forgave her grandmother for the wrongs she had done her but could not forgive the Queen Mother for keeping quiet about the relationship between Charles and Camilla when working hard to arrange Diana's marriage.

In an angry letter to the Queen Mother which has since disappeared (burned probably by Princess Margaret, along with other correspondence to her mother), Diana expressed rage that she had been lured into the marriage by the royal family so they could have an heir.

In her 'Secrets Tapes', Diana said that she hoped to leave England where she had been so unhappy. Lonely, miserable and angry with Camilla, Diana hoped to find another husband and have more children. She wanted to find a bachelor wealthy enough to own a jet aircraft so she could return to England at short notice from wherever she was living to see her beloved boys. She also wanted to find a place where she and her sons would be secure when they went on holiday together.

In search of a replacement husband, Diana had dinner dates in America with various wealthy single men who included the charismatic multi-millionaire Theodore (Teddy) Forstmann. He owned several planes and was a mature man who now needed a wife to travel with him and entertain for him. On a visit to England, Forstmann took Diana to dine at a romantic venue, the Complete Angler restaurant at Marlow, which has views over the Thames.

Having forgotten his reading glasses, Forstmann held the menu at arm's length, close to a lighted candle in the centre of the table. Dazzled by her beauty, he asked Diana why she kept looking at him so intently. Diana showed her sense of humour as she burst out laughing and said she feared he was about to set the restaurant alight.

Forstmann was attracted by Diana's beauty and her quick wit. But what he needed was a 'trophy wife' who would drop everything to travel with him at a moment's notice, rather than a celebrity princess. However, he admired Diana and for several years paid a London florist to make a daily delivery of flowers to her. Teddy Forstmann was a friend to whom Diana was able to confide her troubles, but their friendship never developed into anything more.

Realising that most men did not want the baggage that came with her, Diana exclaimed, 'Who would want me? I'm too much fuss.'

In December 1993, Diana decided to make changes to her life, announcing she was giving up the patronage of a hundred of her charities but would remain the official patron of several hospitals, the National AIDS Trust and the Centrepoint Aid to the Homeless. Having yearned for years to become a ballet dancer, Diana also remained as patron of the English National Ballet and gained immense pleasure from attending their performances.

The announcement that the Princess of Wales was retiring from public life increased the amount newspaper editors would pay photographers for good close-ups of Diana. Having lost her HRH title and having dispensed with the Royal Protection Service's bodyguards, Diana found herself hassled by the paparazzi.

As Diana had cut down her public appearances, there were less photo opportunities and, as a result, the price editors paid for good photos of Diana soared, and magazines like *Hello, Stern, Paris Match* had doubled and even tripled the rate they paid freelance photographers for good quality close-ups of her. Diana, whose photographs adorned more magazine covers than any other woman in the world, was seen as a cash cow by the paparazzi, who waited outside the gates of Kensington Palace for her to appear.

Following the advice from Dr Maurice Lipsedge on how to remain slim, she took regular early morning workouts at the exclusive Chelsea Harbour Health Club, walking there from Kensington Palace wearing a brightly coloured T-shirt, shorts and a baseball cap, which attracted photographers. Diana knew that a photo of herself in shorts was likely to push her husband off the front page, so she would ensure her lip gloss and mascara were perfect before she set off.

The paparazzi wondered who the Princess of Wales was meeting at the Chelsea Harbour Health Club. Why not do workouts in the privacy of Kensington Palace? The Rat Pack, as her pursuers were christened, soon discovered that Will Carling, the good-looking captain of the English football team, was a member of the Chelsea Harbour Health Club and after his early morning workouts would meet Diana at the café attached to the gym for morning coffee. Alerted to this, the 'Rat Pack' soon discovered the couple had secret love trysts in a private hotel in Cadogan Gardens near Sloane Square, where Carling booked a room and Diana entered the hotel through the staff entrance.

Diana seemed to enjoy courting danger, aware her own marriage was past saving. This clandestine relationship continued even after Carling married his fiancée TV presenter Julia Smith. Questioned by the press, the captain of the English rugger team continued to deny there was anything more than friendship between him and Diana but unwisely he boasted about his amorous success with Princess Diana to fellow rugger players in a locker room gossip session.

In July 1995, *Today* magazine ran an article headlined 'Is Will Carling Another Trophy for a Bored, Manipulative, Selfish Princess of Wales?'[87]

A month later, well-known columnist Nigel Dempster wrote an article about Diana's married lovers titled 'Diana, Mistress of Manipulation, the Mental Anguish behind the Fall of Diana the Saint.'[88] After reading the article, Will Carling's wife, Julia, a TV presenter of a women's programme, called a press conference and told the assembled journalists: 'Princess Diana will have a fight on her hands over her association with my husband' which sparked a fresh round of interest.

On 29 September 1995, *The Independent* ran a story that Julia Carling and her husband were living apart as their 'marriage was in difficulties and they needed time to consider their position'. To a *Daily Mirror* journalist, Julia Carling added, 'Of course this has happened before,' mentioning Diana's affair with Oliver Hoare. Later that month, Julia Carling announced she was suing for divorce citing the Princess of Wales as the cause of her marriage breakdown.

A tearful Diana denied this was true, terrified that it would be used against her in her divorce and that she might lose custody of her sons. Several of Diana's school friends who had dared to criticise her friendship with Carling were deemed disloyal, and she never spoke to them again, changing the number of the cell phone on which they called her.

The monarchy suffers, and Diana seeks revenge

With Julia and Will Carling's divorce hot news among sports fans, Diana visited Argentina at the request of the Argentinean Association for the Prevention of Infantile Paralysis. Buenos Aires newspapers ran articles and photos about Diana's visit, and she requested an English translation for her album of press clippings. She was horrified to read articles headlined 'Mission of Charity for the Adulterous Princess Diana', and 'Wives, look after your husbands! Diana the Seductress has arrived.'[89]

Back in London, the tabloids turned on Diana, whose image they had helped to create, pointing out she had spent nearly £2 million on clothes since marrying Prince Charles. They ignored the fact that Diana's patronage of British designers had made millions for the British fashion industry.

---

87 *Today* magazine, 8 July 1995.

88 Nigel Dempster, 'Diana, Mistress of Manipulation, the Mental Anguish behind the Fall of Diana the Saint', *Mail on Sunday*, 20 August 1995.

89 These articles, translated into English, appeared in *The Guardian* of 24 November 1994.

Without any proper evidence, a staff journalist on the *Sunday Mail* suggested that Princess Diana was suffering from a psychiatric syndrome known as Borderline Personality Disorder, a disturbed mental state that borders on schizophrenia. No general practitioner or medical specialist who actually saw Diana professionally endorsed these rumours. They were started by a few members of the Highgrove set and royal aides keen to curry favour with Prince Charles. In fact, Prince Charles was angry about the rumours, and fearing the effect on their young sons, warned Jonathan Dimbleby to remove any references to his wife having 'Borderline Personality Disorder' in Dimbleby's forthcoming biography.

The fact that Diana was not mad was confirmed by loyal friends and after her death was confirmed by medically qualified Dr Hasnat Khan, who had been her lover.

Gossip and innuendo about Diana's dangerous liaisons with Hewitt, Hoare and Carling, and a rumour she had enjoyed a brief affair with King Juan Carlos of Spain, made Diana keen to let the public know her side of the story and to revenge herself on Camilla, who she referred to as the 'Rottweiler who hung onto Prince Charles', the woman who had destroyed her hopes of a happy marriage.

Tiggy & Diana in a stand-off

Towards the end of 1995, several staff at Buckingham Palace were involved in a scheme to promote an amorous relationship between young Alexandra 'Tiggy' Legge-Bourke and Prince Charles, aware talk about Charles and Camilla was harming the monarchy.

Tiggy Legge-Bourke was the attractive daughter of a friend of the Queen, employed by the Prince of Wales to act as a combination of big sister and companion to Prince Harry and Prince William when they were spending time with their father. Tiggy had known Charles since she was a child and Prince William, aged eleven, and Harry, nearly nine, were devoted to her.[90]

After leaving Heathfield with four 'O' levels, Tiggy was sent to the language coaching and finishing school in Switzerland that Diana had hated. Unlike Diana, Tiggy made a success of her time there and, after completing her training as a Montessori teacher, ran her own kindergarten. She named it Mrs Tiggy-Winkle's after Beatrix Potter's famous character, and so acquired the nickname Tiggy.

90 Tiggy Legge-Bourke was born on 1 April 1965, raised at Glanusk Park, her mother's enormous estate in Wales, and educated at Heathfield School, Ascot.

She soon became aware that life in the conflicted royal household was not easy and had no ambitions to make a royal marriage. Her mother, the Hon Shan Legge-Bourke, had inherited a fortune from a very wealthy ancestor, Sir Joseph Bailey, who owned and ran a highly successful Welsh iron foundry.

Tiggy had enjoyed a happy childhood and her sense of fun and stability made life enjoyable for the young princes. Like Diana, Tiggy had been a plump teenager, but she slimmed down dramatically after the onset of celiac disease, which went undetected for a long time. The fact that the young princes loved Tiggy and saw her as a combination of surrogate mother and big sister encouraged courtiers to hope Prince Charles would fall in love with this lovely unspoiled girl and get rid of Mrs Parker Bowles. Tiggy did nothing to encourage this campaign but made William and Harry feel happy and secure.

Diana became jealous of Tiggy, fearing that she was being displaced in her sons' affections, and tried to limit the time that Tiggy spent with her boys and was upset when *The Guardian* quoted Tiggy claiming that Diana took her sons to cinemas and gave them popcorn which was bad for their teeth.

Camilla disliked Tiggy, aware she was younger and prettier and referred to her disparagingly as 'the hired help'. This was ironic since Tiggy was a family friend of the Windsors, while Camilla was at that time banned from royal residences. The only thing on which Diana and Camilla agreed was that Tiggy had to go – as soon as possible.

The thirteen-year-old Prince William, aware of the animosity between his parents, invited Tiggy to attend the Fourth of June celebrations at Eton as his guest which upset Diana who had not been invited.

The Fourth of June is traditionally a holiday when Etonians celebrate the birthday of King George III, a keen supporter of the school. Boys and their relatives and guests picnic in the grounds and watch a procession of boats on the Thames. Like many children with parents who are separated or divorcing, Prince William was worried his parents might argue if he invited both of them. Aware he could not invite one parent without upsetting the other, he settled matters by inviting Tiggy as his only guest. Diana was furious and planned revenge on Tiggy.

Diana and Charles both had offices in St James's Palace. Diana had spies in the enemies' camp so was aware that Tiggy had taken a great deal of time off work that summer, and believed it was because she was pregnant by Prince Charles and had aborted the baby. Diana knew that when she had custody of Harry and William, Tiggy helped out in Prince Charles' office.

Diana confronted Tiggy at the annual Christmas staff party Prince

Charles held at St James's Palace. She approached Tiggy saying with feigned sympathy, 'What a pity, you had so much time off for the baby,'. These words were designed to hurt Tiggy as well as make Camilla jealous. Tiggy, upset by Diana's insinuation she had aborted a child, left the party in tears. She rang her mother, who rang her lawyer Peter Carter Ruck.

Carter Ruck circulated a letter to the media claiming 'malicious lies' were being promoted about his client, Miss Alexandra Legge-Bourke, linking her to Prince Charles and she intended to sue unless she received an apology. Diana's lawyers had no option but to send the required apology.

Camilla was devastated when she did not receive an invitation to Charles' birthday party, allegedly organised by Prince William and Prince Harry, although the actual organising was done by Tiggy who later claimed she had done this at the request of William and Harry who did not want Camilla to be invited.

Tiggy worked for a few more years with 'her boys' as she called the young princes, before becoming engaged to Etonian Charles Pettifer, a boyfriend since she was at boarding school at Ascot. Prince William and Prince Harry attended Tiggy's wedding and have remained close friends up to the present.[91]

'There were three of us in this marriage'

Late in 1995, Diana became involved in talks with an ambitious young television journalist named Martin Bashir, a London-born Pakistani working for the BBC-TV programme *Panorama*. Bashir was keen to make a name for himself by interviewing a major celebrity. He met Diana after holding discussions with her brother about making a TV documentary about Althorp.

Martin Bashir asked Diana if he could interview her and she was keen to appear on his programme as she distrusted the forces of the Establishment and wanted to inform the public she feared her phones were being tapped. Bashir promised to have BBC technicians sweep the Princess of Wales' apartment at Kensington Palace for bugs if Diana agreed to let him interview her there.

---

91 Tiggy's husband, Charles Pettifer, was a former Coldstream Guards officer with two children from a previous marriage. He married Tiggy in the family chapel on her estate in Wales. They now run a bed-and-breakfast called 'The Tiggy Experience' for couples with children. Tiggy has two boys and attended Charles and Camilla's wedding. Prince Harry is godfather to her eldest son and Tiggy's second son, Tom Pettifer, was a page at the wedding of Prince William and Kate Middleton.

Influential friends within the media, Lord Peter Palumbo and Clive James, warned Diana against doing this interview as Bashir would ask embarrassing questions about her private life.

In fact, that was just what Diana wanted, so she did what she always did to those who advised her – smiled sweetly, agreed with them and did the opposite. She had previously refused a request from David Frost to interview her for American and British television.

Frost told me at one of his parties he had entertained Diana to lunch at his home and was disappointed she was to be interviewed by the then relatively unknown Martin Bashir. Frost reckoned Bashir had played on Diana's fears her Kensington Palace apartment was bugged, sent a BBC team to remove any bugs and said he would try to obtain a contract to write a book about her.

Kensington Palace was Crown property, so for security reasons Diana had to advise Buckingham Palace that she was admitting Bashir's television crew to her apartment. Diana ignored this rule, afraid Buckingham Palace would forbid her to make this interview or warn ABC chief Sir Marmaduke Hussey, husband of Lady Susan Hussey, the Queen's lady-in-waiting. Diana enjoyed outwitting Buckingham Palace and was determined to make life difficult for the husband she saw as betraying her.

So, Sir Marmaduke Hussey, Chairman of the BBC was not told that Diana was to be interviewed on the prestigious *Panorama* programme by Martin Bashir. Worried by Prince Charles' evident depression, Lady Susan Hussey had begged Camilla to renew contact with him again. Had Sir Marmaduke known about the Martin Bashir's interview with Princess Diana, it was likely to have been cancelled or heavily edited, with Bashir's questions vetted in advance but this was not the case.

Bashir's interview with Diana was watched with mounting anger by Charles and Camilla at Clarence House and by the Queen and Prince Philip at Buckingham Palace. They were amazed by the pent-up anger Diana revealed when talking about her husband and their marriage.

Before going on air, Diana surprised the BBC make-up girl by insisting on doing her own make-up and applying *kohl*, rather than eyeliner, around her eyes. Unfortunately, *kohl*, a cosmetic invented by the ancient Egyptians, melted under the heat of the television lights and smudged badly. So Diana had tears in her eyes and 'panda eyes' when she claimed, 'I desperately loved my husband and wanted us to share everything together and thought we were a very good team … I found myself more and more involved with people who were rejected by society – drug addicts, alcoholics and found an affinity there… I used to sit on people's beds and hold their hands. People were shocked as they had not seen royalty behave like this before but for me it was natural.'

Diana described how, after learning that her first child was a boy, she felt an enormous sense of relief, aware it was her duty to produce an heir for the House of Windsor.

On her 'Secrets Tapes' made shortly before her death, Diana claimed the reason she was angry with the Queen and Prince Philip was that they had regarded her as a 'baby-factory' but had refrained from making this comment to Martin Bashir.

The wily Bashir had managed to lull the tearful princess into a false sense of security so that she admitted she had been distraught to learn her husband was having an affair with another woman, but Diana refrained from naming Camilla.

During the interview with him, Diana admitted to her affair with James Hewitt, to forestall adverse publicity from his kiss-and-tell book. She looked sad and claimed 'Yes, I was in love with him [Hewitt] I adored him, but I was very let down.' She did not admit she had ended the affair – she wanted viewers to feel sorry for her, as they did.

Viewers knew from Andrew Morton's book that Diana suffered from bulimic vomiting. Now they heard her admitting to cutting her arms and legs with a penknife to ease her inner pain, a practice common among disturbed schoolgirls today but not widely known in the early 1990s.

Bashir glossed over this unattractive picture before asking the question he knew would rivet attention and make him well-known.

'According to the biography by Jonathan Dimbleby, it says that around 1986 your husband renewed his relationship with Mrs Camilla Parker Bowles. Were you aware of this? What was your response?'

Diana told Bashir that discovering her husband did not love her made her feel 'useless and hopeless and as though I had failed'. She added that some of her husband's friends had claimed she was 'unstable and should be put in a home of some sort' as they must have had access to the opinions of royal physicians and Sir Martin Roth's replacement, Dr Michael Pare via some other doctor, as Sir Martin would never have revealed royal secrets.

When Bashir asked the Princess of Wales whether Mrs Parker Bowles was responsible for the failure of her marriage, Diana replied with a witty one-liner that she had rehearsed with her friend the American comedian Ruby Wax: 'There were three of us in this marriage, so it was a bit crowded.'

Bashir then asked Diana what she felt about her husband and his role as the future king of Great Britain.

Diana would have been wise to have refused to answer this loaded question, but she replied, 'It's a very demanding role being Prince of Wales, and an even more demanding one being King,' implying she believed her husband was unfit for what she described as 'the top job'.

Realising she had gone too far, Diana hastily added that she hoped her husband would 'find peace of mind', which suggested he was troubled which made things worse rather than better.

Several Members of Parliament now called Princess Diana a 'loose cannon'. The Hon Nicholas Soames, Minister for the Armed Forces in the Conservative Government, described Diana's interview as 'frightful' on the BBC's *Newsnight* programme. Years earlier, Soames had warned Prince Charles against marrying Diana, and he stated, 'The Princess of Wales is in an advanced stage of paranoia.' This allegation by a Minister of the Crown was widely reported in the press.

As a result, when Nicholas Soames met Prime Minister John Major in the House of Commons, the Prime Minister told his Armed Forces Minister he should keep his mouth shut on royal matters.

The Queen was appalled that Diana would question her son's ability to rule. Princess Margaret, now something of an outsider in the royal family since her marriage break-up, had previously seen Diana as a friend. But Margaret had always kept silent about her love affairs and her husband's infidelity, so found Diana's behaviour disloyal, as it broke the royal family's code of silence.

Princess Margaret ended their long friendship with an angry letter to Diana saying she had disgraced the royal family by breaking their rule of 'keeping silent on matters which should remain private or the monarchy would lose its appeal'.

Diana's mother was horrified by what her daughter had said about the heir to the throne. When Diana phoned her in Scotland, expecting to be congratulated, Frances was so upset she refused to speak to her youngest daughter.[92]

Patrick Jephson had been Diana's Private Secretary for the last seven years and with his degree in political science and wide experience had given her wise counsel. He was shocked as he watched Diana on television, doubting her husband's fitness to rule as king, as she had not told him she was doing the interview. He had been hoping to heal her breach with the House of Windsor and persuade the royal family what an asset Diana was. He realised with dismay that, in spite of all her hard work, Diana would never receive royal recognition for so much humanitarian work. Her implication that Charles was unfit to rule would be seen as deeply

92 Diana and her mother never spoke again. Frances was not advised by the royal family of Diana's death in Paris and only heard that her daughter was dead when she turned on the BBC news.

offensive by the Queen and her husband.

Jephson was tired of Diana's mood swings and that she had not consulted him before doing such a major interview when he was meant to act as her advisor. He resigned and later published a disillusioned book called *Secrets of a Princess* about the difficulties of working for Diana and her violent mood swings.

Patrick Jephson's resignation was followed by that of Australian-born Geoffrey Crawford, the Queen's Deputy Press Secretary, whose difficult task had been to supervise Diana's contacts with the press.

Meanwhile, Camilla and Nicholas Soames felt that the allegations that Diana 'was loopy and ought to be locked up', voiced by Camilla's brother-in-law, Richard Parker Bowles, were justified.

The public did not share their opinion. Her interview had revealed Diana as vulnerable and fallible, and many people loved her more than before. An opinion poll in the *Daily Mirror* showed 92 per cent of their readers supported Diana.

The *Sunday Times* published the results of their latest opinion poll two weeks after the *Panorama* interview. It showed 67 per cent of their readers believed the Princess of Wales had been right to give such a frank television interview. She had rung several friends claiming she had put things right and did not realise how much she had offended the Palace, but it did show she was a more accurate judge of public opinion than anyone had previously believed.

'Never again,' wrote an admiring Canadian journalist Brian Hoey, 'would anyone accuse the Princess of Wales as being as thick as a plank.'

In November 1995, just before Prince Charles held his annual shooting party at Sandringham House, Diana informed Charles that she and the boys would not be attending family Christmas at Sandringham. Diana claimed she could not bear to be near her husband any longer and would be taking an early skiing holiday with William and Harry.

Her abrupt change of plan convinced Prince Charles (backed loyally by Camilla) that dealing with his wife over access to their sons was too difficult. A divorce was the only solution, as it would ensure specific days and times established for each parent to have custody of the boys.

The situation in the royal love triangle had reached crisis point and threatened to harm not only the heir to the throne but the institution of monarchy itself.

CHAPTER ELEVEN

Diana's fight against landmines, and her divorce

There is no way that Diana was mentally unstable. There is nothing wrong with expecting your husband to be faithful and being angry when he isn't. Dr Hasnat Khan, FRCS, October 2013.

When you are happy, you can forgive a great deal. Princess Diana discussing her marriage in 1996 when in love with Dr Khan.

An affair to remember

For Christmas 1995, Diana took her sons on a skiing holiday and was s photographed on the balcony of her ski chalet reading a book titled *Discovering Islam* by Professor Akbar Ahmed. This renewed interest in Islamic art and the Koran, to which she had been introduced by Oliver Hoare, was prompted by Diana's introduction in September 1995 to a brilliant young Muslim heart surgeon.

Diana met Dr Hasnat Khan at the Royal Brompton Hospital. He was Senior Registrar to Professor Sir Magdi Yacoub, the famous surgeon who had done more successful heart transplants than anyone else in the world.

The princess and the heart surgeon first met at the bedside of singer Joe Toffolo, the husband of Diana's Irish acupuncturist and spiritual advisor, Oonagh Shanley-Toffolo. He had just had a triple bypass operation performed on him by Dr Khan and the consultant Professor Magdi Yacoub. Preoccupied by Joe Toffolo's post-operative complications, Dr Khan merely nodded at Diana and then departed, followed by a retinue of medical students as he continued on his ward rounds.

To a beautiful woman like Princess Diana, accustomed to be the focus of attention, the fact that Dr Khan seemed uninterested in her was intriguing. Diana confessed to Oonagh that Dr Khan was 'disturbingly attractive, with those dark-brown velvet eyes you could just melt into'.[93]

The next time Diana accompanied Oonagh on a visit to her husband, she asked the nurses about Dr Khan. She was told he was part of the team

---

[93] The account of Diana's first meeting with Dr Khan and other parts of the film Diana are inaccurate according to Dr Khan, and he wanted it known he had never been involved with the film. Much of the script was based on Kate Snell's book *Diana, Her Last Love,* André Deutsch, London, 2013. (Kate Snell had previously made a documentary film about Princess Diana for London Weekend Television.) Information about Diana and Dr Khan emerged in a detailed interview with Oonagh Shanley-Toffolo by journalist Sarah Ellison titled 'Diana's Impossible Dream' in *Vanity Fair,* September 2013.

working with the famous Sir Magdi Yacoub, Britain's premier cardio-thoracic surgeon who had the largest heart transplant programme in the world. Sir Magdi's team were making ground-breaking discoveries in heart surgery and valve replacement. But what Diana really wanted to know was whether the handsome Dr Khan was single or married.

She discovered Dr Khan was a bachelor, two years older than herself, and one of four children of a wealthy Pathan family from the town of Jhelum, north of Lahore. Like other young surgeons lucky enough to be part of Sir Magdi Yacoub's team, Hasnat Khan was expected to work long hours, cooperate on research papers and write up his PhD thesis. He found the work of Professor Yacoub's unit fascinating and regarded it as a privilege to be allowed to work at London's prestigious centre of cardiac research carrying out research on cystic fibrosis. This was an area in which Diana was interested as she had helped raise money for one of the charities of which she was patron to purchase equipment for cystic fibrosis patients and had visited some of them in hospital.

Princess Diana at Brompton Hospital where she was there to highlight the fact that it was cystic fibrosis week. She looked tanned as she had just returned from a holiday in Barbuda she is pictured wearing a powder blue Versace suit sitting on the bed with cystic fibrosis sufferer Nicky Welsh. 15th April 1997. © Mirrorpix

Professor Yacoub had established his Chain of Hope Charity to treat children with heart defects in Third World countries. It flew them to London for the life-saving operations he performed on them and paid for their post-operative care.

For the next three weeks, Diana and Oonagh paid regular visits to the Brompton Heart Hospital and sat at Joseph Toffolo's bedside. This gave Diana a chance to talk briefly to the handsome surgeon in his green operating gown.

Diana noticed that Dr Khan had deep brown eyes surrounded by laughter lines. She was soon on her battery of cell phones telling young female friends and the more mature Lady Bowker and Lady Annabel Goldsmith that she had just met a fascinating man who resembled the film star Omar Sharif. She code-named him 'Mr Wonderful' and flirted with the handsome heart surgeon, but he did not seem to notice her. This intrigued her even more.

As a way of getting to know Dr Khan, Diana asked if he would be kind enough to introduce her to some of his other patients as she had a special interest in cystic fibrosis and its treatment. He asked her to wait until he came off duty and gave her a brief tour of the wards on which he had patients, and she talked to some of them.

The nurses were amazed that Dr Khan showed Her Royal Highness no special deference. He talked to the Princess of Wales as though she were a colleague, discussing his patients and their problems. She told him she visited several patients on the cystic fibrosis ward on a regular basis, so he knew she was genuinely interested and added that visits from her were reckoned to have a good psychological effect on patients.

Diana was fascinated by Dr Khan and regarded impressing him as a challenge. She took special care with her appearance and visited the Royal Brompton Hospital every day. But it took two weeks before the serious-minded Dr Hasnat Khan unbent enough to invite her to accompany him on a trip to Stratford-upon-Avon to collect textbooks for his doctoral thesis. They were to visit the home of his uncle, Dr Omar Khan, who was married to a young English lawyer. Diana was delighted by his invitation.

When Hasnat Khan arrived at Kensington Palace to collect her, Diana was surprised to see he drove a battered old car and realised he was totally uninterested in status symbols.

On the journey up the motorway, he explained that his father was a graduate of the London School of Economics, owned a factory in Lahore, and had paid for his studies. In order to specialise in heart surgery, he had taken a post at St Vincent's Hospital in Sydney, working for the famous heart surgeon Dr Victor Chang, whose murder had made headlines around

Australia. After having operated successfully on media mogul Kerry Packer, Dr Chang was shot during an attempted kidnap. His Chinese captors believed they could claim a ransom for him, but the hold-up gun went off by mistake killing the famous heart surgeon.

Shocked by the murder of his mentor and friend, Dr Khan had left Sydney for London where he gained a place on the prestigious unit run by Professor Sir Magdi Yacoub and passed his exams to become a Member of the British Royal College of Surgeons.

Lady Annabel Goldsmith, Diana's good friend, had a beautiful daughter, named Jemima, who was twelve years younger than Diana. In a strange coincidence, Jemima had recently married Hasnat's famous cousin, the wealthy cricketer Imran Khan. From correspondence with Jemima, who was now living in one of the Khan family compounds, Diana learned the importance of family bonds in Pakistani society. As the eldest son and his mother's favourite, Hasnat would be expected to marry one of his cousins and bring her to live in the family compound.

What piqued Diana was that 'Mr Wonderful' was not impressed by her celebrity, her title or her ancient lineage. What fascinated Dr Khan was how well his patients were responding to Diana's daily visits.

Diana enjoyed meeting Hasnat's English-born Aunt Jane, who would become a friend. She learned that it had not been easy for Jane and Hasnat's uncle to marry but, eventually, the Khan family had accepted Jane. On that first evening at Stratford-upon-Avon, Diana and Hasnat Khan dined in a small restaurant where no one recognised Princess Diana. They drove back to London happy and relaxed, and that night he accompanied her to her apartment, and their love affair began.

Diana discovered that Hasnat had simple tastes. He enjoyed watching football and liked a glass of wine or a pint of Guinness when he came off duty. His main relaxation was listening to jazz, so Diana asked him to take her to Ronnie Scott's jazz club. She went there disguised in a black wig, dark glasses, an oversize T-shirt and black leggings. She was delighted that no one recognised her and enjoyed the evening and learned a lot about jazz.

With Diana disguised by her wig, they visited Hasnat's local pub, where she queued up to buy pints of beer, the first time she had ever done this. Although his family had money, Hasnat Khan enjoyed a modest lifestyle, and his ambition was to obtain his PhD. Unlike Diana's previous lovers, Hasnat was not interested in money, status or luxury. His priorities were his patients, his research and his doctorate.

Dr Khan rented a small bachelor apartment in Neville Street, South Kensington, a quiet street between Onslow Gardens and the bustling

Fulham Road which lay within easy walking distance to the Royal Brompton Heart Hospital. Diana was shocked to discover how long Hasnat worked each day. He started with ward rounds early in the morning and, if complications developed during surgery, would not finish operating until midnight, by which time he was exhausted. As a senior registrar in the NHS, when rostered for night duty, he slept in a room so small and bare that Diana thought it resembled a monk's cell.

Diana became aware of the fierce competition among young doctors to succeed in the competitive world of heart surgery and the long hours Hasnat and other junior staff worked in order to become consultants, as work and study consumed their lives.[94]

As Diana knew the importance of publicity in raising funds for medical equipment and research through heading various charities, she found it hard to understand Hasnat's intense dislike of any publicity at all for his work. All his attention was concentrated on his patients and obtaining his thesis.

As their relationship deepened, Hasnat gave Diana a key to his apartment, and she would go there to dust and vacuum, do his washing-up and wash and iron his shirts. This was extraordinary considering how privileged Diana was as the Princess of Wales with an army of servants to look after her.

Diana, as a princess was accustomed to everyone doing whatever she wanted. She was annoyed when she phoned Dr Khan, and the switchboard operator refused to put her calls through. Operators were instructed to only put calls from doctors through to surgeons, so she and Hasnat developed a special code whereby Diana would announce she was 'Dr Armani' or 'Dr Versace', and if he was free, Hasnat would accept her call.

This love affair with someone so dedicated to work and study was entirely new for Diana. She instructed Paul Burrell to buy her a copy of the medical textbook *Gray's Anatomy* to try and understand his work.

By a strange coincidence, Hasnat's uncle, the famous heart surgeon Professor Jawad Khan, had operated on her father several years ago. When Hasnat introduced her to Professor Khan, he told Diana he remembered Earl Spencer very well and this gave her a sense of connection to the Khan family.

Hasnat told Diana that his family had already selected one of his cousins, the daughter of a noble Afghan family, as a potential bride for him

---

[94] My late husband, Professor Lawrence Evans, worked as Senior Registrar to the celebrated physician Sir Henry Matthew at the Royal Edinburgh Infirmary, and later for Professor Sir Martin Roth, President of the Royal College of Psychiatrists. Their research teams often worked from 8 a.m. until 8 p.m., so the long hours worked by Dr Hasnat Khan were normal.

when he returned to Pakistan when he would be expected to live in the large family compound in the town of Jhelum. He confessed his ambivalence about the future his family had planned for him and had as yet made no steps towards a betrothal, so Diana was relieved.

Hasnat treated Diana as a fellow humanitarian. He had no interest in her title but saw her as a charming companion with a gift for helping sick people come to terms with their illness. He told her he hoped to return to Pakistan to set up a free hospital for underprivileged children with heart problems. Diana was excited, hoping it was an ambition she could share. She trusted Dr Khan completely, feeling that, unlike other lovers, he would be faithful and never look at other women.

'He won't sell me out like the rest,' she told Oonagh when she invited Hasnat to move into her apartment. He refused, preferring to retain his independence. He was often exhausted after a long stint in the operating theatre and all he wanted was to relax, watch football on television, eat a hamburger and drink a glass of beer or wine. When Diana visited him at the hospital, she often had to wait for hours before he was free to see her, so she would fill in the time by visiting his cystic fibrosis patients. She would visit his patients in recovery, bring them small presents and, if they needed comfort, would hug them and talk to them, and Hasnat was pleased that they did derive comfort from her visits.

Dr Hasnat Khan appreciated and loved what was best about Diana: her compassion and wish to embrace humanitarian causes but could not see himself as the husband of a celebrity and the mother of a future king. He was the only one of Diana's lovers who could understand her and was able to reassure her that he loved her for herself rather than for her status.

Diana found Hasnat Khan an entertaining companion with a sense of humour similar to her own. Hasnat provided comfort at a tense time when details of her divorce settlement were being worked out and made her see that a divorce was preferable to a legal separation in many ways. Coming from a large happy family, Hasnat understood Diana's devotion to her sons and how sad she was that she was unable to have William and Harry with her during the Christmas holidays.

That Christmas, Hasnat was on duty at Brompton Hospital, so Diana ate Christmas lunch alone at Kensington Palace. William and Harry were staying with their father and grandparents at Sandringham.

Journeys to Pakistan

In spite of the fact that Dr Khan had told Diana that a marriage between them would be impossible, she refused to listen to his arguments, hoping she could convince him to marry her. She made several trips to Pakistan, a country that fascinated her. On one trip she was accompanied by Annabel Goldsmith and Lady Annabel's niece, Lady Cosima, ostensibly to visit Lady Annabel's daughter Jemima Khan and the cancer hospital that Hasnat's cousin Imran Khan had funded. She also visited Hasnat's grandmother, with whom she had been corresponding for some time without his knowledge.

On 15 February 1996, a few days before her departure for Pakistan, Diana was driven from Kensington Palace to Buckingham Palace. The purpose of the visit was for Diana to express her wish to retain her title of HRH (Her Royal Highness).

The Queen who Diana greatly respected was kind and sympathetic and assured Diana that she must not worry about the custody of her sons 'Nothing will change the fact you are the mother of William and Harry' she said, adding that her main concern was that her grandsons would not be harmed by the divorce. Diana found this reassuring, being unable to forget what had happened to her as a result of her parent's bitter divorce.

Diana and Lady Annabel and her niece, Lady Cosima Somerset (who was also coping with a stressful divorce), flew to Pakistan, where Diana was hoped to meet Hasnat's family and persuade them she would be a suitable wife for their son. But she did not think it wise to mention this to Hasnat at this juncture.

On this and a subsequent trip to Pakistan, Diana stayed with Jemima Khan, who was living in her husband's family compound in Lahore. As Imran Khan was away, on Diana's first visit they sat up late into the night talking. Jemima tried to warn Diana that every Pakistani mother's worst nightmare was to have a son working in England who would return with an emancipated English bride, let alone a celebrity princess. Jemima also tried to warn Diana about the obstacles to her marriage with Hasnat, having encountered problems in her marriage to Imran Khan.[95]

Diana did not want to listen. She had been convinced by one of her therapists that she was being guided by the spirit of her dead grandmother and that things with the marriage would work out.

Diana was in her element inspecting the imposing new Shaukat Khanum Memorial Cancer Hospital in Lahore – named after Imran Khan's mother who died of cancer, and the reason he raised the money to build the hospital in her memory.

---

95 Jemima and Imran Khan's marriage, cited by Diana as the perfect example of a mixed marriage, ended in divorce in 2004.

At the imposing hospital beside the tranquil lake, Diana insisted on visiting every room and every patient suffering from various types of cancer. She seemed tireless talking to patients and encouraging them they would survive. There was a concert put on for her by children who had cancer during which a little boy, disfigured by a suppurating cancerous tumour, snuggled into her arms. Diana seemed totally unconcerned that the little boy's weeping tumour was ruining her beautiful dress. She found the hospital by the lake inspiring and hoped she and Hasnat Khan might do something similar for children needing heart operations in Pakistan.

Moving towards a divorce

Back in London, Diana agreed to meet Prince Charles for more discussions with their divorce lawyers, as her happiness with Hasnat made her agree that a divorce was preferable to a legal separation. The meeting with Prince Charles did not have the bitterness and anger of their previous discussions, and slowly they began to move forward to a kinder stage in their relationship. Diana said she was now resigned to the idea of Charles and Camilla being together and felt that Camilla was good for him.

Although she was genuine at that moment, occasional resentment still lingered over Camilla's role in her marriage break-up. At this stage in their relationship, Diana introduced Hasnat to her sons and both of them liked him.

In April 1996, one of Sir Magdi Yacoub's complex heart operations was being filmed by Sky TV to raise funds for his charities in Third World countries. Hasnat Khan felt honoured that he had been selected from among all the ambitious young surgeons to assist the famous surgeon operate on a seven-year-old boy with severe heart problems. The little boy had been flown in from Cameroon by Professor Yacoub's charity, as the child's parents were desperately poor.

Diana, always the star, arrived at the operating theatre wearing make-up, complete with mascara and was given a green operating gown and a mask. She was fascinated by the operation as the sight of blood never bothered her. On seeing photos of Diana taken to publicise the charity, journalists were scathing about the princess wearing mascara in an operating theatre.

In June 1996, Diana visited the uncle of Hasnat Khan and his wife at Stratford-upon-Avon. The purpose of the visit was to introduce Diana to Hasnat's grandmother and his cousin who were on holiday in England, as Diana had been corresponding with Hasnat's grandmother and wanted to win her approval.

Some weeks later, Diana invited Hasnat's grandmother and his cousin to Kensington Palace, along with Hasnat's Aunt Jane. Diana served them English tea and gave Hasnat's grandmother a beautiful silver bowl. She was disconcerted when told that Hasnat's father had said that should his son marry her, it would be like a marriage between two people from different planets. This remark left Diana panic-stricken, fearing Hasnat would break off their relationship.

Diana was dogged by journalists, cameramen, bodyguards and hangers-on who followed her every move. The press besieged Dr Khan's apartment, and he was starting to receive hate mail from fanatics who had realised he was in a relationship with the Princess of Wales.

Diana realised with a shock that due to prejudice it would be very difficult to marry Hasnat and live in England.

⁂

However, Dr Khan's support gave Diana the strength to face the divorce she had dreaded for so long. On 4 July 1996, details of the divorce settlement of the Prince and Princess of Wales were announced, with terms more favourable than Diana had imagined. Her lawyers had asked for joint custody of the boys, which was granted. Prince Charles had told his lawyers he wanted to be generous and had borrowed money from a bank, so her divorce settlement was £20,000.000 plus an annual allowance of £400,000 to cover office and travel expenses. Diana realised she was now a very wealthy woman and free to live outside England if she wanted and still hoped to persuade Dr Hasnat Khan to marry her, even if they had to leave England to avoid him being harassed by the press.

On the evening of the day that her divorce settlement was announced, Diana was a guest of honour at a fundraising dinner at London's Dorchester Hotel in aid of the cancer hospital Imran Khan had founded in Pakistan. She arrived looking radiant in an ivory *shalwar kameez*, a long tunic embroidered with pearls over matching trousers, a gift from Jemimah Khan.

On 15 July 1996, the divorce of HRH the Prince of Wales versus the Princess of Wales was heard in a private room at Somerset House. Neither of them was there to witness the ending of their marriage.

In the months that followed, Diana was able to take stock of her life. She was exhausted by the whole divorce process and engaged more therapists to help her face her new life. Supported by Prince William, she decided to sell her ball gowns and outfits she would not need again and donate the money to charity at an auction held by Christie's in New York.

Raising money in Sydney for cardiac research

Diana had agreed to speak at a fundraising event for Sydney's Victor Chang Cardiac Research Institute, hoping that Sydney, where Hasnat had once worked for Dr Chang, could be somewhere they might be able to live together. Diana also wanted to demonstrate that she could raise money for causes dear to Dr Khan's heart. Hasnat's deep admiration for his former mentor explained why Diana was prepared to fly halfway around the world to raise money to continue the work of Dr Chang at his former unit in Sydney's St Vincent's Hospital.

In October 1996, Sydney welcomed Diana with enthusiasm. Her presence and her heartfelt speech at the fundraising event raised a very substantial sum for the Victor Chang Cardiac Research Institute.

As had happened on her previous visit, 'Di-mania' ensured that Diana was mobbed everywhere she went, and the paparazzi would not leave her alone. Diana had naively hoped that Sydney might be a place where she and Dr Khan could live without being harassed by the press, but she was wrong. Aware she was involved with Dr Khan, journalists and photographers would not leave her alone.

While Diana was in Sydney, her love for Dr Khan was revealed by the *Sunday Mirror*. The British newspaper ran a story about the romance of Princess Diana and the man the journalist described as the 'shy caring Pakistani heart surgeon whose babies she wanted to have'.[96]

Once this story appeared, journalists and photographers waited outside the Royal Brompton Hospital in an attempt to interview Dr Khan. They surrounded his apartment in Neville Street, went through his rubbish bins and phoned him at all hours of the night. It was a baptism of fire for a surgeon who had hoped that his privacy might be respected.

Knowing how much Hasnat hated publicity, back in London Diana tried to lessen the impact of the story, but her efforts only served to make matters worse.

Diana told Richard Kay of the *Daily Mail* to whom she often fed stories that she and Dr Khan were 'friends in an entirely professional way'. In an effort to cool the story, Diana told Richard Kay that 'rumours that she and Dr Khan were more than just good friends were bullshit' and, without thinking of the effect of her remarks on her lover, Diana added she and her staff were 'laughing themselves silly at the very idea.'[97] This admission was

---

[96] *Sunday Mirror*, 3 November 1996. This article and Diana's subsequent denial are featured in the 2013 film *Diana*, with Naomi Watts playing the part of Diana to very mixed reviews. Dr Hasnat Khan claimed that it was not the real story of what happened between them.

[97] *Daily Mail*, 4 November 1996.

scarcely flattering to Dr Khan.

Diana's denial of her relationship with Dr Khan spread like wildfire around the West Brompton Hospital. Young nurses giggled and pointed at the doctor in the corridors, and he was annoyed and hated having to walk through a posse of yelling journalists and photographers to reach his front door.

Over the next few days, Dr Khan as a Muslim received death threats, some contained a copy of his photo cut out of the newspaper with a noose in black ink around his neck, as a warning of what could happen to him, and he realised what kind of treatment he could expect in Britain should he marry Diana, the mother of a future king of Great Britain.

Diana's tragedy was that she had finally found a man who loved her for herself and her humanitarian ideals. But there seemed to be too many factors working against a marriage of two people from widely different backgrounds and different lifestyles for it to succeed.

Diana stubbornly refused to recognise this and would be badly hurt. The fall-out from her tactless comments to the press was that Dr Khan refused to speak to her or take her phone calls. Desolate at being ignored by the man she loved, she visited his bachelor apartment, washed and ironed his shirts and vacuumed the floor to demonstrate how much she loved him.

After mediation by Paul Burrell, Diana's 'Mr Fix-It', the lovers resumed their relationship. Diana kept Hasnat Khan's photograph by her bedside, studied verses from the Koran, bought herself a collection of *shalwar kameez,* the embroidered tunics and trousers worn by Pakistani women. She planned another visit to Dr Khan's family to demonstrate that she would be able to 'fit in' with their culture and way of life.

Diana wanted to prove that she could be a valuable asset in raising money for Hasnat's pet project, a unit to help underprivileged Pakistani children with heart problems and hoped they could combine their skills to help treat sick children.

Although Diana claimed she could fit into Muslim society and live in his family compound, Hasnat could foresee problems.

In October 1996, Diana visited Rimini to accept an award for her humanitarian work. After the award ceremony, she was seated next to Dr Christian Barnard, the elderly surgeon who decades earlier had performed the world's first heart transplant. Diana opened her heart to Dr Barnard, telling him she was in love with Dr Khan and hoped to marry him and live far away from Britain and the paparazzi who plagued them.

Diana related details of Dr Khan's curriculum vitae, which included working for the eminent Dr Victor Chang in Sydney and Professor Magdi

Yacoub. Dr Barnard was impressed and wanted to help. Back home, he made a few phone calls to surgeons and paid a visit to Diana at Kensington Palace when next in London. As a result of Diana's intercession with Dr Barnard, Dr Khan was invited to send his CV to the cardiac department of a leading Boston hospital.

A proud man who had succeeded through hard work and talent rather than nepotism, Dr Khan was furious with Diana for meddling in his career and told her that working in America was not an option. He was determined to remain in London and finish his Ph.D thesis under Professor Yacoub. A fierce argument followed and, once again, Dr Khan refused to see Diana or take phone calls from her.

This second break-up left Diana very stressed and unhappy. She flew into a rage and dismissed Oonagh Shanley-Toffolo, who she believed had talked to the press about her and Hasnat Khan without her permission. Diana's mother also angered her daughter by giving an interview to *Hello* magazine. Frances revealed facts about Diana's bulimia as well as stating that her daughter's decision to give a televised interview to Martin Bashir had been unwise.[98]

Diana had a bitter argument with her mother. Frances justified her actions by saying she had only agreed to be interviewed on condition *Hello* magazine paid a very large fee to a Catholic charity she was supporting.

Diana was furious that her mother had dared to discuss her eating disorder and her *Panorama* interview and refused to take any of her mother's phone calls. This final estrangement meant they never spoke again. Diana returned her mother's letters unread.

Diana recovered her equilibrium when she made an excellent speech on eating disorders to the staff at the Priory, a private psychiatric clinic at Roehampton that had just opened an Eating Disorders Unit. Diana spoke

---

98 *Hello* magazine, May 1997. Interview with Frances Shand Kydd. Diana refused to take her mother's calls and they never spoke again. Mother and daughter, alike in so many ways, both had sad lives. Frances endured the deaths of her baby, of her daughter Diana, and of her stepson, Adam Shand Kydd, of whom she was very fond, who died of an apparent drug overdose in Cambodia. Her brother, Lord Edmond Fermoy, committed suicide. Frances, the ultimate romantic, endured the pain of two unhappy marriages and two divorces. The Hon. Frances Shand Kydd, née Roche, was warm-hearted and intelligent but spent her final years alone on a remote Scottish island. In 2002, with her health failing due to a muscle-wasting disease, she had to give evidence to the police in London after Paul Burrell was accused of stealing more than 300 items belonging to Diana from her apartment after Diana's death A last-minute reprieve saved him when the Queen suddenly remembered giving Burrell permission to take the items and Frances did not have to appear in court. Later that year she had had a lucky escape when she crashed her car into a bridge at Oban. There were suggestions she had become an alcoholic, although loyal friends insisted this was not the case. She died on 3 June 2004.

about the anguish caused by bulimia but did not admit that this was her problem.

She started feeling sorry for Camilla, as Charles did not seem to be making any steps to marry her now he was divorced. It seemed highly unlikely at this stage the Anglican Church would allow it to happen. Nevertheless, Diana was only human and was piqued when it was announced that Charles was giving Camilla a lavish party for her fiftieth birthday at Highgrove, her former home.

Meetings with Dr Khan's family

In May 1997, Diana again flew to Pakistan, ostensibly to visit Jemima and Imran Khan and visited the Khans' family residence with its large garden with enough children and grandchildren to form a cricket team. Wearing a pale blue *shalwar kameez* and bringing presents for the whole family, looking very beautiful, Diana was welcomed by Hasnat's father and his mother Naheed. His sisters Aleema and Rhanee liked Diana and took her sight-seeing in their car around the city.

Hasnat's mother, Naheed, had a Master's Degree in Fine Arts. She was a strong-minded woman who disliked the British for their role in the partition of Pakistan and India and questioned the wisdom of Diana marrying her eldest son but said the decision was up to him.

Diana had hoped to win over Hasnat's mother, but his parents, educated and moderated in their views, could see how different both of them were. Even if she moved to Pakistan with Hasnat, Diana would have difficulties in adjusting to the traditional role of a daughter-in-law and she would need to fly back to England frequently to see her sons. Such a marriage would be fraught with problems.

In a desperate attempt to make Hasnat Khan change his mind, Diana appealed to Imran Khan to speak to his cousin on her behalf. From the fraught experience of his marriage to English-born Jemima Goldsmith, Imran Khan was aware of the difficulties in such a marriage, but he liked Diana and agreed to support her and speak to his cousin when he was next in London.

But before Imran Khan could meet with Hasnat, the heart surgeon broke off his relationship with Diana aware of the problems between them.

Disappointed and despairing, Diana began a summer romance with Dodi Fayed, substituting a wealthy playboy for a dedicated doctor. Years later a revealing statement given to the *Paget Inquiry*, Dr Khan revealed that he had been jealous when this happened, as Diana had hoped and admitted that the fact Diana had done this 'had made him mad'.

According to the writer Daphne du Maurier, writing biographies of women is always difficult because most women lie about their relationships if their lover has rejected them. Perhaps having lost her husband to Camilla, Diana did not want to admit she had been dumped by Oliver Hoare and by Hasnat Khan. Always careful to compartmentalise her friends, Diana gave totally different accounts of what had occurred between her and Dr Khan to various friends and to her butler Paul Burrell.

In Dr Hasnat Khan's testimony to the Paget Inquiry, he stated that Princess Diana had ended their two-year relationship. According to Paul Burrell, the final meeting between Diana and the heart surgeon took place amid tears and recriminations in June 1997, and Diana had been in tears when she related what had happened.

It would be Paul Burrell, who had often acted as a go-between in this doomed love affair, who sent the grief-stricken Dr Khan a ticket, so he could attend Diana's funeral.

⁂

Dr Khan did eventually make a very brief marriage to a cousin, but it broke up, and he claimed he thought a great deal about Diana. He spent time in Pakistan setting up a free heart unit designed to serve as a memorial to Diana, who he said 'had a remarkable gift for soothing sick children and helping ameliorate their lives, regardless of colour or creed'.

At the time of writing, Dr Khan is in England working at an NHS teaching hospital and admired as the only one of Diana's lovers who did not betray her, and after eighteen years has just become engaged again to a young Pakistani woman. Those who loved and admired Diana should wish him well as he was a positive influence for good at a dark time in Diana's life.

Diana's finest hour: her crusade against landmines

In mid-June 1996, Diana spoke with authority at a conference on landmines. Chaired by Lord William Deedes, the conference was organised by the Mines Advisory Group and held at the Royal Geographical Society in London where the impact of landmines was revealed in all its horror with graphic shots of civilians maimed or killed when they entered areas where the mines were buried.

Diana made a speech praising soldiers engaged in the dangerous work of mine-clearing and wanted to devote herself to trying to raise awareness of the damage mines were doing. In a corner of her sitting room at Kensington Palace, Diana hung a chart of landmine sites across the world and, with red-topped pins, indicated the areas where the mines were clustered.

On 25 June, Diana flew to New York for a press viewing of the charity auction of a dozen of her evening dresses. The auction conducted by Christie's raised a total of three million, two hundred and fifty-eight thousand, seven hundred and fifty American dollars, which Diana donated to AIDS charities. In New York, she met with Mother Teresa, whom she had previously visited in India. Mother Teresa, admiring Diana's stance against landmines, gave her a rosary.

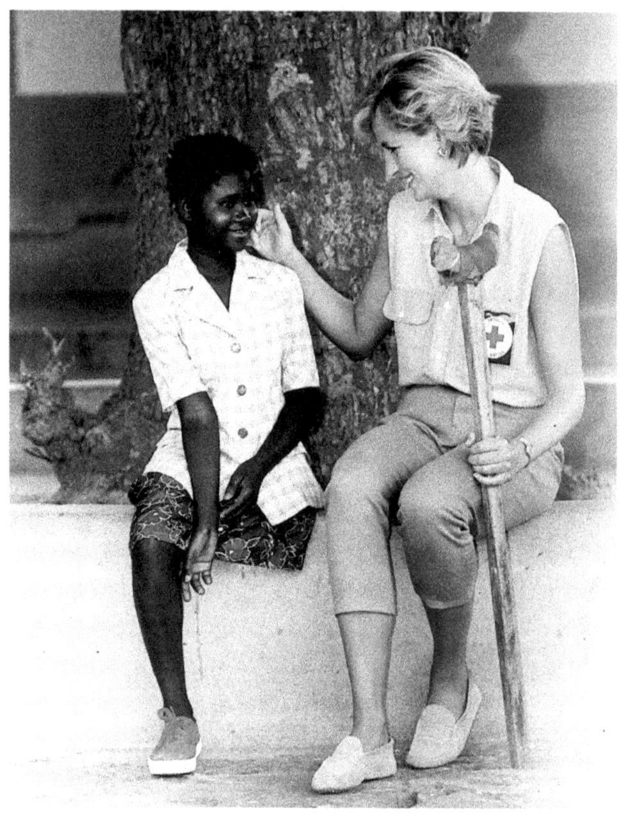

Princess Diana meets a victim of landmines in Angola, January 1997 ©Mirrorpix

In January 1997, Diana insisted on visiting Angola, a country heavily infested with mines. Devoid of make-up, wearing an open-necked cotton shirt, a plastic head shield and a flak jacket with a microphone around her neck, Diana walked through a recently cleared minefield with mine craters around her.

Princess Diana with mine expert Paul Heslop in a land mine field in Huanbo Angola 15th January 1997 during a visit to help a Red Cross campaign outlaw landmines worldwide. © Mirrorpix

A BBC television crew filmed Diana walking through the minefield in a documentary intended to raise money for the British Red Cross Landmines Appeal. The former journalist and *Daily Telegraph* editor, Lord William Deedes, a major advocate of banning landmines since 1992, accompanied Diana. Sandy Gall, the well-known BBC television reporter, described Diana's actions on this trip as being extremely brave. Having encountered landmines in Afghanistan, he knew how dangerous walking through allegedly 'cleared' minefields could be, but Diana was undaunted by the danger and insisted on doing it.

'Nobody took any notice of landmines until Diana came along,' Lord William Deedes

On their visit to Angola, Diana and Lord Deedes were accompanied by cynical members of the press corps who wanted to prove this was merely a publicity gimmick on the part of Diana.

One of the cynics was the *Sunday Times* war reporter Christina Lamb, who was very sceptical about a princess and former fashion icon visiting the battlegrounds of Angola and thought it was a stunt. However, seeing Diana walking through a minefield where observers had been killed only a few days previously by unexploded mines, Christina Lamb was impressed by Diana's sincerity and dedication. Watching her do this changed the opinion of the hardened war correspondent, and she became a supporter of the Princess of Wales.

At a hospital in Huambo, Diana cuddled children with bandaged stumps and was confronted by skeletal figures with missing limbs or gaping wounds. Many of their injuries were so gruesome that Christina Lamb could not bear to look at them, despite years of war reporting. Diana confronted horrific sights without flinching and did her best to comfort victims with terrible injuries.

At the hospital, after the photographers had departed for air-conditioned hotels to wire photos to London, Christina Lamb watched Diana, unaware the journalist was observing her. Diana sat quietly holding the hand of Helena Ussova, a seven-year-old girl whose intestines had been ripped apart by an exploding mine, injuries too harrowing for most war reporters to confront. For nearly an hour Diana sat beside young Helena, continuing to hold her hand or stroke her forehead without the need for words.

When finally, Diana had to leave, this young girl still racked with pain asked Christina Lamb, 'Was the beautiful lady an angel sent by God to soothe my pain?'

The hardened war correspondent realised that Diana, the princess turned humanitarian, was indeed an exceptional young woman who helped those in despair 'with genuine compassion. Christina Lamb, famous for her articles about war and war heroes claimed that Diana, by her presence and her concern for those who had little to live for, brought them new hope and described the morale-raising effect Diana had on those amputees to whom she talked and whose hands she held.

At the end of that nightmare trip to Angola, Diana said that she could never forget that partially disembowelled young girl, a sight so terrible no one was willing to photograph it.

Lord Deedes, a hardened newspaper editor, not easily impressed praised the power Diana had wielded so skilfully to change public opinion on the dangers of landmines.

'Nobody took a blind bit of interest in landmines until Princess Diana came along,' Bill Deedes said praising Diana's courage and determination. He added that she had never once complained on this trip although many journalists were dismayed and horrified by the state of Luanda, Angola's capital city, whose rat and cockroach-infested streets were filled with rotting garbage. The stench was fearsome, but Diana was determined to continue to do what she had come there for, although some journalists in the group talked of leaving as the conditions were so unsanitary and appalling.

The BBC documentary about Princess Diana's trip to Angola was shown worldwide. It resulted in widespread support for the Ottawa Treaty, which would eventually be signed by forty different countries which banned the sale and manufacture of landmines.

This was Diana's finest hour and showed how human beings have the power to change. Lady Diana Spencer, the nervous girl once too shy to answer questions in class and who had panic attacks in exams had just walked fearlessly through a minefield and saved countless people from death or horrible injuries.

Her detractors could not fault Diana's courage in speaking out against the manufacture of landmines sold by armaments dealers who made millions from this grisly trade. With Princess Diana on board the anti-landmines campaign, the British and American governments had to sit up and take notice.

On 8 August 1997, Princess Diana and Lord William Deedes, accompanied by Paul Burrell, flew out to war-torn Bosnia on a jet belonging to multi-millionaire philanthropist George Soros.

On that nightmare drive to Sarajevo over pot-holed roads lined with reeking corpses, they were joined by two American landmine victims: Jerry White and Ken Rutherford. These two brave men had set up the Survivors Network after having lost their legs to landmines and having to walk with crutches.

On her second anti-landmines tour, Diana once more showed her ability to empathise with the maimed and the dying. She was confronted by sights so distressing they were not normally shown to visitors and did not flinch. Miss Stevens would have been proud of her former pupil.

In war-torn Bosnia, Diana also visited a graveyard and embraced and comforted a woman sobbing beside her mother's grave. Diana visited centres where artificial limbs were fitted to landmine victims. She saw hundreds of children who had been maimed by landmines that had remained buried long after fighting had ended; she was photographed comforting survivors and grieving parents.

Diana's commitment to the passing of the Ottawa Treaty was endorsed by Prime Minister Tony Blair. She also met with Foreign Secretary Robin Cook who, after discussions with Cabinet, announced that by 2005 Britain would destroy its stock of landmines and redouble its efforts towards a world ban on mines. This was an important achievement since Britain had previously been a substantial exporter of landmines and other armaments.

Princess Diana's legacy endures in what is now known as the Ottawa Treaty. In her very public and courageous support for banning landmines, Diana found her greatest mission in life.

Diana and the Fayeds

Mohamed Al Fayed and Diana had met at polo matches and when they were both patrons of the English National Ballet; Fayed was a generous benefactor of the company. The Egyptian-born billionaire, a tycoon with a colourful vocabulary, offered Diana a holiday at his walled estate near St Tropez.

Rosa Monckton warned Diana not to accept his offer, as Al Fayed had been accused of bribing members of parliament and had been refused a British passport over his 'cash for questions' Parliamentary scandal. However, Al Fayed had been a kind and generous friend to Diana and given money to her beloved English National Ballet, one of her favourite charities, had been on friendly terms with her father and stepmother in the final years of her father's life, and Diana did not forget his kindness to her family.

The Princess of Wales took an impish delight in riling the Establishment and wanting somewhere safe to holiday with her boy and accepted the invitation from Al Fayed and his Finnish-born second wife to join them at their hillside villa in picturesque St Tropez with William and Harry.

Mohamed Al Fayed, son of a humble school inspector (a fact he preferred to forget), had divorced his first wife, Samira, the sister of Saudi Arabian entrepreneur and arms dealer Adnan Khashoggi and the daughter of the Shah of Persia's private physician. Samira's son Emad (known as Dodi) had been neglected after his parent's bitter divorce and said his childhood had been lonely and miserable. He had been looked after by an uncle in Egypt while his father was working hard to build his fortune, involved with the development of the port of Dubai, which made him immensely wealthy but meant his son rarely saw him. Al Fayed became financial advisor to the Sultan of Brunei, the world's wealthiest man, and he too became extremely wealthy.

Once Al Fayed had made his millions, he moved to London and purchased various assets, including Harrods department store.

Al Fayed had also helped to bring Diana and her stepmother together. After the widowed Raine married a French aristocrat, Diana had surprised everyone by reconciling with her.

Diana had been looking for a secure place in a warm climate to enjoy a holiday with fifteen-year-old Prince William and his younger brother, Prince Harry. She liked Al Fayed's Finnish wife, Heini, who had young children, and a holiday at the Al Fayed private estate near St Tropez with private bodyguards guarding it seemed ideal. So, Diana and her sons flew to the Nice in one of Al Fayed's private jets and were driven to the villa.

On Bastille Day, 14 June 1997, France's national holiday, Diana spent the morning jet skiing with her sons and asked to be ferried across to a motor launch hired by reporters and photographers of various British newspapers.

According to James Whitaker, rather than running away from the press, Diana was now talking freely to them about her failed marriage and her divorce. Diana arrived on board the press launch looking trim and terrific in a revealing swimming costume, giving photographers a chance to take all the photos they wanted.

'You're going to get a big surprise with the next thing I do,' she told Whitaker. 'My boys are urging me to leave the country. They want me to live abroad. In London, I am followed by paparazzi r everywhere wherever I go.'

That night after dinner at Mohamed Al Fayed's villa, the house party watched a display of fireworks that took place over the Mediterranean. Al Fayed felt Diana was sad and summoned Dodi on his mobile phone to come to his villa and amuse her. Dodi was staying on a yacht moored off St Tropez with his American fiancée, a Calvin Klein model named Kelly Fisher, who had no idea a party was taking place at the Al Fayed villa without her.

Dodi and Diana talked at length, and Al Fayed was delighted by how well they interacted. Each had experienced a divorce that scarred their childhoods and been deprived of their mothers in childhood, which aroused Diana's compassion for him.

As the two of them got on well together, discussing favourite films and laughing and talking, Al Fayed began to cherish ambitions that he could end Dodi's engagement, and his son might marry Diana.

The following morning, Dodi appeared at his father's villa and he and Diana once more talked for hours. She learned Dodi had attended a Swiss boarding school with the sons of American and European tycoons, but like Diana, he suffered from learning difficulties and had failed all his exams, so his father sent him to do an expensive course at Sandhurst Military Academy where the sons of military dictators were taught how to take military salutes and wear medals. But this was not how Dodi wanted to spend his life. Al Fayed was aware his son was star-struck, and it was unlikely he would settle down and work at Harrods as he had hoped. In an attempt to compensate for past neglect, Al Fayed had used his wealth to purchase a Hollywood film company for Dodi to manage.

Dodi's role in the company mainly consisted of writing cheques and taking glamorous starlets to dinner. He gained plus points for introducing his father to Heini Wathén, who became Al Fayed's second wife. She had given him four beautiful children and made him happy, and for this, he was grateful to Dodi.

In the artificial world of Hollywood, Dodi developed a fondness for cocaine. So his father sent him back to Cairo in the care of relatives, and he was able to see his mother again before she died of cancer in 1986 when her death precipitated an emotional crisis in her son.

His story interested Diana whose childhood had been scarred by the loss of her mother. During that holiday, she saw a great deal of Dodi, while his fiancée, Kelly Fisher, returned to America. Diana and Dodi found they had much in common.

Dodi had never settled into a proper job, worked briefly in Harrods but found it boring. He loved cars and eventually owned five Ferraris and a Park Lane apartment with a collection of toy soldiers and stuffed animals, including teddy bears. Dodi was always surrounded by private security guards and, as the son of a billionaire, lived with the fear he could be kidnapped and held to ransom.

Diana told Dodi about her trips to visit leper colonies, her meeting with Mother Teresa, and her work on the campaign to ban landmines. Dodi was fascinated; he had never met anyone like her in his world of models and Hollywood starlets.

Dodi had been married to a French model, Suzanne Gregard, but their brief marriage ended in divorce. What Dodi did not tell Diana was that he had given Kelly Fisher an engagement ring and promised to marry her. His father had told him to forget the engagement and concentrate on making Diana happy.[99]

With his father's money, Dodi had recently purchased a five-acre beachfront home in Malibu, the former home of Julie Andrews and her film producer husband, and Dodi invited Diana to come and see it ignoring the fact it was intended to be his home with Kelly Fisher once they were married.

Al Fayed gave an interview to the *Mail on Sunday* telling the journalist that Diana was happy as part of their family and added, aware that Diana was upset Charles was throwing an enormous birthday party for Mrs Parker Bowles, 'As for Camilla, Diana doesn't think about her. Camilla is like something from a Dracula film compared to the beautiful Diana,' he said.[100]

---

[99] At the inquest into Dodi's death, Kelly Fisher claimed that she believed that she and Dodi were to live in the former beachfront home of Julie Andrews, purchased for them by Al Fayed, and she sued Al Fayed for compensation for her broken engagement.

[100] Brian Vine, the *Mail on Sunday*, 20 July 1997.

When Diana and her sons flew back to London, she found that Dodi had filled her Kensington Palace apartment with pink roses. He also sent her a gold Cartier watch. Kelly Fisher had returned to Los Angeles to fulfil a modelling contract, still believing she and Dodi were to marry.

The British media liked to depict Dodi as a blend of Hollywood playboy and cocaine addict, living on an allowance of $100,000 a week from his father. However, the women Dodi had dated in Hollywood were a great deal kinder than the British media and without exception claimed Dodi Fayed was gentle, affectionate and a very considerate lover.

Having failed all his exams, Dodi did not make Diana feel poorly educated and ignorant as Prince Charles had done. Diana told her girl friends all Dodi seemed to want was to make her happy.

On 2 July 1997, Diana flew to Milan to attend a memorial service for the fashion designer Gianni Versace, who had been murdered by a serial killer. Diana was among the celebrities seated in the front row beside Elton John, with whom, six months earlier, she had fallen out but now all was forgiven, and their friendship was restored.

Dodi was now genuinely fond of Diana. He flew to London on a surprise visit to see her but found she had just left for Milan and he had missed her by only a few hours.

On 23 July 1997, Diana joined Dodi in the South of France for a cruise on the *Jonikal* and was photographed kissing and embracing Dodi on board the yacht. According to Paul Burrell, Diana rang him in London to ask if he thought Hasnat Khan had seen the photos of her kissing Dodi aware that Dr Khan purchased a newspaper every morning on his way to the Royal Brompton Hospital.

Lady Elsa Bowker also received a phone call from Diana who admitted that she was flirting with Dodi in front of photographers to make Hasnat jealous. Diana added mischievously it would be amusing if she hid inside the gigantic cake made for Camilla's birthday party, and as the cake was wheeled in on a trolley, she would jump out and startle the guests! Diana admitted she was able to joke about the birthday Charles was holding for Camilla saying blithely 'Now I know what love is'.

On 26 July, Dodi and Diana enjoyed a quiet weekend in Paris together, walking hand in hand along the Seine and dining in small bistros without being bothered by the press.

Later it would be revealed that, to protect her reputation, Diana stayed in the Imperial Suite at the Ritz, while Dodi stayed at his father's apartment in the rue Arsène Houssaye and Diana flew back alone to

London on 27 July.[101]

Mohammed Al Fayed was so enthusiastic about Dodi and Diana's summer romance that he urged Dodi to take Diana on another luxury cruise to Sardinia and Corsica. Al Fayed was a complex, driven man, hated by many but capable of great generosity to those he liked.

On learning she agreed to make another cruise with him, Dodi, using his father's money, gave Diana a magnificent bracelet set with diamonds and other expensive gifts. Dodi was generous by nature and had unlimited funds from his father to do anything that would make Diana happy. Confronted by such generosity, Diana telephoned friends and told them she preferred the warm atmosphere of the Al Fayed family to the cold-hearted Windsors.

However, her new relationship caused tension between her and Prince William. On 29 July, Diana and Hasnat met for the last time. He would not commit to a marriage which he believed would never work, but Diana had not abandoned hope he might change his mind.[102]

She was contacting the press, offering photographers exclusive opportunities to photograph her with Dodi in the South of France. Friends were sure Diana was doing this hoping Hasnat would become jealous and agree to marry her.

August 1997 was a very busy time for Diana. Her complex nature meant she was able to enjoy a summer fling with Dodi, living in luxury while making trips to Africa and Bosnia for humanitarian work amid scenes of the utmost horror. And it is possible all the love and attention lavished on her by Dodi gave her the strength to do this.

Diana received and made long phone calls to Dodi and made arrangements to join a short five-day cruise in the Aegean, which she was booked on to accompany her friend Rosa Monckton, who was head of Tiffany and Co and the wife of editor Dominic Lawson and sister-in-law of TV celebrity Nigella Lawson.

On 15 August 1997, Diana and Rosa flew to Greece in one of Al Fayed's many jets. In an article she wrote about the cruise, Rosa revealed that Dodi phoned Diana frequently and told Diana about expensive presents he had bought her in America.

Diana confided to Rosa, 'That's not what I want… I don't want to be bought… I just want someone to be there for me, to make me feel safe and secure.'[103]

---

101 Information presented to the Scott Baker inquiry held in London after Diana's death.

102 Dr Khan confirmed at the inquest into Diana's death this had been the case.

103 Richard Kay and Rosa Monckton, *Sunday Telegraph*, 7 August 1997.

Cruising the Aegean coast, Diana telephoned Taki Theodoracopulos, the columnist for *The Spectator*. Questioned by Taki as to whether she intended to marry Dodi, Diana assured him marriage was not on her mind. In his column, Taki explained how. 'It took her [Diana] a long time to get out of one loveless marriage, and she's not about to get into another.'

Later that month, Diana flew from London Airport to Nice and was driven to the yacht harbour where she and Dodi departed for another luxury cruise on Al Fayed's yacht, visiting romantic ports en route to Sardinia. At one luxury boutique where Diana admired a cashmere sweater, in a grand gesture, Dodi bought the entire stock of cashmeres in her size in many different colours, a gift worth thousands of dollars. The crew of the *Jonikal* saw the pair of them returning to the Al Fayed yacht laden with packages, giggling happily like children returning from a visit to a fun fair.

From the *Jonikal*, with its crew devoted to fulfilling Diana and Dodi's s every wish, Diana phoned Lady Bowker and said she was enjoying herself but was missing Hasnat Khan. She added that Dodi was treating her exceptionally well, but marriage was not on her mind.

Diana had always loved the warmth of the Mediterranean and was enjoying her summer romance with Dodi. On the phone to female friends, she told them she was having a 'blissful' romantic time with Dodi who was attractive, kind and generous.

Since Dodi had no job and was supported by his father, he was able to devote all his time to keeping Diana – the only one of her lovers to do this.

Encouraged by his father, Dodi was deceiving his American fiancée. Kelly Fisher was unaware of his summer romance with the Princess of Wales and still wore Dodi's engagement ring while doing modelling assignments in America.

On 26 August, Diana, phoned Hasnat's uncle, Professor Jawad Khan, reassuring him that there was 'nothing in her relationship with Dodi'. Professor Khan warned her that attempts to make Hasnat jealous would not work.[104] But he was wrong. Years later, Hasnat would confess in his written statement to the Paget Inquiry into Diana's death that her relationship with Dodi had made him 'mad as hell'.

---

104 Kate Snell, *Diana, Her Last Love,* Andre Deutsch, 2013, p 225. The existence of this call has not been confirmed by Dr Hasnat Khan.

CHAPTER TWELVE

Diana's tragic death & her legacy

Diana, the very essence of compassion, ... of style and of beauty. From the speech of Diana's brother, Charles, Earl Spencer at her funeral.

Millions of those who had never met Diana felt that they knew her and will never forget her. Queen Elizabeth II.

By late August 1997, it was clear Diana and Dodi were fond of each other. They enjoyed many of the same activities: swimming, dancing, water-skiing and were happy watching old movies and TV soaps in the private cinema aboard the *Jonikal* or in Dodi's Mayfair apartment.

On their second cruise aboard the *Jonikal*, while anchored off the coast of Sardinia Diana arranged for a leading photographer named Mario Brenna to take photos of her and Dodi, sun baking and embracing.

Brenna would sell these exclusive photos for record prices, as editors of newspapers and magazine went into a bidding frenzy to purchase the rights to reproduce them.

On 30 August 1997, Mario Brenna's photos were featured on the front pages of the London and Paris papers accompanied by a story about Princess Diana's Mediterranean cruise with her latest lover.

Diana's ploy worked. When Dr Khan saw the photos, he rang Diana, but her cell phone was engaged. When he rang back, a recorded voice message told him the number he wanted had been changed but offered no alternative. Cutting off her mobile number was a frequent ploy used by Diana.[105]

Had they managed to talk, it could have left the way open for Diana to fly back to London and she might still be alive. Instead, persuaded by Dodi, she agreed to spend another night in Paris which would be her last.

Diana's last days, 30 & 31 August 1997

On the morning of 30 August, Dodi and Diana rose early and left the *Jonikal* at its berth in Sardinia. They were taken to the airport by car and flown to Paris in one of Al Fayed's private jets. They arrived at Le Bourget

---

105 *The Operation Paget inquiry report into the allegation of conspiracy to murder Diana, Princess of Wales and Emad El-Din Mohamed Abdel Moneim Fayed,* London, 14 December 2006. Dr Khan did not appear in person but co-operated by giving written information to the Paget Inquiry held in London.

Airport on a hot and humid summer afternoon when Paris was crowded with tourists.

As Dodi and Diana crossed the scorching airport tarmac, they were surrounded by sweating photographers toting cameras. The paparazzi were excited by the fact that Mario Brenna's photos of Diana and Dodi were alleged to have earned him half a million pounds for first publication rights for one morning's work.[106]

Encouraged by Brenna's success, they were prepared to risk a great deal of time and money to obtain good shots of Diana and Dodi while the courting couple were hot news.

Media attention was very different from their previous incognito visit a few weeks earlier when they had walked hand in hand along the banks of the Seine and enjoyed a quiet relaxed dinner at Chez Benoit, a bistro in the rue St Martin. Dodi hoped to create the same romantic mood for this visit, intending to propose to Diana later that evening. He had made another reservation at *Chez Benoit,* planning a romantic dinner *à deux* before they returned to his apartment and he would give her a ring engraved with the words 'Tell Me Yes', with the promise of a much more expensive engagement ring later.

Mohamed Al Fayed had been busy masterminding their visit from London.[107] He arranged for Diana and Dodi to be driven from Le Bourget Airport to the Ritz in the Place Vendôme which he owned. A hairdressing appointment had been made for Diana, and they would be driven to Dodi's apartment, where they would change for dinner, enjoy a bottle of chilled champagne and the view over the Champs Elysées before dining informally at the romantic *Chez Benoit* bistro.

Philippe Dourneau, the head chauffeur employed by the Ritz, was to meet them at Le Bourget Airport in the hotel's black Mercedes. Their luggage would be taken to Dodi's apartment near the Arc de Triomphe in a Range Rover driven by Henri Paul, Head of Security.

Everything had been carefully planned by Al Fayed. Dourneau had instructions to make a detour so the couple could have another look at the Villa Windsor whose lease had been purchased by Al Fayed from the French Government in 1986 after the death of the Duchess of Windsor. The mansion had lain empty since then. Al Fayed had sent most of the

---

106 This amount was paid by Mirrorpix to Mario Brenna. A further £100,000 for second rights was paid by *The Sun* and the *Daily Mail* and still more was paid by other French, American and Italian papers.

107 Tom Bower, *Fayed the unauthorised biography*, Pan, London, 2001, states that Mohamed Abdel Fayed, son of a primary school teacher, was born in 27 January 1929 in Alexandria. In the early 1970s he added the prefix 'Al', which denotes aristocratic birth, although his eldest son, Dodi, was happy to be styled simply 'Fayed'.

furniture to auction but, impressed by royalty, had kept Wallis' love letters from Edward VIII, the king who had abandoned his throne for love. If Diana were to marry, Dodi Fayed hoped they would live at the Villa Windsor.

Diana, an aristocrat whose family possessed an ancestral mansion, had no wish to be associated with the Duchess of Windsor and was regarded by most of the British aristocracy as a social climber. Growing up amid the restrained Georgian elegance of Althorp, Diana found the opulent décor of the Villa Windsor glitzy and saw it as a place full of sad memories.

While Dodi was phoning his father, Diana called Lady Annabel Goldsmith, worried that Dodi had mentioned buying her a ring in Paris. Diana feared accepting the ring could compromise her and upset her sons. She asked Lady Annabel how to deal with this tricky situation. Dodi had been very generous; Diana had grown fond of him and did not want to hurt his feelings by refusing his gift. However, she told Lady Annabel 'I need another marriage like a rash on my face'.

The older woman suggested Diana thank Dodi for his gift, place the ring anywhere but on the fourth finger of her left hand where engagement rings are worn. This would prevent any confusion that accepting the ring meant she had agreed to marry Dodi.[108]

Diana's visit to the former home of the Duke and Duchess of Windsor took exactly twenty-eight minutes, but later, Al Fayed's PR officer Michael Cole embellished the story. He claimed Diana and Dodi had spent two hours looking at the Villa Windsor, accompanied by an interior decorator, which was an invention.[109]

At the Ritz, one of the most luxurious hotels in the world, Diana was to have her hair done by the top stylist in the Imperial Suite to ensure her privacy.

As their car headed towards the Ritz, paparazzi riding pillion on motorbikes wove in and out of the traffic, approaching dangerously close to the black Mercedes as they attempted to take photos with special flashguns designed to capture photographs through tinted glass. Dodi, upset by the flashes and the roaring of motorbike engines, screamed at Philippe Dourneau to go faster. Used to rich temperamental guests, the chauffeur ignored his demands.

Arriving at the Place Vendôme, the couple hurried through the glass doors of the Ritz and into the lobby with the papparazzi in hot pursuit.

---

[108] Tina Brown, *op. cit.*, p15, mentions the phone call to Rosa Monckton in which Diana declared she had no plans to marry Dodi. Her call to Lady Annabel Goldsmith features in *Diana* by Sarah Bradford, *op. cit.*

[109] *The Operation Paget inquiry report, op. cit.*

Diana was jostled by burly men thrusting camera lenses in her face, shouting and gesticulating to gain her attention. The manager escorted Diana to the tranquillity of the elegant Imperial Suite, where her hair was washed and blow-dried by the establishment's best hairdresser.

Meanwhile, Dodi had slipped out to visit a branch of Repossi's at Number 6 Place Vendôme to collect the engraved ring he planned to give Diana which had been sized to fit the princess.[110]

Dodi had the ring in his pocket when the couple left the Ritz at 7 p.m. in the black Mercedes, driven by Philippe Dourneau, heading for Dodi's apartment in the rue Arsène Houssaye. The paparazzi, thinking how much money they could make, once again rode dangerously close to the Mercedes, using flash guns to photograph the couple through the tinted windows of the Mercedes.

At Dodi's apartment, the couple were met by more paparazzi, shoving and pushing them. Diana was rushed inside the apartment block by two of Al Fayed's security guards.

Dodi's butler had already unpacked their cases, so they showered and dressed for the informal dinner that Diana always liked in a traditional bistro. With Dodi's arm around her, informally dressed in a black linen blazer, white trousers and high heels, Diana emerged from his apartment around 9.30 p.m. to drive to Chez Benoit. Once again, bodyguards had to clear a path so they could get to the car.

Dodi had left the Repossi 'Tell Me Yes' ring with Rene Delorm, his butler, planning to give it to Diana after dinner and instructed the butler to place a bottle of champagne on ice. Dodi, always good at romantic touches, instructed Delorm to place a love poem engraved on a silver tablet under Diana's pillow.

En route to *Chez Benoit*, they were joined by more paparazzi, swerving dangerously close to the Mercedes on their bikes. Dodi, flustered by the roar of motorbike engines, abandoned the idea of a quiet dinner at the bistro and ordered Philippe Dourneau to drive back to the Ritz. Unaccustomed to coping with the paparazzi, Dodi did not call ahead on his cell phone to inform the hotel management of his revised plan so they could arrange for additional security guards to prevent photographers from entering the hotel. Neither did he make a booking for the famous *L'Espadon* restaurant.

---

[110] The Paget Inquiry elicited the information that the ring had not been previously sighted in Monaco but was being worn by Madame Angela Repossi, from whom Dodi purchased it at the Paris showroom at No 6, Place Vendôme, with the expectation that Dodi Fayed would purchase a much more expensive ring later for Princess Diana. Monsieur and Madame Repossi altered their statements when interviewed for investigators working for the Paget Inquiry.

Dodi and Diana entered the lobby of the Ritz at 9.50 p.m. and found it filled with guests and men with cameras. The noise and confusion made Dodi so nervous he yelled at the Fayed bodyguard Kez Wingfield, 'This whole thing's a fuck-up. It's your fault.'[111]

Once again, Diana was jostled and harassed before the paparazzi were ejected by security guards. The CCTV film shows Diana looking tense, realising she was no longer in the experienced hands of Scotland Yard's Protection Squad.

Henri Paul, Head of Hotel Security, having driven the couple's luggage in the Range Rover to Dodi's apartment, had returned to the Ritz and installed himself with a glass of *pastis* in the Bar Vendôme and was chatting to Fayed's bodyguard Trevor Rees-Jones awaiting orders from Dodi, in charge of revised plans for the evening.

Henri Paul was a balding, middle-aged man recovering from a failed love affair. He was taking antidepressants and an anti-anxiety drug and should have been informed that drinking alcohol and driving while on medications was dangerous. He kept quiet about the fact he had been drinking when asked to drive Dodi and the princess to Dodi's apartment. The Head of Security was not the model employee he seemed. To earn extra cash, he accepted cash from French Intelligence for supplying information about guests in whom they or the police were interested.[112]

Henri Paul had not eaten but in the bar of The Ritz Hotel ordered another glass of pastis claiming it was 'pineapple juice' before he was to drive Dodi and Diana to Dodi's apartment. Dorneau, the hotel's official chauffeur, who had started work early that morning, was now off duty.

Dodi's revised plan involved dining at *L'Espado*n, the main restaurant of the Ritz famous for employing some of France's leading chefs, which meant that the restaurant was fully booked. But as Dodi's father owned the hotel, they had to find him a table.

It took some time for a table of the right height to be found, brought down to the restaurant and laid up while Diana and Dodi waited impatiently in the hotel's magnificent Imperial Suite, a replica of the room designed for Marie Antoinette at Versailles.

By now, it was almost ten o'clock. Diana was tired and on edge, having risen at dawn to fly from Sardinia to Paris, and she had not eaten since midday. They finally arrived at *L'Espadon* at ten o'clock and were shown to their table.

---

[111] Trevor Rees-Jones, *The Bodyguard's Story: Diana, The Crash and the Sole Survivor*, Time Warner Books, London, 2001.

[112] Revealed to the French and Metropolitan police working for the Paget Inquiry when they examined Henri Paul's bank accounts.

Diana who had dressed for an informal meal in white trousers and a linen blazer over a matching T-shirt, found herself dining in one of most exclusive restaurants in Paris among wealthy women in *haute couture* dresses and impressive jewellery and felt embarrassed.

CCTV cameras in the restaurant showed Diana annoyed by being stared at by the other diners picking listlessly at the food on her plate, by now too tired to eat, her eyes misted with tears.

Pushing her plate aside, the worlds' most photographed woman rose from the table and, with Dodi's arm around her, left the restaurant and re-entered the lift to the Imperial Suite which had a copy of the canopied bed similar to the one the ill-fated Queen Marie Antoinette had used on her last night at Versailles. Whether Diana and Dodi rested on this bed, on their last night, has never been disclosed.

The couple left the Imperial Suite around midnight on Sunday, 31 August 1997, joined in the lift by Trevor Rees-Jones and Henri Paul, the Security Officer who was to drive the hired Mercedes. The other Mercedes, with its tinted windows masking the occupants, would be used as a decoy and was to leave from the front entrance, luring the paparazzi on a wild goose chase. While the photographers were occupied, Dodi and Diana would escape via the hotel's rear entrance in the rue Cambon.

Diana, Dodi, Henri Paul and the Al Fayed bodyguard entered the glass lift which descended to the rear entrance. A CCTV camera in the lift recorded the time as 12.20 a.m. and shows Diana tense and unsmiling.

All four climbed into the hired Mercedes. Diana and Dodi sat in the back of the car, Diana on the right-hand seat with Dodi on her left. The bodyguard and the driver, Henri Paul, were in the front. For reasons never explained, Henri Paul was the only one to fasten his seat belt.

The paparazzi, alerted by friends with cell phones at the rear entrance, now realised they had been duped. They turned their motorbikes around and roared into the rue de Cambon in hot pursuit of the hired Mercedes.

Henri Paul did not take the direct route to Dodi's apartment along the rue de Rivoli and the Champs Elysées, aware traffic lights would slow them down or force them to stop. Keen to escape from the paparazzi and avoid red lights, Henri Paul took a longer route along the wide avenue called the Course de la Reine, where he could drive much faster.

The fatal crash

In the excitement of trying to evade the paparazzi, Henri Paul ignored the speed limit and entered the Pont de l'Alma tunnel with a squeal of tyres travelling way over the speed limit.[113]

Bodyguard Rees-Jones later claimed he had fastened his seat belt and warned his passengers to fasten theirs, but if this was true, his words were ignored. Had Diana and Dodi fastened the seatbelts, it might have saved their lives.

Ken Wharfe, Diana's former protection officer, always claimed the first responsibility of royal bodyguards was to ensure the safety of their royal passengers. Wharfe later blamed Rees-Jones for not doing his job properly, insisting the role of a bodyguard was 'to take a bullet for Diana, not to try and prevent her from being photographed'. He also said Rees-Jones should have insisted Princess Diana fasten her seat belt.[114]

The hired Mercedes approached the entrance to the Alma road tunnel doing more than 75 miles (120 kilometres) an hour. A CCTV camera at the entrance to the tunnel, the only one of fourteen that was working that night due to inadequate maintenance, showed Princess Diana covering her face with her hands.

From skid marks and other evidence, the French police and the investigators for the Paget Inquiry reckoned the Mercedes was doing double the speed limit. Witnesses recorded that the rear mudguard of the Mercedes was hit a glancing blow by a small white Fiat whose number plate was not recorded. Both cars were going far too fast before the black Mercedes skidded and crashed headlong into the tunnel's Pillar Number 13.

The impact of the crash sent the rented Mercedes hurtling headlong across the oncoming traffic into the opposite wall of the tunnel. The heavy car finished up facing the direction in which it had come, its front a crumpled mass of twisted metal, blocking all traffic.

Dodi Fayed and Henri Paul died instantly, Trevor Rees-Jones and Princess Diana were severely injured. Grey smoke poured from the engine of the mangled Mercedes. The tunnel reeked of burning metal. The horn kept on blaring because Henri Paul's corpse was pinned against it, his stomach and liver crushed to a pulp.

A member of the paparazzi, aptly named Monsieur Rat, was the first to arrive at the site of the crash, riding pillion on a friend's motorbike. He leaped off the bike, crossed the road, opened the rear door of the wrecked car and took the first photographs of Diana. Romuald Rat testified that the impact of the crash had thrown Diana onto the floor of the car, and her head was wedged in the gap between the front seats. One of her legs rested

---

113 Complex tests carried out in the Alma tunnel on behalf of Paget Inquiry ascertained that Henri Paul was already over the speed limit as he entered the tunnel before the black Mercedes was struck by the white Fiat Uno.

114 Detailed in Ken Wharfe, *op. cit.*

on the rear seat while the other was twisted underneath her. Diana's eyes were closed as though asleep.

Apart from a small cut on her forehead, her beautiful face was unmarked. She was moaning in pain but had no visible injuries other than this small cut.

Monsieur Rat tried to move Diana but found this impossible, took more photos, then signalled to his friend on the motorbike that the job was completed, and he was ready to leave.

This gesture gave rise to conspiracy theories promoted by Al Fayed to cover up the fact his employee had been driving far too fast. Al Fayed was backed by a witness who claimed two men on a motorbike had used a powerful hand-held laser which blinded Henri Paul, causing him to crash the car; the white Fiat Uno that clipped the Mercedes, throwing it into a skid, had been hired by MI6 as part of a conspiracy to murder Dodi and Diana. This proved to be wild conjecture. (Many years later, a Vietnamese migrant named Van Thanh admitted he had been the driver of the Fiat Uno but had been too scared to contact the police for fear he would be arrested and deported).[115]

Just after midnight on 31 August 1997, Dr Frederic Maillez, a thirty-six-year-old specialist in emergency medicine, was driving through the Alma tunnel and saw the wrecked Mercedes. He stopped and called an emergency hotline and was told that an ambulance was on its way.

Dr Maillez established that the driver and the man in the rear seat were dead and the passenger in front was badly injured. He examined the semi-conscious female passenger but failed to recognise the Princess of Wales. He fetched an oxygen cylinder and mask from the boot of his car, moved the young woman's head to make certain her airway was clear and fitted the oxygen mask. Diana's pulse was weak, she was moaning in pain and had difficulty breathing. He thought she may have been bleeding internally, but he could do little other than carry out very basic emergency.

The bodyguard employed by Al Fayed was semi-conscious with severe injuries to his head. He was the only one wearing a seatbelt.

An autopsy performed in Paris confirmed Diana's pulmonary vein had ruptured, as had the pericardium or protective sac that surrounds the

---

115 Many years later the driver of the white Fiat Uno, who had resprayed the car after the crash, fearing trouble from the police, was identified as a migrant worker named Le Van Thanh. He refused to give evidence to the Paget Inquiry, saying he did not want to be held responsible for the accident and was in fear of retribution if his name were revealed. The French police claimed that as Henri Paul's blood showed that he was over the alcohol limit Van Thanh would not be prosecuted for dangerous driving. For more details see Dennis Rice and Peter Allen, 'Owner of white Fiat Uno refuses to give evidence at Diana inquest', *Daily Mail*, 1 September 2007.

heart. Diana's chest cavity was filling with blood from a ruptured vein although outwardly she appeared untouched. Blood was slowly accumulating in her chest cavity and her long and slow journey to the operating theatre, lasting almost two hours, did not help matters.

Meanwhile, the horn of the Mercedes was still blaring as were the horns of other cars blocking the tunnel. The wailing of police sirens added to the noise and confusion. A French police officer recognised Princess Diana and advised Police Headquarters of the presence of foreign royalty, aware protocol had to be followed and the French Government notified.

Dr Maillez remained at the crash until the ambulance arrived, delayed by heavy traffic. Trained staff placed the unconscious princess on a stretcher. Whether the decision as to which hospital she was to be sent to was made by the ambulance authorities or by senior French Government officials was never clarified, although Dr Maillez appeared to think that this decision was left to Dr Martino, in charge of the coronary care ambulance.

Diana's accident occurred just after midnight, but the ambulance did not arrive until 12.40 a.m. due to heavy traffic. Before she could be transferred by stretcher, Diana suffered a massive heart attack and was given heart massage by Dr Martino, who specialised in cardiac resuscitation, and he inserted a tube into her mouth to keep her airway clear.

In a road tunnel blocked by traffic, it was impossible for a rescue helicopter to have reached Diana. In Paris, it was standard practice to take accident victims to hospital in medically supervised coronary care ambulances rather than the helicopter ambulances used in America.

French authorities believed that transferring Princess Diana to a stretcher, to an ambulance and then making a third transfer to a helicopter outside the tunnel would have risked a fatal jolt to her heart. They were convinced they were doing the best thing by keeping Diana in the coronary care ambulance and driving very slowly.

Once Diana was inside the ambulance, it took over an hour for Dr Martino to stabilise her badly damaged heart. To complicate matters, her blood pressure was still low. Worried about potholes in the road which could jolt Diana's damaged heart, the ambulance drove at a snail's pace to the large public hospital known as Pitié-Salpêtrière, six and a half kilometres from the Alma tunnel on the opposite side of the Seine. Reaching it entailed crossing a traffic-laden bridge.

Dr Maillez later admitted he would have preferred that Princess Diana had been sent to the much nearer, well-equipped Val de Grace Military Hospital at Boulevard Port Royal. on the same side of the Seine. But he was powerless to influence events as an observer.

Due to heavy traffic, it took almost two hours to transport Princess

Diana the six and a half kilometres to the cardiology dept of La Pitié-Salpêtrière University Hospital on the opposite side of the Seine to the Alma road tunnel. An unscheduled halt outside the French Natural History Museum, ten minutes from the hospital, was deemed necessary after Diana suffered a second heart attack. On that desperately slow journey to the La Pitié-Salpêtrière, Diana's blood pressure dropped dangerously low, making it necessary to use a ventilator. At the hospital, an experienced surgical team were awaiting the arrival of the Princess of Wales.

Within minutes of her arrival, Diana suffered a massive cardiac arrest and was virtually dead on arrival in the operating theatre. Her medical team did not give up and doggedly continued their attempts to resuscitate her.

By 2.10 a.m. Diana's heart had stopped completely, and her chest cavity was opened. A tear was found in the pulmonary vein and stitched up. The impact of the crash had displaced her heart from the left side of her body to the right. In spite of more massage of her heart and defibrillation procedures, Diana's damaged heart had given out.

Three and a half hours after the Mercedes crashed into a pillar in the Alma tunnel, Diana, Princess of Wales, the world's most admired female humanitarian, was declared dead and the news was broadcast worldwide.

Receiving the tragic news at Balmoral

At 3.15 p.m. the British Ambassador Sir Michael Jay called Balmoral from Paris to confirm Diana's death. Prince Charles was reported to be in shock at the news. Prince William and Prince Harry, who were on holiday with him, were not told of their mother's death until early the next morning. It was decided that it was best for the young princes to remain at Balmoral with the Queen, Prince Philip and Princess Anne and her children rather than return to London. Prince Charles, deeply upset by Diana's death and probably feeling guilty, expressed his fear that the public would blame him for Diana's death.

Prince Charles had the grim task of telling his sons that their mother was dead. For Prince Harry, still only twelve years old and frantic with grief, this was his first close experience of death. Prince William, showing the fortitude of his character, was calmer but also deeply affected, as he and his mother had been very close.

At first, the Queen and Prince Philip wanted the Spencer family to deal with all the funeral arrangements. They claimed that Diana was no longer a member of the royal family, so this was her family's responsibility.

Prince Charles, to his credit, defied his parents in this matter. He insisted that, as the mother of a future king, a royal flight should return

Diana's body to London where the princess should be given every honour and lie in state in the Chapel Royal of St James's Palace. Finally, after some discussion, this argument was accepted by the Queen.

'I always thought she would come back to me, needing to be cared for,' Charles told his Private Secretary Mark Bolland. This revealing comment demonstrates the complexity of Charles' feelings for Diana, the wife who had given him two fine sons.

Charles was deeply concerned for the young princes, who were at a very vulnerable age to lose their mother. Tiggy Legge-Bourke flew to Aberdeen and was driven to Balmoral to help organise diversions for them and their cousins to help take their minds off their grief.

Arrangements had been made for an aircraft of the Royal Air Squadron to fly Prince Charles from Aberdeen to Paris with Diana's sisters to bring back her embalmed body. Possibly the idea of a lying in state was why the body was embalmed. This was never explained properly.

No one bothered to contact Diana's mother in Scotland. Although Diana had refused to speak to her mother for months, Frances was distraught with grief when she heard the announcement of her daughter's death on the BBC's morning news broadcast.

A post-mortem carried out at Hammersmith Mortuary on the evening of Sunday 31 August 1997 attributed the cause of Diana's death 'to catastrophic injuries sustained in a car crash' but did not investigate any further.

Prince Charles told Camilla and other friends that seeing Diana dead in the mortuary in Paris was 'quite the worst sight I have ever had to bear. I could only remember the girl I had first met, and I wept for her – and for our two boys.'[116]

Funeral of the 'People's Princess', 6 September 1997

The Queen suggested that a private family funeral be held at Windsor and Diana be buried at Frogmore royal cemetery, close to Windsor Castle where minor royals including the Duke and Duchess of Windsor were buried. Diana's family would have preferred a quiet funeral at Althorp with Diana buried on an island in the middle of the lake in the grounds, and this did become her burial ground.

Diana's coffin lay in state in the Royal Chapel in St James's Palace. Initially, no flowers were allowed, but this order was rescinded after complaints from Lucia Flecha de Lima and other friends of the princess.

---

[116] Caroline Graham in *Camilla, Her True Story*, John Blake Publishing, London, 2003.

They filled the area with white lilies as well as other flowers that had been her favourites. Diana's last night was spent at St James's Palace before the funeral service that, by popular demand, was held in Westminster Abbey in the first week in September.

The Queen and Prince Philip felt it wiser that they remained at Balmoral to look after their bereaved grandsons until just before the funeral. There had been disquiet over the Queen's silence over the death of Diana and her absence from grief-stricken London. This would later be justified as necessary for the princes' grandparents to provide stability for Diana's grieving sons. The empty flagpole adorning the roof of Buckingham Palace became a focus of public concern and aroused anti-royal feeling.

Prime Minister Tony Blair did his best to mediate with the Queen, and finally, she agreed that the Union Jack should be flown at half-mast until she returned to Buckingham Palace, when the Royal Standard would be raised.

Princess Margaret was annoyed to be summoned from a holiday in Italy for Diana's funeral. The two former friends had never healed their breach after Diana's television broadcast on *Panorama* with Martin Bashir.

The area outside the gates of Kensington Palace was piled high with flowers as well as children's toys and cards containing affectionate messages from people who had admired and loved Diana. More flowers were left outside Buckingham Palace; so many flowers were left there that the sentries could no longer perform their normal sentry duty.

The Queen did not arrive in London from Balmoral until the day before the funeral amid growing disquiet. She rescued the situation by making a very moving televised speech about the Princess of Wales, written with the help of Diana's brother-in-law, Sir Robert Fellowes.

Dressed in black, the Queen told the public she was speaking as a grandmother and referred to Diana as 'an exceptional and gifted human being, with lessons to be drawn from her life and from the extraordinary and moving reaction to her death.'

Diana's televised funeral procession was watched by billions of people all over the world. The Princess of Wales was seen as a symbol of social change, a compassionate, caring woman in what was hopefully a more compassionate society.

The coffin of the Princess of Wales, draped in the royal standard, was mounted on a gun carriage. Behind it walked her husband, her father-in-law, her sons and her brother, Charles, the ninth Earl Spencer, followed by representatives of the many charities of which Diana had been a patron, a terrible walk for her young sons to endure.

On top of the flag-draped coffin was a large bunch of white freesias, Diana's favourite flowers, holding a white envelope with the one emotive word, 'Mummy', written by the twelve-year-old Prince Harry. Inside the envelope was his personal message of love to her.

Thousands of weeping mourners lined the streets to watch the procession wend its way to Westminster Abbey. At the funeral service, Prime Minister Tony Blair read the lesson and, following a suggestion from Prince William, Elton John sang an adaptation of his song 'Candle in the Wind', originally written about Marilyn Monroe and now rewritten for Princess Diana as 'Goodbye English Rose'.

Wearing dark glasses to escape the unwelcome attention of the press, a grieving Dr Hasnat Khan was also at Westminster Abbey, an entry pass having been sent him in a kind gesture by Paul Burrell, Diana's grief-stricken butler.

Diana's brother, Charles, had been in South Africa when Diana died. The ninth earl returned for the funeral in Westminster Abbey where he gave an emotional speech invoking Diana, goddess of the hunt, after whom Diana had been named. He described his sister as 'the most hunted human being in England', referring to the way the paparazzi had followed her and saw them as playing a part in her death.

Her brother spoke from the heart describing Diana as 'the very essence of compassion, of duty, of style, of beauty. All over the world, she was a symbol of selfless humanity…someone with a natural nobility who was classless and who proved in the last year that she needed no royal title to continue to generate her particular brand of magic.'

The ninth Earl Spencer praised his sister's concern for HIV AIDS sufferers, for the homeless, for lepers and landmine victims. He claimed that Diana, 'remained a very insecure person at heart, almost childlike in her desire to do good for others so she could release herself from deep feelings of unworthiness.'

Diana's brother made an emotive speech, and the Queen's godson hinted that the royal family had not dealt well with his sister. His speech was followed by what sounded like a shower of rain but in fact was the sound of thousands of people outside the Abbey clapping before the two thousand-strong congregation inside also applauded. This was a remarkable response, as normally clapping is never heard at funerals.

As Diana's favourite music, Verdi's Requiem, was played, her coffin was placed in a hearse laden with flowers for the long journey to her ancestral home via Marble Arch, the Edgeware Road and the M1 with its turnoff at Wootton to Althorp.

At one point in the county of Northamptonshire, where the Spencers are very popular, so many flowers were thrown onto the bonnet of the hearse that the chauffeur could not see out of the windscreen so had to stop the car and remove them in order to finish his sad journey.

Many hundreds of people with links to Althorp lined the route and stood there for hours to see the cortege pass. Large numbers wept, as Diana was greatly loved in the area where she had spent her teenage years.

The 'People's Princess' was buried on a small island in the middle of an ornamental lake on the Althorp estate. Later Diana's brother opened a Diana Memorial Museum containing photos, letters, dresses and other memorabilia of his sister which is now closed.

In 2013, under the terms of Diana's will, when Prince William and Prince Harry turned thirty, their mother's possessions reverted to them. Accordingly, the Diana Museum at Althorp became dedicated to telling the long and colourful history of the Spencer family.

The long vendetta of a distraught father

In 1999, two years after the crash, French judge Hervé Stephan exonerated the paparazzi for the death of Diana. The judge insisted that Al Fayed's employee, Henri Paul, whose blood alcohol reading was found to be high, was to blame. However, Al Fayed refused to admit this. Stricken by grief, Mohamed Al Fayed was unable to accept that a Fayed employee driving over the speed limit in a car hired to a Fayed company had been responsible for the death of his son and Princess Diana.

On several occasions, he claimed in front of witnesses that Prince Philip, aided by MI6, had killed the pregnant Princess Diana to prevent her marrying his son, as Dodi was a Muslim.

The statement that Prince Charles was happy was a cruel one for the Prince of Wales who was devastated by Diana's death. He and Diana had been getting along much better and she had written her ex-husband a very sweet letter of consolation when Laurens van der Post died in December 1996. Even when things were bad between them, Diana sent Charles birthday and Christmas cards stating she would always love him as the father of her beloved boys.

Using a team of lawyers and a barrister, Al Fayed presented one hundred and seventy-five 'conspiracy to murder theories' to various French courts, which delayed further investigations in England.[117]

---

[117] Martin Gregory, 'Stranded on Planet Fayed: a legal circus dominated by Fayed', *The Spectator*, 27 June 2007.

Incompetence among the French police

For some strange reason, the French police seemed totally uninterested in tracing the driver of the white Fiat Uno. However, they did express an opinion that the driver of the Mercedes had been at fault for entering the Alma tunnel too fast, skidding and slamming into the pillar but failed to discover the car had been stolen from its original owner, crashed. written off and rebuilt and, according to another Ritz chauffeur, was a dangerous vehicle none of them liked driving.[118]

Journalists from the *Daily Mail* and from *The Scotsman* investigating the crash claimed the French police were inept. It was, however, hard to be accurate about the speed of the Mercedes as, due to the crash, the speedometer of that particular model of Mercedes automatically returned to zero.

Several British journalists became critical of French police procedures and claimed the Paris police force was so inept that those in charge resembled Peter Sellers' bumbling Inspector Clouseau in the amusing *Pink Panther* films.

Unfortunately, none of the cars driving through the tunnel at the time of the accident recorded the number plate of the white Fiat Uno. Several tourists in the tunnel volunteered to provide witness statements and were surprised they were never questioned by the French police. For reasons known only to themselves, the French police initially denied a second car had glanced off the speeding Mercedes or caused damage to its paintwork.

A decade later, staff working for Operation Paget found scratches on the rear mudguard of the Mercedes containing white paint from another car. Using sophisticated tests, they identified the approximate year of manufacture of the white Fiat Uno and did their best to trace it, but without success.

The French police and ambulance authorities were later accused of issuing a statement that covered up the forty-minute delay in the arrival of the ambulance and its further delay in reaching the operating theatre. How much of the delay was due to a decision by senior French Government officials to send Princess Diana to a hospital six and a half kilometres from the Alma tunnel has also been covered up to save reputations. There were two equally good hospitals considerably closer to the Alma road tunnel.

Neither the ambulance driver Michael Masseboeuf nor the resuscitation specialist Doctor Martino were called to give evidence at the

---

118 Witness reports of a second car driving dangerously close to the Mercedes were conflicting. Some witnesses claimed the Fiat Uno was black, others said that it was white, none of them took the registration number.

French inquest. This seems extraordinary in view of the witness statement from Dr Maillez that, had Diana reached hospital without great delay, her life could have been saved.

Once he regained consciousness, the bodyguard employed by Al Fayed, Trevor Rees-Jones, would claim that the driver of the missing white Fiat Uno was at fault. The 'glancing blow' the Fiat gave the Mercedes caused it to swerve and skid as the driver of the smaller car was also driving dangerously. Al Fayed spent a great deal of money trying to trace the white Fiat Uno, convinced that his son and Princess Diana had been assassinated and the driver of the Fiat Uno was implicated and could have been paid by MI6.

His investigations turned up a French photographer called James Andanson who had at one time photographed Diana and owned a white Fiat Uno. However, Andanson was not in Paris at the time of the crash. This line of inquiry became even more complex when Andanson was found shot dead in 2000.

As part of Al Fayed's campaign against the Duke of Edinburgh and MI6, Dodi's grieving father helped fund a documentary film titled *Unlawful Killing*. The film was shown at Cannes but not in England or America, where large sums were demanded by insurers before the film was screened for fear of expensive litigation. The film echoed some of Al Fayed's legal complaints and suggested (without any evidence) that Diana had been assassinated on the orders of Prince Philip and the crash arranged by MI6 (or even rogue members of the SAS) using a dazer or hand-held laser, whose beam was used to stun Henri Paul at the entrance to the Alma tunnel.

Conspiracy theories continued to proliferate, each one wilder than the next. It was claimed the target was Dodi Fayed, murdered by one of the many enemies Al Fayed made in his spectacular rise to great wealth.

To complicate matters in this complex case, eight months before the crash, Diana penned a note addressed to no one in particular in which she claimed her husband was planning to kill her by arranging a car crash, so he could marry someone else. (A space was left blank to be filled in with the name of the woman Prince Charles wished to marry.)

An individual known to the French police under multiple identities ranging from Levi, Levick and Levestre claimed to have seen a brilliant flash of light in the tunnel when he was driving through at the time of the accident. This not very credible witness claimed the flash came from a dazer (hand-held laser) held by someone on a motorbike. Other witnesses saw the brilliant flash guns used by professional photographers to obtain good photos through tinted windows.

Monsieur Levi/Levick/Levestre (an individual not considered as credible by the Paris police) initially contacted Al Fayed via the Ritz rather than contacting the French police direct. He was produced as chief witness to support Al Fayed's claim that Diana had been murdered, and he had seen a man riding pillion on a motorbike dismount, approach the crashed Mercedes, open the door, look inside and then signal to the driver of the motorbike, giving him a 'mission completed' gesture.

Subsequent inquires suggested the man making the alleged 'mission completed' signal was likely to have been Romuald Rat, the first photographer to reach the scene of the crash and take photos. Monsieur Rat admitted he had signalled the driver of the motorbike that had brought him to the crash after he had finished taking photos. This 'mission completed' gesture was discredited by the Paget Inquiry and the inquest held in London a year later in 2007.

The Operation Paget Inquiry

Back in 1997, the allegation of murder against Prince Philip and Prince Charles using Ml6 was raised by the grief-stricken Mohamed Al-Fayed keen to shift blame for the accident from his employee, Henri Paul, in a car hired by a hotel that he owned.

The fact all the CCTV cameras inside the tunnel were found to be out of commission at the time of the accident was cited as proof of a plot, but this did not ring true. Since the shortest route to the Al Fayed apartment was via the Champs-Elysées and not through the Alma tunnel, it is unlikely anyone planning an assassination would have bothered to tamper with those particular CCTV cameras on the off-chance Diana's driver would use the Alma tunnel rather than taking the more direct route.

The fact that Henri Paul was taking antidepressants and an anti-anxiety drug, one of the benzodiazepines, was established. These medications rendered driving or operating machinery dangerous when combined with the *pastis* Henri Paul had consumed in the bar before he got behind the wheel of the Mercedes.

One important question that remained unanswered was why Princess Diana's body was embalmed immediately after her death. Since this practice is illegal in France, on whose authority was it done? And for what reason? Embalming fluids are likely to mask a pregnancy, but even now no one wants to discuss this question.

The second question is why Princess Diana, normally so very security conscious, did not fasten her seat belt in a built-up area of Paris when driving in a speeding car.

Due to public disquiet about Diana's death, between 2003 and 2006, a British inquiry into accusations of a conspiracy to murder Diana, (the Paget Inquiry) was held in London. It was conducted by Lord Stephens of Kirkwhelpington, a former head of the Metropolitan Police who had headed a major investigation into terrorism in Ireland.

The 'flash before the crash' statement provided to Mohamed Al Fayed was dismissed by the police. The fact the informant had initially contacted the Ritz Hotel rather than the police aroused suspicion. In her book, *The Diana Chronicles,* Tina Brown described Francois Levi's statement as 'the invention of a pathological liar with a criminal record'.[119]

Mohamed Al Fayed's claim that Diana was pregnant was denied by Dr Hasnat Khan. In a written statement to the Paget Inquiry, Dr Khan said that Diana was always scrupulous about taking the contraceptive pill each night.

Diana's close friend, the Hon Rosa Monckton, with whom Diana went on a short cruise around Greece in August 1977, confirmed that Diana was taking the contraceptive pill in Greece and was meticulous about taking it. Rosa Monckton stated that Diana had menstruated while she was with her on the Greek cruise, so could not have been pregnant by Dodi. She also said that Diana had told her she would never have considered marrying Dodi.

Between 27 and 29 August 1997, Diana had telephoned close friends Rosa Monckton, Lucia Flecha de Lima, Lady Elsa Bowker and Lady Annabel Goldsmith. To each of them, she said she was not planning to get engaged to Dodi but was having a wonderful time and was very happy.

The shock of Diana's death was so profound that conspiracy theories abounded, fuelled by those who remained convinced that the car crash was an assassination rather than an accident. These theories have given rise to many books and conspiracy websites. 'Every year around the time of Diana's death Buckingham Palace receives fresh conspiracy theories,' claimed Dickie Arbiter, a former press spokesman for the Queen.

The report of the Paget Inquiry, published late in 2006, dismissed much of the 'evidence' produced by Al Fayed, including the statement by Francois Levi/Leveck/Levestre, a pathological liar with a police record, that a laser beam blinded the driver of the black Mercedes.

The general consensus was that any blinding flash could have come from a power flash used by one of the paparazzi.

The Paget Inquiry discounted the claim of Mohamed Al Fayed that Diana was pregnant and about to become engaged to Dodi and that Prince Philip ordered Diana's death so Charles could marry Camilla. Since Charles and Diana were already divorced, there was no legal impediment

---

[119] Tina Brown, *op. cit.*, p460.

to Charles marrying Camilla as long as the Queen did not object.[120]

The inquiry concluded that the accident was caused by Henri Paul driving too fast in a built-up area with passengers who were not wearing seatbelts. Several experts claimed that had they been wearing seatbelts, it was probable Diana and Dodi would have survived.

The Paget Inquiry found Al Fayed's accusations without foundation, and he was made to withdraw his claims. However, his withdrawal received far less publicity than the original conspiracy theories. The report issued by the head of the Paget Inquiry, Lord Stephens of Kirkwhelpington, was regarded as meticulous.

What complicated matters was the note allegedly written by Diana in or around October 1996, nearly a year before her death, claiming Prince Charles was planning her death. It was unsigned and was not addressed to any particular person. It was authenticated by Paul Burrell as having been written by Diana, although its veracity has been queried by several eminent historians. Burrell was known to write messages in Diana's Christmas cards for her when she was busy and was good at simulating her handwriting.

In the note Diana expressed the fear that the brakes of her car would be tampered with so as to cause an accident, resulting in a serious head injury or death. Diana stated she believed this would occur in order to get her 'out of the way' so Charles could marry again.

The note was lodged with her divorce lawyers, Mishcon de Reya, and given to Scotland Yard, but for reasons never properly explained, it was never produced at the French or the British inquests by Diana's lawyers.

When Paul Burrell's book *A Royal Duty* was published in 2003, the note was printed in it. As part of the Paget Inquiry, Prince Charles was interviewed by Lord Stevens of Kirkwhelpington in 2005, the year he married Camilla.

The Paget Inquiry took several years to make their investigations. In December 2006, the Inquiry concluded that the Princess of Wales and Dodi Fayed died due to catastrophic injuries sustained in a car accident caused by the extreme intoxication of the driver, Henri Paul, and the fact he was well over the speed limit.

An inquest that had begun in 2004, which had been suspended while the Paget Inquiry did its work, recommenced in October 2007 at London's Courts of Justice, finishing in April 2008.

The verdict of the inquest handed down on 7 April 2008 was that Diana and Dodi had been unlawfully killed through the grossly negligent

---

[120] Information from the Rt. Hon Michael Alison, former Member of the Queen's Privy Council.

driving of chauffeur Henri Paul.

Lawyers for Al Fayed finally accepted that there was no medical evidence to support the theory that Diana was illegally embalmed to cover up a pregnancy. Al Fayed stated he was abandoning his campaign to prove that Diana and Dodi had been murdered and would accept the findings of the inquest.

Mohamed Al Fayed dealt with his grief by constructing a monument to Dodi and Diana in Harrods but sold the Knightsbridge department store in 2010 for £1.5 billion to Qatar Holdings, the sovereign wealth fund of the Emirate of Qatar.

Diana's lasting legacy

In memory of Diana and his son, Al Fayed generously endowed the former West Heath School so that it is now a home and school for traumatised children, a project that would have been close to Diana's heart and was most apt of all the memorial projects set up at this time.

Diana was a strong supporter of AIDS victims who were shunned by the public until she began supporting AIDS charities in 1987. At the time Diana was daring in her support of AIDS victims as the efficacy of drugs dealing with HIV had not been developed. She became the first member of the royal family to be photographed kissing someone who had the HIV virus. Photographs of this compassionate gesture helped educate the public that AIDS could not be transmitted by touch, as many people had feared.

In the final year of her life, Diana made trips to Bosnia and Angola as part of her crusade to ban the manufacture and sale of landmines. She spoke out fearlessly in Washington and London against those who manufactured and dealt in arms and urged her supporters to donate money to help injured victims rebuild their lives.[121]

A Princess of Wales Memorial Fountain and a Memorial Walk were set up in Hyde Park, and a Diana Memorial Fund was set up within hours of Diana's death. In her spirited support for banning landmines, Diana had found her greatest mission in life, helped by the psychological support

121 The splendours of Althorp are open to public from 1 July to end August. For more details see http://www.althorp.com, which gives a detailed history of the house and the Spencer family. The Diana Memorial Museum (now closed) documented her childhood, adolescence and her wedding, with glass cases displaying her clothes. Some of the thousands of condolence books the Spencer family received from all over the world are still on view. Diana's grave cannot be visited, but there is a special area on the edge of the lake where a memorial has been erected to her, and visitors can see this. The Spencer family museum records the lives of many fascinating Spencer women, including exhibits about Diana.

given to her by Dr Hasnat Khan, an important witness to Diana's state of mind in the final year of her life. He affirmed she was very emotional but was certainly not mad, as her critics have suggested.

When disaster befell the Diana Memorial Fund

At one point, the Diana Memorial Fund was receiving thousands of cheques each week from all over the world. Trustees were appointed, including Diana's sister Lady Sarah McCorquodale. Some of the donations caused blistering rows among the Trustees as to who should or should not be given money in Diana's memory.

Public donations totalled a staggering £20 million, topped up by money from corporate donors. Over the following decade, the Memorial Fund would receive publicity for the quarrels among its Trustees where gigantic egos clashed. Meetings were stormy, as the Trustees seemed incapable of agreeing which projects should be funded or what Diana would have wanted.

As the proverb goes, 'Hell is paved with good intentions.' What caused the Fund to close was an ill-judged attempt to assert moral superiority and take on the powerful American organisation Franklin Mint in the American courts to stop them selling Diana dolls without paying a licence fee. The attempt even had the backing of a legal opinion from the Fund's lawyers, but it would ultimately lead to financial disaster.

Several of the Trustees had decided misguidedly they should act as guardians of Diana's image. They accused Franklin Mint of designing and marketing Princess Diana souvenir dolls without their permission. The Fund claimed compensation from this profitable American company, which specialises in selling souvenirs and collectables in decorative boxes.

Litigation proved staggeringly expensive, and the court case dragged on and on. The prolonged legal battle cost the Diana Memorial Fund all its reserves. When finally, the Diana Memorial Fund was forced to make an out-of-court settlement with Franklin Mint, it was bankrupt and had to close amid a welter of recriminations.

In 2011, in recognition of Diana's outstanding support for charities and hospitals for sick and disabled children, the Diana Princess of Wales Memorial Award for Inspirational Young People was created.

One of Diana's most moving epitaphs was contained in a speech given by Queen Elizabeth II on the occasion of Diana's funeral when the Queen observed, 'Millions of those who had never met Diana felt that they knew her and will never forget her.'

The legacy of Diana has been enormous. It has taken twenty years for the world to realise just how much she changed the monarchy with her modern approach. She pioneered taking royal children on overseas tours and crouching down and talking to children on walkabouts instead of walking around wearing white gloves and waving at the crowds like the Queen Mother.

Diana was the first to shake hands with and even kiss AIDS victims, shake hands with people in leper colonies, although warned against doing this; she cuddled victims of landmines and cuddled children with suppurating sores from cancer. Many young European royals and Meghan Markle and Duchess Catherine are modelling themselves on her as is Australian-born Princess Mary of Denmark and several other princesses.

Out of her own personal pain as a teenager and a young wife, she developed a style of dealing with people that is now widely imitated: the 'Diana' effect, the way she would lightly touch a sick child on the cheek and create a bond, all this is special to her. Diana's' style has even influenced the Queen on walkabouts so that now she is much less formal than her mother ever was on royal occasions.

Diana's influence on the royal family has been enormous and should never be underestimated. Diana, Princess of Wales, made it acceptable to talk about depression and AIDS, and at the end of her life, she could talk about her bulimia which she had kept hidden from everyone for so many years. Her courage and determination in overcoming her initial psychological problems deserves to be acknowledged. Diana's influence on her sons was enormous, and they treasure the time she spent with them.

Madonna gave a striking tribute to the late Princess of Wales when she claimed, 'The bravest and most dignified thing about Diana was that while she exposed herself to the public, she admitted that she had problems, was flawed and vulnerable and the public loved her for it and anyone who had a chance to meet her never forgot her.'

The twentieth anniversary of Diana's death focussed on her achievements in the final years of her life in succeeding in banning the manufacture of landmines as well as on her modernisation of the monarchy. In their mother's memory in August 2017, Prince William and Prince Harry arranged for the creation of an all-white, sunken garden at Kensington Palace filled with their mother's favourite flowers – white tulips and freesias. Her sons and Duchess Catherine entertained representatives of charities with which Diana was connected to celebrate her life with them, and have plans for a statue of her, close to Kensington Palace.

Diana's greatest legacy lies in her sons who are undertaking humanitarian work of which she would approve.

The final word on his mother should come from Prince William speaking on the anniversary of Diana's death.

> *Twenty years seems like a good time to remind people of the difference that she made not just to the royal family but also to the world.*

As Prince William observed, his mother will never be forgotten. This beautiful portrait photo of Diana was taken in the month in which she died, August 1997. She was photographed at Sarajevo where she was met by Ken Rutherford, founder of the Landmine Survivors Group and with him she made visits to more survivors of landmines, which they found both comforting and inspiring. (Mirrorpix, London)

CHAPTER THIRTEEN

Camilla – Princess Consort or Queen?

My darling Camilla has stood by me through thick and thin and in difficult times. From Prince Charles' wedding speech.

Camilla has been… and always will be the love of Charles' life. She's been discreet and loyal and deserves recognition for this. Princess Diana, 1996.

The period following Diana's death was a very difficult one for Charles. He was devastated by the failure of his marriage and the difficulties he experienced in understanding the complexity of Diana's nature and her problems. He sought consolation from Camilla, the only person with whom he could discuss his feelings.

In the outpouring of grief for Diana, Camilla once again more became an object of hatred, seen by many as responsible for the break-up of Diana's marriage and, by extension, her death.

Having taken tentative steps into the public arena after her lover's divorce from Diana, Camilla was warned to keep out of the limelight for her own safety and received sacks of hate mail.

Prince Charles, no longer vacillating, soon made it absolutely clear that Camilla was a 'non-negotiable' part of his life, but Camilla was still effectively in limbo, her position undefined.

The Queen, as the head of the Church of England, believes in the sanctity of marriage and disapproves of divorce. After Diana's death, the Queen still refused to meet Camilla.

In 1998, there were numerous celebrations to mark Charles' fiftieth birthday when it would have been possible for the Queen and Camilla to meet. However, at the express wish of Buckingham Palace, this did not happen. Camilla was not invited to the birthday reception the Queen organised for her son, and celebrations that Camilla attended or organised at Highgrove or at Clarence House – where she now had her own suite – were ignored by the Queen and the Queen Mother.

That same year, a government-run poll showed that 88 per cent of the British public was violently against Charles marrying his mistress. Some fifty-four per cent of those interviewed claimed Charles should renounce the throne in favour of Prince William, something which was, still is, highly unlikely.

For some time, Camilla lay low. The couple's first joint public appearance was seventeen months after Diana's death in January 1999, at a birthday party for Camilla's sister, Mrs Annabel Elliot, at the Ritz Hotel in Piccadilly.

Camilla's first kiss in public by Prince Charles was merely a small peck on the cheek, stage-managed by Mark Bolland, Charles' Secretary-turned-spinmeister of Operation PB, (Parker Bowles) with additional advice from spin-doctoring expert, Peter Mandelson. The huge problem facing Prince Charles was the need to change the public perception of Camilla from wicked witch and marriage breaker to that of the woman he had loved when he was young and been forbidden to marry by the rules governing royal marriages.

Camilla used her divorce settlement to buy Ray Mill, a large house with plenty of grounds, but had sustained substantial losses at Lloyds after two syndicates failed in which she had invested money left to her by her grandmother.

So by now Camilla was living above her income. The Prince of Wales, who received an annual income of twelve million pounds from Duchy of Cornwall revenues, had given most of his money to Diana as a divorce settlement and borrowed from the bank to do this. But Prince Charles could not afford to let it be known that that the woman whose reputation he had ruined was in debt due to a divorce in which he was implicated. So, Charles came to the aid of Camilla and he paid the staff wages at Ray Mill and her monthly grocery bill.

However, parliament and some sections of the media were scathing when they learned that Duchy of Cornwall funds were paying Mrs Parker Bowles' living expenses and public funds were used to provide police protection for Camilla's private residence, so strong were the feelings against her.

In June 2000, the Queen hosted a party to celebrate the 100th birthday of the Queen Mother. Due to the antipathy of the Queen Mother to divorcées in general, the woman who had supported Prince Charles when he was at his lowest ebb and who he loved was not invited.

Although Camilla's parents enjoyed a devoted marriage, but the Shand and Cubitt families were riddled with adultery and divorce. Camilla's paternal grandfather, Philip Morton Shand, and her maternal grandfather, the Hon. Roland Cubitt (the future Baron Ashmore) were each divorced three times. Camilla's wealthy Cubitt uncles had eight wives between them as well as several mistresses and illegitimate children – an embarrassing background for a royal wife.

Very slowly British society was changing its attitude to divorce. Between the years 1960 and 2000, divorce had increased by a staggering five hundred per cent. At the start of the twenty-first century, a newspaper poll found that sixty-eight per cent of the British population felt that Prince Charles and Mrs Parker Bowles should be allowed to marry.

A former Archbishop of Canterbury, Dr George Carey, warned that should this royal marriage be allowed to proceed it could cause a crisis in the Anglican Church. The fact that Camilla's former husband was alive made it harder for the church authorities to authorise a church wedding. However, within the hierarchy of the Anglican Church, there was a growing opinion that it would be preferable to have the heir to the throne and future head of the Anglican Church married, rather than living in sin.

The Queen finally recognises Camilla

Camilla was now firmly ensconced in the prince's life. Charles insisted staff and visitors acknowledge her as though she was his wife, addressing her as 'Ma'am'. Even Camilla's closest friends were required to stand as she entered or left the room.

Prince Charles used a birthday party he was hosting for his cousin, ex-King Constantine of Greece, to bring matters to a head with his parents. He sent them an invitation which made it clear that Camilla was acting as his hostess.

Prince Philip's office excused him from attending the birthday party on the grounds he had a prior engagement. However, in a volte-face that surprised many of her subjects, the Queen accepted the invitation. The hostility of some senior Anglican bishops towards divorce made it difficult for the Queen to meet the divorced Mrs Parker Bowles officially and condone what the Church believed was a sinful relationship. However, this was an informal rather than a formal occasion.

When the Queen arrived at Highgrove for the party, she was greeted by Prince Charles, who presented a very nervous Camilla to his mother. The Queen gave Camilla a brief nod of acknowledgement and a tight-lipped smile but was careful to keep her son's mistress at a distance and avoid being photographed with her.

This brief meeting of the monarch and the 'scarlet woman' made the front page of the *Daily Telegraph*, which bore the headline: 'Finally The Queen Recognises Mrs Parker Bowles'.

King Constantine's birthday party had a welcome outcome. Prince Charles was invited to bring Mrs Parker Bowles to Buckingham Palace for a private meeting with the Queen.

A catalyst for change was the death of the Queen Mother on 30 March 2002. She had refused to invite Camilla to Clarence House or Birkhall but remained good friends with Camilla's husband, the philandering Brigadier

Andrew Parker Bowles, who escorted her to various race meetings.

The Queen Mother's death left the way open for a rapprochement between Buckingham Palace and Highgrove. Mrs Camilla Parker Bowles received an invitation to attend the Queen Mother's funeral but was seated far away from Prince Charles to ensure there would be no photos of the two of them together. Camilla was allocated a seat at the extreme rear of Westminster Abbey, while Prince Charles was seated in the front row with the Queen, Prince Philip and other members of the House of Windsor.

Emotive funeral orations included one by Prince Charles, who described the Queen Mother's fortitude in World War Two and her morale-boosting visits to bomb-blasted areas in the East End consoling Londoners who had lost their homes. For Prince Charles, the death of his beloved grandmother marked the end of an era. In a televised address to the nation, he praised his grandmother's 'panache, style and unswerving dignity'.

The Queen Mother's funeral was followed by the Queen's Golden Jubilee Service of Thanksgiving in late 2002. Charles assumed that he and Camilla would be seated together, but once again, the Buckingham Palace mandarins seated Mrs Parker Bowles ten rows behind Charles and the rest of his family.

The Prince of Wales could barely hide his fury at what he regarded as a public humiliation of the woman he loved. He was so angry he told Buckingham Palace staff he would have nothing to do with planning the next big occasion, which would take place ten years later in 2012 for the Queen's Diamond Jubilee celebrations.

After the death of his grandmother, Clarence House became Prince Charles' official London residence. Charles also inherited some superb antiques and paintings from his grandmother.

Clarence House was renovated to Charles' specifications, regardless of cost. Figures presented to parliament showed that the Prince of Wales spent over £6 million renovating Clarence House. This included redecorating a luxurious suite for Mrs Parker Bowles. The cost raised a few eyebrows at Buckingham Palace, where the Queen and Prince Philip live much more modestly than Prince Charles, as they have to meet the cost of the upkeep of other royal residences. Thanks to his Duchy of Cornwall revenues, Prince Charles is by far the wealthiest member of the House of Windsor.

The final indignity for Camilla occurred in front of friends in November 2004. It happened in front of over 600 wedding guests, when Edward van Cutsem, Prince Charles' 29-year-old godson, married heiress, Lady Tamara Grosvenor, the eldest daughter of the Duke of Westminster. Prince Charles was seated in the front row beside the Queen, Prince Philip and Princes William and Harry but Camilla was sidelined, seated several rows back on the side of the church reserved for the bride's family, rather than beside Prince Charles on the side of the groom. The van Cutsem and Grosvenor families insisted the separation of Prince Charles and Mrs Parker Bowles was dictated by protocol, as Charles' mistress could not be seated next to the Prince of Wales with the Queen at the wedding.

A dance to the music of time

In 2005, the Queen, hoping to restore harmony with her heir, agreed to a second private meeting with Prince Charles and his 'constant companion' Mrs Parker Bowles at Buckingham Palace.

The Queen was faced with a dilemma, and she needed to discuss the situation with her heir. Although the royal family was supposed to set a moral example to the nation, over time entrenched attitudes to sexuality and divorce had changed. A large proportion of the British public was now divorced and in new relationships. By refusing to recognise divorce or to remarry divorcées the Church of England risked becoming irrelevant to the lives of many of its adherents.

It finally dawned on the most conservative members of the Anglican Church that, should the Queen die unexpectedly, the Archbishop of Canterbury would have to crown a king who, according to the Church, was 'living in sin' with Camilla, a divorced woman.

By now several members of the Privy Council, as well as senior members the Anglican Church, were feeling that Charles had paid a high price for doing his duty and marrying Diana to produce an heir. Several senior figures in the church were prepared to change the rules. Charles and Camilla could have a ceremony of blessing, *provided* they acknowledged they had sinned in the eyes of God. This was a tricky situation without precedent in British history.

After much agonising, the Anglican Church hierarchy finally agreed that Prince Charles and Mrs Parker Bowles should marry as soon as possible, but *not* in an Anglican church. As a compromise – the British being good at compromises – after a civil ceremony, a ceremony of blessing would be allowed at Windsor Castle, in which the couple must acknowledge they had sinned in the eyes of God.

On receiving this advice from the Archbishop of Canterbury, the Queen decided to allow the marriage, and purely as a matter of form, the Prime Minister added his approval.

With the consent of the Queen, thirty-four years after they first met and began their love affair, after numerous setbacks Prince Charles was finally able to ask the woman he loved to marry him. He proposed to Camilla (allegedly on bended knee) at Birkhall, the Scottish house on the Balmoral estate he inherited from his grandmother. Charles gave Camilla a diamond engagement ring consisting of a large diamond surrounded by smaller baguette diamonds that had once belonged to the Queen Mother, who must have been turning in her grave.

In her first press interview, Camilla told journalists how happy she was that 'the two of us can now be together as man and wife'.

'Operation PB' designed to 're-brand' Camilla

The major hurdle Prince Charles faced was to persuade the British public to accept his mistress as his second wife. For years Camilla had been vilified after the disclosures about her in Andrew Morton's book and over 'Camillagate'. When it was revealed that public money was being used to provide a police guard for Camilla's private residence, this caused a furore similar to the one aroused centuries earlier when it was revealed that Charles II had taken Treasury funds to maintain soldiers to support his mistresses. It seemed the maxim, 'The more things change, the more they stay the same' was true.

To prepare the British public for Camilla's impending marriage to Prince Charles, Operation Parker Bowles, code-named Operation PB, was set up on the advice of former MP Peter Mandelson, considered to be a master spin doctor. *The Daily Express* was outraged and claimed that those who had adored Princess Diana were appalled at the idea of Prince Charles marrying an adulteress who might become Queen.

However, Prince Charles remained sanguine in the belief that, given time, the public would change their perception of Camilla and they would recognise her intelligence, integrity and loyalty. The difficulty was how to get them to accept Mrs Parker Bowles as someone who had supported the prince through difficult times and enabled him to perform his royal duties with a sense of purpose.

The fact that Princess Diana was still greatly loved made Camilla's transition from royal mistress to royal wife difficult. Diana's influence was still so powerful that Camilla chose to be styled Duchess of Cornwall rather than take the title of Princess of Wales, which was so closely associated with Diana.

Diana had been a young and beautiful bride. Having lived through years of criticism, Camilla, at the age of fifty-seven, knew she was being compared with Princess Diana, who had died in her early thirties at the height of her beauty and elegance. Like Marilyn Monroe, Diana would remain young and beautiful in the memories of those who loved her.

Camilla was and is more attractive in real life than her photographs, which often showed her in hunting gear grimly urginge her horse over high fences, her bouncy blonde hair confined under a black velvet riding hat.

Other photographs showed Camilla working in her garden, her hair unkempt, wearing an old shapeless sweater and muddy jeans. Photos of Camilla at hunt balls show a more glamorous figure in sexy off-the-shoulder ball gowns that revealed her magnificent cleavage.

Between 2001 and 2002 the transformation of Camilla's public image from a country woman obsessed with horses and gardens into a well-groomed, elegant royal consort, went into overdrive. Charles had been deeply hurt by the criticisms of Camilla and unfavourable comparisons with Diana. Money was no object.

Operation PB was assisted by a team which included the brilliant British clothes designer Anna Valentine, beauty specialists and dieticians. Decades as a heavy smoker and holidays in the sun had taken their toll on Camilla's complexion. However, treatments by a beauty therapist who administered expensive 'bee-sting' facials by injection (considered more effective than injections with Botox) gradually smoothed away some unwelcome lines.[122]

The Belgravia workshop of the Irish hat designer, Philip Treacy, created large picture hats, similar to the hats worn by Mrs Keppel and the Queen Mother, which were very flattering to mature women. However, Camilla is relatively petite, so it was vital the brims of her hats were not too large, or she would resemble a giant mushroom.

Her first official portrait photographs show Camilla in a flattering lilac dress. Her hair had been restyled and lightened to a silvery blonde, and her teeth had been whitened. Giving up smoking was difficult, and it took several years before Camilla finally succeeded. Flattering outfits and good hairdressing were important, but a great deal of Operation PB's success was ascribed to the fact that when people met Camilla, they came to realise that she was a very pleasant woman who was easy to get along with and devoid of snobbishness.

A Windsor wedding for the Duchess of Cornwall

On 10 February 2005, with the approval of the Queen and Her Majesty's Privy Council, Clarence House announced that Mrs Camilla

---

[122] This skin cream contains a percentage of bee-venom that increases blood flow to the skin and aids the elasticity of the skin by mimicking the effects of a bee sting.

Parker Bowles and Prince Charles were to marry on 8 April 2005.

At the last moment, the date had to be changed due to the death of Pope John Paul II. The ceremony was postponed by twenty-four hours to enable Prince Charles to attend the Pope's funeral as the Queen's personal representative.[123]

Finally, on 9 April 2005, Charles and Camilla were married in a civil ceremony in Windsor's Guildhall, which served as the town's registry office, followed by a ceremony of blessing in St George's Chapel in the grounds of Windsor Castle.

This was the first time a Prince of Wales had legally married his mistress. Since many people regarded Camilla as responsible for the breakdown of Diana's marriage, there were fears of hostile demonstrations outside the Guildhall. A band was hired to drown out any possible noise from demonstrators. In the event, it was not needed as there were no protests.

Several British colonies issued commemorative stamps recording the wedding of Prince Charles and the newly created Camilla, Duchess of Cornwall

For her civil wedding, instead of a veil, Camilla wore a large flattering hat by Philip Treacy, whose hats were now her trademark. Her wedding hat was a superb confection trimmed with a fountain of feathers that toned with her newly silvery-blonde hair and she looked very elegant.

The Queen, as Supreme Governor and Defender of the Faith, for reasons of protocol did not attend her son's second wedding at the Windsor Guildhall. Also, for reasons of protocol, since the Queen and

---

123 Legal opinions have suggested that modifying this appellation to 'Defender of Faiths' would be open to challenge by the Church of England.

Prince Philip did not attend, Camilla's widowed father, Major Bruce Shand was also absent.

However, Prince William, Prince Harry and Camilla's children, Tom and Laura Parker Bowles, acted as witnesses at the ceremony. The contretemps between Tiggy Legge-Bourke and Camilla was long over, and Tiggy – or to give her correct title, Mrs Pettifer – and her new husband were guests.

Following the registry office ceremony, a Service of Prayer and Dedication took place in St George's Chapel, Windsor Castle, under the colourful banners of knights of old suspended from its magnificent vaulted ceiling. It was one of those ceremonies British royalty do so well.

For the second event in her big day, Camilla confounded her critics by appearing at the ceremony of blessing in an elegant floor-length silk coat, embroidered with gold thread, over a silk chiffon dress in similar tones, also designed by Anna Valentine.

The 'Service of Prayer and Dedication' held in St George's Chapel was attended by the Queen, Prince Philip and Camilla's widowed father. To mollify devout members of the Anglican Church, a clause had been inserted into the ceremony in which Camilla and Charles were made to acknowledge their 'manifold sins and wickedness'. This phrase, taken from the Anglican Book of Common Prayer, referred to their former adulterous relationship.[124]

At the reception in Windsor Castle, Prince William gave his new stepmother an affectionate kiss. In his wedding speech Prince Charles thanked, 'My darling Camilla, who has stood by me through thick and thin and in difficult times.'

The Queen made a witty speech, in which she referred to the famous high jump known as Beecher's Brook in the annual Grand National horse race, saying, 'Camilla and Charles have overcome Beecher's Brook and all kinds of terrible obstacles. They have come through. I am very proud and wish them well. My son is home and dry with the woman he loves.'

Camilla received a personal coat of arms from the Queen, and as well as becoming Duchess of Cornwall, also received the title of Duchess of Rothesay. She uses this ancient Scottish title north of the border, where Charles is known as the Duke of Rothesay. Camilla also gained the right to be addressed as Her Royal Highness, ensuring her royal status was recognised.

---

124 'Adultery' is defined by the *Oxford English Dictionary* as 'a sexual relation of a married person with one who is not his or her lawful spouse, whether unmarried, or married to another'.

As Duchess of Cornwall, Camilla became the second highest ranking royal female in the United Kingdom but was placed fourth in order of precedence below the Queen, Princess Anne and Princess Alexandra, who were born royal.

A Duchess' nervous public appearances

While old friends were delighted to see Prince Charles happier than he had been for years, friends of Diana were unable to forgive Camilla for the misery she had caused to the young Princess of Wales. Prince Charles' net worth in land and property was estimated at £210 million, and her critics felt that Camilla was reaping the rewards of her adulterous relationship by marrying for money as well as status.

During the first two years of her marriage, public feeling against Camilla still ran high. She was nervous about appearing in public so did not accept many public engagements. In 2007, Camilla's appointments diary showed only 137 public engagements and four foreign visits with her husband, and she made no speeches in public. In the same year, the Queen turned eighty-one and carried out 425 public engagements. Prince Charles had 498 engagements, which led Camilla's critics to call her 'The Duchess of Dolittle'. Mark Bolland, Prince Charles' Deputy Private Secretary and spin doctor, was frustrated by Camilla's reluctance to speak in public. In a moment of exasperation, Mark Boland described her as 'the laziest woman in Britain', a comment seized upon with glee by Camilla's critics.

However, laziness was not Camilla's problem. Mark Bolland failed to realise how nerve-wracking Camilla found public appearances, having lived through years of scathing criticism of her relationship with Charles.

Camilla's father defended his daughter and claimed, 'We brought Camilla up to take on new challenges. She won't fail, but she will take things slowly.'

It took many years for people's perceptions of Camilla to change and for them to see her not as a scarlet woman but a loyal wife trying to do a good job as patron of various charities. Some of her enemies insisted they would never accept her as Queen. A large proportion acknowledge she is working hard at her charities and are happy to accept her as long as she remains Duchess of Cornwall or Princess Consort but do not want her to become Queen.

Diana was helped by voice coach Peter Settelen to project her voice in public and made her 'Secrets Tapes' for him and Camilla, who has an attractive husky voice, also took professional tuition in the art of public speaking. Her initial nervousness overcome, Camilla is now a confident speaker and advocate for the causes she espouses.

Mark Boland recanted his previous criticism of Camilla and later described her as 'a lovely woman, kind and patient. She has no desire to be famous or popular but doesn't want to be hated. Being demonised by the newspapers has been upsetting for her and also upset Prince Charles, as he feels responsible for it.'[125]

With her growing schedule of public engagements, Camilla needed her own office and staff. Instead of selecting a titled lady-in-waiting to assist her, Camilla chose Mrs Joy Camm, a highly efficient former theatre sister at St Bartholomew's Hospital and wife of a senior London heart specialist.

Joy-Maria Camm had had plenty of experience in stressful situations and proved to be unflappable with a keen eye for detail and shared Camilla's sense of humour. Mrs Camm was given two assistants to help her with Camilla's extensive programme of talks and public engagements. Camilla acquired her own dresser and personal hairdresser to accompany her on official tours. Later she admitted she found touring very tiring in countries with hot climates.

With a generous clothing allowance from Prince Charles, Camilla was helped by the talented British designer Anna Valentine, whose flair for creating stylish, beautifully-cut clothes transformed Camilla's wardrobe. With good grooming and a flattering hair colour and styling, Camilla has demonstrated that women of her age can look very good indeed.

A major test for Camilla was her first overseas tour, accompanying her husband to the United States. There were fears at Clarence House that there might be demonstrations against her, as Princess Diana had been so popular there. These fears proved groundless.

Those who met Camilla on her first tour of the United States reported that the Duchess of Cornwall was refreshingly natural. She has a keen sense of humour, is naturally outgoing, and has the ability to put people at their ease.

The purpose of the visit was for the Prince of Wales to receive a medal for environmental awareness and to visit New Orleans in the aftermath of Hurricane Katrina. However, critics pointed out that the couple's flight to Philadelphia with an entourage of thirty people had discharged a great deal of pollution into the atmosphere; on environmental grounds, it might have been better to have stayed in England – a criticism which could be applied to all international environmental conferences where delegates arrive by air. Prince Charles' response to this sort of criticism is his funding

---

[125] Mark Boland, *PA Magazine.* Date unknown.

and support of reforestation projects.

At an official function held in Philadelphia, a city with a large working-class population, the Duchess of Cornwall raised eyebrows by wearing a heavy necklace of diamonds and rubies the size of quails' eggs. Ingrid Seward, editor of *Majesty* magazine, observed that 'rubies dangling in the cleavage was not a good look' for women of Camilla's age.

The necklace, worth over £2 million, had been a gift to Camilla from Saudi Arabian Prince Al-Waleed bin Talal. The prince, one of the world's richest men, owned London's Savoy Hotel as well as having shares in Apple, Twitter and Murdoch's News Limited. A confirmed Anglophile, the prince had been introduced to Camilla in London. He met the Duchess again when she visited the Persian Gulf with Prince Charles. Greatly impressed, he called her 'an exceptional woman' and made her this valuable gift.

Diana's memorial service – Camilla's nightmare

In July 2007, over one hundred and fifty guests attended a party at Highgrove to mark the Duchess of Cornwall's sixtieth birthday. The year 2007 was also the tenth anniversary of Princess Diana's death.

Prince William and Prince Harry had organised a memorial service for Diana in August and invited Camilla. Staff reported that Camilla and Charles argued over whether she should go. The service was to be held at the Guards Chapel in Wellington Barracks on 31 August 2007.

Camilla felt that accepting her stepsons' invitation to a memorial service for Diana was unwise, but Charles insisted that his wife accompany him. Camilla was caught in a double bind – damned if she did attend and damned if she didn't. Her husband's advisors repeatedly told her it was appropriate for her to attend. Against her better judgement, Camilla agreed to do as her husband and his advisors wished and accepted the invitation.

When it became known that Camilla would be at the memorial service, there was a public outcry, with an avalanche of angry letters to newspaper editors and vitriolic comments on social media. Memories of Diana and resentment of Camilla were still too fresh in people's memories to accept her presence at the memorial.

The Queen was consulted. She made it known that she would support Camilla's decision if she decided not to attend. It was hastily announced that the Duchess of Cornwall would not attend the Diana Memorial Service as she did not wish to 'divert attention from the purpose of the occasion, which was to focus on the life and service of Princess Diana'.

In spite of her dignified withdrawal, Camilla must have felt humiliated that once again she was the object of criticism. Anti-Camilla websites had a field day – one describing her as 'an avaricious adulteress'.

Camilla spent the day of the Diana Memorial at Birkhall, while Charles attended the service with his sons. The adverse publicity was a setback for the rebranding Camilla campaign. All the old accusations against her were recycled. Camilla struggled to hide her distress as she was once again exposed to criticism.

Prince William and Prince Harry were in a difficult position. They knew they had to invite Camilla, as ignoring her would be interpreted as a deliberate slight. In their childhood, they had witnessed their mother's unhappiness and had disliked Camilla. But as young adults they realised there were two sides to the story in every unhappy marriage: they had to accept Camilla as their father's wife, the woman who made their father happy and who was now part of their extended family.

In 1998, years before they were married, Charles and Camilla accepted an invitation to attend a dinner and music recital at Spencer House on 14 November in honour of Charles' birthday. This was hosted by Lord Rothschild, whose renovations had saved the Spencers' stately home, and now held a one hundred and twenty-year lease on the property.

The Diamond Jubilee and Camilla's total acceptance by the Queen

In 2012, Queen Elizabeth demonstrated her acceptance of Camilla as a member of the royal family by giving her daughter-in-law a public role at the Diamond Jubilee celebrations. When Prince Philip was unexpectedly admitted to hospital, Prince Charles and Camilla took his place beside the Queen in the royal carriage. The Duchess of Cornwall was seated beside the Queen at several Jubilee events.

From the ease with which the Queen and the Duchess chatted away, it was apparent that Her Majesty had come to approve of Camilla. The appearance of the Queen, Camilla and Charles together and in accord with each other, sent the public the message that, should anything untoward happen, Prince Charles and the Duchess of Cornwall would be there to stand in.

Proof that the Queen was pleased with her daughter-in-law's hard work was the fact she bestowed on Camilla a Membership of the Royal Family Order of Queen Elizabeth II. The Royal Family Order is worn only by female members of the royal family. It consists of a miniature portrait of the Queen painted on ivory, set in diamonds, suspended from a yellow ribbon to be worn on state occasions. The Royal Family Order is the Queen's highest personal honour and was awarded to Camilla on the occasion of her and Charles' seventh wedding anniversary, in recognition of her service to the Queen.

In April 2012, the Duchess of Cornwall was made Dame Grand Cross of the Royal Victorian Order (GCVO) with a medal presented to her by the Queen, and she also received the Queen's Diamond Jubilee Medal. Peter Mandelson was correct when he told Mark Boland at the start of Operation PB, 'Time heals many wounds and changes everything.'

Sadly, Princess Diana, who yearned for praise and recognition from Buckingham Palace and who achieved a great deal as a humanitarian, never received an official award from the Queen, her mother-in-law.

Camilla and Highgrove

The gardens of Highgrove, largely designed by Charles and Camilla with advice from two keen female gardeners, are now considered to be some of southern England's finest gardens.

House guests at Highgrove House are served organic food grown on the home farm and in the vegetable garden of the main house. The Prince of Wales' parties are more extravagant than those of the Queen and Prince Philip, who are more concerned with economy than their heir. In the lavish mode of Edward VII and the Queen Mother, Prince Charles entertains in the grand style and hires additional staff when he gives a party so that house guests have their own personal butler.

Former house guests at Highgrove confirm that Camilla is an accomplished hostess. Weekend visitors have included actors Stephen Fry, Rupert Everett, Richard E Grant and Joanna Lumley, all of whom have enjoyed Camilla's dinner parties and noted her ability to put people at their ease and to soothe a tired prince.

Another house guest was Alexander McCall Smith, the popular Edinburgh author of the *Number One Ladies' Detective Agency* novels and other amusing books. McCall Smith, Emeritus Professor of Medical Law at the University of Edinburgh, is an excellent judge of character. A few years ago, he told his aunt, Dr Janet Irwin, that when he and his wife were invited as weekend guests to Highgrove, he found Camilla 'delightful, intelligent, easy to talk to and a very considerate hostess'.[126]

---

126 Dr Janet Irwin, personal communication to the author. Dr Irwin, a dedicated supporter of women in developing countries and women's refuges, died in New Zealand after devoting her life to university medicine.

A writer who speaks highly of Camilla is the effervescent Australian Kathy Lette, married to the well-known human rights barrister Geoffrey Robertson. Kathy praises Camilla as 'down-to-earth and entirely natural, a warm, intelligent and compelling person'. She says that one of the most endearing things about Camilla is her ability to laugh at herself.

Charles and Camilla share an off-beat sense of humour. Camilla has a wide circle of friends from many different walks of life and tells the occasional risqué joke at the dinner parties she hosts.

One wife of a Lord Lieutenant of an English county (who does not wish to be named for obvious reasons) used to dread having to entertain Prince Charles and Princess Diana but enjoys entertaining him with Camilla. She describes Charles as being much more relaxed with Camilla beside him.

When together at official functions the royal couple laugh at private jokes and seem genuinely happy. Of course, they have occasional disputes as on occasion they have different preferences – as do most married couples. Prince Charles is obsessively neat, while even Camilla's closest friends admit she is woefully untidy. He likes to sleep with the windows open (to which he became accustomed to as a boarder at Gordonstoun), while Camilla prefers a warm bedroom.

Support for charities & worthy causes

The Duchess of Cornwall has become involved with charities that reflect her interests. Her name is associated with raising money for the prevention and treatment of osteoporosis, as well as supporting women's crisis centres, animal welfare organisations and organisations promoting literacy.

Camilla has done much to raise public awareness of the terrible effects of osteoporosis and has raised a great deal of money for this cause. She has been President of the National Osteoporosis Society since 1997 and chaired meetings and calling for more government assistance to the victims of this terrible condition in which bones become honeycombed and crumble; sufferers used to die in great pain without substantial pain relief.

The commitment of the Duchess of Cornwall to this organisation was the result of how she and her family watched helplessly as their mother, Rosalind Shand, died a slow and painful death in 1994.

The Duchess has described how, 'Seeing someone you love die slowly, in agony and knowing nothing about the disease that killed them is heart-breaking. My family and I watched in horror as my mother literally shrank in front of our eyes. She lost about eight inches in height and became so bent that she was unable to digest her food properly.'

In an effort to help, the Duchess of Cornwall has opened bone scanning units and osteoporosis centres to help sufferers. She has been honoured with an award from the Royal Society and has a Centre for Treatment of Osteoporosis at the Royal Cornwall Hospital named after her in recognition of her work to improve treatment of this distressing condition. The National Osteoporosis Society has created an annual Duchess of Cornwall Award to reward those who raise funds to bring relief to sufferers from this painful disease that afflicts so many of the elderly.

Camilla is very concerned about illiteracy in adults and children. Her lifelong enjoyment of reading and belief in the importance of literacy has motivated Camilla to accept the post of patron of the National Literacy Trust. She has launched campaigns to promote literacy among adults and visits schools and libraries in order to give readings to young children. The Duchess of Cornwall constantly stresses the importance of literacy and how difficult life is for those who are illiterate. She urges children to turn off Facebook and open a real book.

Camilla has also won praise for her support and assistance for battered wives and rape victims. Her valuable work began in 2009, after visiting nine rape crisis centres and hearing harrowing stories from rape victims. Camilla is practical in her approach to problems and suggested ways in which money could be raised to help victims of assaults.

In 2010, Camilla joined Boris Johnson, then Mayor of London, to open a rape crisis centre in the London suburb of Ealing, followed by the opening of more rape crisis centres in Fulham, Hillingdon, Hounslow and Hammersmith.

In 2013, Camilla broke new ground by holding a meeting at Clarence House to bring together victims of domestic violence and the various support groups for them. Having recently visited nine different rape crisis centre in Derbyshire, she asked a group of abused and battered wives who had fled from violent homes what they needed, and they told her their most pressing need was for wash bags and toiletries. They had left their homes with no possessions and no money and were unable return for fear of more violence. Camilla paid helpers to assemble seven hundred and fifty wash bags containing toiletries, a face flannel and other necessities, so each victim of domestic violence would receive a practical gift.

The Duchess of Cornwall is a keen supporter of animal welfare organisations, providing help for dogs and other animals who are victims of cruelty, and she visits the animal shelters to see how the animals are cared for. Animal lovers are aware that visits to shelters for homeless dogs are harrowing as they are confronted by the imploring eyes of many dogs and cats that have been victims of cruelty and know it is impossible to give every one of them a home.

In 2011, Camilla adopted a Jack Russell puppy when visiting London's famous Battersea Dogs and Cats Home, which finds homes for rescued and abandoned animals. Photos of the Duchess with her new puppy resulted in a surge of rescue dogs being adopted. The following year the Duchess of Cornwall opened two veterinary facilities at Bristol University providing treatment for sick animals. Since 2006 she has been President of the Brooke Hospital for Animals, the largest equine charity in the world.

Camilla is a keen supporter of the adoption of abandoned cats and dogs as Patron of the Battersea Dogs and Cats Home and has taken home some abandoned animals herself.

The Duchess of Cornwall's passion for gardening led her to accept the role of official Patron of Scotland's Garden Scheme, which opens some of Scotland's most beautiful private gardens to the public in order to raise money for various charities. Her interest in horticulture is reflected in her support of the United Kingdom Vineyards Association since winemaking is once again thriving in various parts of England, just as it did when the Romans occupied Britain.

As the daughter and former wife of army officers, Camilla enjoys close links with military organisations.[127] She has been praised for the

---

[127] She has been appointed Royal Colonel of the 4th Battalion of the Rifles, Honorary Air Commodore, Colonel-in-Chief of the Royal Australian Corps of Military Police and is Colonel-in-Chief of the Queen's Own Rifles of Canada.

kindness and empathy she has shown grieving widows and families of soldiers killed in Iraq and Afghanistan.

Conquering her initial nervousness, the Duchess of Cornwall has spoken on a range of subjects ranging from the value of soil conservation and the importance of the freedom of the press in a democratic society – a magnanimous gesture from someone who has suffered greatly at the hands of the tabloid press.

A loyal supportive wife rather than a rival

Marriage to Camilla has given Prince Charles the peace and happiness his earlier life lacked. Mindful of the rivalry that developed between her husband and Diana when Diana was the main attraction on their visits overseas, Camilla is always careful to remain in the background to allow the cameras to focus on her husband.

When married to the volatile Princess Diana, Charles often had difficulty controlling his temper as they argued about so many things, including Camilla. On one occasion, according to his valet Ken Stronach, Charles threw his boot jack at Diana. (This is a heavy wooden clamp designed to hold a boot while the wearer removes it.) Things are very different today as Camilla's calm nature defuses difficult situations and several of his friends have confirmed that Charles is a much happier person. He seems to have developed anger management strategies and acknowledges that in Camilla he has a wonderful even-tempered wife.

Should the situation at Highgrove become tense for any reason, Camilla can resolve matters by spending a few days in her private residence, Ray Mill House. Like her great-grandmother, the Duchess of Cornwall remains calm in a crisis.

This was evident when the Rolls Royce in which she and Prince Charles were travelling was attacked by students protesting against the trebling of university fees. Some of the protesters (not all of them students) broke windows and threw paint on the royal car after it became separated from its police escort. Through the open window of the royal limousine, a long stick was jabbed in the Duchess of Cornwall's ribs by an angry protester. The Duchess sat stoically, ignoring the attack while surrounded by an angry mob.

When the danger was over, Camilla dismissed the attack with the comment, 'Ah well, there's a first time for everything.'[128]

---

128 Report in *The Guardian,* 10 December 2010, headed 'Prince Charles and Camilla caught up in London violence after student fee vote'.

Camilla has admitted to close friends she sometimes finds the formality of royal life annoying and misses her privacy. Her husband insists on strict protocol, enjoys a formal lifestyle and is used to being surrounded by servants. Camilla dislikes the fact that protocol requires even her closest friends to curtsey to her when they visit Highgrove or Clarence House and at public functions.

Camilla's family home, Ray Mill House, a gabled stone manor house on the outskirts of Laycock, the unspoiled picture-book village preserved by the National Trust, is where Camilla can forget protocol and formality, kick off her high heels and relax with family and friends.

Ray Mill, like her previous homes, has been decorated and furnished in the relaxed but elegant style associated with English country houses.

By agreement with her husband, Camilla often spends much of the Christmas holidays with her children and grandchildren at Ray Mill House rather than at Sandringham or Balmoral, which gives Prince Charles the opportunity to go shooting and deer stalking with his father and his sons.

At last a 'marriage of true minds'

Before he married Diana, Charles told friends that 'a marriage of true minds' was what he was looking for, and this is what he has found with Camilla. They share so many interests including a love of country life, horses, riding, dogs and gardens, enjoy classical music and opera, and take European holidays together.

Charles and Camilla have enjoyed holidays in Italy and Turkey and have cruised around the Greek coast on the yacht of Greek billionaire, John Latsis – ironically the same yacht on which Charles and Diana spent that failed attempt at a reunion. They have visited Alice Keppel's former home with its magnificent view over Florence. Tuscany is a favourite place for Charles and Camilla, as both of them are keen amateur artists. Prince Charles has encouraged the development of drawing skills through his Prince's Drawing School, an important London teaching centre founded at a time when drawing was no longer being taught to aspiring artists.

Prince Charles and the Duchess of Cornwall have made official tours together to various areas of the Middle East. In March 2009 they made a ten-day tour of the west coast of South America, including parts of Chile and Ecuador and the Galapagos Islands off the coast of Ecuador, and a visit to Brazil to promote British trade and raise concerns on environmental issues and the problems of climate change.

In Santiago, Chile's capital city, flags were flying in honour of Prince Charles and his wife. They visited the home of Lucia de Santa Cruz, who originally introduced Prince Charles to Camilla and was a guest at their wedding.

The Duchess of Cornwall has faced health problems and needed a hysterectomy in 2007. Camilla's health has improved since she gave up smoking, which was causing her to suffer from rhinitis or hay fever. She succeeded with the help of Dr Mosaraf Ali, who also treated her for back pain, a legacy of falls from her fox-hunting days.

The Duchess has accompanied her husband on official visits to former Iron Curtain countries and represented the Queen at the 2010 and 2018 Commonwealth Games, visited the Pope and paid a visit to Germany where Prince Charles visited relatives on his father's side of their family.

In April 2011, Camilla broke her left leg while hill-walking with Prince Charles in Scotland but with her leg in plaster nevertheless fulfilled most of her official engagements. In the past few years, the Duchess of Cornwall and her husband have made official visits to numerous counties in Europe, South Africa and Tanzania and several to the Persian Gulf and other areas in the oil-rich Middle East and in November 2017 to Delhi during a thick smog which blacked out the city and stopped traffic.

Camilla's first visit to Australia took place in November 2013. The Duchess and Prince Charles were representing the Queen on a gruelling tour that included visiting five states in six days.

Encouraged by Camilla, Prince Charles works hard on a variety of projects as chairman of the Board of the Prince's Charities in Britain, Canada and Australia to aid disadvantaged youth. He is also involved in a wide range of environmental projects. His work on valuable heritage projects deserves special mention, such as saving the Georgian architecture of Dumfries House in Scotland from becoming a spa hotel. He personally brought together the consortium that is preserving Dumfries House and bringing prosperity to the surrounding area of Cumnock, which previously had one of the highest rates of unemployment in Scotland.

During an average year, Charles and Camilla and their support staff entertain a staggering three thousand, five hundred people at Clarence House associated with their various charities, they open the gardens at Highgrove House to various groups of visitors and produce from Highgrove, and other Duchy enterprises grown without pesticides can be bought in the Highgrove Shop.

Camilla, a grandmother with family loyalties

Camilla and her first husband, Andrew, managed the task of parenting after their divorce without the bitterness that often accompanies a marriage break-up. They remained on excellent terms with each other and their children. Unlike many Anglican wives of Catholics, Camilla was never made to convert to Catholicism, nor did her two children attend Catholic schools. Tom went to Eton, like Prince William and Prince Harry, although he was senior to them. Laura attended a Church of England boarding school, took a degree in art history at Oxford, and worked as an intern at the Peggy Guggenheim Museum in the Palazzo Venier in Venice before managing a London art gallery.

In 2006, Laura married Harry Lopes, a chartered accountant, in the local Anglican Church in the Wiltshire village of Laycock. Camilla organised her daughter's wedding and the reception at Ray Mill House. The 400 guests included Prince Charles, Prince William, Prince Harry, and Princess Margaret's daughter Lady Sarah Chatto. Camilla and Andrew Parker Bowles were joint hosts.

Laura and Harry Lopes have a daughter and twin boys; Tom Parker Bowles and his wife Sarah have three children. Camilla is a doting grandmother and has converted the top floor of Ray Mill House into a children's suite where she can spend time with her grandchildren without worrying whether their noise is disturbing her husband.

Each year Camilla organises a special 'Groovy Grannies Day' picnic for her grandchildren, their friends and other grandparents. There are games and a special high tea, which includes sausages and assorted jellies prepared by kitchen staff at Highgrove and delivered in heat-proof containers to Ray Mill House, twenty-five miles away. At her dinner parties at Ray Mill House Camilla usually serves roast meat and organic vegetables grown at Highgrove.

Tom Parker Bowles is Prince Charles' godson. Malicious rumours that he is Prince Charles' natural son is ridiculous; Prince Charles was overseas on naval service when Tom was conceived. When Prince Charles created a substantial trust fund for both of Camilla's children, it was his attempt to compensate for the unhappiness they were caused by his long-running affair with their mother. Charles stated that since William and Harry have become millionaires after inheriting money from Princess Diana, he wished to be even-handed and see that Camilla's children had their financial futures assured.

After leaving Eton, Tom Parker Bowles went to Oxford and eventually became a food and travel writer. The first of his many best-selling books was *E is for Eating: an Alphabet of Greed* (2004), followed by *The Year of Eating Dangerously, A Global Adventure in Search of Culinary Extremes,* which appeared in 2007 to good reviews. Writing seems to run in Camilla's family. In 1990, her father, Major Bruce Shand, published a memoir about his war time exploits titled *Previous Engagements*, which was praised by military historians. Her son's books continue to be sought-after.

Andrew Parker Bowles married his long-term companion, divorcée Mrs Rosemary Pitman, and the two couples remain friends. In 2008, the four of them holidayed together on the island of Antigua in the West Indies. Rosemary died of cancer two years later, and Camilla attended her funeral.

The Duchess as University Chancellor

On 10 June 2013, the Duchess of Cornwall became the first female Chancellor of Aberdeen University, a non-academic appointment. Looking elegant in a black velvet robe edged with gold for her induction as Chancellor, the Duchess said she was 'honoured' by the appointment.

With self-deprecating humour, Camilla confessed to the audience of academics that she had left school at sixteen with only one 'O' level – a confession which took some courage to make to a gathering of some of Scotland's leading minds who do not tolerate fools.

What Camilla did not mention is that extensive reading on a wide range of subjects and her travels, had, over the years, provided her with an education in 'the university of life'.

The Duchess of Rothesay (as Camilla is known in Scotland) told the assembled audience that the area was dear to her as her father's family hailed from Banff in north-eastern Scotland. However, she did not mention that her famous great-grandmother, Alice Keppel (née Edmonstone) was born in Duntreath Castle deep in the Highlands, an estate granted to distant ancestors by a king of Scotland.

Camilla told her audience that she looked forward to awarding degrees to students at the end of each university year, praised Aberdeen University as a world-class institution and talked about its multi-million-dollar library, for which Prince Charles chaired a campaign to secure funding. She expressed the hope that the University of Aberdeen would encourage research to reduce adult illiteracy, describing this 'as one of life's severest handicaps that needed addressing in this day and age'.

The Vice-Chancellor awarded the Duchess of Cornwall an honorary degree of Doctor of Laws. He told the audience she was following in the footsteps of two former prime ministers who had held this prestigious post.

Camilla has confounded her critics by making the difficult transition from royal mistress to royal wife. Many people see Camilla as a warm-hearted, caring woman who has made Prince Charles happy. Although with his life of privilege and luxury, he is not always an easy man to live with. Others can never forgive her, no matter how hard she works

On 8 May 2013, Camilla sat beside the Queen, her mother-in-law, at the opening of parliament, acknowledging her role as the wife of a future king. The Duchess of Cornwall wore a long white lace dress offset by the blue and gold sash of a Dame Commander of the Royal Victoria Order, an award signifying personal service to the monarch. Her status was reinforced by a diamond tiara that had once belonged to the Queen Mother.

The medal of the Royal Victorian Order was bestowed on Camilla by her mother-in-law on the seventh anniversary of her marriage to Prince Charles. It confirmed that the Duchess of Cornwall is now a respected member of the inner circle of the royal family.

From hated to feted, will there be a crown for Camilla?

In spite of her age, there are no signs Queen Elizabeth wishes to retire. When Queen Beatrix of the Netherlands resigned in favour of her eldest son, Queen Elizabeth said she found retiring a strange thing to do. But with Prince Philip retired suffering from health problems, the Queen has welcomed the fact that Prince Charles and Duchess Camilla are able to take over more of her official duties.

The Diamond Jubilee in 2012 saw a huge outpouring of affection and admiration for Queen Elizabeth II. After she was hospitalised in March 2013 with a stomach complaint, the Queen was advised against making long overseas trips and sent Prince Charles and Camilla to the Commonwealth Heads of Government Meeting (CHOGM) in Sri Lanka in November 2013 in her place. The Duchess of Cornwall has stated on several occasions that she would be happy to take the title of Princess Consort when her husband ascends the throne, which it appears is a popular choice.

Legal authorities continue to insist that present laws ensure the wife of a king automatically becomes his queen, and this law would have to be amended by a special Act of Parliament to make Camilla Princess Consort. Nor can Prince William leapfrog the succession and become king, with Duchess Catherine as his queen – a measure that would please many young people – without the law being changed.

On his official website, Prince Charles stated his position on Camilla's title under the section Frequently Asked Questions.

To the question: *'Will the Duchess of Cornwall become Queen when the Prince becomes King?'* the prince's website carried the following reply though by 2017 it had disappeared. (This disappearance is clearly very significant, indicating Charles' determination to have Camilla as his queen.) *'At the time of the wedding of Charles and Camilla in April 2005, it was intended that the Duchess be known as HRH, the Princess Consort when the Prince of Wales accedes to the throne.'* Prince Charles hopes time will mellow opposition to Camilla and she will take the title of Queen, which, unless a special law is passed to prevent it, is hers by right.

⁂

In 2014, there was sympathy for Camilla when her brother Mark died in a freak accident in New York on 24 April. He was there to preside over a Sotheby's charity auction to raise money to save endangered Asian elephants. For years Mark had headed the London-based charity Elephant Family, which he had founded.[129]

A man of many parts, Mark Shand made documentary films about elephants in the wild to draw attention to the fact that these highly intelligent animals are under threat of extinction. Poachers kill mother elephants for their tusks, leaving their baby elephants to die from starvation. Mark Shand's sustained efforts to help were aided by whole-hearted support from Camilla and from Prince Charles, who paid a visit to his brother-in-law after attending the CHOGM conference in 2013 and they continue to be involved with his charity.

Camilla and Mark Shand promoting the work of his charity Elephant Family

---

[129] Mark Shand enjoyed romances with Caroline Kennedy, Bianca Jagger and supermodel Marie Helvin. An income derived from the Cubitt family trust helped Mark travel and fight against ivory poachers. Camilla helped her brother raise funds for Elephant Family and she and Charles continue to do this.

Mark Shand's premature death, aged sixty-two, was announced as Charles and Camilla were preparing for an official tour of Canada. His death was shocking for an adventurous man who had braved many dangers.

Camilla's brother stepped outside the Grammercy Park Hotel, where the auction was being held, to smoke a cigarette, slipped on an uneven pavement and cracked his skull. He never regained consciousness and died in the intensive care ward of a New York hospital.

His family consoled themselves that he died raising funds for the cause to which he had devoted such a large part of his life. He died at a moment of triumph, as the charity auction had succeeded in raising almost a million dollars for the Elephant Family.

Camilla's son, Tom Parker Bowles commented how tragic it was that an adventurer who had survived being chased by African cannibals and Dyak head-hunters had died from something as mundane as slipping and falling on a pavement.

On 1 May 2014, the grief-stricken Duchess of Cornwall joined the mourners at her brother's funeral at the Anglican Church in the Dorset village of Stourpaine, where her parents are buried.

In Britain, opinions about Camilla's title when Charles succeeds to the throne are divided. As Duchess of Cornwall, Camilla supports over 90 charities as Patron or President. She attends functions to meet their members and raise funds for them in different ways. Camilla has taken over the patronage of several charities from the Queen including Dr Barnardo's, the Battersea Dogs and Cats Home and and the Royal School of Needlework. Her other charities are mainly concerned with children's health, adult literacy, and the topics royals once never faced like rape, sexual abuse and domestic violence and empowering women.

Although Camilla does not like flying she has made numerous trips abroad with her husband and is photographed here in 2018 in one of her trademark large hats, walking though Brisbane's Botanical Gardens pursued by the press. (Photo by Jacqui Miller)

CHAPTER FOURTEEN

Kate – childhood & adolescence

The Queen's decision to allow Prince Charles to marry Mrs Parker Bowles changed the ancient precepts that Crown Princes had to marry aristocratic virgins or princesses. At one stage in this long relationship, it was felt that Prince William, as heir to the throne, would unlikely be allowed to break with centuries of tradition and marry a girl who certain snobbish Buckingham Palace officials described as a 'commoner' rather than an aristocrat.

Kate Middleton came from a respectable middle-class family who through hard work and bequests from relatives had acquired a beautiful country house and enjoyed a very pleasant life. Held against them by some old-fashioned die-hards was the fact that Carole Middleton, Kate's mother, had working-class ancestors including a road sweeper, domestic servants and a butcher – something the press enjoyed mentioning whenever a royal marriage for Kate was discussed.

Since the wedding of Duchess Catherine, more details have emerged about her father's ancestors. Her father's family were related closely to the Luptons who were Yorkshire-landed gentry with two cousins married to aristocrats one of whom, Baroness Airedale, was a guest at the coronation of King George V and Queen Mary.

⁂

As Nancy Mitford, daughter of Lord Redesdale, noted in her book, *Noblesse Oblige, an Enquiry into the Identifiable Characteristics of the English Aristocracy,* many British aristocrats look down on the middle classes who they find pretentious and vulgar. But in view of some genealogical research, those snobbish members of the royal household have to eat their words. Catherine, Duchess of Cambridge through her father, Michael Middleton, is related to several members of the landed gentry and aristocracy of Yorkshire. The Queen authorised the grant of a coat of arms to Michael Francis Middleton on 19 April 2011.

Some genealogical researchers attempted to link Duchess Catherine with Lady Elizabeth Knollys (daughter of Catherine Carey, the alleged love child of Henry VIII and his mistress Mary Boleyn, sister of the more famous Anne).[130]

Lady Catherine Knollys is buried in a handsome tomb in Westminster Abbey, unlike her husband who did not achieve that honour. It makes a stronger case for Catherine Knollys being of royal birth, but only a DNA test could establish a connection between the wife of Prince William and the illegitimate daughter of Henry VIII. While some historians believe this to be true, others say the links between the pair of them are genealogically weak.

⁂

It has been proved that Michael Middleton is a relative through marriage of heiress Olive Lupton, one of the Luptons of Leeds, a wealthy family. Olive had two cousins who married into the peerage, giving her a link to the aristocracy, which should satisfy those snobs who were nasty enough to mock the former Kate Middleton when she became the regular girlfriend of Prince William in their student days by focusing on the fact that her mother had been an air hostess.

Kate's father, Michael Middleton, is the son of Oxford-educated Peter Middleton who served as a fighter pilot in World War One which makes Peter Middleton Kate's grandfather. His father, Noel Middleton, married Olive Lupton, the wealthy heiress and philanthropist daughter of Francis Martineau Lupton, so Olive Lupton was Kate's great-grandmother.

Francis Martineau Lupton was a wealthy mill owner and industrialist turned philanthropist who owned Potternewton Hall in Leeds and later lived in Georgian splendour in a rural mansion known as Beechwood.

Francis Lupton made his second fortune as a property developer in Leeds and, with more money than he needed, harnessed his energies into becoming a noted philanthropist dedicating himself to alleviating the living conditions of slum dwellers. Francis Martineau Lupton and his wealthy brothers were important in the establishment of the University of Leeds and endowed it with several buildings known as the Lupton Residences.

Francis Lupton was a firm believer in the power of education to change lives and sent his three sons to Cambridge. In mid-life his life was blighted by tragedy as his wife died of peritonitis, and all three of his sons died fighting on the Somme in World War One, leaving him without a male heir and only his daughter named Olive who married Noel

---

130 *The National Dictionary of Biography* according to Charlotte Eager and Marlene Eilers Koenig who have both written on Catherine Carey has cited the wrong birth date for Catherine. A full story of Catherine of Katherine Knollys is by S.B. Watson published by Chronos Books and the story of Mary Boleyn inspired Philippa Gregory's historical novel *The Other Boleyn Girl.*

Middleton whose family were established family solicitors in Leeds.

The philanthropic Frances Lupton died in 1921 leaving a fortune to his daughter, Olive Middleton, and her descendants. This money was tied up in a series of family trusts so that the descendants of his only surviving child, Olive Middleton, could have the best education that money could buy, and she grew up to be a very accomplished woman. One of Olive's Lupton cousins married into the peerage and became the Baroness Airedale, photographed with her husband in ermine-trimmed coronation robes before the coronation of George VI, and they owned a rural mansion in Yorkshire and entertained royalty.

In contrast to the affluent Luptons and Middletons, Kate's mother, Carole Goldsmith and her family were working-class battlers, coal miners and hard-working domestic servants and even a convict sent to Tasmania. Carole has never tried to cover this up, but when Kate was older and involved with Prince William, learning that her mother had a working-class background, certain sections of the press in class-conscious Britain claimed that Kate Middleton was an unsuitable bride for Prince William.

What Kate's detractors did not know was that her father, Michael Middleton, came from a very wealthy family that had once been part of the landed gentry of Yorkshire.

Kate's grandfather, Peter Middleton, was a student at New College, Oxford, with his fees paid for by the family trust and served as a fighter pilot in World War Two. He married Valerie Glassborow, a clever and attractive young woman who, during the Second World War, was one of the dedicated female code breakers at Bletchley who helped defeat the Nazis by cracking their coded telegraphic messages in what was known as the Enigma code.

Francis Lupton strongly believed in the power of education, and the educational trusts established by him paid for Kate and her sister, Philippa, to attend Marlborough College (one of England's finest co-educational schools) and for Kate to attend the fee-paying St Andrew's University and for Philippa to attend Edinburgh University.

Kate Middleton – school days & university

Catherine (Kate) Elizabeth Middleton was born on 9 January 1982 in the Royal Berkshire Hospital and baptised into the Anglican Church.

She was the first child of an attractive young couple of airline employees, Michael and Carole Middleton. Michael Middleton had decided against following his father and studying at Oxford and, fancying a life of travel and excitement, joined British Airways where he met and married flight attendant Carole Goldsmith when they worked together as cabin crew.

When little Catherine turned four, her parents took her to Amman in Jordan for two years while her father was appointed temporary manager of British Airways. In September they returned to England where they lived near Pangbourne, and Kate attend a primary school.

In 1995, they were doing well and were able to move to a village called Chapel Row on the outskirts of the pleasant Berkshire village of Bucklebury where the Middletons still live but in a much larger house called The Manor.

Kate and her siblings, Philippa (a year younger than Kate) and James (born in 1987), have always been very close. Their mother, Carole, worked hard running their Internet mail order business, Party Pieces, from home. Eventually her husband joined her in the business which prospered when it was difficult to buy attractive items for a children's party.

Kate attended several day schools before having a couple of terms at Downe House, an all-girl boarding school. At this stage, she was a very tall, shy reserved child with braces on her teeth and a bad case of eczema. Kate's exceptional height made her a target for bullies and she was so unhappy and eating so little her worried parents transferred her to the co-educational, £28,000 a year Marlborough College in Wiltshire.

At this beautiful campus, where she was known as Catherine, she was happy and gained confidence excelling at swimming, netball, hockey and tennis. She eventually gained the school record for the high jump and was voted the best all-rounder at sport.

At Marlborough College, Catherine Middleton was now almost a different girl. She was deemed highly responsible and made good friends who have remained close to her in adult life. While her gangling limbs and above-average height had made her a target for bullies at Downe House, at Marlborough College she gained confidence and plenty of good friends. She changed from an awkward lanky teenager to a beautiful girl whose height and willowy figure was that of a top model with impeccable manners, an attractive speaking voice and a natural dignity.

As a boarder at Marlborough College, Catherine, as she was known, gained friends and confidence. When she and her friends were old enough to go out together at night, she drank very little as she is sensitive to alcohol. She was always the sensible one in any group, the one who drove her friends home. She never smoked, calling cigarettes 'cancer sticks' and never experimented with drugs.

Her family enjoyed sport, and calling herself Catherine, her baptismal name, she and Pippa enjoyed several winter sports holidays with their parents and learned to ski well. The family's company, Party Pieces, in which Catherine's father was now involved, was prospering thanks to their website. They could afford an expensive family holiday to the island of Mustique, made famous by Princess Margaret, where villa rentals cost as much as two hundred and fifty thousand American dollars a week complete with staff.

In Kate's gap year in 2000, she was able to spend time in Florence, the cradle of the Renaissance with its numerous art galleries which was ideal for a girl about to study art history at university. She did a twelve-week course in history of art and Italian language at the British Institute.

Kate's parents paid Raleigh International for her to join a working party run by the organisation. They send small groups of young people overseas to help villagers in underdeveloped countries gain access to clean, unpolluted water and sanitation and improve their educational facilities.

By coincidence, Kate worked in Patagonia in the same area where Prince William had been working only a month earlier. She had once seen him play hockey at Marlborough College and thought him very handsome. She learned that William had insisted on being treated just like all the other volunteers who lived under very basic conditions. In Kate's group, no one complained and they all 'mucked in' together and helped to build a children's adventure playground in a remote village and do some extensions to the small schoolhouse.

However, Kate and William did not meet until the autumn of 2001 when both of them arrived as first year students of art history at St Andrew's University. Studying art history seemed a sensible choice for William, as his grandmother, the Queen, owns one of the world's most prestigious art collections.

St Andrew's has eleven halls of residence, and in another coincidence, Prince William and Kate were both assigned to live at St Salvator's Hall but on different floors as the sexes were segregated. Some female students spent a lot on clothes and wore full make-up attempting to attract the handsome prince. William managed to dodge their attentions and mixed with his school friends from Eton, playing pool in the evenings or spending time with Carley Massey-Birch, daughter of a West Country landowner who lived near his country home, Highgrove.

Prince William values his privacy and dislikes having anything to do with the media unless it is strictly necessary. The Press Office at Buckingham Palace negotiated an agreement whereby the media would leave William alone in return for a photo opportunity and a press interview on his arrival at St Andrew's. But this did not prevent some rogue photographers stalking him with their long lenses.

Kate and William knew each other by sight when attending art history lectures and because they were both keen swimmers who swam in the same pool and went jogging before breakfast. At that time, St Andrew's lacked a heated pool, so in the chilly, wintery Scottish climate, both of them paid to swim in the heated pool of a local hotel. Having been out running, they often arrived late to breakfast in the large dining hall with its rows of long tables, and sometimes Kate was invited to join William and his male friends for a healthy breakfast of muesli and fresh fruit.

In 2001, there were fears of many bomb threats and kidnapping by the IRA. Prince William's room was specially designed so if the Queen's grandson was under attack by any terrorist group, he could take refuge in his bulletproof bathroom. In the four years he and Kate were at university, a detective from the Royal Protection Squad of Scotland Yard hovered around discretely as there were fears for Prince William's safety.

Many girls made eyes at William fancying a serious relationship with the 'Prince Charming', but the prince was quoted as saying, 'I just want to go to university and have fun. I'm young and not interested in serious relationships…I'll probably marry around twenty-eight or even thirty.'

Kate and William often bumped into each other at lectures where Kate was a dedicated student who took copious notes. On a couple of occasions when the prince had to miss a lecture, she let William borrow her notes so he would be able to study them when it came to revising for end-of-term exams.

Kate was dating Rupert Finch, a handsome, dark-haired law student in his final year who was part of the St Andrew's cricket team. Prince William was dating Carley Massy-Birch, and he and Kate were just good friends. The sports-loving Prince William invited Kate and Rupert Finch as a couple to a party in his room while Carley Massy-Birch was present as the prince's regular girlfriend.

William was also fond of blonde *sportif* Jecca Craig whose father, Ian Craig, owned a vast property near Mount Kenya where William had been a guest for part of his gap year. She was at one stage linked romantically with Prince William by the tabloids.

Part of Jecca Craig's attraction for William was the happy holiday he had spent at Lewa Downs, the vast Craig family property in Kenya where African wildlife is protected. William was fascinated by the opportunity to study Africa's wild animals at close quarters with Jecca and her father, Ian Craig.

William and Harry had loved Africa since their boyhood visits there with Prince Charles before he made a second visit with Tiggy Legge-Bourke, who had been employed by Prince Charles to 'nanny' them during their parents' separation. For William and Harry, Africa had become a land of romance, the place which represented, and still represents, an escape from what they both hated – the relentless intrusion of the paparazzi who they felt had been so callous at pursuing their mother.

Before William left for university, Prince Charles warned him against drinking too much, taking drugs or being caught in compromising positions with female students. It was feared that the paparazzi might attempt to break the agreement negotiated with Buckingham Palace that they would not photograph William while he was at St Andrew's in return for a photo opportunity when he arrived there.

Perhaps the cold, damp weather of Scotland in November affected William who was now missing Highgrove and dancing the night away at Bouji's, the exclusive South Kensington nightclub for the affluent young. Both princes were coping in their own ways with teenage *angst* and their intense grief and anger over the death of their mother.

Kate and William were no more than friends, but he found Kate interesting and valued her opinion. One day, he admitted to her that he was not enjoying university as much as he had hoped and was thinking of dropping out and joining Harry on his army training at Sandhurst. Kate tactfully suggested that William might enjoy studying geography more than art history. The knowledge gained from this course would be of use to him when he travelled to other countries.

The Dean of St Andrew's was worried when he learned that William was thinking of dropping out, aware it would not look good for the university. It was suggested to Prince William that changing courses would not be a problem.

Returning to Highgrove, William discussed this option with his father who was sympathetic and supportive, as Charles initially had found life at Cambridge difficult. So, after some discussion, William decided to stay at university and study geography.

In March 2002, Kate took part in a student fashion show to raise money for charity. William purchased an expensive front row seat to the show which included a champagne party afterwards. Kate, normally demure in the way she dressed, stole the show wearing a black lace see-through dress over a black bra and black bikini pants that highlighted her long, shapely legs.

As she sashayed down the catwalk with coloured ribbons threaded through her long chestnut-brown hair, William was mesmerised, suddenly aware what a sensational figure and long shapely legs his studious fellow student possessed.

'Wow, Kate's hot!' William was alleged to have told the male friend who accompanied him.

At the champagne party afterwards, William made a bee-line for Kate and congratulated her with a kiss on the lips in a spontaneous gesture of admiration. She was stunned and slightly embarrassed and did not respond, aware that her boyfriend, Rupert Finch, a handsome dark-haired, law student in his final year was watching them.

However, this electrifying moment changed their relationship from friendship to something deeper. Eventually, Rupert Finch faded into the background to be replaced by the equally handsome, muscular Prince William. But the three of them remained friends for the rest of the academic year until Rupert graduated and left St Andrew's.

Many years later when Rupert Finch was a successful lawyer, he married Lady Natasha Rufus Isaacs, the dress designer and daughter of the Marquis of Reading. Interestingly enough, there is a marked resemblance between Kate and the more petite Lady Natasha who has the same beautiful smile, stunning figure and long brown hair.[131]

Six months after William gave Kate a passionate kiss after that student fashion show, they were in love and celebrated the end of first year with a typically rowdy student party where everyone drank far too much.

They kept their relationship a secret on campus for fear the paparazzi would find out. Discretion has always characterised their relationship, unlike Harry and Meghan who held hands and embraced the first time they appeared together in public at the Invictus Games.

At the start of their second year at St Andrews in September 2002, Kate and William rented a share house at 13a Hope Street in the centre of St Andrew's with Fergus Boyd, one of William's classmates from Eton, and another student Olivia Bleasdale.

Used to servants at Kensington Palace and Highgrove, living in a rented share house was a challenge and a new way of life for Prince William. The quartet, with the aid of some occasional help with house cleaning, divided the domestic chores between them. William took out the garbage while Kate did most of the cooking aided by Fergus Boyd. William insisted on taking his turn cooking but sometimes needed a helping hand from Kate.

In 2003, during their third year at university, William and Kate turned twenty-one. Kate's parents were proud of her results at university and wanted to give her a really good party, so they hired a marquee which was erected in the grounds of their house. It was arranged for William to slip in

---

131 Lady Natasha Rufus Isaacs is known for her humanitarian work with Indian girls who have been trafficked. To help them create new lives, she founded the fashion label of *Beulah* which sells dresses made from Indian silk created by women and girls who have been the victims of trafficking.

unnoticed and join the birthday celebrations.

On 21 June 2003, Kate attended William's twenty-first birthday party held at Windsor Castle. She drove through the great arch that led to the courtyard where there was reserved parking for guests, mounted the great stairs leading to one of the castle's magnificent reception rooms, which was originally remodelled for George IV by the great architect Wyatville. Under the great crystal chandeliers, gilded ceilings and surrounded by priceless oil paintings in heavy gold frames, family and friends celebrated the coming of age of the second in line to the throne after his father, Prince Charles.

On this occasion, Kate was not presented to the Queen. Kate was thankful that the media ignored her as the journalists and photographers covering the event believed that William was seriously interested in Jecca Craig from Kenya.

In September 2003, wanting more privacy, Kate and William rented a cottage on the large walled Strathtyrum estate on the outskirts of St Andrew's which was owned by a distant cousin of Prince William. His security officers also lived on the estate, and Scotland Yard ensured the cottage was bombproof.

Kate and William enjoyed entertaining friends, installed a bar fridge and filled it with bottles of champagne and good wine, and they enjoyed a wonderful summer away from the lenses of the paparazzi.

Kate and William made history by being the first royal couple to live together before marriage. They were in love, but on campus, they were still very careful not to show their affection for each other, and Kate played the role of platonic friend.

William taught Kate to shoot, the sport he enjoyed, and like all sports Kate undertook she quickly became good at it. As part of their lease of the cottage, they were allowed to shoot grouse on the estate which was then prepared by Kate for dinner guests.

Some weekends were spent at Balmoral where the Queen allowed them to stay in a smaller cottage on her estate surrounded by heather covered hills. They took long walks and went shooting and fishing in the River Dee.

In the evenings, they would cook a meal together and share a bottle of wine. Sometimes they were joined by university friends or Kate's brother, James, and her sister, Pippa, who was studying at Edinburgh University. It was at Balmoral that Kate stalked her first stag and was 'blooded' by having its blood smeared on her forehead, as is the custom with novices with their first kill – something Diana would have hated.

In April 2004, Kate was invited to join Prince Charles's annual skiing holiday at Klosters, the Swiss ski resort, with William and Harry. As was his usual custom, Prince Charles had hired a chalet. The media horde covering Prince Charles's skiing holiday was now alerted to the fact that Kate Middleton was William's girlfriend of the moment.

The fact that William was seeing other girls on campus distressed Kate, but she didn't make an issue of it. William's childhood and teenage years had been fraught by jealous scenes between his parents, and Kate distracted herself by immersing herself in her studies to obtain a good degree.

One of the girls William fancied was a blonde, beautiful twenty-two-year-old American shopping centre heiress whose father had been killed in a shooting accident near Nashville in Tennessee. William met Anna Sloan through friends who were studying with her at Edinburgh University, and the fact that they had both lost a parent formed a bond between them.

That summer, William was going to on a trip to Greece with male friends but also accepted an invitation to join a house party Anna Sloan was throwing at her family estate. The fact William had not asked Kate to join him during this Greek holiday or in America wrongly convinced Kate that Anna Sloan had set her sights on Prince William. In fact, this was not true. When William arrived at Anna's Tennessee mansion, he found she had a steady boyfriend, and they remained good friends for years. And eventually Anna Sloan would attend the wedding of William and Kate.

Kate spent that summer university vacation in France with student friends to whom she confided that she and William were going to have some time apart as he was saying that he found their relationship 'confining' and wanted space.

After their respective vacations, they returned to St Andrews for their fourth and final year. William made it clear that he had no intention of committing himself in his early twenties. He talked about returning to Kenya to spend time on Jecca Craig's family property and game reserve after graduating. He had had a few dates with the attractive Isabella Gough-Calthorpe which upset Kate, but he reassured her that this relationship was platonic. Both he and Kate were still concentrating on passing their final important exams.

Kate looked very elegant when she attended Prince Charles' fifty-sixth birthday party at Highgrove in November at the end of the autumn term. Prince Charles and Camilla liked Kate and saw she was good for William.

William and Kate saw little of each other in the Christmas holiday of 2004 and New Year which he spent at Sandringham with his grandparents, but in March 2005, Prince Charles invited her to join him, William and Harry for a family skiing holiday in a villa he had rented at Klosters. This was one month before Charles' marriage to Camilla.

William is a strong skier, but athletic Kate easily kept up with him on the slopes. The press was alerted to their romance because William was spotted tenderly kissing the back of Kate's neck while standing in the queue for the ski lift. A shot of the two of them on the ski lift smiling affectionately at each other appeared in *The Sun* on 1 April 2004 under the headline: 'FINALLY PRINCE WILLIAM GETS HIS GIRL'.

From then on, the lovers were followed everywhere by photographers. Kate hated the media attention but adjusted quickly and, from the beginning, refused to speak about William to the press who pestered her.

Prince Charles and Camilla, now given the title of Duchess of Cornwall on her marriage, attended Prince William's graduation ceremony in June 2005 in the company of the Queen and the Duke of Edinburgh. The Middleton family travelled north to St Andrews to see their twenty-three-year-old daughter, wearing a black academic gown and mortar board, receiving her MA Hons degree in art history. Michael Middleton photographed William and Kate with their arms around each other. Neither Kate nor her family were presented to the Queen.

The speech made by Vice-Chancellor Brian Lang must have resonated with Kate when he told the new graduates, 'You may have met your future husband or wife. Our reputation as the top matchmaking university in Britain signifies much that is good about St Andrews.'

That evening at the graduation ball, Kate and William looked happy and carefree as they danced together. But some of William's friends scoffed at the Vice-Chancellor's speech about meeting a future marriage partner and were convinced the affair between Kate and William would end once he left St Andrew's. Princes' *always* married girls with titles or royal blood and there had never been a middle-class princess.

CHAPTER FIFTEEN

Kate – leaving university for adult life

After the graduation ceremony, William and Kate were both invited to stay with Jecca Craig on her parent's Kenya estate where William was again involved in the Craig's conservation work.

He and Kate returned to England and saw in the New Year of 2006 together. Later William left for his officer training at the Royal Military Academy at Sandhurst, where Harry was about to graduate, and William was only in his first year.

In March 2006, Prince Charles and Camilla invited Kate to join them in the Royal Box to watch the Cheltenham Gold Cup. William had military duties at Sandhurst from which he could not be released. But the fact that Kate was invited to the Royal Box by Prince Charles was an indication that he approved of her relationship with William.

Military training kept William very busy, and Kate did not see much of him in London. Unlike many graduates, she was not sure what she was going to do now her studies were over. In contrast, William's days were crowded as he was undertaking his first overseas visits to Wellington, New Zealand, on behalf of the Queen. Back at home, he was undertaking a round of visits to hospitals and civic functions on behalf of his grandmother who turned eighty in April 2006.

Obtaining an entrée to a good job in the field of art history is not easy. Kate had graduated as an art historian and unsuccessfully applied for a couple of jobs with various galleries. Instead she began to work for Party Pieces, the company owned by her parents. She was labelled 'Waity Katie' for deciding to take a job which would give her plenty of free time if she was going to go on seeing William who would ring at the last moment to see if she was free to join him.

Kate realised William was having a difficult time as, having lost his mother, he was now coming to terms with having Camilla, his mother's nemesis, as his stepmother. The official inquest into Princess Diana's death had just been published reviving old wounds. The inquest concluded that the crash in which Diana died was a tragic accident and not part of any plot on the part of the royal family, as had been insinuated by Al Fayed's lawyers.

In April 2006, Kate and William had a carefree holiday on the romantic Caribbean island of Mustique where they stayed in a villa belonging to friends of Kate's parents. The Robinsons established the highly successful fashion chain 'Jigsaws' where Kate was offered a job as a junior fashion accessory buyer. Dressed in some of their latest fashions, Kate's high media profile was an asset. She was allowed a large degree of freedom as to the hours she worked which suited her as it enabled her to accompany William on some of his official duties and on his overseas holidays.

Back in London, the tabloids speculated that the handsome pair were about to announce their engagement, but each time they printed this, it was denied by the Press Office at Buckingham Palace.

2006 was spent on a series of exciting holidays such as joining William on a cruise on Richard Branson's yacht as William was friends with Branson's children.

Speculation about a royal engagement was rife in the press. No one seemed to remember that a year earlier in March 2005, William had told the press that he had no intention of getting married before he turned twenty-eight.

In December 2006, expectations were heightened when the press revealed that Kate would attend William's Sandhurst graduation ceremony which was known as the passing-out parade, when William would receive his commission with the rank of Second Lieutenant.

The Queen was to inspect the newly commissioned officers, and this was the first royal ceremony to which Kate had been invited. She was accompanied by her parents, and they were seated next to Prince Harry to watch William's passing-out parade as an officer. Once again, Kate was not presented to the Queen which scotched the rumours that an engagement was imminent. The press had started calling her 'Waity Katie' which was distressing for Kate because William still had not said anything.

On the parade ground, the tall blonde prince looked handsome in his scarlet dress uniform while Kate also wore scarlet. Her photograph wearing a black very flattering hat standing beside Prince Harry and her parents was featured on the front pages of many newspapers with more speculation of an impending engagement.

Unfavourable media attention was focused on Kate's mother, Carole, who was on a diet and was spotted chewing gum. This *faux pas* was compounded when she asked for directions to the 'toilets', which was considered lower class, instead of her using the upper-class term 'lavatory'. The criticism upset Carole Middleton, who had just attended the funeral of her mother closely followed by the funeral of Michael Middleton's mother, Valerie, the wartime Bletchley code-breaker who had died at the age of eighty-two. She was also upset by the press description of her daughter as 'Waity Katie' implying Kate was desperately hanging onto William when, in fact, there were other eligible young men who would have been happy to date Kate.

After two bereavements, the Middletons decided to get away for Christmas and rented a beautiful Georgian mansion in Perthshire where it was unlikely photographers would find them as William had accepted an invitation to spend Christmas with them. At the last moment he rang up apologising as he was obliged to spend Christmas at Sandringham with the royal family. It was traditional to only invite married couples to Sandringham for Christmas, so Kate could not be invited. Instead, she spent Christmas 2006 with her family and saw the New Year in with them without William.

January 2007 saw William commissioned into the Blues and Royals Regiment in the steps of Prince Harry who had skipped university and was now in the army. During their first four weeks in camp, young officers were not allowed to leave the camp, so Kate celebrated her twenty-fifth birthday without Prince William.

Kate had moved out of her parents' home to live in their Chelsea apartment with her sister, Pippa, who had left university. On 9 January 2007, she celebrated her twenty-fifth birthday, but the day was spoiled when on walking out of her apartment she was blinded by camera flashes from scores of paparazzi demanding, 'When's the engagement Kate?'

Kate lacked 'minders' or security officers to protect her from the paparazzi. She was tired of journalists rifling through her rubbish bins searching for anything on which they could base a story. For the first time she understood what Princess Diana must have suffered. Kate decided that enough was enough and made an official complaint alleging invasion of her privacy to the Press Complaints Tribunal.

Clarence House issued a statement that Prince William was unhappy with the media harassment of his girlfriend which was the first official acknowledgement of their relationship.

⁂

Meanwhile, William who was now in London with his regiment, was spending many evenings at Bouji's nightclub in Thurloe Place, South Kensington which charged entry fees ranging from £500 to £1,000 for a table in the VIP section near William and his friends. A bottle of French champagne here cost between $300 and $350. William and his party drank what they believed was French champagne or the club's specialty, Crackababy cocktails – a mixture of vodka, passion-fruit juice topped up with Dom Perignon. The owner recognised that the young princes would lure affluent patrons to his expensive nightclub, so very rarely did the royal party pay for their drinks.

Many years later, allegations that Bouji's staff were substituting cheap Italian *prosecco* for French champagne emerged during a court case after violent fights had exploded outside the club. Several staff called to the witness box swore on oath that the three hundred and sixty pound bottles of Dom Perignon had been filled with *prosecco* only costing nine pounds a bottle. Cheap supermarket vodka was substituted for the very chic Grey Goose, the most expensive vodka in the world. None of Bouji's young patrons could tell the difference, and the club was fined and received a warning. (A few years later, a second court case with more evidence of substitution of drinks for cheaper brands ensured. Bouji's closed its doors forever but all that lay ahead).

On the night of 14 April 2007 in what became the couples' second major breakup, Kate was photographed by the paparazzi leaving Bouji's in tears and climbing into a taxi alone. This led to press comments that the reason for Kate's tears was that William was still in love with Jecca.[132] This seemed unlikely, as later Kate and Jecca were photographed chatting happily at a charity event in London in which William was involved.

⁂

Kate and William attended the races together for the Cheltenham Gold Cup as they had done on previous years, but both of them looked miserable as their body language made it clear.

Compromising photographs had been published in the press of William enjoying a night out at the Elements nightclub near Bovingdon Army Camp with a young Brazilian named Ana Ferreira. Kate later learned that he had danced the night away with another pretty girl.

Seeing the photographs in the press the next day, Kate had had enough and delivered another ultimatum. Either she had William's full commitment or they should take another break from the relationship. She hoped her stance would bring William to his senses, but he was not yet ready to make a commitment.

Prince William was still living in army barracks and spending off duty evenings with his army mates drinking in the local pubs. Back in London at his old haunt, the Polynesian-themed Mahiki club, he celebrated his newfound 'freedom' by dancing with a series of pretty girls and after drinking too much yelled 'I'm free, I'm free.'

---

[132] When I lived in South Kensington in the 1950s and 1960s, the nightclub Bouji's in Thurloe Place was a large bookshop which became the expensive nightclub where William, Harry and Kate spent many evenings, and Harry was sometimes the worse for wear outside the club and fought with photographers.

Kate did not retaliate by having her own fling with another man, although there were plenty of eager young and eligible men ready to step into William's shoes.

Instead, a tanned and trim Kate was photographed also enjoying herself at private parties and the night clubs she had previously attended with William. She was often accompanied by Pippa, her younger sister.

Learning about the breakup, William's male friends divided into two groups. The snobs said they always knew the relationship would never last and Kate was far too middle-class for Prince William. But close friends of the couple who knew Kate was good for William believed he would eventually tire of one-night stands and return to Kate.

Much later, William would explain his conduct saying, 'We were both very young … were both finding ourselves.' For William, the memory of his parents' turbulent marriage made him cautious about making any commitment to Kate. He was intelligent and sensitive and did not want to hurt her, but the combination of his parents' divorce followed by his mother's terrible death had made him wary. At the age of ten while at boarding school, he had to cope with the shattering news delivered by his adored mother that she and his father, Prince Charles, were going to divorce. At the age of fifteen, William attended his mother's funeral and had to help Harry, three years younger than him, who was a childish blend of sensitivity and boisterous exuberance and even more vulnerable.

Of course, Kate was upset when she heard about William shouting, 'I'm free, I'm free' after all their years together, but she chose to ignore his outburst and kept herself busy. She was tired of being labelled 'Waity Katie' by the press and made it clear she was not prepared to resume her relationship with 'Prince Charming' unless he made a firm commitment that eventually they would marry. She paid a visit to Dublin with her mother to attend the opening of a friend's art exhibition and spent an enjoyable time exploring the Irish National Gallery.

Back in London, Kate attended another round of parties and dances with eligible attractive young men. She was pursued by the paparazzi, something she hated, but press photos showed Kate looking attractive, happy and carefree.

To keep her mind off William, Kate became involved in a fund-raising project for charity with twenty-one good looking sporty girls. The group planned to row a dragon boat from Dover to Cap Gris Nez near Calais.

The training was demanding, but it was just what Kate needed. However, the paparazzi continued to follow her asking for details about her and Prince William, but Kate resolutely ignored them.

At his army camp at Bovington, William was having second thoughts.

Freedom had been exhilarating for a few nights on the town, but this soon palled. He missed Kate's sunny nature, their close friendship and could not find the same rapport with any other girl.

As the end of Kate's rowing training drew closer, the attention from the media was so intrusive that Kate decided to pull out of the race. William had been ringing her on her cell phone several times a day and urged her to continue. But Kate had no minders or bodyguards and felt too exposed.

Kate and William's reunion took place at a fancy-dress party at William's barracks. Kate went as a 'naughty nurse' and William wore a policeman's helmet and hot pants. They danced together all evening and spent the night together in his quarters. The relationship was back on its former footing.

The news had been leaked to *The Mail on Sunday*, and it ran the story on 24 June 2007. The following week on 1 July would have been Diana's forty-first birthday, and the princes had organised a memorial concert at Wembley Stadium to raise money for charity. It was decided that Kate should not sit with William or Harry, as it would take the focus off Diana and onto Kate. The Who's Who of the pop world were performing including Sir Bob Geldof and Sir Elton John who sang *Candle in the Wind.* William made a speech telling the audience 'This event is all about what our mother loved in life: her music, her dancing, her charities and friends.'

The concert proved to be a turning point for William, and he finally decided his future lay with Kate. Organising the concert had involved an enormous amount of work for the princes, and William decided that they should holiday that summer on the idyllic island of Desroches in the Seychelles. The couple lazed in the sun, swam, went scuba diving and returned to London having reached an understanding that they would marry.

In December, Kate gave up her job at Jigsaw and started working on the website for her family's firm, Party Pieces, where her role included catalogue design, marketing and photography as she is a skilful photographer.

In July 2008, Kate appeared as number 4 in the International Best Dressed List of the influential American magazine *Vanity Fair.*

⁂

William had to complete a total of sixteen months military service in the army after which he moved to the Royal Navy where he trained at Dartmouth Naval Academy and was then posted for duty on a frigate patrolling the Caribbean. When William's ship neared the island of

Mustique where Kate was holidaying with her family, the couple was able to snatch a couple of days together when he was off duty. William told Kate that he adored flying and had decided to become a full-time pilot with the RAF Rescue Force. Kate was delighted, as it meant that William would be posted back to Britain and they would have some time together.

The Queen recognised the importance of the emotional support Kate had given William over many years, and the two first met in May 2008 at the wedding of Princess Anne's son, Peter Phillips, to Canadian-born Autumn Kelly – a girl who, like Kate, did not come from a titled family.

Kate and William were in the seventh year of their relationship when the Middleton family, which had studiously avoided any contact with the press, were engulfed in a major scandal involving Gary Goldsmith, Carole Middleton's younger brother.

In the early summer of 2009, the couple flew to Ibiza to stay with Kate's millionaire uncle, Gary Goldsmith. He had just made millions selling his company and, unknown to William, was leading a louche life in his villa named *La Maison de Bang Bang* where life was one continual party and drugs were freely available – although Kate and William certainly did not partake. Perhaps William foresaw this would be a problem, and he hired a yacht so that he and Kate were cruising around the island when photographers discovered they had been staying at the Villa Bang Bang.

On their return to England, it was hugely embarrassing to find Kate's uncle and his Villa Bang Bang featuring in a front-page story in *The News of the World* with the headlines 'Kate Middleton's Uncle, Drugs and Vice Shock' alleging his involvement in drug parties attended by hookers. Other newspapers ran the headlines 'Kate's Drug Shame' and 'Royal Outrage'.

Kate's parents worried that courtiers would use these headlines to declare Kate an unsuitable match for Prince William. There was also a degree of snobbery and class prejudice as Gary's 'crimes' in the eyes of the media included the fact he was covered in tattoos, had a juke box in his villa instead of antiques and had a cockney accent having been born in Southhall. But what galled them even more was that he had somehow managed to make money and wind up a multi-millionaire.

⁂

After a very long courtship, William finally proposed to Kate in October 2010 while they were on a ten-day safari in Kenya. They were both twenty-eight. They were staying in a remote log cabin, 10,000 feet up the northern slopes of Mount Kenya overlooking a lake where they fished for trout in the evening to have for dinner. They drank champagne by candlelight as there was no electricity. Later William revealed the reason for his choice of where to propose saying 'Africa holds a special place in my heart. The locals haven't a clue who I am, and I love that Africa is my second home.' William's many trips to Africa involved work for the Tusk Trust, a wildlife conservation organisation and other African charities.

William gave Kate something very dear to his heart, his mother's eighteen carat gold engagement ring with a huge sapphire surrounded by fourteen diamonds. Significantly, although they had broken up briefly on two occasions, they had no serious involvements with anyone else since their first meeting at university at the age of nineteen.

William visited Kate's parents to tell them the news. Later he explained why he hadn't asked Kate's father for permission before proposing. He confessed that he feared Michael Middleton would say no because he knew that Kate might be happier if she married someone who was not the object of constant surveillance by the media.

Their engagement was formally announced on 16 November 2010 and that they would marry in the spring or summer of the following year. They were to live on the remote isle of Anglesey in north Wales where William was training to be a rescue pilot with the Royal Air Force.

Prince Charles said that he was thrilled by the engagement and added jokingly, 'After all, they *have* been practicing long enough.'

In accordance with the Royal Marriage Act, the Queen had to give her formal consent to the marriage and inform her Privy Council she had approved the marriage of a future king.

The official engagement photographs were taken in the State apartments of St James's Palace by Mario Testino, then in high favour but eventually to fall from grace over a sex scandal involving young male models.

This was Kate's first media engagement, and she was naturally apprehensive. Unlike the stilted interview following the official announcement of Prince Charles' and Lady Diana's engagement, William and Kate were clearly in love and very warm with each other. Prince Harry declared himself to be delighted saying that he had always wanted a sister.

While Prince Charles and Diana had over a thousand wedding presents, all of which had to be unpacked and acknowledged, this young couple announced that they would prefer those who wanted to give a wedding gift to donate money to one of the twenty-six nominated charities they planned to support.

CHAPTER SIXTEEN

Kate – a royal wedding at last

The date of the wedding of the popular couple the press referred to as 'Wills and Kate' was confirmed as Friday, 29 April 2011. The Queen declared the day a public holiday in the United Kingdom and various Commonwealth countries.

The huge cost of security would be borne by the government, but the cost of the wedding was to be split between the royal family and the Middletons which, in a time of financial stringency in Britain, was appreciated. Australia's *Herald Sun* estimated that the cost for security, including anti-terrorism measures, would be in the region of thirty-two million Australian dollars while the Middletons contributed their share of the flowers and trees that decorated Westminster Abbey, as well as the music.

In earlier centuries, a dowry was essential for any princess or aristocratic girl marrying a prince. But some European papers misunderstood the situation and described how the Middletons had paid a large dowry for Catherine to marry Prince William.

⁂

Some 1,900 guests were invited to the ceremony in Westminster Abbey of whom half would be friends of the couple. The rest were politicians, Commonwealth prime ministers and various heads of government. Catherine, created Duchess of Cambridge on her wedding day, spent the days before her wedding surrounded by her close-knit family as the Middletons reserved several suites at the luxurious Goring Hotel near Westminster Abbey.

Unlike Princess Diana's enormous billowing silk wedding gown, Duchess Catherine's stunning wedding dress was a slim-figure-flattering Alexander McQueen gown with a demure V-neckline and long fitted sleeves. It was made of satin overlaid by delicate white lace which fitted the new princess like a glove.

The Queen lent her new granddaughter-in-law a diamond tiara to hold her veil in place. To prevent the tiara from falling off (as nearly happened to Princess Diana who wore the Spencer tiara), Catherine's hair stylist back-combed her hair and made a tiny plait in it. She attached the tiara to the tiny plait and then sewed it on with a firm thread.

The bride was driven to the Abbey in a Rolls Royce Phantom VI accompanied by Michael Middleton. On her father's arm, she walked up the nave towards Prince William who was standing on the alter steps, resplendent in the scarlet uniform of an officer of the Irish Guards and across his chest the handsome prince wore the deep blue sash of the Order of the Garter. Prince Harry stood beside him in his role of 'supporter' – the correct title for the best man at a royal wedding. In a special pocket sewn into Harry's uniform so he could not lose it, was the wedding ring made of Welsh gold.

In their marriage vows, the couple vowed to 'love, comfort, honour and keep' each other. The Bishop of London ended his sermon with a prayer composed by the newlyweds who promised to 'keep our eyes fixed on what is real and important in life and to be generous with our time, love and energy.'

After signing the register, Prince William and the new Duchess of Cambridge walked down the aisle, pausing so that each of them could bow or curtsy to the Queen.

As the couple left the church, the bells of Westminster Abbey rang out joyously. The popular couple were greeted by cheers from the excited crowd who had watched the service on huge television screens.

The bridal couple were driven in the state landau drawn by four white horses and escorted by the prince's regiment – the Blues and Royals – as they rode through more cheering crowds to Buckingham Palace.

Prince William and his wife after their wedding ceremony in Westminster Abbey with Prince Harry as best man (courtesy Reuters)

At the palace, they appeared with the Queen and the rest of the bridal party. Contrary to the dire predictions of snobbish aristocrats that Carole Middleton would not know how to behave in front of royalty, she was one of the most elegant women in the Westminster Abbey, and throughout this stressful day, the Middleton family conducted themselves with great dignity.

Six hundred guests were invited to the wedding luncheon at Buckingham Palace hosted by the Queen.

That evening, the Prince of Wales gave a dinner for 300 family members and friends, followed by dancing and a display of fireworks in the grounds of Buckingham Palace.

A few days later, the couple slipped out of the country very quietly on a private jet heading for the islands of the Seychelles off the coast of Africa in the Indian Ocean. As part of William's quest for privacy, they stayed on Desroches Island, one of the most remote islands in the Amirantes group, but the destination was a closely guarded secret.

When they returned to Britain, the newlyweds learned their wedding had been watched by a global audience of some two billion viewers – a genuine love match and a fairytale wedding of a couple in love with each other.

The wedding sparked an immense wave of affection for the royal family which followed a period of coolness after the Queen's delayed appearance in London following the death of Princess Diana so she could be with William and Harry at Balmoral. This may have annoyed the public, but Diana's sons have recently admitted that in the depths of their grief, it was vital for them to have had that time at Balmoral where the Queen, in her role of a loving grandmother, refused to allow newspapers to be within sight of the young princes, then fifteen and twelve, respectively. And should they see the television, this would only intensify their grief rather than assuage it.

Showing a similar sensitivity as she had shown then, the Queen now allowed the newlyweds to have two years away from public life to enjoy their marriage. Possibly she recalled she had been able to do this before she became Queen in her first two years of married life with Prince Philip when he was a naval officer stationed on the island of Malta.

CHAPTER SEVENTEEN

Duchess Catherine, Prince William & family

William and Catherine, now the Duke and Duchess of Cambridge, rented a pleasant but not luxurious five-bedroom farmhouse from Sir George and Lady Meyrick on the isle of Anglesey. The island lies off the Welsh coast where William was to serve as a search-and-rescue pilot with the Royal Air Force. They newlyweds lived quietly and modestly, cooking their own meals, and Catherine could be seen pushing a shopping trolley up and down the aisles of the local supermarket.

Prince Harry joked that his brother had 'become boring' since he married, and there were no more evenings drinking champagne and vodka cocktails at Bouji's.

Locals on the isle of Anglesey respected the couple's privacy, and they were not bothered by the paparazzi and had protection officers who lived in the area. Catherine, Duchess of Cambridge, sometimes went south to see her parents and had meetings with the committees of charities she had chosen to support, which were mainly concerned with child welfare, hospitals, mental health and education. Her arts interests were reflected in her support for the National Portrait Gallery and for the Kensington Natural History Museum. As part of her new role, Catherine also had private tutorials with senior representatives of the government, the media and the arts.

As a member of the royal family who in today's world are often under threat from terrorist groups, Catherine had to complete a course run by the Special Air Services (SAS), a special unit of the British Army concerned in counter-terrorism. She had to learn how to use a revolver, how to behave if kidnapped or held hostage – which in today's world is a danger faced by royalty, the mega-rich and celebrities.

When visiting London, the couple stayed at tiny Nottingham Cottage in the grounds of Kensington Palace (affectionately referred to as 'Nott Cott' by the royals and the former home of Diana's sister Lady Jane Spencer who had married the Queen's Private Secretary) while they waited for the extensive renovations and redecoration to be completed on Apartment 1A. This apartment had been standing empty for some time and had once been the residence of Princess Margaret and Tony Armstrong-Jones, the Earl of Snowdon.

Since William's salary as a part-time air-sea-rescue pilot did not cover all their expenses, Prince Charles covered the shortfall. This included the cost of his daughter-in-law's designer outfits for official occasions since Kate is not allowed to accept 'freebies' from fashion houses that, in fact, love her to wear their creations. She looks so good in them that sales are enormous and provide a huge boost to the British fashion industry. However, the new Duchess remained thrifty and continued to buy clothes from retail outlets like Topshop and various discount stores. When photographs of the Duchess of Cambridge appear in the press wearing High Street fashions, they sell out immediately. In the early days of their marriage, Duchess Catherine did her own hair but now, as a mother and with many royal duties, she has a personal hairdresser, a secretary and a press officer.

The Duchess' beauty routines are very simple, and she insists on applying her own make-up. Instead of Botox, the Duchess has the same bee-sting facials recommended by Camilla, which keep her complexion looking young and fresh.

To lose weight before her wedding and to keep slim after having babies, the Duchess of Cambridge follows the diet created by the Parisian general practitioner and nutritionist Dr Pierre Dukan. The Dukan diet is based on eating lean meat, poultry, fish and other seafood, eggs, tofu and low-fat dairy products. The Duchess eats plenty of raw vegetables, goji berries and tabbouleh. She also enjoys roast turkey, prawn or lobster salad and roast parsnips.

Kate's mother also keeps very slim and follows this diet. She recommends keeping peeled prawns and cottage cheese in the fridge to avoid eating starchy or sugar-laden snacks. An essential part of the Duchess' diet is eating oat bran which has the ability to absorb twenty-five times its volume of water. This means that as the bran reaches the stomach, it swells giving a feeling of fullness. Doctors claim that oat bran reduces cholesterol and protects from diabetes and colon cancer. The Duchess has always been very keen on walking, which forms an essential part of the Dukan diet.

Dr Dukan's theory is that limiting carbohydrates makes the body burn fat. Catherine is living proof that this diet works, and one of its good points is that food does not need to be weighed. The food groups selected by Dr Dukan can be eaten in large quantities preventing a feeling of hunger.

But like most people, the Duchess has a sweet tooth and sometimes eats desserts. One of her favourites is sticky toffee pudding which she enjoys making for family and friends.

A favourite meal Catherine enjoys preparing for her family is curry with plenty of vegetables in it accompanied by homemade chutney – a batch of which she made as a Christmas present for the Queen because the royal family give each other fairly inexpensive gifts at Christmas, and she was pleased to see that her chutney was on the table the next time she visited Sandringham.

Royal tours, public engagements & babies

In 2011, the Duke and Duchess of Cambridge undertook their first royal tour. They visited Canada and California and in Hollywood drew larger crowds than any of the movie stars. This was the first of several tours to Canada, a country they always enjoyed visiting.

In 2012, the young couple undertook an official tour of Malaysia, Singapore, the Solomon Islands and Tuvalu on behalf of the Queen for her Diamond Jubilee celebrations. Unlike Princess Diana who rarely read her briefing notes, Catherine is assiduous in studying background information on the countries they visit on their overseas tours.

After moving into their newly decorated Apartment 1A, Kensington Palace, the young couple had plenty of space and privacy behind the high walls of the palace where many members of the royal family have apartments or small cottages.

The Duke and Duchess of Cambridge who enjoy a wide variety of sports, attended many events at the London Olympic Games in the summer of 2012. The Duchess of Cambridge and Prince William were guests of honour at a gala at the Royal Albert Hall hosted by the British Olympic Association. They and Prince Harry are official ambassadors for the British Olympic delegation and the British Paralympics. Many of the Olympic athletes at the gala, at which Kate wore a stunning turquoise floor-length gown, felt that the young royal couple brought excitement and glamour to the evening and to the sporting events they attended.

Two years into their marriage, the young couple announced that Kate was expecting their first baby. Her first pregnancy was not an easy one as she suffered from a severe form of morning sickness, known as *hyperemesis gravidarum,* which was so debilitating she spent three days in hospital. This severe morning sickness would also affect her during subsequent pregnancies.

After the birth of Prince George on 22 July 2013 in the Lindo Wing of St Mary's Hospital, Prince William collected his wife and new-born son in his car, placed little George in the baby capsule and drove them home to Kensington Palace.

Before they married, Prince William had promised Kate's parents, the Middletons, they would play a large role in the upbringing of their grandchildren. So, instead of following the normal royal pattern and engaging a nanny who would care full-time for the royal baby, he and Kate went to stay with the Middletons at their home in Bucklebury. Kate and her mother looked after the baby themselves. Only when they had moved back to Kensington Palace and discovered that caring for a new baby meant many sleepless nights did they engage a Spanish nanny.

Early in April 2014, the Duke and Duchess of Cambridge and the eight-month-old Prince George and his Spanish nanny, Maria Theresa, made a three-week tour of New Zealand and Australia. A large part of the tour was intended to focus on the role of the Anzacs in World War One and various events to recall this.

Their first stop on their New Zealand tour was Government House in Wellington where they stayed as guests of the Governor and his wife. The Duke and Duchess of Cambridge unveiled a formal portrait of Queen Elizabeth II. It had been arranged that Prince George and his Spanish nanny would remain at Government House while his parents toured some of highlights of this beautiful country.

On the following day, they attended a wreath laying ceremony at the War Memorial at Blenheim, New Zealand, and saw historic war planes at the Omaka Aviation Heritage Centre. Auckland provided excitement for the *sportif* couple as they took to the water in a friendly but competitive sailing race with Kate photographed wearing jeans, a striped *matelot* sweater and a yachting cap.

The Duchess had her first solo engagement meeting terminally ill children at the Rainbow Place Children's Hospice in Hamilton.

Their New Zealand itinerary was a varied one. It ranged from a meeting with the All Blacks in Dunedin to tasting local wines, followed by an exciting ride on a jet boat at Queenstown where the couple, wearing lifejackets, enjoyed a thrilling journey.

The royal couple wrapped up their ten-day tour of New Zealand receiving a warm farewell during their final walkabout in Wellington before flying to Australia on a Royal Australian Airforce jet.

On 17 April 2014, they arrived at Sydney Airport for their first official visit to Australia. Duchess Catherine looked stunning in an elegant yellow dress carrying Prince George off the plane. At an informal reception on the tarmac, the couple waved to the spectators and local dignitaries who greeted them. Everywhere they went on their Australian tour, the photogenic couple drew vast crowds.

Sydney's beautiful Government House overlooking the harbour acted as their base where they were once again able to leave Prince George with his nanny while they fulfilled their busy schedule.

At an official function on the steps of the Opera House, enthusiastic school children waved small flags and offered flowers to Duchess Catherine. In an emotive speech, Prince William told the inhabitants of Sydney how much he and his wife had been looking forward to visiting their beautiful city and added how pleased he was to have a chance to show this beautiful city to his wife.

Prince George had a very special visit scheduled to Taronga Park Zoo where a baby bilby was to be named after him. Prince William joked that he suspected his baby son's first new word uttered in Australia might be 'bilby' as he would find it too hard to say 'koala!'

Among the huge crowd that greeted the popular couple at the Opera House were four hundred young leaders of arts, sports and community organisations who were excited to see the Duke and Duchess on their ten-day Australian tour.

On the third day of the tour, 'Kate and Wills', as Australians call them, visited the Royal Easter Show. As a tribute to Australia's fashion designers, Kate wore a stunning white lace dress designed by the Zimmerman sisters, Nicky and Simone, who have just opened a store in New York and are known for designing glamorous casual wear, the kind of clothes that the Duchess loves.

The couple paid a visit to the Blue Mountains and saw the spectacular peaks of The Three Sisters towering above the Jamison Valley. They also met survivors of the bush fires that had ravaged the area the previous October.

In Brisbane, they were greeted by huge crowds along their route to the Royal Australian Air Force base at Amberley. They returned to Sydney for an Anzac commemorative service in St Andrew's Cathedral and the following day flew to Canberra. Kate was able to relax and play with Prince George in the gardens of Government House and take her toddler for a walk by the lake to see his first kangaroos.

The following day, they flew to what was once known as Ayers Rock, which is now known by its Aboriginal name, Uluru. Later they met a group of indigenous artists at Yulara. In South Australia, they visited Elizabeth, a suburb named after William's grandmother, Queen Elizabeth II.

In Canberra, they planted a tree in the beautiful grounds of the Australian National Arboretum, with its many different species of native and exotic trees.

The following day was Anzac Day, a public holiday in memory of the Anzacs who died fighting in World War One at Gallipoli, on the Somme and in subsequent wars. It was officially planned that the Duke and Duchess would have a rest in the morning, but they insisted on making an unscheduled appearance at the 5 am Dawn Service attended by over 37,000 Australians.

To beat Canberra's early morning chill, the Duke and Duchess wore warm clothes and Prince William wore his service medals as they stood beside Governor-General Peter Cosgrove. The dawn service was made even more emotive as huge blow-up photos of those who died in World War One were projected onto the walls of the War Memorial.

Kate and William explained they had wanted to join Australians in this commemorative service on what was a very special day of the year for Australians.

Later, the royal couple were welcomed at the Anzac Day morning service held at the Australian War Memorial by Prime Minister Tony Abbott, who said that though Australia no longer regarded Britain as the mother country 'we are still family'. He added that the presence of Prince William who had served in the army and as an Air Force rescue pilot reminded Australians of their comrades in arms.

Duchess Catherine looked dignified in a blue and white tweed coat dress which highlighted the colour of the red poppy badge presented to her by a war veteran. The Duchess laid a large wreath of poppies at the Shrine of Remembrance, and inside the Hall of Memory, they placed more poppies on the Tomb of the Unknown Soldier and paused to reflect on the huge losses suffered by Australia in World War One.

A handwritten message from the Duchess was placed on the Tomb of the Unknown Soldier. As her relatives, the three Lupton brothers, died young serving in France in World War One, her note was written with great emotion and read, 'In every second of every day, you will be remembered for your courage and your bravery. Thank you for your sacrifice and for what you did for us. For that, I am truly grateful'.

Duchess Catherine then placed a scarlet poppy on the huge granite Wall of Memory which has long lines of poppies and the names of many thousands of dead Anzacs engraved on it.

Inside the lecture hall of the War Memorial, images of the forty Australian soldiers killed in Afghanistan were projected onto a screen while Lieutenant Commander Desmond Woods and Squadron Leader Sharon Brown read dramatic accounts of their experiences during their war service in Afghanistan. The Duchess planted a tree, cultivated from the historic Lone Pine, the last tree left standing on the site of the battle on the Gallipoli Peninsula where so many young Australians lost their lives.

The royal couple flew home with young Prince George and his nanny. Back in London, the second pregnancy of Duchess Catherine was announced on 8 September 2014. Once again, she suffered very badly from a severe form of morning sickness and was hospitalised, so was unable to carry out any official engagements.

On 2 May 2015, Catherine was taken to St Mary's Hospital in Paddington where Princess Charlotte was born at 8.34 am. It was announced that her full name would be Charlotte Elizabeth Diana. 'Charlotte' (as a feminine version of Charles) honours Prince William's father; 'Elizabeth' honours the Queen, her grandmother and 'Diana' honours William's mother.

Back at Kensington Palace, mother and baby received visits from Prince Charles and Camilla, the Queen and Kate's parents. Prime Minister Tony Abbott sent a Tasmanian merino wool blanket.

On 5 July, Princess Charlotte was christened in the small church of St Mary Magdalene at Sandringham village (where Princess Diana was christened when the Spencer family lived at Park House on the Sandringham estate). By now, the Duke and Duchess and their children were spending most of their time at Anmer Hall near the village of Anmer close to the main Sandringham estate – a Georgian house the Queen had given them.

Anmer Hall when it was the residence of the Duke and Duchess of Kent (Private collection)

Prince George, the adorable 'little rascal' as his father calls him, had his first birthday party with its central theme chosen by his mother. The room was decorated with pictures of Beatrix Potters' well-known characters, Peter Rabbit and Jemima Puddleduck. This reflected Kate's interest in her ancestors, the Luptons, who were relatives of the famous children's author, Beatrix Potter.

In 2016, Prince George was photographed with President Obama who had given him a rocking horse when he was born. His encounter with the little prince prompted Obama to joke that 'Prince George showed up at our meeting in his bathrobe, clearly a breach of protocol!' Prince George had his first taste of school at the Westacre Montessori Nurse School near his parents' country home, Anmer Hall in Norfolk. The little prince goes to school, usually taken by one or other of his parents, wearing a backpack labelled 'George Cambridge' although his actual family name is Mountbatten-Windsor. He and Princess Charlotte are very devoted to each other, and Kate loves spending time with them.

Duchess Catherine and her daughter Princess Charlotte (courtesy Reuters)

⁂

Twenty years after Diana's death, Catherine, Duchess of Cambridge, the beautiful young woman who prior to her marriage was known as Kate, together with her husband, opened a Memorial Garden dedicated to the mother-in-law she never knew. Sheltering under an umbrella from a slight drizzle, Catherine and her husband, Prince William, walked through the white garden planted with Diana's favourite flowers: white freesias and lilies. It was here that Diana used to bring her young sons, William and Harry, to feed the carp in the lily pond in the centre of the garden.

Invited to this ceremony were representatives of some of Diana's favourite charities. Duchess Catherine, pregnant with her third child, said, 'I would have loved to have met Princess Diana as she was such an inspirational woman.'

Also present at the official opening of the Diana Memorial Garden was a representative of one of Diana's favourite charities, the Royal Marsden Trust for Cancer Research of which Prince William became President in May 2007, a position previously held by his late mother. In his speech, Prince William said that the Royal Marsden did an outstanding job 'treating thousands of cancer patients each year with standards of care and compassion that are unsurpassed.' The Trust is currently funding research into more than seven hundred diagnostic tests concerned with the prevention, diagnosis and the treatment of cancer (Prince William has made many visits to the Marsden Hospital and opened its important Ralph Lauren Centre for Research into Breast Cancer).

Another guest, Peter Waddup of the Leprosy Mission, reminded Prince William and Duchess Catherine how on her Indonesian visit, Diana insisted on shaking hands and touching lepers in spite of being warned by her 'minders' to avoid any contact with them. This was typical of Diana's fearless commitment to her humanitarian work which her sons and Duchess Catherine are continuing.

Catherine's charities reflect her special interests and focus on issues surrounding the physical and mental health of children, treatment of addiction and the charity Heads Together concerned with recognition of the awareness of mental health issues. She is also the patron of the Royal College of Obstetricians and Gynaecologists and involved with Nursing Now, a campaign to raise awareness of the profile of nurses as Catherine's grandmother and great-grandmother were both nurses. With a degree in art history and a keen photographer she is interested in the role of art helping disadvantaged children express themselves through art therapy. With her knowledge of art history she is a valuable and knowledgeable patron of the National Portrait Gallery where she curated an exhibition of the work of Victorian photographers of children and has recently accepted to become patron of London's fascinating Victoria and Albert Museum.

William and Harry were convinced the paparazzi contributed to their mother's death, which explains why William's highest priority is protecting his privacy and that of his family. Prince William as a child saw his mother crying over the way the paparazzi were hounding her, and he is determined to protect his wife and children from them. He and the Duchess of Cambridge sued a French magazine for invasion of privacy for publishing a photograph of her sunbathing topless on holiday at a private villa in Monaco. They realised how embarrassing these photos would be if published when William becomes King William V and Duchess Catherine becomes Queen Catherine.

The court ruled that these photos were an invasion of privacy. On 5 September 2017, it awarded Prince William a total of ninety-one thousand, seven hundred pounds in damages, a significant victory in his ongoing battle against the paparazzi who had hounded his mother to her death.

When Meghan Markle and Prince Harry announced their engagement, they were congratulated by the Duke and Duchess of Cambridge. In a public statement, they said 'We are very excited for Harry and Meghan. It has been wonderful getting to know Meghan and to see how happy she and Harry are together.'

On 23 April 2018, the Duchess and Prince William welcomed their third child, a health baby boy and once again Prince William was present at the birth. The news that Kate was expecting a third baby was a shock to many royal watchers who thought that the Wales had completed their family.

After a few days, it was announced that the baby's name is Prince Louis Arthur, and these names are intended as a tribute to Prince Charles.

As the Duchess emerged from the Lindo Wing carrying her beautiful baby, royal watchers noted that Kate was wearing a scarlet maternity dress with a white collar, repeating the same colour as Princess Diana had worn after the birth of Prince Harry.

As he climbed into the car, Prince William, when asked by journalists how he felt, smiled and said, 'It's wonderful. But it triples your worry.'

Kate and William are stoic faced with worries about death threats from terrorists against them and their children. The danger the young couple face with courage and composure was highlighted in July 2018 when Lancashire resident Husain Rashid was jailed by Judge Andrew Lees at Woolwich Crown Court for inciting terrorist attacks on members of the British royal family. Sentencing Rashid to 25 years in prison Judge Lees stated, 'The message you wanted to convey was clear when you posted on line the name and address of Prince George's school with a threat that he and other members of the royal family should be seen as targets for terrorist attacks.'

CHAPTER EIGHTEEN

Meghan – a very modern romance

Meghan Markle on a walkabout with Prince Harry (courtesy Reuters, London)

I am proud to be a woman, bi-racial and a feminist. Meghan Markle.

A prince in love

The official announcement of the engagement of Meghan Markle to Prince Harry marked a major change to long tradition governing British royal marriages. Prince Harry's American fiancée was a divorced actress, with a mother of African-American heritage, whose ancestors had been shipped to America to work as slaves on a cotton plantation in the state of Georgia.

In the not so distant past, just one of these facts would have precluded Ms Markle from marrying into the British royal family.

Some commentators on Prince Harry's engagement to Meghan Markle drew parallels with the Abdication crisis of 1936 (eight decades earlier) when the Windsors, backed by the Archbishop of Canterbury, the British Prime Minister and his Cabinet, refused to allow the uncrowned Edward VIII to marry the twice divorced American socialite Wallis Simpson.

Eight decades later, changes to the status of women, the sexual scandals and divorces of three children of Queen Elizabeth II including her heir to relax the precepts that stipulated brides of princes must be virginal, of royal blood or aristocratic. She was happy to welcome the divorced bi-racial Megan Markle into the royal family.

Although Meghan Markle had a wide following in Canada and America after her success on the Netflix television programme *Suits* not many people knew much about her in Britain, Australia or other Commonwealth countries.

Several European Crown princes had already broken the ancient rules about marrying aristocrats, and made successful marriages to what had previously been described as 'commoners'. Just like Prince Harry with Meghan Markle, two European princes had met their glamorous university-educated wives under unusual circumstances.

Crown Prince Frederick of Denmark had met his Australian bride, advertising executive Mary Donaldson, in a pub at the Sydney 2000 Olympic Games and introduced himself as 'Fred'. Mary Donaldson had no idea 'Fred' was a prince when she fell in love with him and only later discovered the truth.

Crown Prince Wilhelm-Alexander of Holland met his Argentinian bride, Maxima Zorreguieta, when celebrating a fiesta in Seville with friends. He was introduced as 'Wilhelm' to Maxima, a glamorous blonde merchant banker working for the United Nations in New York. She had no idea he was heir to Queen Beatrix of Holland. On their second date when friends revealed his identity, Maxima thought they were playing a practical joke and refused to believe them. But this transatlantic romance led to a happy marriage and three children and today Maxima is Queen of Holland.

⁂

In the first week of July 2016, Prince Harry, having broken up amicably with his girl friend, the aristocratic Cressida Bonas, by arrangement met Californian-born television star Meghan Markle on a blind date at London's exclusive Soho Club.

The blind date had been arranged by a mutual friend who believed they had a lot in common. Both of them were fascinated by Africa and the preservation of its unique wildlife, were involved with charities that worked to improve the health of African children, and were not romantically involved with anyone else.

Meghan Markle had made a film for Canada's World Vision, a charity which was building wells and pipelines to provide clean water to remote Rwandan villages where children were dying of typhoid and cholera. Prince Harry had spent his gap year in the tiny kingdom of Lesotho and been horrified to learn how many children were orphaned as their parents had died of AIDS. A few years later, aided by his friend, the Crown Prince of Lesotho, Harry had set up his own charity there called Sentebale in memory of his late mother.

At their first meeting Meghan's exotic beauty, long dark hair and soft Californian accent proved irresistible to the russet-headed prince. Recounting the story of their romantic first date Harry described Meghan as the 'beautiful girl who fell into my life.' During the first months of their transatlantic romance, Harry and Meghan managed to keep their relationship secret. Harry travelled *incognito* to Toronto with a woolly beanie over his distinctive copper coloured hair.

The couple spent a few romantic days together at an environmental resort in Botswana, watching the wildlife and getting to know each other. Harry flew to Toronto and worked on the next Invictus Games to be held there and saw Meghan and she flew to London for quiet dinners with Harry at his bachelor cottage in the grounds of Kensington Palace.

Their secret romance was exposed five months later by Britain's *Sunday Express* who ran a front page article headed 'Prince Harry's Secret Romance with TV Star.' The article described Meghan as a divorced actress with an African-American mother which sparked a media furore. Some comments on social media were racist and highly offensive while others queried how someone like Meghan Markle could possibly fit into the royal family.

In reality Meghan Markle was a talented young woman with a university degree and substantial financial earnings from her starring role as Rachel Zane in the Netflix series *Suits* and various sponsorships. Meghan was two years older than Harry, a humanitarian and a feminist with a keen interest in improving the lives of women and children in underdeveloped counties. Years of experience as an actress and public speaker had given her the ability to handle the media with charm, poise and dignity.

Meghan: ancestry, childhood & adolescence

The public learned that Rachel Meghan (Meg) Markle had been born on 4 August 1981, in a Los Angeles hospital, just days after Harry's parents, Prince Charles and Lady Diana Spencer were married in St Paul's Cathedral.

Meghan's father, Thomas Markle, was divorced from her mother and was a former award winning Hollywood director of lighting and photography now retired and living in the port of Rosarito in Mexico. More details emerged when journalists interviewed Markle relatives and were told Thomas Markle's ancestor, Heinrich Martin Merckel, had emigrated from Alsace on the French-German border to America, anglicised his name to Markle and also had Irish blood.

On her mother's side Meghan's ancestors were African, captured by slave traders and, packed together in the dark fetid holds of English slave ships transported to America and sold to plantation owner, William Ragland. They worked on his cotton plantation in Georgia, the state which figures prominently in the dark history of American slavery. According to custom, as William Ragland's slaves, they were given his family name.

Ironically, Prince Harry's distant forbear, James, Duke of York (later King James II) had headed the Royal Africa Company, an English mercantile company set up by the Stuart royal family and a group of London merchants. The company was given a monopoly of all English trade with Africa between 1666-1689, including the highly profitable trade in African slaves, shipped in English vessels, many owned by the company to English-owned sugar plantations in the Caribbean and to the Americas. Like Meghan's distant ancestors many of the kidnapped slaves ended up working the cotton plantations of America's Deep South.[133]

All slaves in America were freed by law in 1865, once the American Civil War ended. In search of a better life the Raglands left Georgia and went north to Cleveland, Ohio and eventually moved to California.

---

133 Originally known as the Company of Royal Adventurers Trading to Africa under a charter established in 1660 the company established to deal in gold next established large slave forts on the West African coast to hold slaves sold them by slave dealers and transported to the West Indies and the Americas. King James took a large share of the profits from the slave trade in which the Trading to Africa Company held a monopoly as well as profits from the compulsory sale of any ships that violated its monopoly. The original company still connected with King James II changed its name to the Royal Africa Company. For further details see G.F. Zook, *The Company of Royal Adventurers Trading in Africa,* New Era Printing Company, Lancaster, Pennsylvania, 1919; K.G. Davies, *The Royal African Company,* Routledge, London, 1996 and Hugh Thomas, *The Story of the Atlantic Slave Trade 1440 – 1870,* London, 1999.

Meghan's grandparents, Alvin and Jeanette Ragland lived in Los Angeles where they owned a small antique-cum second-hand shop.[134] Their daughter, Doria, was born in 1956. A sweet-natured intelligent child her education was adversely affected by the 1971 San Fernando earthquake which severely damaged many schools in Los Angeles. Normal lessons were disrupted: students had to be relocated to makeshift classrooms and attend lessons in shifts.

After leaving school Meghan's mother, Doria worked in her father's antique shop. She held several other jobs before becoming an apprentice make-up artist at a Hollywood film studio where she met the recently divorced Thomas Markle.

Thomas Markle had two children from a previous marriage when in 1979 he married Doria Ragland. Doria, baptised a Protestant became a devotee of the Hindu guru, Yogananda (regarded by some Hollywood luminaries as the greatest teacher of yoga techniques). Doria and Thomas married at Yogananda's Self-Realization Fellowship Temple in Hollywood.

Thomas was well paid as a director of lighting and photography on various film and television series and had won an Emmy Award for his work. He and Doria and the children of his first marriage, Samantha and Tom Junior lived in a large comfortable house overlooking the Pacific Ocean.

Thomas Markle thought his baby daughter Meghan, born in 1981, was beautiful and was proud of her. He was earning good money but was working exceptionally long hours at the studios. Left alone much of the time Doria found her teen-age step-children resentful and difficult to cope with by herself.

Meghan's teenage half-sister, Samantha, an aspiring actress, was unhappy about her father's second marriage and jealous of the attention he paid to his new baby daughter.

The marriage as far as Doria was concerned was not working as she had hoped. When Meghan turned two, she took her curly headed toddler and returned to live with her mother, as by now Doria's parents were divorced. Money was tight. Jeanette Ragland cared for her little granddaughter while Doria did a variety of jobs to support them and at one stage worked as an air stewardess and later as a travel agent.

Thomas Markle was shattered by the break-up of his second marriage and the abrupt departure of Doria. But both parents wanted their little daughter to grow up feeling loved and secure so kept in close contact for her sake and did not divorce until Meghan was six. They agreed that once

---

[134] For a full description of Meghan's ancestry read Andrew Morton *Hollywood Princess,* Grand Central Publishing, New York, 2018 and Michael O'Mara Books, London, 2018.

Meghan started school she could spend weekends with her father. Meghan said she never heard her parents say anything unkind about each other.

Family photo albums show Meghan was a cute little girl with a mop of black curls and a gap between her front teeth, later fixed by an orthodontist. She was sent to the prestigious Little Red House kindergarten and primary school, an expensive Hollywood institution with its own swimming pool, attended by the children of Hollywood's lawyers, accountants and film stars. The school's most famous pupil was the late Elizabeth Taylor.

As a bi-racial child growing up in a predominantly white affluent area and attending a private kindergarten and primary school with almost exclusively affluent white pupils, Meghan witnessed her mother's humiliation when Doria was mistaken for a paid nanny.

A $700,000 win in a lottery enabled Thomas Markle to set aside money to pay Meghan's school fees at the Immaculate Heart High School in Los Angeles and her fees at university. The Immaculate Heart was known for the quality of its tuition and for the high standard of the theatrical events in which its students including Meghan took part. Thomas Markle helped by acting as their lighting director and from an early age Meghan showed a talent for acting.

Although the Immaculate Heart School is Catholic Meghan was not made to convert. Her mother was born a Protestant and her father an Episcopalian (the American equivalent of the Church of England).

Aged eleven, Meghan first became aware of the sexist language used in advertising when her class was asked to comment on several commercials. The tag-line of a Proctor & Gamble commercial for Ivory Clear Dishwashing liquid was 'Women face a problem with greasy pots and pans in the kitchen.'

The boys in Meghan's class agreed with the commercial's message that women's role was in the kitchen doing the dishes. Meghan, a thoughtful intelligent student, raised by a single mother with feminist principles, was incensed. She wrote to the soap manufacturers, asking them to change the sexist tag-line.

When Proctor & Gamble changed the wording to '*People* are worried about greasy pans in the kitchen', a local television station followed up the story and sent a camera crew to Meghan's home to film her reactions.

Thomas Markle had been working on an adult television series with the occasional risqué scene and Meghan would arrive at the Hollywood film studio for a lift home with her father.

During a television interview, Meghan later recalled how 'Everyday, after school for ten years, I was on the set of *Married with Children* — an unusual place for a little girl wearing the uniform of a Catholic schoolgirl.'

Thomas Markle was protective of his young daughter and whenever suggestive scenes were being shot for the television series *Married with Children* her father would suggest she go outside and help the staff in the catering room.

Unlike the motherless Prince Harry, seen as a 'difficult' pupil at Eton College, Meghan was a model student at her Catholic high school. Classmates remember Meghan as 'a lovely girl, very hardworking and dedicated'. Her olive complexion, freckles and delicate facial features led many of them to assume she was Italian.

Taught yoga and meditation by her mother, a discipline known for calming minds and bodies, Meghan became a proficient practitioner, posting a photo of herself in a yoga pose on Instagram.

Meghan's excellent exam results gained her a place at Evanston's fee-paying Northwestern University, near Chicago, which had an attractive campus and good library facilities. Thomas Markle helped pay his daughter's university fees from the money he had set aside from his lottery win. But subsequently he went bankrupt as a result of a bad investment with a friend. On retirement from the film business he moved to the Mexican port of Rosarito.

At university Meghan enrolled in English studies with the intention of becoming a writer but changed her mind. She switched courses and enrolled in the university's Department of Communications and while studying hard worked for several community service projects. In 2003 she graduated with a double major in international relations and theatre studies.

In a subsequent interview Meghan revealed that to earn credits to complete her junior year, an uncle on her father's side in the State Department helped her gain an internship at the US embassy in Buenos Aires.[135] She enjoyed her work as an intern but was shocked by the huge gap between rich and poor in the Argentine capital, having already witnessed poverty in Jamaica and Mexico where her mother had taken her on holiday while working for a travel agency.

Having graduated from Northwestern University, Meghan flew to Spain where she completed a semester in Madrid to improve her Spanish and sat for the entrance examination for America's diplomatic service. After failing this competitive exam, (the first she had ever failed), Meghan decided to concentrate on acting but hoped to combine it with humanitarian work.

---

135 *Vogue* magazine, October 2017.

In the eleven years between leaving university and winning a starring role in *Suits*, unlike most aspiring actresses who work as waitresses, Meghan supported herself as a freelance calligrapher. She designed and produced beautiful hand-written invitations for wealthy clients. She did this while waiting to audition for film roles explaining to a journalist from *Vogue* how, 'I would sit there with a little white tube sock on my hand, so no hand oil got on the card, while auditioning.'

To earn serious money Meghan worked as what was known as a 'briefcase girl' in a television quiz show. The job entailed donning a figure-hugging scarlet costume with a low-cut bodice and painfully high stilettos. Working in what feminists would consider a degrading job was not the career that Meghan, as a feminist, had ever envisaged for herself. But she was determined to continue supporting herself and trying to gain a lucky break in films.

Years later, Meghan recalled how miserable and frustrated she felt at missing out on roles for which she had auditioned, aware that being bi-racial made it harder to succeed in Hollywood.

In an interview with a journalist from *Elle* magazine, Meghan commented wryly that she had been what she called an 'ethnic chameleon'. 'I wasn't black enough for the black roles or white enough for the white ones, leaving me in the middle — an ethnic chameleon who couldn't book a job.'

Meghan had been raised by her mother to be proud of her African heritage and made the point, 'I have come to embrace this, and [take] pride in being a strong, confident mixed-race woman.'

In 2004 Meghan began dating Trevor Engelson, a tall fair-haired New York film producer, son of a wealthy Jewish orthodontist and a speech therapist. Trevor's parents approved of their relationship. They lived together in a yellow-painted Los Angeles bungalow high above Sunset Boulevard. Photos she took on vacation and placed on Instagram (later removed) showed two of them vacationing in beauty spots like the Greek island of Santorini.

Meghan managed to obtain small parts in two films, *Get Him to the Greek* and *Horrible Bosses* and in 2010 appeared in *Remember Me*, a film shot in English with a dubbed French edition, still available on Netflix.

After living together for five years, on 10 September, 2011 Trevor and Meghan had a bohemian version of a Jewish wedding on the beach of Ochos Rios, on the island of Jamaica. According to Jewish custom, the newly-weds were hoisted aloft on chairs by guests with dancing and music. The party lasted for four days with beach games and more dancing. Meghan was also celebrating the fact that she had just obtained an important part in the Netflix television series *Suits*. She was to play an ambitious trainee lawyer or paralegal and was so busy with rehearsals for the first episodes she had to employ a wedding planner for her Jamaican wedding.

Meghan's starring role in *Suits*

Meghan almost missed out on the role that jetted her to fame and fortune: her agent omitted to tell her she was auditioning for a television series set in a lawyer's office. She arrived for her audition and screen test wearing black jeans and a skinny top with spaghetti-thin straps before realising with horror that she was unsuitably dressed for the part.

She raced out of the studio to the nearest branch of H&M stores, bought a little black dress for $35, wore it for her screen test and won an important role in the series.

Aaron Korsh, creator of *Suits*, later revealed that the casting directors had spent time and money searching for an actress who was beautiful in an unconventional way. For the part of Rachel Zane it was necessary to find someone with the intelligence to play the role of an ambitious young trainee lawyer from a wealthy background. The actress selected had to convey Rachel's toughness and attitude as well as a certain sweetness of character. The casting directors had been searching for the right actress to play Rachel Zane for some time without success. Selecting Meghan Markle for this important role was a unanimous decision as her screen test was excellent.

Due to generous tax concessions, *Suits* was to be shot in Toronto so Meghan had to move there while Trevor's work kept him in Hollywood. As a Californian she found it difficult to become accustomed to the long cold Canadian winters. She rented an inner city apartment before moving to a pretty little house in Toronto's Seton Valley, with a garden for her two much loved rescue dogs, Bogart and Guy. Had Meghan not adopted them they would have been put down as strays.

Although initially their marriage seemed happy, unlike the proverb where absence makes the heart grow fonder, in their case this did not happen. It soon became apparent that Meghan and Trevor were very different in personality and attitudes to life. The fact that during the five years they lived together Meghan was only given one part in films her husband produced has been claimed as a factor in their eventual break-up but neither of them commented on the failure of the brief marriage.

Meghan's house in Vancouver, later listed by Freeman Real Estate

Trevor's work as a producer continued to keep him in Hollywood and their lives in two different cities continued until August two years later, when Meghan petitioned for a no fault divorce. This was finalised the following year without complications as the marriage was childless.

Trevor was later seen dating several beautiful women in Hollywood and on June 1, 2018 announced his engagement to a beautiful blonde Hollywood dietician declaring he was very happy.

With her evenings free Meghan started a lifestyle blog which was praised by *Elle* magazine as one of the best on line. The blog was called 'The Tig' (short for Tignanello, Meghan's favourite Chianti, a well-known variety of Tuscan wine). Meghan's blog was so informative and lively it soon had thousands of followers. She wrote about foods and wines and the latest upmarket restaurants as well as fashion trends.

On her blog Meghan praised Cory Vitiello's Harbord Room restaurant, visited by friends in the acting world and in the arts. It led to her friendship with restaurant owner and celebrity chef Cory Vitiello, Toronto's answer to the innovative television personality, Jamie Oliver but without the laddishness and Cockney accent of the British chef.

Cory's warm Italian charm attracted high flyers to his restaurant and through him Meghan acquired new friends, including Jessica Mulroney, a fashion and design expert, wife of Ben Mulroney, the son of Canada's former Prime Minister. Meghan also became a good friend of tennis star Serena Williams.

Meghan was invited to become a fashion ambassador for Ralph Lauren and met Violet von Westenholz, daughter of Baron Piers von Westenholz. Violet handled the media for Ralph Lauren and, although this has never been confirmed, she is believed to have been the discrete friend who arranged Meghan's blind date with Prince Harry.[136]

Meghan also met Markus Anderson, a director of the Soho House Club which has branches all over the world and went on a holiday with him and Cory Vitiello. Megan and her friends were frequent visitors to the Soho House Club in Toronto and she became an ambassador for the international organisation.

Cory and Meghan kept their relationship low key. They preferred to spend their free time relaxing at home and enjoyed cooking for each other. Cory Vitiello, who has an Italian father and a Scandinavian mother, is not unlike Prince Harry with similar red hair, stubbly beard and muscular frame. Meghan's relationship with Cory was approved of by his parents and many of their friends thought it would end in marriage.

When interviewed, Cory's mother said she would have welcomed Meghan as a daughter-in-law and had no idea why they broke up. He has remained loyal to Meghan and has turned down large sums from journalists to tell his side of the story. Meghan's blind date with Prince Harry at the Soho House Club took place three months after she stopped seeing Cory.

A year after her divorce from Trevor, Meghan's horizon were expanding rapidly. While working on *Suits* she had been invited to join a panel at the United Nations Young World Summit in Dublin to speak on gender equality and human rights and met the former United Nations Secretary, Kofi Annan. Meghan's passionate speech concerned the under-representation of women in the world's parliaments, the need for women not only to find a voice (as they already had a voice) but to use it to good advantage. She would later meet Canada's Prime Minister Justin Trudeau and discuss these ideas with him.

In February 2016, having noted her celebrity resulting from her appearances in *Suits*, World Vision of Canada approached Meghan Markle to star in a feature film to promote their charitable work in Africa. In February, 2016 she was flown to landlocked Rwanda in East Africa and was filmed watching the construction of wells and pipelines funded by World

---

[136] Many years ago living in Chelsea I was invited to a party at the beautifully decorated London apartment of Baron Piers von Westenholz by his friend Richard Salm, then at Cambridge as we were all keen skiers. At that time he was working as an interior designer and his own apartment was impressive with terracotta walls and beautiful antiques including two enormous antique globes which fascinated me and style is integral to this family.

Vision as well as dancing and singing with Rwandan children which she clearly enjoyed. In the film she showed children how to paint with water based paints using water from a newly-installed pipeline This film was placed on YouTube to raise more funds for World Vision.

Exterior shots for the film were taken in searing heat. They showed Meghan dressed in a plain dark grey cotton robe so the clouds of dust would not show. Technical staff liked working with her as no matter how tough the conditions Meghan never complained. She was not just a token celebrity who jetted in and out as a paid fund raiser but someone who cared passionately about the project.

The film featuring Meghan raised substantial sums for World Vision to assist its valuable work of bringing unpolluted water to Rwandan villages and helping out in other disaster areas.

As a Global Ambassador for World Vision for two years[137], Meghan worked to raise awareness of the vital importance of clean water to prevent typhoid, cholera and dysentery, responsible for the high mortality of babies and children in underdeveloped countries. She pointed out other benefits of piped water which many people today take for granted in the developed world, claiming 'Having clean water available keeps young girls in school because they aren't walking for hours each day to source water for their families.'

On her return to Toronto, in her own time Meghan organised an exhibition of children's drawings to raise money to construct more wells in Rwanda. She later returned to Africa on a fact-finding mission for the United Nations.

Meghan's other interests include fashion and interior design. In 2016 she worked with designers from the Canadian fashion chain Reitmans on her own line of ready-to-wear clothes. She was photographed wearing these outfits for publicity shots. Meghan who loves shoes owns a large collection including many by the celebrated Jimmy Choo. While working on fashion designs she was shooting successive episodes of *Suits*, which now had high ratings on Netflix.

Meghan and her mother have always been close. Doria has a strong

---

137 World Vision is concerned with the health and education of children and the money given to it is put to good purpose. I donated royalties from two of my books to World Vision of Australia after writing *Blue Ribbons, Bitter Bread* the biography of Australia's most decorated humanitarian Joice NanKivell Loch. Joice worked in refugee camps after World War One and raised the money to bring a pipeline of unpolluted water to a Greek refugee village by writing a best-selling children's book which was sold in America. Meghan's work for World Vision bringing unpolluted water to Rwandan villages had echoes of this and aroused my interest in her and led me to write her story.

work ethic and a social conscience. Meghan described how 'My mother raised me to be a global citizen, with my eyes open to the often harsh realities of life. I have never wanted to be a lady who lunches but preferred to be a woman who works.'

In March, 2017 Doria accompanied her daughter when Meghan addressed the United Nations Women's Organisation as a UN Advocate for Female Leadership with Hilary Clinton in the audience seated near Doria.

Harry: from angry rebel to heroic prince

Both Prince Harry and Meghan were children of divorced parents, educated at expensive fee-paying schools and had close relationships with their mothers but other than that their lives were very different.

Harry, second son of Princess Diana and Prince Charles, born 15 September, 1984 had also been very close to his mother. Diana insisted Charles help out in the nursery with bottle feeding and changing his nappies, something Prince Charles would recall in an amusing speech at Harry's evening wedding event.

Princess Diana wanted both her sons to have a broader range of experiences than previous royal children rather than being relegated to nurseries and mothered by nannies. Diana broke with tradition and took Harry and William to McDonald's and Disney World, to AIDS clinics and shelters for the homeless as well on skiing holidays in Austria. Her sons loved the time spent with their mother with no idea it would end.

The brothers were staying with their grandparents at Balmoral when Princess Diana died in a car crash in Paris. Prince Charles had to come north to Balmoral to break the news. For those terrible days immediately after they were cared for by the Queen and Prince Philip, before returning to London for their mother's funeral, distraught they had been unable to tell her how much they loved her before she died.

At twelve, Harry was required to walk in front of more photographers to read the grief-stricken messages pinned to a sea of floral tributes placed in front of Kensington Palace by mourners who had never met his mother, but felt they knew her. Once again the world and the paparazzi watched as Harry walked behind his mother's hearse on which had been placed a bouquet of Diana's favourite white roses and a handwritten card from her son saying only the word, 'Mummy'.

When sent as a boarder at Eton College, England's most exclusive private school, Harry was a 'difficult' and rebellious student but excelled at sport. His academic results were poor, but with a great deal of help from certain teachers, he qualified for entry to Sandhurst Military College.

Harry spent his gap year at the age of 19, working on a cattle station in Australia and in Lesotho in South Africa where he worked in a hands-on capacity in a home for children orphaned by AIDS. Lesotho is a tiny landlocked country bordering South Africa. This independent African kingdom, (formerly known as Basutoland), was being devastated by the AIDS scourge. Harry had been shocked to find thousands of children infected with AIDS, and another 300,000 orphans whose parents had died from the disease. Visiting a home for orphaned children, Harry befriended a young boy called Mutsu Potsane, whose parents had died of AIDS. This was a life-changing experience for Harry.

After he turned 21 and had money of his own, with the help of his friend, Prince Seeiso, a member of Lesotho's royal family, in memory of Princess Diana, Harry founded the charity, Sentebale to help homeless children affected by AIDS. Sentebale was able to build a large centre to house some of these children. Eventually Harry returned there on a long visit, met Mutsu again and played football with the younger children.

Over the years Harry raised money for his charity by speaking at functions in Britain and Dubai as well as organising special polo tournaments to raise money from wealthy polo addicts. He also produced a documentary film about the ravages of AIDS in Lesotho, titled *The Forgotten Kingdom* and appeared briefly in it, something he had in common with Meghan when they met.

Inspired by his mother's humanitarian work in Angola, Harry also visited the area with the Halo Trust, the charity for which Diana had walked through minefields.

⁂

In her mid-thirties when finally she met Harry, Meghan had the necessary empathy and emotional maturity to understand the unresolved grief and anger Harry had locked inside him over his parents' marriage breakup and the shock and devastation he suffered over his mother's death.

It was clear that as an adolescent Harry had been smoking and drinking too much in an effort to forget Diana's death. He was photographed reeling out of London nightclubs and engaging in drunken scuffles with members of the paparazzi who he still blamed for harassing his mother, pursuing the car in which she died and filming her as she lay dying.

On his return to England from Lesotho, Harry was sent to Sandhurst Military Academy for officer training. He graduated and was eventually promoted to lieutenant in the Blue's and Royals regiment.

Harry served in Canada and on the frontline in Afghanistan where he commanded a platoon in the frontier area, lived rough with his men and was popular with them. He was deployed in Helmand Province in Afghanistan where he helped Gurkha troops from the Himalayas repel attacks from Taliban insurgents and was awarded an Operational Service Medal in 2008.

Harry was reluctantly forced to leave the frontline when his presence was revealed by a newspaper making his platoon a prime target for the Taliban who issued death threats against him. Killing a member of the royal family would have been a major coup for the Taliban.

Captain Harry Wales was sent back to Britain but was eager to return to Afghanistan in a different capacity. He took a helicopter training course with the RAF at Shawbury, joining his brother who was also training to be a helicopter pilot. Harry gained his Apache Flying Badge in April 2011, coming top of the course and had his wings presented to him by his father. Also present was Harry's long-term girlfriend, Chelsy Davy, the daughter of a Zimbabwean business man. When their relationship ended Chelsy was replaced by the aristocratic blonde Cressida Bonas, a granddaughter of Edward Curzon, the sixth Earl Howe. Cressida shared Harry's deep love of Africa but also hated being harassed by the paparazzi.

Harry, promoted to captain returned to Afghanistan. On 10 September 2012, within days of arriving in Afghanistan the Taliban again threatened his life. Taliban spokesman Zabiullah Mujahid spoke to Reuters and was quoted as saying, 'We will use all our strength to get rid of him, either by killing or kidnapping, and our commanders in Helmand will do whatever they can to eliminate him.'

Leaving behind the horrors of the war in Afghanistan, on much needed R&R leave in August 2012, Harry and army friends went to Las Vegas on a 'boys only trip' and partied as though there was no tomorrow. Invited to a strip-billiards party in a Las Vegas hotel by total strangers Harry unwisely accepted and was set up with girls and caught on their cell phones, bollock-naked, cavorting with topless hookers. These photos were leaked or sold to the American celebrity website TMZ on 21 August 2012 and picked up worldwide the following day.

Respecting Harry's bravery during his service in Afghanistan, the British press initially refused to publish the photo but *The Sun* had no such qualms. On 24 August *The Sun* published the photos which shocked some people. Harry later apologised, explaining that at the time he had been 'more army than prince'.

However this escapade did not dint Harry's huge popularity. A UK poll taken a few months later revealed he was now the third most popular member of the royal family after Prince William and the Queen.

In January 2014, having witnessed horrific injuries and deaths of army colleagues, Harry completed his attachment to No. 3 Regiment Army Air Corps and was posted back to London. Captain Wales returned to England in a plane full of badly wounded men, some of whom had their amputated limbs wrapped in plastic beside them and this tragic sight affected him badly.

After his second tour of duty in Afghanistan, Harry needed a new purpose in life. He wanted to do something of which he felt his mother would have approved. While visiting various Army Recovery Units and hospitals where injured and disabled army soldiers were having treatment he realised how difficult it was for wounded veterans or those with psychological damage to adjust to civilian life and felt he must do something to help them.

Harry is a young man of action and raised funds and publicised what became his brainchild, the first Invictus Games (*invictus* is Latin for unconquered). On 6 March 2014, he launched this Para-Olympic style sporting event for injured service men and women announcing that running this first games in Britain was now his full-time job. Harry oversaw the first Invictus Games which was very successful and a second Invictus Games was scheduled for Toronto in 2016.

In April 2015, Prince Harry flew to Darwin for a month long secondment before flying to Perth to train with the Special Air Service Regiment (SASR). In Sydney he undertook urban operations training with Second Commando Regiment and participated in counter-terrorism training in Sydney Harbour with the Royal Australian Navy.

In June 2015, he completed his term of army service having been awarded the Atlantic Council's Distinguished Humanitarian Leadership Award. He then spent time in Malawi with African Parks and Wildlife and joined a team of volunteers and professionals carrying out one of the largest elephant resettlements in history in order to repopulate areas decimated by poaching. The team managed to move 500 elephants from the Liwonde and Majete National Parks to a wildlife reserve. He visited other environmental reserves to learn about their operations and this made him a passionate advocate for the conservation of African wildlife.

Back at Nottingham Cottage his bachelor residence in the grounds of Kensington Palace, where William and Kate had their apartment, seeing William happy with Kate and his young family made Harry think it was time to think about marriage and children.

While Chelsy Davy and Cressida Bonas had shared his interest in African wildlife and night-clubbing at the Makati Club and at Bouji's, they had hated the media attention and neither of them fancied spending the rest of their lives in the royal goldfish bowl and this had ended the relationships.

That first blind date

A close friend warned Harry that only a very special girl would be willing to take on the role of a princess, always in the public eye, subject to constant criticism and pursued relentlessly by the paparazzi.

In the first week of July 2016, on a blind date at London's exclusive Soho House Club in Mayfair, Harry finally met that 'special girl'. Meghan Markle had the poise and maturity to cope with the media and stay calm, helped by her training in yoga. She admitted she did not know a great deal about the British royal family but like thousands of young girls had wept as she watched Diana's funeral.

Harry admitted that he had never watched *Suits* so only knew what his friend had told him, that Meghan was a talented actress with exotic looks who had worked with World Vision in Rwanda. A shared interest in Africa and the plight of children there helped provide a topics of conversation when they first met.

Before their meeting Meghan had asked her friend if her blind date was 'nice' as she feared that a prince might be arrogant. On meeting Prince Harry she found him more sensitive and thoughtful than she had expected. Both of them claimed it was love at first sight, the attraction of physical opposites as well as recognition they had met someone very special with that vital spark of physical attraction between them.

Aware that time was short, as Meghan was due to fly back to Toronto on 5 July to resume filming they re-arranged their schedules and arranged to spend the following day together. Much later, in an interview on BBC World News, Meghan revealed how 'Very early on we realised we were going to commit to each other and had to invest the time, the energy and whatever it took to make that happen.'

A secret courtship

After two transatlantic dates, Meghan accepted Harry's invitation to visit the Meno a Kwena Safari Retreat in Botswana on the edge of the Kalahari Game Reserve. Their romantic two-day camping or 'glamping' break took place in a luxuriously outfitted tent with ensuite bathroom and solar-powered hot water. The secluded wildlife resort, owned by conservationist David Dugmore, a good friend of Prince Harry, gave them privacy and a chance to talk at length without distractions.

After dusk Harry and Meghan sat under the stars and watched elephants, giraffes and zebras come to drink at the lake at the bottom of the hill. Harry described this as 'a wonderful opportunity where they got to know each other well'.

The couple managed to keep their relationship out of the news for some months. Harry remained unrecognised when he flew to Toronto and continued to keep his woollen 'beanie' pulled down low to cover his red hair and travelled as 'Harry Wales'.

But on 31 October 2016, after a tip-off, Britain's *Sunday Express* exposed the couple by publishing close-up photographs and an article about their secret transatlantic romance.

Immediately a media storm erupted over the fact that Harry's new girlfriend was a divorced, bi-racial American actress. The name Meghan Markle, once known only to those who watched Netflix or who read her blog, was now a topic for discussion. A friend told the media Harry was 'besotted' about Meghan. A few social media posts wrongly assumed that Meghan's mother was a dreadlocked African-American from the wrong side of the tracks and even claimed Meghan had grown up with criminals in Los Angeles. Trolls hiding behind pseudonyms unleashed racist and sexist abuse and some websites carried defamatory stories.

Harry felt guilty that his position had unleashed so much racist commentary on the young woman he loved.

Substantial sums were offered for a tell-all story to Meghan's former boyfriend, Cory Vitiello who ignored all offers. Germaine Greer, the Australian feminist author who enjoys being controversial predicted gloomily, 'She'll bolt. She's bolted before'.

Harry, aware how badly the press had treated his mother was determined to protect Meghan and so consulted his brother, aware Kate had been subjected to years of media abuse before their marriage.

On 8 November, 2016, a week after news of the couple's relationship became public knowledge, Kensington Palace issued a formal statement confirming Meghan Markle was Prince Harry's girlfriend, requesting her right to privacy be respected and asking the press and social media to stop the 'wave of abuse and harassment' of Meghan's family, co-workers and friends.

The communiqué mentioned how Meghan's mother had to struggle past photographers blocking her front door, attempting to force their way inside her house, searching her rubbish bins in the hope of finding information or personal letters.

All this distressed Meghan, always close to her mother. From the money made from *Suits* and various sponsorships Meghan had paid the fees for her mother to study at the University of Southern California where Doria, aged 61 had obtained a post graduate degree as a therapist and she still works as a social worker and grief counsellor as well as teaching meditation as a part-time yoga instructor.

This photo appeared on Megan's Instagram site and shows how happy both of them were when Doria received her degree.

In the third week of December 2016, Meghan flew from Toronto to London and was spotted by the paparazzi holding hands with Harry walking through London's West End admiring the Christmas decorations but the couple spent Christmas apart.

Following tradition, Harry spent Christmas with the Queen and his family at Sandringham. Meghan flew the Atlantic to spend Christmas with her mother before flying back to London and saw in the New Year with Harry. In January he took her to Norway to show her the romantic Northern Lights, and they stayed with a friend who owns a property in Tromsø. As their relationship was now an open secret Harry no longer flew incognito.

The year 2017 was a frantically busy one for Meghan. She had a tight film schedule for *Suits*, was in constant demand for charity appearances, wrote her lifestyle blog each night, and did all this in the middle of a transatlantic romance which was now at a serious stage.

During Meagan's February visit to London Harry introduced Meghan to Prince William, his sister-in-law and their children. Meghan and Kate, who are the same age, got on famously. In March 2017 the couple travelled to Jamaica, to attend the wedding of Harry's childhood friend Tom 'Skippy' Inskip and guests described them as radiantly happy and much in love.

Later that month they made their first official public appearance in Britain at the annual Audi Polo Challenge at Ascot. Harry played polo while Meghan cheered him from the sidelines. They were captured on camera after the game kissing and holding hands, criticised by some as not exactly royal behaviour.

On 16 April, Harry at last felt confident enough to speak in public about the intensely personal struggle he endured after his mother's death and how 'Losing my mother at twelve and shutting down all my emotions for the past twenty years has had a serious affect on my personal life' before he finally sought professional counselling. The understanding and love Harry had found in his relationship with Meghan finally enabled him confront his mother's death and publicly admit the reason for his troubled adolescence.

Early in May, Meghan was escorted from Heathrow Airport by security and driven to Kensington Palace to stay at Nottingham Cottage with Harry. Speculation mounted about an engagement. On 20 May, Meghan attended Pippa Middleton's wedding reception at which the criteria was supposed to be 'no ring, no bring' and only married or engaged couples were invited. Clearly this was a serious relationship.

Meghan's appearance at the Duchess of Cambridge's family celebrations alerted everyone to the fact the couple were now on the brink of an engagement if the Queen would permit this.

In August 2017, a year after that first brief stay at the Meno a Kwena Safari Retreat, Harry once again took Meghan to Botswana for a three-week romantic get-away to celebrate her 36th birthday.

By then Harry was planning how best to approach his grandmother to obtain her permission to marry a divorced, bi-racial actress rather than a young woman from their own social circle. But it is an open secret that the Queen and Prince Philip love Harry very much and they were thrilled to see him so happy and filled with purpose.

Meghan meets the Queen

The prospect of a royal meeting over tea and cucumber sandwiches at Buckingham Palace must have been intimidating. Harry had briefed his grandmother as she along with his grandfather, Prince Philip, had looked after him during the terrible days after Diana's death. He had shown the Queen a copy of the film Meghan had made for World Vision in Rwanda, explained what an exceptional young woman she was and the reasons he wanted to marry her.

Perhaps he mentioned that Meghan had stopped him smoking and that he had lowered his consumption of alcohol. The Queen is very fond of her grandson and agreed to a meeting which went well, helped by the Queen's corgis who recognising Meghan as a dog lover sat at her feet wagging their tails instead of barking and snarling as they often did with strangers. Harry later admitted with a rueful laugh, 'I've spent the last thirty-three years being barked at. This one walks in, and absolutely nothing!'

After talking to the couple at length the Queen approved of Meghan and gave her permission for their marriage which was necessary under the recent Act of Succession. As Kate was pregnant with the birth of her third child Harry would drop back to sixth in the line of succession so what he did with his life or who he married was no longer vitally important constitutionally.

An engagement at last

Having received the Queen's approval Meghan felt sufficiently confident to speak openly about her relationship with Prince Harry. The October 2017 issue of *Vanity Fair* featured her on its front cover with an eight page spread under the banner heading 'She's Just Wild About Harry'. Meghan was quoted as saying, 'We're a couple. We're in love.'

Her *Vanity Fair* interview aroused a storm of criticism in the British tabloids, probably annoyed they had not been the first with the story, claiming Meghan Markle had broken a long standing taboo against royal girlfriends talking to the press (the faux pas that had ended any chance of a relationship between Lady Sarah Spencer and Prince Charles)

At Toronto's Invictus Games held from 23-30 September 2016, Meghan appeared with Prince Harry. Both were dressed casually, Meghan in expensive, designer jeans, tastefully ripped at the knees, an oversized freshly laundered white 'husband' shirt designed by her friend Misha

Nonoo and enormous Hollywood sunglasses.

The couple were openly affectionate, clearly in love, holding hands and laughing at private jokes which sparked media speculation that an engagement would follow.

Doria Ragland, attending the Invictus Games as Prince Harry's guest, met him for the first time. Meghan was very close to her mother and it was important to her that Harry liked and admired Doria who could see for herself how happy the couple were. Later Meghan phoned her father in Mexico to tell him about the situation, received his blessing and he promised to attend her wedding.

Meghan had appeared in almost one hundred episodes of *Suits*. The producers realised that if this romance ended in marriage, as seemed likely, Meghan would be unable to continue filming so gave instructions to write Rachel Zane out of the series by marrying her off to her fiancé. This meant Meghan was free to leave Toronto.

⁂

Prince Charles finally announced the engagement of Prince Harry to Meghan Markle on Monday, November 27, 2017 from Clarence House, and expressed his delight over his son's happiness.

'America's loss is our gain,' added Camilla, no doubt relieved that there would be another royal couple to take on some of the many duties that she and Prince Charles undertake.

The newly-engaged couple met the press in the sunken garden at Kensington Palace on a bitterly cold November afternoon. Meghan, her dark hair loose wore a belted white cashmere coat by a British designer, designer heels but bare legs and no stockings which broke protocol. She posed for photos and confirmed how happy they were, describing Harry's proposal of marriage as 'sweet and very romantic.'

Harry said he was 'thrilled and over the moon.' He laughed boyishly as he recalled going down on one knee to propose to Meghan while she was cooking a roast chicken in the kitchen of Nottingham Cottage in the grounds of Kensington Palace. He had given his fiancée a diamond engagement ring which he had helped design. It incorporated two diamonds that had once belonged to Diana and a much larger diamond from Botswana. It is sobering to realise that at the time they announced their engagement, Meghan was 36, the same age as Princess Diana when she died in a car accident.

When questioned about her whirlwind romance Meghan queried this description, saying, 'I don't think that I would call my romance a whirlwind ... we had five or six month's privacy which was amazing (in fact they had just under five months). We were able to have time just to connect and we never went longer than two weeks without seeing each other. Early on we realised we were going to commit to each other; we knew we had to invest the time and the energy and whatever it took to make that happen.'

Days later, Harry and Meghan's first appearance as an engaged couple in Britain was greeted with great excitement.

⁂

Following the formal announcement of their engagement many things changed for Meghan. She resigned from her position as Global Ambassador for World Vision Canada, from the United Nations Organization for Women and other organisations concerned with raising the status of women in undeveloped countries. Meghan had already shut down 'The Tig', the lifestyle blog she had founded three years earlier. She was made aware that members of the royal family are not allowed to have blogs, comment on or endorse products or express political opinions.

There would be other changes as Meghan prepared for her new role as a member of the royal family. Like Kate Middleton she took instruction in the Anglican faith as she needed to be a confirmed member of the Church of England before she could be married in an Anglican church with the Queen's official title as the defender and protector of the Anglican church.

Meghan received the same 'princess' lessons in protocol as Kate before she became Duchess of Cambridge. She had to learn that a strict order of royal precedence governs the order in which individuals arrive at public and private functions so everyone is in their places when finally the Queen appears. Etiquette lessons were an essential part of 'princess training' so that Meghan would know the correct form of address for everyone she meets including dukes, duchesses, ambassadors and bishops. It was agreed that for the first six months a representative of the Queen would accompany them on all official duties to help Meghan adjust to the terms of royal protocol which are very different to those prevailing in Hollywood.

Used to memorising longs scripts Meghan had no problems with these formalities which had sometimes daunted Princess Diana.

Meghan learned that once she was married court circulars would refer to her by her official title of 'Her Royal Highness the Princess Harry', but never as Princess Meghan as she had not been born royal like Princess Anne although some American papers continued to do this. When she became a duchess she would be formally addressed as 'Your Grace'.

Meghan also had to master the art of curtseying which includes the quick bob which requires her to bend her knees which can be difficult when wearing very high heels. But the full deep royal courtesy is rarely performed today. She would be expected to curtsey to family members who are senior to her as well as become familiar with their correct titles and forms of address.

Another important course Meghan had to undergo was on personal security. It included how to use a pistol and how to react if taken hostage — the grim side of being royal today when terrorism is an ever present threat, especially since Harry has been singled out by the Taliban. Other royals had needed speech training but as Meghan was confident speaking to the media she had no need of coaching in this important aspect of being royal today.

⁂

After her engagement was announced Meghan vacated her Toronto house, said a sad goodbye to her fellow actors who she regarded as family, and flew across the Atlantic. She moved into Harry's bachelor home, Nottingham Cottage (known as Nott Cott) in the grounds of Kensington Palace with her beagle, Guy. Her other rescue dog was considered too old to travel by air so Meghan found a home for him with Canadian friends.

Meghan also brought her electric blender which she used to make health drinks from fruit and vegetables. She went through Harry's kitchen cupboards and his refrigerator and threw away all the junk food. She had persuaded Harry to attend a gym on a regular basis, reduced his consumption of alcohol and he had given up smoking.

Meghan enjoys cooking. One of the things she had enjoyed doing when writing her lifestyle blog was the research she undertook into food and restaurants. She associates food and home cooking with love and happiness and perhaps it is no coincidence that Harry proposed as she was preparing an evening meal of their favourite roast chicken for which she has her own special recipe. Having a girlfriend who was a good cook and having home-cooked meals was a new experience for Harry after years spent at boarding school and in the army.

Christmas 2017 with the royal family

In what is seen by some commentators as a modern fairy-tale, the Queen went out of her way to welcome Meghan at the Buckingham Palace staff Christmas party. As she had no family in England the Queen invited her to Sandringham for a family Christmas. Over the Christmas holidays Harry and Meghan stayed with Prince William and his wife and family at Anmer House and the four of them walked to morning service at the nearby Sandringham Church where Diana had been christened.

Photo taken on Sunday morning outside Sandringham Church. Meghan seemed to be enjoying herself as she accompanied her fiancé, Kate and William on a walk to Sandringham Church on Christmas Day. She was warmly wrapped up against the British winter in a pale camel coloured coat and knee length brown leather boots. The locals greeted her with enthusiastic cries of 'Meghan, Meghan' and were thrilled to see her. (Photo courtesy Reuters.)

That Markle sparkle & the family debacle

Royal weddings have traditionally featured long lace trains, tiaras and tantrums. This wedding would be no different. But this time it was not the bride throwing tantrums but her step-brother and step-sister who made headlines for the wrong reasons while the royal family maintained a dignified silence.

Things started well when Samantha Markle, Meaghan's step-sister seemed happy about Meghan's engagement to Prince Harry but was annoyed when Harry said Meghan had never had a proper Christmas and said they had always tried to give her a family Christmas even after the divorce.

Samantha who had three children and lives in Florida had reverted to her maiden name after her divorce. Her life is obviously difficult as she is confined to a wheelchair after being diagnosed with multiple sclerosis and things went badly wrong between the half-sisters. When Samantha announced that she intended to write a revealing book about their childhood and Meghan's subsequent career, with the controversial title *The Diary of Princess Pushy's Sister* it was obvious there was no love lost between them.

Tom Markle Junior, a divorced window fitter, was quoted in Britain's *Daily Mail* saying their father was happy for Meghan and proud of her.

The situation darkened in January 2018, when Meghan's half-brother made headlines after police charged his current fiancée, Darlene Blount with assaulting him during a drunken quarrel in their home on New Year's Eve 2017. Tom Markle bailed his fiancée out of jail, and paid the $1,000 good behaviour bond on her behalf. He blamed press harassment following the announcement of Meghan's engagement and announced that he and his fiancée would attend alcohol and relationship counselling.

Tom Markle explained that the stress of being thrust into the limelight had contributed to their problem with alcohol by saying, 'It hasn't been easy when your sister is engaged to royalty. It adds a whole new level of scrutiny. We've been under a lot of stress because of all the attention. At some point you find yourself drinking too much to escape the pressure.'

Bizarrely, Meghan's half-brother wrote an open letter to Prince Harry, which was published in a US celebrity magazine urging Harry not to marry Meghan, describing the forthcoming royal wedding as 'the biggest mistake in royal wedding history'. He later apologised claiming the letter had been written during a time of great stress.

A Los Angeles based gossipy website issued a stream of regular updates about whether or not Meghan's father would be attending the wedding as it appeared he had heart problems and a bad knee.

Days later, Tom Markle was in Los Angeles being photographed having a fitting for a new suit for the wedding, looking at books on England and delivering a bunch of flowers to the home of his former wife. A staff reporter for Rupert Murdoch's News Corp released the news Meghan's father had earned $180.000 for staging this series of photos with a News Corp photographer Jeff Rayner. Later Samantha Markle admitted doing this had been her idea 'to improve her father's image before the wedding.'

By now Samantha rarely had a good word to say about Meghan and posted negative messages on social media. Meghan's half-brother Tom Markle told Australia's Channel 7 that Samantha had an 'ongoing resentment since Meg (Meghan) was born.' He added that his family 'was normal as sibling rivalry is not uncommon … Everyone has secrets in the closet and hatreds. This wedding has brought them out into the open.'

Samantha was critical of Meghan's treatment of her father and declared that all he wanted was peace and quiet. He had been pursued by press cars and had panicked on the freeway in a dangerous situation. She exposed the fact photographers had rented the house next to his home in the sleepy run-down Mexican port of Rosarito and added 'He can't open his blinds and can't go anywhere without being followed. It's atrocious and intrusive.'

Samantha described her father as stressed out and having 'heart pains'. In hindsight it might have been wise for Meghan and Harry to have paid for a security firm to guard the homes of both parents who were harassed by the paparazzi. Meghan's father had been declared bankrupt in 2016 so it was unclear who would pay his fare to fly to London for the wedding.

Meghan's twenty-something nephews, Tyler and Thomas Dooley, were the next family members to hit the headlines. They announced they were going to fly to England for the royal wedding to launch a strain of cannabis called 'The Markle Sparkle' with their mother Mrs Dooley, but when they arrived with t-shirts extolling cannabis Mrs Dooley was not asked to act as a commentator for British television as she had hoped.

Just days before the wedding Meghan's father announced that due to all the embarrassment the family had caused he would not be attending. He apologised to his daughter for the trouble he had caused and gave her his best wishes for her big day.

As her father was not attending her wedding Meghan was left with no one to walk her up the long aisle of St George's Chapel. Her suggestion that her mother walk her up the aisle did not receive official approval. It is claimed she asked Prince Charles if he would act in lieu and he was delighted to agree. It was decided he should leave his seat and take her halfway down the aisle and present her at the altar to her future husband which did not please strict feminists.

Like all royal brides Meghan was facing an ordeal under a barrage of television cameras. Princess Diana was nineteen when she married Prince Charles and suffered from agonising shyness and was terrified just before her wedding although conducted herself brilliantly during it. The most timid royal bride in the royal family was seventeen year old Princess Augusta of Saxe-Gotha who at her wedding to Prince Frederick of Wales, son of George III, on catching sight of her husband's infamous mistress, Anne Vane, in the congregation was overcome by nerves, threw up and ruined her silk wedding dress.

The announcement of Meghan and Harry's engagement enchanted the media but this changed after publication of Andrew Morton's unflattering biography, *Hollywood Princess*. Morton, author of an important biography of Diana, now lives in America and interviewed Meghan's childhood friends including Niniki Priddy, her former 'bestie' who confided Meghan had ditched old friends for newer ones in order to clamber up the greasy celebrity pole after critical and financial success playing Rachel Zane in *Suits*.

Journalist Piers Morgan, presenter of the popular television programme *Good Morning Britain*, described Meghan 'setting her cap at a prince who she captured' after their blind date arranged by a mutual friend' and ruthless in pursuit of fame and fortune. In an interview on BBC TV Meghan insisted she had known 'very little' about Prince Harry before their first date at a chic London club for people in the arts and media. Niniki Priddy claimed Meghan had read a biography of Diana and watched television and film about Harry's mother. Comments on social media called Meghan a 'gold digger' as she must have known Princess Diana had left each of her sons around £20,000,000.

Another rejected friend is believed to have leaked to *The Sun* newspaper an email from Meghan. The email revealed that, before her wedding to Trevor Engleson, Meghan packed gift bags for younger guests with marijuana-filled cigarettes that she had rolled by hand. Since Harry had smoked pot as a teenager, he would not have been shocked at this disclosure. But in 2011 at the time of Meghan's first wedding, pot was still illegal in Jamaica. Had Meghan been jailed for breaking the law, it is highly unlikely she would have been allowed to marry her Prince Charming.

When the love-struck Harry introduced Meghan to Prince William, he warned his hot-headed younger brother against rushing into marriage with a divorcee, about whose family background Harry knew very little. Subsequent unsavoury stories involving members of the Markle clan (pages 371-372) and the threat of a tell-all book by Meghan's vociferous half-sister, made Prince William's warning seem prescient.

A damaging leak, from an unnamed source at Buckingham Palace, alleged Meghan had refused the Queen's suggestion the couple sign a pre-nuptial agreement. In an era of easy divorce, 'pre-nups' are relatively common when the wealth of one party greatly exceeds that of the other. Once again social media contained allegations Meghan was a 'gold digger' but royal protocol prevented Meghan from defending herself and she had to remain silent.

A second palace leak alleged Meghan was furious when the Queen refused to lend her the exquisite Boucheron tiara studded with emeralds to hold her wedding veil in place. Prince Harry's insistence that 'What Meghan wants, Meghan gets,' cut no ice with his grandmother who is loyal to those who work for her. Meghan received a royal rebuke for the way she had spoken to a member of the Queen's staff.

CHAPTER NINETEEN

Meghan & Harry:
A modern royal wedding – all about love

She chose me and I chose her, whatever we have to tackle will be as a team. Prince Harry, 2018

St George's Chapel, venue for a royal wedding

The wedding date had been set for 19 May, 2018, the start of the English summer, due to fears about Prince Philip's health as he had recently undergone a hip replacement and doctors advised it would be easier for him now in his nineties to attend a wedding at Windsor Castle rather than in London. Harry was very keen that his beloved grandfather was at the ceremony.

Meghan and Prince Harry wanted to share their special day with members of the royal household, representatives of charities with which they are involved and community representatives. Invitations were sent to over 1,000 people from various groups which allowed them to enter the Castle precincts on the day of the wedding and hopefully feel part of it. They were advised to bring folding chairs or stools, a picnic lunch and issued with souvenir bags complete with a commemorative booklet, a few small treats and a bottle of spring water which was useful as the day was unusually warm.

Those present said they felt privileged to share in this happy event, they watched the arrivals and departures, felt part of the event and could watch the service on their mobile devices or on giant screens.

Another difference between this and previous royal weddings was that no ministers of state, foreign dignitaries or foreign royalty were invited to the wedding other than Prince Seeiso of Lesotho who is involved with Prince Harry in his charity Sentebale.

Invitations went out to many of those who had worked with the bride on *Suits* and on various charitable endeavours.

The cost of the wedding was borne by the royal family. The overall costs of catering, flowers, music and security, (a major concern) were expected to be around £32 million. It was predicted that a tourism boom generated by the wedding would boost the British economy by around £500 million with increased tourism to the Windsor area which would last several more years. As many as three billion people worldwide are estimated to have watched this royal wedding on television or on various electronic devices.

It was announced that the bride was buying her wedding outfits and there was huge speculation as to who would be chosen to design her wedding dress and another one that she would wear to the evening party.

Boosted by media and American interest in the royal wedding with Meghan as a modern and affluent Cinderella, over 120,000 visitors descended on the small town of Windsor. Many wore mock tiaras and waved small British and American flags. Some had camped out overnight in order to watch the bride and groom drive along Windsor High Street and down the Long Walk in Windsor Great Park in an open-topped horse-drawn coach on a perfect English summer day.

St George's Chapel located inside the gated precinct of Windsor Castle seats 600 people and was ideal for the intimate wedding that Harry and Meaghan wanted in this beautiful fourteenth century church. The carved woodwork and magnificent fan vaulted ceiling are considered one of the glories of Gothic architecture.

St George's Chapel was rarely used for royal weddings in the past until Queen Victoria who was in permanent mourning for Prince Albert refused to leave Windsor Castle. So the wedding of her eldest son, Bertie, Prince of Wales to Princess Alexandra of Denmark took take place at St George's Chapel as did the weddings of four of her daughters. These weddings had all been arranged by Queen Victoria who claimed she had married off her children to the sons and daughters of the main crowned heads of Europe.

At these arranged marriages Queen Victoria, still mourning for Prince Albert to whom as queen regnant she had made a love match was a grim figure dressed in black. She issued orders that guests were to wear grey, lilac, purple or black — out of respect for her late husband.

In contrast to the muted colours at the weddings of Queen Victoria's children, the wedding of Harry and Meghan was a riot of colour as their friends wore stylish clothes and hats in brilliant colours. Security was as strict as at any major airport and guests arrived in special coaches rather than by car through gates manned by armed police and security staff.

Meghan was helped in selecting the designer for her two wedding gowns by her close friend, Canadian stylist Jessica Mulroney, whose twin sons were pages at the wedding. The ten small flower girls and pages included Prince George and Princess Charlotte and Meghan's Canadian god-children.

Meghan and Harry gave their closest friends and relatives a short list of wedding presents, among which was a large brass bed. However the couple requested well-wishers among the public make donations to one of seven charitable organisations. These included one that supports young people living with HIV, one that works with homeless people, another based in Mumbai that helps empower women, a charity that supported children whose fathers had been killed serving with the British Armed Forces, a conservation body working to protect beaches and oceans, and the Wilderness Foundation of the United Kingdom.

However many commercial firms chose to ignore the message and sent expensive 'gifts' of clothing, household items, furnishings and sports goods, aware of the immense celebrity value of the glamorous couple which manufacturers wanted to claim used their products in advertisements. Under the circumstances it was felt wiser to return these unsolicited gifts with a polite note saying that they could not be accepted, only donations to charities were acceptable. It was later estimated some £12 million pounds worth of goods were returned to various manufacturers such was the 'pulling power' of this charismatic royal couple and any charity which has Meghan and Harry as patrons will benefit enormously and the couple will be effective ambassadors for British-made goods, as Meghan is aware now that she is choosing clothes by British designers, like Princess Diana and Duchess Catherine.

The Queen's gifts included the expenses of the wedding and Meghan's formal wedding dress. She had given Prince William and his bride Anmer House at Sandringham and will give Prince Harry and Meghan a country house which, at the time of writing, is believed to be York Cottage on the Sandringham estate. The reason for the Queen's gift of country houses to close relatives has been described as 'the need for a secure and private retreat from media intrusion.'

As the new Duke and Duchess of Sussex hope their marriage will be blessed with children they will be given a larger apartment in Kensington Palace to act as combined home and office. Using their own money Meghan and Harry, like the Duke and Duchess of Cambridge will work hard for the causes they espouse.

⁂

On the morning of his wedding, Prince Harry looked dashing in the uniform of a major in the Blues and Royals regiment with his pilots' wings pinned to his close-fitting dark blue jacket. He walked from the castle to the wedding venue with Prince William who was also wearing his regimental uniform.

Only carefully selected media and television camera and lighting operators had security clearance into St George's Chapel to record the arrivals of members of the royal family. First came Prince Andrew, Duke of York, and his daughters, Beatrix and Eugenie, known for wearing weird hats. Princess Eugenie wearing a tight-fitting blue dress was escorted by her fiancé and distant cousin Jack Brooksbank, the next royals to marry in St George's Chapel, in October.

The divorced 'Fergie', Duchess of York once known for her fashion disasters had lost weight. She looked slim and very elegant in a navy blue ensemble with a pale pink collar. Protocol did not allow her to sit with her divorced husband so she was seated beside Princess Diana's brother, Earl Spencer. It is rumoured that the Duke and Duchess of York hope to remarry now that the queen only needs to approve of the marriages of the first six candidates in line for the throne. The birth of Prince Louis means Prince Andrew is now out of the line of direct succession.

Beside Earl Spencer sat Diana's elder sisters, Lady Sarah McCorquodale and Lady Jane Fellowes. Earl Spencer, Diana's brother is remembered for his fiery speech at her funeral criticising the royal family for their behaviour to his sister.

Dora Ragland, Meghan's mother wearing a diamond nose stud and an elegantly embroidered coat and matching dress in soft pistachio green sat beside Prince Charles and Camilla, whose picture hat resembled a large pink chrysanthemum with a matching coat-dress in a flattering shade of pale pink.

In a ceremony full of innovations, this royal wedding highlighted how times have changed. Sporting celebrities like Serena Williams, the Beckhams, and Hollywood stars like George and Amal Clooney, elegant in brilliant yellow and Meghan's co-stars from *Suits* sat near the bride and groom while the older royal relatives were relegated to seats behind the choir.

At previous royal weddings, aristocrats, ambassadors and politicians were always given the best seats. At this wedding these groups were notable by their absence other than former Prime Minister John Major, invited as he had been appointed 'special legal guardian' to Harry and William after the death of their mother.

The last to arrive, according to protocol, was Her Majesty the Queen in eye-catching lemon yellow with the Duke of Edinburgh in a morning suit. The former naval commander bravely refused to use a stick but was clearly in pain as he made his way down the aisle. It was later revealed he was suffering from a cracked rib after another fall, but was determined to attend the wedding of his much-loved grandson.

The bride arrived by car with her mother and entered the West Door of St George's Chapel with her twin seven year old pageboys, the sons of her friend Jessica Mulroney, dressed in miniature versions of Prince Harry's uniform holding her train.

The bride looked very beautiful as she walked up the steps under a four metre high arch of green leaves and white flowers. Meghan's dress was simple but very elegant, created by British designer Clare Waight Keller, artistic director of the House of Givenchy, the French couture house famous for designing stunning outfits for Audrey Hepburn. It was made from a dazzlingly white silk so heavy that it would not crease. Her veil was kept in place by the splendour of the Queen Mary diamond bandeau tiara loaned by Queen Elizabeth with Meghan's matching diamond earrings as a gift from her husband.

The bride's tiara although very beautiful and valuable presented a problem. Princess Diana and the Queen both stated that the weight of a tiara can cause a headache in the wearer in the same way as a heavy crown, which has always been a problem for queens at coronations.

It was later revealed Princess Diana suffered a headache at her wedding from wearing the Spencer tiara at her wedding. The beautiful and very valuable bandeau tiara made for Queen Mary, (great-great-grandmother of Prince Harry) which Meaghan was loaned by Queen Elizabeth has a large diamond brooch embedded in its centre and is even heavier than the Spencer tiara.

In the past royal brides had worn wedding dresses heavily ornamented with crystals, seed pearls, overlaid with lace and silver and gold thread embroidery. Waists were tightly fitted and many royal brides had been so tightly corseted to achieve a wasp waist some brides almost fainted during the service.

Previous royal brides including the Queen had chosen silk dresses encrusted with seed pearls and Princess Diana had thousands of them sewn to the billowing silk taffeta fabric of her dress which rustled beautifully as she moved. The drawback to using silk taffeta was that it crumpled badly as the inexperienced designers had not allowed for the fact the narrow doorway of the royal coach crushed the delicate fabric. Captured on television, Meghan was serene and smiling as she walked up the aisle alone. Her princess-line dress of heavy uncrushable silk fabric had a boat-shaped neck-line and floor-length skirt with an organza underskirt which kept the skirt in soft folds. The dress was elegance personified and accentuated the bride's slender figure.

An official communiqué stated that the bride's father was unable to give his daughter away because only days before he had a stent inserted in hospital to treat symptomatic coronary artery disease and would be watching the ceremony on television from his home in Mexico.

The orchestra accompanied a soprano who sang Handel's '*Eternal Source of Light Divine*', as Meghan advanced towards the altar looking very calm and smiling, her long hair was swept up into a loose chignon. Her five metre long veil, embroidered with the floral emblems of Britain and fifty-three Commonwealth countries, was held in place by the heavy bandeau diamond tiara made for the wife of King George V.

As the bride reached the half-way point, Prince Charles in a grey morning suit, met her and with gentle gallantry took her arm. He walked with her to the altar where Harry was waiting.

Harry, the war hero, had tears in his eyes as he whispered to his bride, 'You look amazing. I missed you.'

The Archbishop of Canterbury turned to the congregation and said 'I am required to ask anyone present who knows a reason why these persons may not lawfully marry to declare it now.'

There was an awkward silence. Clearly some people in the congregation had wondered whether a Markle relative would burst in and in a scene reminiscent of the novel *Jane Eyre* shout an objection. Fortunately there were none.

Diana's sister, Lady Jane Fellowes, read the first lesson taken from what is referred to as a Biblical love poem, *The Song of Solomon*.

The bridal couple sat together on heavily gilded, chairs upholstered in red velvet, and held hands while they listened to Bishop Michael Curry's passionate speech about the redemptive power of love he equated to the power of fire. 'We were made by the power of love and our lives were meant to be lived with love' he claimed.

The Rev Michael Curry is the first African-American to preside over the American Episcopal Church. To the bemusement of some of the congregation he launched into an animated sermon in Deep Southern preacher style, quoting from Martin Luther King and overran his allotted time by eight minutes.

In recognition of the fact this was a multicultural wedding, the Kingdom Choir from south-east London, whose ancestors came from Commonwealth countries, sang their own African-American gospel interpretation of '*Stand by Me*'.

The bridal couple made their vows and Meghan promised to 'love, comfort and keep' her husband, but as a feminist omitted the word 'obey'. Meghan placed a platinum wedding ring on Harry's finger, another break with royal tradition as no other males in the royal family wear a wedding ring. Prince Harry placed a ring made of Welsh gold on his bride's finger and made his vows.

As she replied 'I will', Meghan Markle became the Duchess of Sussex, Countess of Dumbarton, a Scottish town, and Baroness of Kilkeel after a small northern Irish town, to honour the three countries which make up the United Kingdom while Prince Charles' full title honours Wales.

As Harry kissed his bride Doria Ragland had trouble keeping back tears of happiness for the daughter who she had raised with love and care.

During the signing of the register, Faure's beautiful *Après une Rêve* and an arrangement for cello and orchestra of Schubert's moving *Ave Maria* were performed by the 19-year old cellist Sheku Kanneh-Mason. Prince Charles has a keen interest in classical music and may have chosen the music for the ceremony. A harp engraved with the name 'Prince of Wales', normally kept in the drawing room at Clarence House, had been transported to St George's Chapel to be played by the orchestra's harpist.

The wedding ceremony concluded with the singing of the British National Anthem 'God Save Our Gracious Queen'. As the bride and groom approached the Queen, Harry bowed and Meghan curtseyed but the cameras were occupied elsewhere causing unjustified media criticism of the bride for not curtseying to the Queen.

Queen Elizabeth II, now Meghan's grandmother by marriage will be her sovereign when eventually Meghan is granted British citizenship.

⁂

The ceremony over, the bride and groom walked down the aisle, out of the great West Door and paused under an enormous floral arch to exchange a kiss before the invited guests in the castle precinct.

A very special moment between bride and groom under gigantic arch of hornbeam branches, white roses (Princess Diana's favourite flowers) and white peonies, the favourite flowers of the bride. Photograph courtesy Reuters.

Prince Harry and the two twin page boys assisted the new Duchess of Sussex with her long delicate veil as she mounted the steps of the open horse-drawn landau. Pulled by the famous matching Windsor grey horses it was driven along Windsor High Street and through Windsor Great Park, where thousands of cheering people, waving small flags had gathered to see the newly-weds.

There had been fears of a terrorist attack on the open landau in Windsor High Street where balconies overlook the street from which grenades could be thrown into the landau. Days before the wedding police had arrested a suspect believed to be linked to previous terrorist attacks. Over 3,000 police from Scotland Yard were present, backed by 40 armed soldiers from the SAS to ensure there was no repeat of the assassination of President Kennedy in an open car in Dallas.

The wedding guests were invited by the Queen to a luncheon reception in the vaulted ceilinged St George's Hall, adjacent to St George's Chapel. Speeches were made and the health of bride and groom toasted in Pol Roger champagne. Elton John serenaded the bride and groom while Prince Charles moved the guests to tears as well as laugher with an emotional speech about Harry's childhood.

The bridegroom delighted guests with a speech in which he praised his bride for 'navigating everything with such grace. We make such a great team, I can't wait to spend the rest of my life with you.'

⁂

That evening a party with dancing and a display of fireworks took place in a gigantic marquee pitched outside the superbly decorated Frogmore House, former home of the mother of Queen Victoria. The party was for 200 special friends and was held in the marquee as Frogmore House was not suitable for a party with dancing.

Prince Harry was debonair in a black tuxedo and the couple looked more like vintage Hollywood stars than royalty as they arrived at their evening party in a pale blue open topped electric powered version of the elegant 1968 E-type Jaguar with its spectacular long bonnet.

Meghan looked stunning in a slinky white-halter-neck gown designed by English designer Stella McCartney and wore a gift from her husband, an enormous aquamarine ring formerly owned by Princess Diana.

At the party Harry once again commended Meghan for performing throughout the wedding with such grace.

Later one guest said, 'Meghan stole the show. It is traditional for the bride's father to make a speech, but in his absence Meghan spoke for herself, something brides at royal weddings have never done before. She said that she wanted to give a very big thank you to the queen for the wedding and the royal family for their understanding and acceptance. She also thanked her mother, for not only being at her wedding, but for being there her entire life.

As another innovation Meghan read a very personal and moving poetic tribute to her husband, which she had written, describing how blessed she had been to meet him. She read her poem so movingly that it left some guests in tears.

Meghan's speech was a fitting end to this unusual, very emotional love story and a wedding which was all about love.

⁂

Meghan Markle's royal fairy tale ended in January 2020 with an announcement from Buckingham Palace that the couple had decided to step back from royal duties. As they will no longer represent the Queen they cannot use the titles His and Her Royal Highness. Harry and Meghan have agreed to repay the two million pounds spent on renovating a home for them in the grounds of Windsor Castle and will live in Canada or America. Estimated to be worth well over $40 million, they surprised their admirers by announcing they wished to work towards becoming 'financially independent'. Meghan has often admitted her long-term goal is to enter politics.

Nineteenth century lithograph after a watercolour by Caleb Stanley shows Adelaide Cottage in the grounds of Windsor Castle which was used by Queen Adelaide as a get-away from royal life. The picturesque cottage with a fountain in the garden was lived in by royal equerry Captain Peter Townsend during his passionate affair with Princess Margaret. A Crown lease rather than the freehold has been given to Harry and Meghan who will use Adelaide Cottage when they visit his grandmother at Windsor.

ACKNOWLEDGEMENTS

Thanks to Philippa Lester-Wilson, a classmate from St George's, and as the wife of the late Vere Davidge of Little Houghton House, near Althorp, a friend of Earl and Countess Spencer. Philippa was a volunteer guide at Althorp when Diana was a teenager. Philippa and another school friend Sylvia Alison (wife of the Hon Michael Alison, former members of the Queen's Privy Council) encouraged me to write this book.

I am very grateful for the help of creative editors Linda Funnell and Marusia McCormick, line editors Lyn Crowley of Mackenzie Editorial and Secretarial Services and Carole Castle, cover designer Lee Burgemeestre, and Andrew Farrell of Dennis Jones who also worked on the MS and converted the text into an e-book. My thanks to Bill Zang for photography and computer expert Wayne O'Connor of Bonza IT of Ipswich who provided vital assistance when needed, and to David Wilkinson of Reuters London for his help with picture research.

Selwa Anthony, literary agent and loyal friend and Andrew Farrell at Dennis Jones of Melbourne offered advice and encouragement at a critical time when my late husband was suffering from cancer and, with their support and that of Marusia McCormick, following his death I finally finished this book a few days after the wedding of Meghan Markle and Prince Harry.

About the Author

Susanna lives in sub-tropical Brisbane in a house with a colourful garden visited by red and green King parrots, white cockatoos and kookaburras. She writes with two rescue dogs in a basket beside her. She has nine de Vries grandchildren and a rapidly increasing number of great-grandchildren.

She was born in London and has Scottish and Irish roots. She attended St George's, Ascot as a boarder and visited Windsor Castle frequently on weekend outings. On the many days when it rained, her parents took her to see the royal art collection at Windsor and these visits encouraged her interest in art. She studied French history and art at the Sorbonne in Paris, became a fluent French speaker, won a scholarship to study art history in Spain. In her late twenties, she married into an Edinburgh medical dynasty.

While her late husband Dr Larry Evans, MRCPsych undertook post-graduate studies in psychiatry, she studied psychology. He worked on the research team of Professor Sir Martin Roth, President of the British Royal College of Psychiatrists who was consulted professionally by several senior members of the royal family. Professor Larry Evans died in Brisbane.

Susanna married the Dutch-born Jake de Vries, City Architect of Brisbane. Together they wrote and published book on Australian art and history and Susanna wrote five anthologies of women's history. She was awarded an Order of Australia for services to literature and a Winston Churchill Fellowship which enabled her to do research in the Royal Library at Windsor Castle. In 2012, the New South Wales Society of Women Writers gave Susanna the Alice Award as one of Australia's leading biographers. Details of her books are on www.susannadevries.com or www.goodreads.com and Amazon.

www.ingramcontent.com/pod-product-compliance
Ingram Content Group UK Ltd.
Pitfield, Milton Keynes, MK11 3LW, UK
UKHW020058200726
13856UKWH00002B/267

9 781925 283624